C++ *for* Programmers

Third Edition

Leen Ammeraal
Hogeschool van Utrecht

John Wiley & Sons, Ltd
Chichester • Weinheim • Brisbane • Singapore • Toronto

Reprinted June 2000, March 2001

Other Wiley Editorial Offices

John Wiley & Sons, Inc., 605 Third Avenue,
New York, NY 10158-0012, USA

Weinheim • Brisbane • Singapore • Toronto

British Library Cataloguing in Publication Data

ISBN 0-471-60697-9

Produced from author's PostScript files. Printed and bound in Great Britain by Bookcraft (Bath) Ltd, Midsomer Norton. This book is printed on acid-free paper responsibly manufactured from sustainable forestry, in which at least two trees are planted for each one used for paper production.

Contents

Preface

Since the first and second editions of this book, published in 1991 and 1994, respectively, the C++ language and its standard library have improved considerably. This third edition has therefore been completely revised, in accordance with the revision of the C++ language itself, now crystallized in the ANSI/ISO C++ Standard. For example, the new, important type *string* is introduced in Chapter 1 and used throughout the book instead of C-style strings, which, incidentally are briefly discussed as well because practical programmers will often need them, for example, in view of existing function libraries. I have also introduced some aspects of the Standard Template Library (STL) in Chapter 1, while discussing this in more detail in Chapter 9.

It is possible to download all example programs and the solutions to the exercises from the website http://home.wxs.nl/~ammeraal/. For some of these exercises, marked by an asterisk, their solutions are also included in Appendix C.

I am grateful for some discussions, mostly by e-mail but also by personal contact, on the yearly C & C++ European Developers Forum in Oxford, with C++ experts such as Bjarne Stroustrup, Dan Saks and especially Francis Glassborow, who was the first to draw my attention to the STL.

Leen Ammeraal
l.ammeraal@consunet.nl

1

Introduction

1.1 About C++ and Other Languages

The C++ programming language was designed by B. Stroustrup and published in his book *The C++ Programming Language* in 1986. C++ was derived from the well-known programming language C. The name C++ is related to the expression `C++`, which we can write in a C(++) program to increment a variable C.

C++ offers good facilities for object-oriented programming (OOP), but, as a hybrid language, it also permits the traditional programming style, so that programmers can shift to object-oriented programming if and when they feel the need to do so. In this regard, C++ differs from some purely object-oriented languages, such as Smalltalk, Eiffel, and Java. Viewed from the angle of many C programmers, C++ is simply 'a better C.' Besides the important class concept, essential to OOP, there are many other useful language concepts and facilities that are available in C++, not in C. To mention just a few, related to functions, we have function overloading, inline functions, default arguments, type-safe linkage, function templates, and the very simple requirement that functions be declared before they are used. The use of undeclared functions is allowed in C, but not in C++.

The point just mentioned and some others make C++ much 'safer' than C, but unlike some other languages, C++ offers the same flexibility as C. This use of the word *safe* refers to what happens with incorrect programs. In this regard, assembly language is extremely 'unsafe', but this does not mean that programs written in assembly language cannot be perfectly correct and reliable. They can, and so can C programs. Most experienced programmers want as much control over the computer system as is possible and will therefore prefer C or C++ to, say, Basic. It is fine if a language is safe, as long as this does not make it restrictive. C++ is safer but not more restrictive than C. The oldest

1

well-known professional programming languages are Fortran and Cobol. They have been very durable: revised versions are still widely used by application programmers.

Fortran and Cobol already existed in 1960, the year of birth of Algol 60, which was a milestone in the world of scientific programming languages. In the sixties, Algol 60 was a very elegant and modern language, and it was as popular in academic circles as Fortran was in industry. For many years, new algorithms written in it were published in *Communications of the ACM* and in many other scientific journals. This language and its defining report inspired many experts to design successors to it. The best known among these are PL/1 (also based on Fortran and Cobol), Pascal, Simula 67, and Algol 68. Because of the extreme complexity of its defining report, Algol 68 was far less popular than Pascal, for which good compilers and books were soon available.

The notion of data hiding by means of classes, as used in C++, has been borrowed from Simula 67; the possibility of defining operators for new types, another important feature of C++, was already available in Algol 68. Some newer languages are Modula, designed by N. Wirth, and ADA, from the American Department of Defense, which was also the birthplace of Cobol. Modula and ADA are based on Pascal, while C and C++ have more in common with Algol 60 and Algol 68. For example, conditional expressions (to be discussed in Section 3.1) were available in Algol 60 and Algol 68, but not in Pascal, Modula or ADA; the compact notation used for them in C (and C++) is similar to that in Algol 68. Another common aspect of Algol 60, Algol 68, C, and C++ is the fact that values returned by functions can be ignored so that such functions can be used as procedures. As for their general acceptance outside the academic world, those of the above languages with a purely American origin (Fortran, Cobol, PL/1, Basic, C, C++, ADA) have done better than most of the others (Algol, Simula, Pascal, Modula).

Realistic and easy-to-use programs are not always easy to read. It is very difficult not to make errors when complicated programs need to be modified. With C++, this situation is much better than with some other languages in that we can define our own language extensions, known as classes. We write these in separate modules, and simply use such language extensions in our main programs, or rather, in our application modules, which can then be kept much simpler than would be the case otherwise. For example, a program that performs arithmetic with very large numbers is likely to be complicated if it is to be programmed in a language that does not support a data type for such numbers, with its associated operators +, −, *, /. Although C++ has no such built-in data type, we can define it ourselves in such a way that application programs can be written exactly as if this data type were supported by the language itself. We can say that in this way we are extending the language. User-defined language extensions have the advantage of greater flexibility. The alternative of built-in facilities often leads to the availability of things other than what we actually want. Before discussing all this in detail, we must be familiar with more elementary language aspects, most of which are also available in the C language.

If you have no experience with other programming languages, you have the advantage of not being confused by language differences, but you must know that it takes time to become a skilled programmer; programming can only be learned by doing, so don't ignore the exercises. Incidentally, this also applies to those who have such experience. There are many exercises in this book, but you can also use other sources, or invent programming problems yourself; the more programs you write the better.

1.2 An Unrealistic Program

Most example programs in this book are unrealistic because each illustrates just some subject that we are discussing. They are therefore shorter than real programs, which combine a great many of such subjects. In this section we will deal with a program that is even more unrealistic than most others because each action prescribed by it is performed exactly once. For those who are already more or less familiar with programming, this is about the same as saying that the program does not contain any conditional statements or loops. This program, shown below, reads two integers a and b from the keyboard to compute both $u = (a + b)^2$ and $v = (a - b)^2$:

```
// example1.cpp: A program to compute the squares of both
//               the sum and the difference of two given
//               integers.
#include <iostream>
using namespace std;

int main()
{   cout << "Enter two integers: "; // Displays input request.
    int a, b;
    cin >> a >> b;                   // Reads a and b.
    int sum = a + b, diff = a - b,
    u = sum * sum, v = diff * diff;
    cout << "Square of sum        : " << u << endl;
    cout << "Square of difference: " << v << endl;
    return 0;
}
```

After typing this program by using a program editor, we save it as the file *example*1.*cpp*, that is, if we are using some compiler for MS-DOS, such as those from Microsoft and Borland. For C++ compilers under the UNIX operating system, the file-name extension *.C* instead of *.cpp* is normally used. Most C++ compiler packages for the PC actually consist of both a C and a C++ compiler, and it depends on the file-name extension which one is used. Since our program contains several elements that are specific to C++, it must be compiled with a C++ compiler; a compiler for plain C would display many error messages.

After compiling and linking, we can execute the program. Then the following text appears on the computer screen:

```
Enter two integers:
```

We can now enter, for example,

```
100 10
```

After we press the Enter key, the following appears:

```
Square of sum       : 12100
Square of difference: 8100
```

We can easily check these values: with $a = 100$ and $b = 10$, it follows that *sum* = 110 and *diff* = 90, and by squaring these we find 12 100 and 8100 as the values of *u* and *v*, respectively.

We will now briefly discuss some C++ language rules, which apply to our example. It is good practice to start any program with a *comment*. This can be done in two ways. If (in a reasonable position) we write a pair of successive slashes (//), this pair and the rest of the program line are ignored by the compiler. This explains the first three program lines, repeated below:

```
// example1.cpp: A program to compute the squares of both
//               the sum and the difference of two given
//               integers.
```

We can also use comment at the end of a program line, to explain the preceding portion of that line, as is the case in

```
cin >> a >> b;                 // Reads a and b.
```

As we will see in Section 1.8, there is a different, older way of writing comments, based on the character pair /* at the beginning and the reverse, that is, */, at the end.

The two comment lines at the top of the program are followed by

```
#include <iostream>
```

We say that *<iostream>*, referred to as a *header*, is *included* by this program line. Although this need not literally be the case, we imagine that there is a file *iostream*, the contents of which logically replace this *#include* line. Each *#include* line always requires a program line of its own. For example, you cannot write the program text *int main( )* at the end of a *#include* line.

In this regard *#include* lines form an exception to a general rule, which says that, as far as the C++ compiler is concerned, program text may be split up over several lines as we please. For example, we can replace the line

```
int sum = a + b, diff = a - b;
```

with the following two lines:

```
int sum = a + b,
diff = a - b;
```

We can even split these lines further, but that would obviously not improve readability. When splitting a line into two new lines, we say that we insert a newline character.

Similar characters are the space character and the tab. Collectively, these three characters are referred to as *white-space characters*.

The program line

```
using namespace std;
```

is required because we use the names *cout*, *cin*, and *endl* (to be discussed in a moment) which belong to the C++ Standard Library. We could have omitted this program line, provided we replace these three short names with their complete versions, *std::cout*, *std::cin*, and *std::endl*. Yet another possibility is to replace the above line with these three lines:

```
using std::cout;
using std::cin;
using std::endl;
```

Every C++ program contains one or more *functions*, one of which is called *main*. (Note that we do not use the term *function* in the abstract, mathematical sense; instead, a function denotes a concrete program fragment, that is, a sequence of characters!) In our example, the *main* function is the only one. It has the form

```
int main()
{  ...
   ...
   return 0;
}
```

Functions may or may not have parameters. If they have, we write them between parentheses, as we will see later. If not, we still use the parentheses, with nothing in between, as is done here. The 'body' of every function is surrounded by a pair of braces { }. It is good practice to write the two braces of such a pair in the same (vertical) column, with everything in between indented, as is done here.

After the opening brace { of a function, we write so-called *statements*. As long as we are not using compound statements (to be discussed in Section 2.4), any statement ends with a semicolon. In the *main* function of program *example1.cpp*, we can count seven semicolons, each of which is the end of a statement. We very often write precisely one statement on a line. However, there may be more than one statement on a line, and a statement may take more than one line, as this statement shows:

```
int sum = a + b, diff = a - b,
u = sum * sum, v = diff * diff;
```

This kind of statement is called a *declaration*. It says that the variables *sum*, *diff*, *u*, and *v* have type *int*, which means that they denote integers. Every variable and constant has a *type* (or *data type*), which will turn out to be a very important concept. The values of type *int* are limited: with most computers, these values range from -2^{31} (= -2147483648) to

$+2^{31} - 1 \, (= 2\,147\,483\,647)$. In the above statement, we not only declare the variables *sum*, *diff*, *u*, and *v*, but we also initialize them, using the values of *a* and *b*. As is usual in programming languages, the asterisk * denotes multiplication. These variables *a* and *b* are declared themselves in the statement

```
int a, b;
```

without being initialized: immediately after this declaration their values are undefined. A completely different statement is

```
cout << "Enter two integers: ";
```

This is the typical C++ way of displaying some piece of text on the video screen. We say that *cout* is the *standard output stream*, to which we can send characters by means of the operator <<. Note that this operator is written as a character pair which looks like an arrow head that points to the left. It therefore suggests that the characters between the double quotes in *"Enter two integers*: " are sent to the stream *cout*. Instead of saying that we send characters to the output stream *cout* (or to the video screen), we sometimes say that we *print* these characters. Analogously, the statement

```
cin >> a >> b;
```

reads two values from the standard input stream (that is, from the keyboard), and stores them into the variables *a* and *b*. The character pair >> may be associated with an arrow head pointing to the right, so the values go from the input stream *cin* to the variables *a* and *b*. When executing this statement, the machine will be waiting for input, so we can now enter the two integers as requested.

After *u* and *v* have been computed, the values of these variables, preceded by some text and followed by a newline character, are displayed by the following statements:

```
cout << "Square of sum       : " << u << endl;
cout << "Square of difference: " << v << endl;
```

We use *endl* to indicate that we are at the end of the line. Instead of *endl*, we could have written '\n', or "\n", as we will see in Section 1.5. The notation *endl* itself will not be explained until Section 10.2. In the meantime, we will use it freely. If *endl* (or one of these alternatives) had been omitted in the first of these lines, the output would have been

```
Square of sum       : 12100Square of difference: 8100
```

In the actual output, shown in the following demonstration of the program, you may notice that the numbers 12100 and 8100 are not properly aligned: since their first digits are in the same position, their final ones are not. We will see how to improve this in Sections 2.5 and 10.2:

```
Enter two integers: 100 10
Square of sum       : 12100
Square of difference: 8100
```

1.3 Memory Organization and Binary Numbers

Both compiled programs and data are stored in (the computer's) memory. In addition to this, our computer has registers, which can temporarily contain data. We can regard the memory as a long sequence of *bytes*, each usually consisting of eight binary digits or *bits*. A bit can only have two values, 1 and 0. Since one byte is not large enough for most integers that we will deal with, a number of bytes are combined, forming a *machine word*, or briefly, a *word*, to contain one integer. These days, it is realistic to use four bytes for one word, which, with eight bits per byte, implies that type *int* values take 32 bits. We number these bits 0, ..., 31, from right to left, as shown in Figure 1.1.

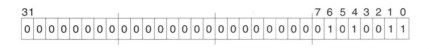

Figure 1.1. A word of 32 bits

This machine word contains the following bit sequence:

```
00000000 00000000 00000000 01010011
```

We can interpret these 32 bits in (at least) two ways: either as four characters (each represented by 8 bits) or as one integer of 32 bits. Which of these interpretations applies depends on the program that manipulates this word. If the word should be regarded as an integer, we use the 1 bits to compute its value. Omitting leading zeros, we have 1010011 here, which is the binary representation of 83. This value can be computed as follows:

$$1 \times 2^6 + 0 \times 2^5 + 1 \times 2^4 + 0 \times 2^3 + 0 \times 2^2 + 1 \times 2^1 + 1 \times 2^0 = 83$$

Instead of 'binary representation of a number,' the shorter (but less precise) term *binary number* is more often used, and we will conform to this usage. The value of a binary number is found by using powers of 2, as this example shows. We say that 2 is the *base* or *radix* of the binary number system. Similarly, 10 is the radix of the usual decimal number system. For example, we can compute the value of the decimal number 8241 as follows:

$$8 \times 10^3 + 2 \times 10^2 + 4 \times 10^1 + 1 \times 10^0$$

If we use all 32 bits of a (32-bit) word the same way, we can represent these 2^{32} numbers:

```
00000000 00000000 00000000 00000000 = 0
00000000 00000000 00000000 00000001 = 1
00000000 00000000 00000000 00000010 = 2
00000000 00000000 00000000 00000011 = 3
           ...
11111111 11111111 11111111 11111111 = 2^32 − 1 = 4294967295
```

We use the term *unsigned int* (or, briefly, *unsigned*) for this representation. In many applications we also want to use negative numbers. The usual way of doing this is by means of the two's-complement method. Using 32 bits, we can in this way represent the integers $-4\,294\,967\,296$, ..., $+4\,294\,967\,295$ as follows:

$$10000000\ 00000000\ 00000000\ 00000000 = -2^{31} = -4\,294\,967\,296$$
$$10000000\ 00000000\ 00000000\ 00000001 = -(2^{31} - 1) = -4\,294\,967\,295$$
$$...$$
$$11111111\ 11111111\ 11111111\ 11111110 = -2$$
$$11111111\ 11111111\ 11111111\ 11111111 = -1$$
$$00000000\ 00000000\ 00000000\ 00000000 = 0$$
$$00000000\ 00000000\ 00000000\ 00000001 = 1$$
$$...$$
$$01111111\ 11111111\ 11111111\ 11111111 = 2^{31} - 1 = 4\,294\,967\,295$$

If the numbers we are dealing with can also be negative, as is the case here, the type of these numbers is *signed int*. As integers are signed by default, we usually write *int*, rather than *signed int*. Note that, with word length n, the unsigned and signed interpretations of any bit sequence with a 1 bit at the extreme left differ by 2^n. For example, using word length 32, the value we associate with the bit sequence

$$10000000\ 00000000\ 00000000\ 00000000$$

is 2^{31} if it is interpreted as *unsigned int* and -2^{31} if it is interpreted as *signed int*. The difference between these two values is $2^{31} - (-2^{31}) = 2 \times 2^{31} = 2^{32}$.

There are also (signed and unsigned) short integers, which usually consist of 16 bits. In that case, their maximum values are $2^{16} - 1 = 65\,535$ for type *unsigned short* and $2^{15} - 1 = 32\,767$ for type *signed short int*.

We conclude this section with another important way of interpreting bit sequences, namely by means of the hexadecimal representation of numbers. We can divide a machine word into groups of four bits. In the hexadecimal number system, the radix is 16, so there are 16 digits, which, with their binary representations, are given below:

$$0000 = 0$$
$$0001 = 1$$
$$...$$
$$1001 = 9$$
$$1010 = A\ (= 10)$$
$$1011 = B\ (= 11)$$
$$1100 = C\ (= 12)$$
$$1101 = D\ (= 13)$$
$$1110 = E\ (= 14)$$
$$1111 = F\ (= 15)$$

Now consider, for example, the following word of 32 bits, divided into eight groups of four bits:

1000 0000 0000 0000 1111 0000 1010 0011

This sequence of bit groups corresponds to the following hexadecimal number

8000*F0A*3

Recalling that we have $F = 15$ and $A = 10$, we can use this to compute

$$8 \times 16^7 + 15 \times 16^3 + 10 \times 16 + 3 = 2\,147\,545\,251$$

This is another way of computing the value of the given 32-bit word, when interpreted as an unsigned binary number. If we want to interpret it as a *signed* binary number, we reduce this value by 2^{32}, obtaining

$$2\,147\,545\,251 - 4\,294\,967\,2956 = -2\,147\,422\,045$$

The contents of memory locations (either bytes or words) are variable: they can frequently change during program execution. In contrast to this, each location has a fixed number, its *address*, to indicate its position. In high-level languages we do not normally know the addresses of our variables. This also applies to C++, but in this language we use a symbolic notation for such addresses. For example, &*a* denotes the address of variable *a*, as we will see in Chapter 5 and elsewhere.

1.4 Identifiers and Keywords

Variable names are technically known as *identifiers*. An identifier is written as a sequence of characters in which only letters, digits, and underscores (_) may occur, while its first character must not be a digit. It is wise to choose only identifiers that begin with a letter (not with an underscore), because there may be system functions with names that begin with underscores to distinguish them from other identifiers. Upper case and lower case letters are different, so there are 52 distinct letters. All characters of an identifier are significant. Here are some examples of valid identifiers:

```
a
largest_element
table1
```

The following identifiers are reserved as keywords, so we must not use them for variable names and similar purposes of our own:

```
asm, auto, bool, break, case, catch, char, class, const,
const_cast, continue, default, delete, do, double,
dynamic_cast, else, enum, explicit, export, extern, false,
float, for, friend, goto, if, inline, int, long, mutable,
namespace, new, operator, private, protected, public,
register, reinterpret_cast, return, short, signed, sizeof,
static, static_cast, struct, switch, template, this, throw,
true, try, typedef, typeid, typename, union, unsigned, using,
virtual, void, volatile, wchar_t, while.
```

In addition, the following alternative representations of certain operators must not be used for purposes of our own either. After each of these, the operator in question, which we will discuss in due course, is listed between parentheses:

```
and (&&), and_eq (&=), bitand (&), bitor (|), compl (~), not
(!), not_eq (!=), or (||), or_eq (|=), xor (^), xor_eq (^=).
```

1.5 Literals

Besides variables, there are also *literals* (or *constants*), an example of which is the number 123 in the following statement:

```
x = a + 123;
```

There are several kinds of literals.

Integer literals

Here are four examples of integer literals:

`123`	(decimal)
`0777`	(octal)
`0xFFFFFF3A`	(hexadecimal)
`123L`	(decimal, long)

If the first character of an integer literal is 0 and is immediately followed by another digit, the literal is interpreted as an octal number (with radix 8); only the digits 0, ..., 7 may then occur in it. If the literal begins with 0x or 0X, it is taken to be a hexadecimal integer. We use A, ..., F (or a, ..., f) as hexadecimal digits with values 10, ..., 15. A letter L (or l), which means *long*, at the end of the literal is a *suffix*. We can also use the suffix U (or u), which means unsigned. The order of L and U is irrelevant if they both occur. The *unsigned* suffix means that the number in question has type *unsigned int* (or *unsigned long* if there is also a suffix L). As we have seen in Section 1.3, the value of an unsigned type can be about twice as large as a value of the corresponding signed type but cannot be negative. A suffix U does not increase the size of the value, that is, the number of bytes the value takes. This may be different for a suffix L.

It is important to know the *type* of a literal. Usually, each of the types *long int* and *unsigned long int* takes four bytes. These days this also applies to the types *int* and *unsigned int*. If no suffix *L* or *U* occurs in a very large integer literal, the type of that literal may yet be *long*, *unsigned*, or *unsigned long*. The precise decision rules for these cases are somewhat tedious, but they have been carefully devised so that they are in accordance with what is both convenient and efficient:

- A decimal integer literal without any suffix has type *int*, unless it is too large for that; in the latter case it has type *long int*. In other words, it has the first of these types in which it can be represented: *int, long int*.
- A hexadecimal or octal integer literal without any suffix has the first of these types in which it can be represented: *int, unsigned int, long int, unsigned long int*.
- An integer literal with suffix *U* has the first of these types in which it can be represented: *unsigned int, unsigned long int*.
- An integer literal with suffix *L* has the first of these types in which it can be represented: *long int, unsigned long int*.

Character literals

We use single quotes at the beginning and end of a character literal, as, for example in 'A'. In C++ character literals have type *char*. (This might seem to be obvious, but they have type *int* in the C language!) If we want, we can easily use the numerical value of a character literal. This value is simply that of its internal representation. Although, strictly speaking, such values are system dependent, with most C++ implementations they are as listed in the ASCII table, included in this book in Appendix B. For 'A' we find the value 65, or 41 in hexadecimal. The latter is useful if we want to write down the actual bit string: 41 hex = 0100 0001 binary (= 65 dec). In C the notations 65 and 'A' are really equivalent (if the ASCII table is used). This is not the case in C++, in which 'A' has type *char*, but an expression such as 'A' + 1 is allowed and is equal to 65 + 1 = 66. This is possible because the type of 'A' is converted from *char* to *int* to make the adding operation possible. We will discuss type conversion in more detail in Section 3.7 and elsewhere.

Some special characters can be represented by escape sequences, in which the backslash character (\) occurs:

`'\n'`	newline, go to the beginning of the next line
`'\r'`	carriage return, back to the beginning of the current line
`'\t'`	horizontal tab
`'\v'`	vertical tab
`'\b'`	backspace
`'\f'`	form feed
`'\a'`	audible alert
`'\\'`	backslash
`'\''`	single quote
`'\"'`	double quote
`'\?'`	question mark
`'\ooo'`	octal number
`'\xhh'`	hexadecimal number

Note that the newline character should really be written as '\n'; the notation *endl* can only be used after << in output operations.

In the final two literals above, *ooo* and *hh* denote at most three octal and two hexadecimal digits, respectively. We can use these forms conveniently if bit strings are actually given. For example, we can write '\x4F' to denote the bit string 01001111. However, we must be careful if the leftmost bit of such a bit string (of length 8) is 1. If type *char* is converted to type *int*, the eight bits of type *char* are extended on the left to the size of type *int*, which is, say, 32 bits. If the compiler regards characters as signed (as is usual), the leftmost bit is used as a sign bit. The value of '\x80' may therefore be –128 instead of 128, because extending the corresponding bit string 1000 0000 to 32 bits may give

```
11111111 11111111 11111111 10000000
```

instead of 00000000 00000000 00000000 10000000. Fortunately, this problem does not occur with normal characters, since their leftmost bit is always 0.

An important special case is '\0', the so-called *null character*, which consists of only zero bits. Note that '\0' has the value 0. By contrast, the ASCII value of '0' is 48, as Appendix B shows.

Floating literals

A floating literal represents a real number. It can have a fractional part, and its value can be much greater than those of integer literals. However, in its internal format it normally only *approximates* the real number it represents. For example, the literal 0.1 may be stored internally as a value that is actually closer to 0.0999999999999999 than to 0.1. A floating literal always contains a period or the letter *E* (or *e*), as, for example, in

```
82.347
.63
83.
47e-4
1.25E7
61.e+4
```

These literals have type *double*, which means 'double-precision floating point.' We can insist that they be (single-precision) *float*, by writing a letter *F* (or *f*) at the end of the literal. By contrast, we can write *L* (or *l*) at the end as a request for more precision than that of type double. If this is done the literal has type *long double*. Actually, the distinction between the types *float*, *double*, and *long double* is used more frequently for variables than for literals. With some compilers (such as Visual C++), the types *double* and *long double* are identical, but with others they are really different. For example, the values shown in the following table apply to Borland C++·

Type	Number of bytes
float	4
double	8
long double	10

String literals

A string literal is a sequence of characters written between double quotes, as, for example, in

```
"How many numbers?"
"a"
```

The string literal "*a*" must not be confused with the character literal '*a*'. A string literal is, technically speaking, an array of characters. An array (to be discussed in detail in Chapter 5) is a sequence of elements of the same type. Since, internally, a null character '\0' is always stored after the final character written in the string literal, the length of the character array used for a string literal is one more than what we may expect. For example, the string literal

```
"ABC"
```

has type

array of 4 const char

where the length 4 is equal to the number of characters stored plus one position for the terminating null character. The word *const* as used here indicates that the characters of string literals cannot be changed, so that we cannot replace the characters *A*, *B*, or *C* in the string literal "*ABC*" with others.

If we want to write a double quote inside a string, it must be preceded by a backslash, so we write \". We can also use other escape sequences, as in

```
cout << "The character\n\\\nis called a \"backslash\".";
```

This statement produces the following output:

```
The character
\
is called a "backslash".
```

Note that each escape character counts as one character, despite the fact that we write it as two or more characters in our source code. For example, the string literal "\n\n\n" has the same length as "*ABC*", so its type is also *array of 4 const char*.

Without special measures, we cannot write a string on more than one program line. However, two or more successive string literals, possibly with white-space characters in between, are logically pasted together. For example, writing

```
"ABC"    "DEF""GHI"
"JKL"
```

literally in our program is just another way of writing the following string:

```
"ABCDEFGHIJKL"
```

As we will see later in this book, we normally use indentation when writing our programs, so it may happen that a long string literal, which starts, say, at the middle of a program line, does not fit into that line, especially if we want our program lines to be rather short. Then we can simply use two double quotes in the same way as those between *I* and *J* in the above example.

There is an older solution (dating back to the first version of the C language) for the same problem. It consists of writing a backslash at the end of the line that is to be continued, as, for example, in

```
cout << "This is a string that is regarded \
as being on one line.";
```

A drawback of this older method is that we must not indent the second of these two lines: any blanks preceding the word *as* in this example are inserted between this word and the preceding word *regarded*, in addition to the blank that there is already after the latter word. The newer method is therefore to be preferred. For example, the following two program lines have the same effect as those just shown:

```
cout << "This is a string that is regarded "
        "as being on one line.";
```

Boolean literals

There are two Boolean literals, written as *true* and *false*. Their type is *bool*. For example, these literals are used in the first two of the following program lines (and in a comment of the third):

```
bool b1 = true,
     b2 = false,
     b3 = 3 < 4;    // that is, b3 = true.
```

1.6 The Standard Type *string*

Besides computation, *text processing* is a very important subject in programming. Unlike older C++ compilers, the newer ones and the C++ standard now offer a very convenient and easy-to-use *string* type. The following program demonstrates this, by reading two lines of text and displaying them in alphabetical order:

```cpp
// twolines.cpp: Application of type string.
#include <iostream>
#include <string>
using namespace std;

int main()
{   cout << "  Enter two lines of text: \n";
    string s, t;
    getline(cin, s);
    getline(cin, t);
    cout << "  Output in alphabetic order:\n";
    if (s <= t)
        cout << s << endl << t << endl;
    else
        cout << t << endl << s << endl;
    return 0;
}
```

The header *<string>* is required for any program that use type *string*. To read a line of text from the keyboard and place this in a *string* variable *s*, we write

```cpp
getline(cin, s);
```

As one would expect, the conventional comparison operators, such as <= (meaning less than or equal to) can be applied to two strings to compare them. Here is a demonstration of this program:

```
  Enter two lines of text:
programming
examples and exercises
  Output in alphabetic order:
examples and exercises
programming
```

Although a string literal is an array of characters and an object of type *string* is not, forms such as

```cpp
string s = "John", t;
t = "Mary"
```

are possible. All this and much more will be discussed in greater detail in Chapter 5, but in the meantime we can already use this *string* type in the programs that we write.

1.7 Some Elements of STL

One of the most important new aspects of Standard C++ is the Standard Template Library, or STL, for short. Although sensible use of this library requires some knowledge of language elements to be discussed in detail later, we will now deal with a program that shows some of the exciting possibilities of it. This program asks the user to enter some lines of text, followed by a line consisting only of the word *stop*. The lines just entered then appear on the screen in sorted order. Let us start with a demonstration of this program:

```
   Enter lines of text to be sorted,
   followed by the word stop:
program, 8
computer, 10
language, 12
compiler, 15
stop
   The same lines after sorting:
compiler, 15
computer, 10
language, 12
program, 8
```

Although this is by no means required, each input line here consists of a word and a number, as is the case when a book index is to be generated. In the output the words *compiler*, *computer*, *language*, and *program* appear in alphabetic order. There are two intriguing aspects in this application:

1. There is (in principle) no limit to the number of input lines.
2. The input lines are sorted very quickly (even if there are a great many of them), although efficient sorting is traditionally considered a rather difficult programming task.

As a consequence of these two points, a program to perform this task would be rather large and far too difficult to discuss at this stage, if STL were not available. When we use this library, the resulting program is comparatively simple:

```
// introstl.cpp: Introduction to STL.
#include <iostream>
#include <string>
#include <vector>
#include <algorithm>
using namespace std;
```

```
int main()
{   vector<string> v;
    cout << "  Enter lines of text to be sorted,\n";
    cout << "  followed by the word stop:\n";
    for (;;)
    {   string s;
        getline(cin, s);
        if (s == "stop")
            break;
        v.push_back(s);
    }
    sort(v.begin(), v.end());
    cout << "  The same lines after sorting:\n";
    for (int i=0; i<v.size(); ++i)
        cout << v[i] << endl;
    return 0;
}
```

The program lines

```
#include <vector>
#include <algorithm>
```

indicate that we are using STL. The notion of *vector* is used for a sequence of elements, stored in a single block of memory, and with the possibility of adding and removing elements efficiently at the back. By writing

```
vector<string> v;
```

we indicate that all elements of this sequence will be *string* objects, as discussed in the previous section. Statements that begin with the word *for* contain actions that are to be executed repeatedly. We can use the simplest form, starting with

```
for (;;)
```

if we program a signal to end the loop inside it, as is done here as follows:

```
if (s == "stop")
    break;
```

This implies that the loop is terminated as soon as the string *s*, just read, is equal to the word *stop*. If this is not the case, this string *s* is added at the back of the vector *v* by means of

```
v.push_back(s);
```

Besides *containers*, of which a *vector* is an example, STL also has facilities known as *algorithms* to perform certain often occurring actions. Perhaps the most useful STL algorithm is *sort*, which we use as follows to sort all elements of the vector *v*:

```
sort(v.begin(), v.end());
```

The expressions *v.begin*() and *v.end*() refer to the position of the first element and that *just after* the final element, respectively. It may look strange that we should specify this, but it makes it possible to sort not the entire vector *v*, but only some part of it, which is occasionally desirable.

The number of elements of the vector *v* is equal to

```
v.size()
```

and these elements themselves can be identified as

```
v[0], v[1], ..., v[v.size() - 1]
```

Precisely these elements are addressed in the following for-loop:

```
for (int i=0; i<v.size(); ++i)
   cout << v[i] << endl;
```

Here *int i* = 0 obviously specifies that we start with *i* = 0. The final value of *i* follows from the condition *i* < *v.size*() in combination with the expression ++*i* to increase *i* by one in each step.

We will discuss for-loops in greater detail in Section 2.5. As will be clear in Chapter 5, expressions such as

```
v[i]
```

were originally only used for *arrays*, which are more primitive than STL vectors in that their maximum size must be specified beforehand.

1.8 Comments

As we have seen in Section 1.2, comments can have two forms:

```
// ...
/* ... */
```

A comment that begins with // terminates at the end of the line on which it occurs. If, instead, it begins with /*, it ends with the character pair */. The latter type of comment is not restricted to one program line. Within a // comment, the comment characters //, /*, and */ have no special meaning. Similarly, the comment characters // and /* have no special meaning within a /* comment, so comments cannot be nested. In the (very confusing) program line

```
/*a/*b/*c/*d//*/x = 0;
```

the comment starts at the character pair /* at the beginning and ends at the first pair */ that follows, which happens to appear just before the statement

```
x = 0;
```

so that the latter (simple) program line and the former (confusing) one are equivalent.

If you want the compiler temporarily to skip program fragments in which comments occur, you can enclose that fragment by the line #*if* 0 at its beginning and #*endif* at its end, as will be discussed in Section 4.12. These two lines have the same effect as the character pairs /* and */ would have if nested comments were possible. This method is to be preferred to using a special compiler option (available with some compilers) which enables nested comments. It is always a good idea to use standard language elements rather than special features that have no real advantages.

Comment cannot occur within a string, so the statement

```
cout << "/* ABC */";
```

causes the following to be printed:

```
/* ABC */
```

Exercises

An asterisk following an exercise number indicates that a solution to the exercise can be found in Appendix C. Solutions to the other exercises are available from the website mentioned in the Preface.

1.1* Write a program that prints your name and address. Compile and run this program on your computer.

1.2* Write a program that prints what your age will be at the end of this year. The program should request you to enter both the current year and your year of birth.

1.3* What numbers do the following bit sequences represent, with the two's-complement method and 32-bit word length?

   a. 00000000 00000000 00000000 00001111
   b. 11111111 11111111 11111111 11110000
   c. A sequence of $32 - k$ zero bits followed by k one bits ($0 \le k \le 31$)
   d. A sequence of k one bits followed by $32 - k$ zero bits ($1 \le k \le 31$)

1.4* Use a word length of 32 bits and the two's-complement method to write the following numbers in the binary number system:

    a. 19
    b. −8.

1.5* Use the operator << only once to print the following three lines:

```
One double quote: "
Two double quotes: ""
Backslash: \
```

1.6* Find the errors in the following program, and correct them:

```
include <iostream>

int main();
{   int i, j
    i = 'A';
    j = "B";
    i = 'C' + 1;
    cout >> "End of
        program/n";
    return 0
}
```

1.7* Use a hexadecimal literal to assign the following binary number to a variable *i*:

```
01010101 01010101 01010101 01010101
```

Display the value of *i* in the normal way, that is, as a decimal number.

1.8* What does the following statement print?

```
cout << "Single quote: \'\nDouble quote: \"\n"
        "Backslash: \\\nThe End.\n";
```

2

Expressions and Statements

To discuss the C++ language in an efficient way, we must be familiar with some more technical terms than those discussed in Chapter 1. For example, each of the following three forms is called an *expression*:

```
a + b
1
x = p + q * r
```

It may make sense for an expression, such as the last of these three, to be immediately followed by a semicolon (;). Then the result is no longer an expression but a *statement*. The characters +, *, and =, as used here, are called *operators*. In the first of the above three expressions the variables *a* and *b* are *operands*.

2.1 Arithmetic Operations

As we have seen in Chapter 1, we use the plus and minus operators + and – to add and subtract. In the expression

```
a - b
```

the minus operator has two operands (*a* and *b*).This operator is therefore said to be a *binary* one. The situation is different with the minus sign in

```
(-b + D1)/(2 * a)
```

which is a *unary* minus operator, because this operator has only one operand (*b*). We can also use + as a unary operator, so we can write, for example,

```
neg = -epsilon;
pos = +epsilon;
```

which, for reasons of symmetry, looks nicer than without the plus sign.

With the binary operators +, −, and *, the result of the computation is integer if both operands are integer; if at least one of the operands has floating-point type, so has the result. We should bear in mind that there is a maximum *int* value, which we can denote in our program as *INT_MAX*, provided that we use the header *<climits>*. If machine words consist of 32 bits, we have

$$INT\_MAX = 2^{31} - 1 = 0x7FFFFFFF = 2\,147\,483\,647$$

Let us assume that this value of *INT_MAX* applies. Then all computations with type *int* are done modulo 2^{32}, in such a way that the result is not less than -2^{31} and less than $+2^{31}$. This is equivalent to saying that we simply take the last 32 bits of the result and interpret these in the usual way. For example, if we write

```
int k = 4 * INT_MAX;
```

we can find the resulting value of *k* by thinking of the binary representation of

$$INT\_MAX = \quad \texttt{1111111111111111111111111111111 (31 bits)}$$

Multiplying this by 4 means that two 0-bits are to be added at the end, so if there were no maximum, we would find the mathematically correct product

$$k_0 = \quad \texttt{111111111111111111111111111111100 (33 bits)}$$

Taking the final 32 bits (by omitting the first bit) of k_0, we find

$$k = \quad \texttt{11111111111111111111111111111100 (32 bits)}$$

which happens to be the representation of −4 according to two's complement notation. In other words, the value of *k* will be equal to −4. We could also have found this value by computing

$$k_0 = 4 \times (2^{31} - 1) = 4 \times 2^{31} - 4 = 2 \times 2^{32} - 4$$

Working modulo 2^{32} means in this case that we have to add or subtract 2^{32} as many times as is required to obtain a result *k* that satisfies

$$-2^{31} \le k < +2^{31}$$

It follows that we have to subtract 2^{32} twice from k_0, which again gives the value

$k = -4$

Except for this modular arithmetic (in cases that are sometimes referred to as *integer overflow*), the results of +, −, and * will be what anyone would expect. This may be different with the division operator /. As with the three previous operators, the result of

```
a / b
```

has integer type if both *a* and *b* have integer type, and floating type if *a* or *b* has floating type. This implies, for example, that

```
39 / 5     is equal to 7
39. / 5    is equal to 7.8
```

We see that there are in fact two essentially different division operators, one for integer and one for floating type. Which one is used depends on the operand types. Beginners often make the mistake of writing, for example, 1/3 (which is equal to 0) instead of 1.0/3.0 with the intended value 0.333.... Instead of 1.0/3.0 you can also write 1.0/3 or 1/3.0, and in each of these three expressions the zeros may be omitted.

When using integer division, we are sometimes interested not only in the quotient (obtained by /), but also in the remainder, which we obtain by using the operator %. For example:

```
39 % 5     is equal to 4
```

The % operator must not be applied to floating types. For any integers *a* and *b*, where *b* is nonzero,

```
a % b     is equal to   a - b * (a / b)
```

Unfortunately, the results of the integer division operators / and % are only implementation-independent if both operands *a* and *b* are nonnegative. For example, with most implementations the result of 39 / −5 will be equal to −7 (the preferred behavior), so that 39 % −5 = 39 − (−5) * (−7) = 4, but the C++ standard also allows the result 39 / −5 = −8, combined with 39 % −5 = 39 − (−5) * (−8) = −1.

The three operators *, /, % have the same precedence, which is higher than that of + and −. If addition or subtraction should precede multiplication, we must use parentheses:

```
(8 - 1) * 2   is equal to 14
8 - 1 * 2     is equal to 6
```

Very often we want to increase a variable by some value. Instead of doing this by means of, for example,

```
x = x + a
```

we can write the following shorter and more efficient expression:

```
x += a
```

Once we are used to this new notation, we prefer the latter expression to the former also because it is more closely related to the way we think and speak: we say that we 'increase *x* by *a*' , not that we 'assign the sum of *x* and *a* to *x*'.

Note that the above two forms are expressions. They would have been statements if they had been followed by a semicolon. Both expressions not only assign a value to the variable *x*, but also yield this value. For example, this whole line is an assignment statement, while $x += a$ is an assignment expression with the value assigned to *x* as its value:

```
y = 3 * (x += a) + 2;
```

Combining arithmetic operations with assignments is not confined to the addition operator. We can also use the following expressions, the meaning of which is obvious:

```
x -= a
x *= a
x /= a
x %= a
```

It often occurs that the value 1 is to be added to (or subtracted from) a variable. For these special cases there is an even more compact notation. Instead of, for example,

```
i += 1   and   i -= 1
```

we can write

```
++i   and   --i
```

The unary operators ++ and −− are called *increment* and *decrement* operators, respectively. We can also write these operators after the operand, as in

```
i++   and   i--
```

Although the variable *i* is updated in this way as was done before, there is an important difference: the value of the whole expression is now equal to the old value of *i*. In other words, if we write such an operator before its operand, it is applied before its value is taken; if we write it at the end, it is applied only after its value has been taken. For example, after the execution of the statements

```
i = 0; j = (i++);
m = 0; n = (++m);
```

the four variables used have the same values as they would have if the following statements had been executed instead:

```
i = 1; j = 0;
m = 1; n = 1;
```

The parentheses in the above statements can be omitted. They were used here to illustrate the fact that those surrounding *i*++ do not cause *i* to be incremented before its value is taken, as is sometimes thought.

If we use *i*++ or ++*i* only to increment *i*, ignoring the values of these expressions, it does not matter which form is used: the statements *i*++; and ++*i*; (with semicolons!) are equivalent.

2.2 Types, Variables, and Assignments

In C and C++, the operator =, when used in an expression, indicates *assignment*: we use it to assign a value to a variable. If this variable has been assigned a value previously, that value is lost. Every variable has a fixed size, which is the number of bytes it occupies in memory. The size of a variable depends on its *type*. For example, the elementary types may have sizes as listed in the table below.

Type	Number of bytes
char	1
bool	1
short (or *short int*)	2
int	4
enum	4
long (or *long int*)	4
float	4
double	8
long double	10

The types *char*, *short*, *int*, and *long* may be preceded by one of the keywords *signed* and *unsigned*. Writing only *unsigned* is equivalent to writing *unsigned int*. Actually, we can distinguish between sequences of certain keywords, known as *type-specifiers*, and *types*. Some types can be represented by different sequences of type-specifiers, as shown below:

Type	*Type-specifiers*

`int`	`int`
	`signed int`
	`signed`

`unsigned int`	`unsigned int` `unsigned`

`short int`	`short`
	`short int`
	`signed short`
	`signed short int`

`long int`	`long`
	`long int`
	`signed long`
	`signed long int`

`unsigned short int`	`unsigned short` `unsigned short int`
`unsigned long int`	`unsigned long` `unsigned long int`

In the second column of this table, the type-specifiers may occur in any order. For example, instead of

```
unsigned short int i;
```

we may write the following, rather unusual declaration, if we like:

```
int unsigned short i;
```

As this table shows, the word *signed* is superfluous for the types *int*, *short int* and *long int*, since for each of these three there are exactly two variants, and *signed* is implied unless the word *unsigned* is used. By contrast, *signed* is not superfluous when used for *char*, since there are three distinct *char* variants:

```
char
signed char
unsigned char
```

Type *char* may behave like *signed char* or like *unsigned char*, depending on the implementation, but formally it is a different type. We will discuss the difference between *signed char* and *unsigned char* in Section 3.7.

We can inquire the size of a type by using *sizeof*. This is a unary operator, which can be applied either to a type name (written between parentheses) or to an expression.

The following program shows how *sizeof* can be used, and many other things besides, such as the way we can format numbers:

```
// typvar.cpp: Types and variables.
#include <iostream>
#include <iomanip>
using namespace std;

int main()
{  char ch = 'A';
   double ff = 5.0/3;
   float f = ff;
   bool b = (f > 1);
   int i, j;
   j = 2 * (i = 5.0/3);  // i = 1, j = 2
   cout << "ch = " << ch
        << "    ASCII value: " << int(ch) << endl;
   cout << fixed << setprecision(10);
   cout << "f = " << f << "    ff = " << ff << endl;
   cout << "i = " << i << "    j = " << j << endl;
   if (b)
      cout << "The variable b is equal to true.\n";
   cout << "Number of bytes for type 'bool':    "
        << sizeof(bool) << endl;
   cout << "Number of bytes for type 'char':    "
        << sizeof(char) << endl;
   cout << "Number of bytes for type 'int':    "
        << sizeof(int) << endl;
   cout << "Number of bytes for type 'float':  "
        << sizeof(float) << endl;
   cout << "Number of bytes for type 'double': "
        << sizeof(double) << endl;
   return 0;
}
```

Although this is not a practical program, it offers us the opportunity to discuss some important new points. In their declarations, the four variables *ch*, *ff*, *f*, and *b* are initialized, while this is not the case with the variables *i* and *j*, which are assigned values in subsequent statements. The variable *ch* is initialized to '*A*', with ASCII value 65 (see also Appendix B). We can obtain this value (of type *int*) by using the expression *int*(*ch*). If, until further notice, we want all floating-point values to show ten digits after the decimal point in the output, we write the following statement:

```
cout << fixed << setprecision(10);
```

For this use of *setprecision* the following line is required at the top of the program:

```
#include <iomanip>
```

We will discuss this in more detail in Section 10.2. With Visual C++, the above program produces the following output:

```
ch = A    ASCII value: 65
f = 1.6666666269    ff = 1.6666666667
i = 1   j = 2
The variable b is equal to true.
Number of bytes for type 'bool':   1
Number of bytes for type 'char':   1
Number of bytes for type 'int':    4
Number of bytes for type 'float':  4
Number of bytes for type 'double': 8
```

When we look at the program, it seems that the three variables *f*, *ff*, and *i* are assigned the same value, namely 5.0/3. Yet these variables assume different values: because of their types the exact value of 5.0/3 is approximated reasonably by *f*, very well by *ff*, and very badly by *i*. This program also demonstrates that an assignment expression, such as *i* = 5.0/3, may occur in a more complicated expression. Since *i* has type *int*, the computed value 1.66... is truncated to the integer 1. Since *f* is greater than 1, the *bool* variable *b* is given the value *true*. The operator *sizeof* is applied to a type in this program, as in

```
sizeof(double)
```

We might have omitted the parentheses if we had applied this operator to a very simple expression, such as in

```
sizeof ff
```

Because of precedence rules for operators, to be discussed in Section 3.6, parentheses are required in less elementary expressions, such as in

```
sizeof(2 * ff)
```

Since both *ff* and 2 * *ff* are of type *double*, all these three uses of *sizeof* yield the same value.

Enumeration types

The keyword *enum*, which occurs in the table of types at the beginning of this section, is normally used when we need some constants with names that say what they mean and with values that are irrelevant. For example, we can write

```
enum days
{  Sunday, Monday, Tuesday, Wednesday, Thursday,
   Friday, Saturday
}  yesterday, today, tomorrow;
```

After this declaration, we can use

- The enumeration type *days*. We can declare some more variables with it, as, for example, in:

```
days the_day_after_tomorrow, my_birthday;
```

- The enumeration constants *Sunday*, *Monday*, ..., *Saturday*, which are the values of type *days*.

- The variables *yesterday*, *today*, and *tomorrow*, which can be assigned values of type *days*.

Enumeration-type values can be converted to type *int*, so that such values can be assigned to *int* variables. In the above example, these *int* values for *Sunday*, *Monday*, ..., *Saturday* are 0, 1, ..., 6, respectively.

It is not correct to assign an *int* value to an enumeration-type variable. Each enumeration type is a unique type; we cannot convert one enumeration type to another. The comments in the following fragment, based on the above type *days*, illustrate all this:

```
int i;
enum color {black, white, red} pen = red;
i = yesterday;  // OK: conversion from days to int.
today = i + 1;  // Error: no conversion from int to days.
today = pen;    // Error: no conversion from color to days.
```

We can also specify numerical values ourselves for enumeration constants. The following example demonstrates this. It also shows that the declaration of variables (*great*, *greater*, *greatest*) can be separated from the declaration that specifies the enumeration type (*mathematician*) itself:

```
enum mathematician    // Numerical value = Year of birth
{  Cauchy=1789,
   Euler=1707,
   Fourier=1768,
   Gauss=1777,
   Hesse=1811,
   Hilbert=1862,
   Kronecker=1823,
   Laplace=1749
};
mathematician great, greater, greatest;
```

If we specify a value for a constant, and none for some that follow, that value is repeatedly incremented for those constants that follow. For example, after

```
enum example {aaa, bbb, ccc=48, ddd, eee, fff=1, ggg};
```

we have

```
aaa = 0, bbb = 1, ccc = 48, ddd = 49, eee = 50,
fff = 1, ggg = 2
```

This example also shows that two constants of an enumeration type may have the same value, as is the case here with *bbb* and *fff*. However, all constant names must be distinct. This is also the case if they belong to different enumeration types, for it would otherwise not be possible to tell the value and the type of a given constant name.

In the above examples, we have used integer literals after the equal sign, such as 48 in *ccc* = 48. In general, we may use 'integral constant expressions' or enumeration constants for this purpose. It should also be mentioned that the enumeration type may be absent. Here is an example that illustrates these points:

```
enum {a = 'A', b = 123, c = a} x, y, z;
```

After this, we can write

```
x = a; y = b; z = c;
```

Register variables

Computers usually have some registers and can work faster with registers than with memory locations. It may therefore be advantageous for some variables, which are used very frequently, to be kept only in registers, not in memory. We can ask the compiler to do this by using the keyword *register* when we declare the variables in question, as, for example, in

```
register int i;
```

The compiler will then use a register instead of a memory word for *i*, if this is possible. If not, the keyword *register* is ignored. You may wonder why not always use this keyword. The first reason is that the number of registers is normally very small, and they are also used for all kinds of other work, which we do not want to slow down because of too few free registers being available. Second, only memory locations have addresses, registers do not. Therefore the *address-of* operator & (to be discussed in Section 4.3) must not be used for register variables. Incidentally, there are compilers that try to keep variables in registers anyway, so when we omit the register keyword, the generated code may still be very efficient.

The *const* and *volatile* keywords

We can use the word *const* to define constants. Here is an example of how we can use this keyword:

```
const int weeklength = 7;
```

or, equivalently,

```
const int weeklength(7);
```

In both declarations initialization is applied, so the equal sign in the first one does not denote assignment. Initialization is really required here. We cannot assign values to constants, so

```
weeklength = 7; // Error
```

would not be a valid assignment statement. For constants such as *weeklength*, initialization is therefore required. We will see in Chapter 4 that we can use *const* also when specifying formal parameters of functions.

The keyword *volatile* is rarely used by ordinary programmers. Syntactically, we use it in the same way as *const*, but, in a sense, it has the opposite meaning. In principle, it is possible for volatile variables to be changed not only by ourselves but also by hardware or by system software. Another point is that volatile variables are not kept in registers, as may be the case with normal variables.

2.3 Comparison and Logical Operators

When programming decisions and repetitions, we often need the following operators:

Operator	Meaning	
<	<	(less than)
>	>	(greater than)
<=	≤	(less than or equal to)
>=	≥	(greater than or equal to)
==	=	(equal to)
!=	≠	(not equal to)
&&	*AND*	(logical *and*)
||	*OR*	(logical *or*)
!	*NOT*	(logical *not*)

The operators <, >, <=, and >= are known as *relational operators*, while == and != are referred to as *equality operators*. The former have higher precedence than the latter. We may collectively use the term *comparison operator* for these six operators. A comparison, such as $a < b$, is an expression with two possible values, *true* and *false*. Comparisons (and logical expressions in general) have type *bool*. In an arithmetic context, the *bool* values *true* and *false* are automatically converted to the *int* values 1 and 0, respectively. For example,

$$(3 < 4) + (7 < 9)$$

is a valid integer expression, and its value is 2. A very funny example is

$a < x < 2$

This is interpreted as

$(a < x) < 2$

Regardless of the values of a and x, the value of this expression is *true*, because the *bool* value of

$a < x$

is converted to either 1 or 0, which is less than 2 in either case.

The unary operator ! is normally used to turn *true* into *false*, and vice versa. For example, the values of the following two expressions are equal for any x and y:

```
x < y
! (x >= y)
```

When used in a logical context, any nonzero arithmetic value is interpreted as *true*, while 0 is interpreted as *false*. For example, if i is of type *int*, the expression

```
!i
```

is valid. A zero value of i is taken as *false* and any nonzero value of i as *true*. Since the operator ! performs negation, the value of the expression !i is *true* if $i = 0$ and *false* if $i \neq 0$. Note that we can write

```
i = !!i;
```

if we (only) want to overwrite any nonzero value of i with 1.

We can combine comparisons (and other logical expressions) by using the logical operators && and ||, as is done, for example, in the test

```
x > a  &&  x < b
```

to check that x lies between a and b. (The example $a < x < 2$ above shows why we cannot write $a < x < b$ here.) With the two forms

```
operand1 && operand2
operand1 || operand2
```

it is guaranteed that *operand2* will not be evaluated if the value of the result is already known after the evaluation of *operand1*. After all, for any value of *operand2*,

```
0 && operand2   is equal to false
1 || operand2   is equal to true
```

This behavior of && and ‖ is important, not only because (with complicated *operand2*) it may save computing time, but also because it may prevent undesirable actions, such as division by zero. For example, in the following expressions the division by *n* will not take place if *n* happens to be zero:

```
n != 0  &&  q < 1.0/n
!(n == 0  ||  q >= 1.0/n)
```

(Note that these two expressions are equivalent!)

Beginning C++ programmers often make the mistake of writing one equal sign instead of two. Doing this in the last example would cause division by zero instead of preventing it! Remember that *n* = 0 is an expression, which, after assigning 0 to *n*, also yields a value. As this value, 0, means false, the second operator in

```
n = 0 || q >= 1.0/n
```

will be evaluated, which will cause a division by zero.

2.4 Compound Statements and If-statements

Compound statements

It will by now be clear that statements describe actions. In contrast to expressions, they do not yield values. Many statements, such as those below, consist of an expression followed by a semicolon:

```
cin >> n;
x = a + b;
cout << "The End.\n";
```

We can use braces { } to build complex statements from simpler ones, just as we can use parentheses ( ) to build complex expressions. For example, the line

```
{x = a + b; y = c + d; z = e + f;}
```

contains a *compound statement*, built from three simpler statements. We often use compound statements in syntactic positions that allow only one statement, but in which we want to write more than one. We will apply this idea shortly.

Compound statements are also called *blocks*, especially if we declare variables in them. A declaration in a block is valid from this declaration until the closing brace of that block. This portion of the program is called the *potential scope* of the variables declared by that declaration. A variable can be used (and is said to be *visible*) in its *scope*, which is equal to its potential scope from which any inner potential scopes of other variables with the same name are excluded. The following program illustrates this:

```cpp
// scope.cpp: Illustration of 'scope' and 'visibility'.
#include <iostream>
using namespace std;

int main()
{   double x = 3.4;
    {   cout << x << " ";       // 3.4
        int x = 7;
        {   cout << x << " ";   // 7
            char x = 'A';
            cout << x << " ";   // A
        }
        cout << x << " ";       // 7
    }
    cout << x << endl;          // 3.4
    return 0;
}
```

Note that a variable declared in an outer block can be hidden in an inner block only if its name is the same as that of another variable. For example, if we had declared *double y =* 3.4 instead of *double x =* 3.4, the variable *y* would have been visible in the inner blocks. This program produces the following line of output:

```
3.4 7 A 7 3.4
```

If-statements

We often want the execution of a statement to depend on a condition. This is achieved by an if-statement of the following form:

```
if (condition) statement1
```

We can also use the following extended form of the if-statement:

```
if (condition) statement1 else statement2
```

Figures 2.1(a) and (b) show how these if-statements work. Here the *condition* is either an expression or a declaration with initialization of a variable (without a terminating semicolon). Examples are

```
x > y
bool choice = a < b && c >= d
int dif = a - b
```

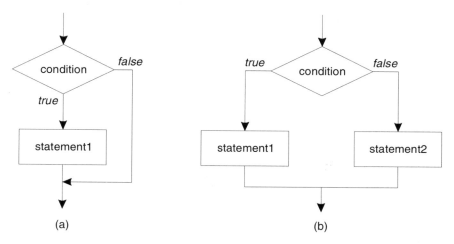

Figure 2.1. If-statements: (a) without else; (b) with else

The first of the three examples just shown is more usual than the second and third. The values of $x > y$, *choice* and *dif* are used as the value of the condition in question. If this value is *true* (or nonzero), *statement*1 is executed and *statement*2, if present, is ignored. In the opposite case, with *condition* equal to *false*, *statement*1 is ignored and *statement*2, if present, is executed. The following examples should be studied carefully.

Example 1

In this example, *statement*1 is a compound statement and there is no *statement*2. It swaps the values of x and y if x is greater than y:

```
if (x > y)
{   w = x;
    x = y;
    y = w;
}               // Now x <= y
```

Example 2

This example demonstrates that the *condition* can consist of the declaration of a variable. This variable must be initialized and its (potential) scope extends to the end of the if-statement:

```
if (int dif = a - b)
{   cout << "dif = " << dif << " (nonzero)\n";
    x = 1;
    y = 2;
}
else
{   cout << "dif = " << dif << " (zero)\n";
    z = 3;
}
```

In logical contexts, arithmetic values are converted to *false* or *true*, depending on whether they are zero or nonzero. In this example this implies that *statement1* is executed if *dif* is nonzero, and *statement2* if *dif* is zero.

Example 3

The statements in an if-statement can again be if-statements, as is the case here with *statement2*:

```
if (x > 0) cout << "Positive"; else
if (x < 0) cout << "Negative"; else cout << "Zero";
```

A pair of (superfluous) braces can clarify this, as the following, equivalent version shows:

```
if (x > 0) cout << "Positive"; else
{  if (x < 0) cout << "Negative"; else cout << "Zero";
}
```

Example 4

We can also take an if-statement for *statement1*, as in

```
if (x <= 0)
if (x < 0) cout << "Negative"; else cout << "Zero";
```

In this example we have two *if* keywords, and at first sight it may not be clear to which of these the *else* keyword belongs. This ambiguity is resolved by the rule that, in case of doubt, the *else* belongs to the most recent *if*. Therefore the above line should be read as

```
if (x <= 0)
{  if (x < 0) cout << "Negative"); else cout << "Zero";
}
```

not as

```
if (x <= 0)
{  if (x < 0) cout << "Negative";
}  else cout << "Zero";
```

Note that the only essential difference between the last two versions consists of the position of the closing brace }. The difference in layout, however important it may be for us humans, is ignored by the compiler.

Example 5

This example shows that even in complicated situations we can make a program readable by paying attention to the layout and, in particular, to the way indentation is used:

```
if (a >= b)
{   x = 0;
    if (a >= b+1)
    {   xx = 0;
        yy = -1;
    }
    else
    {   xx = 100;
        yy = 200;
    }
}
else
{   x = 1;
    xx = -100;
    yy = 0;
}
```

This method of indentation, with matching braces in the same column, is frequently used in this book. As early as 1960, this style was very common in Algol 60 programs, in which the words *begin* and *end* occurred instead of the braces { and }. This style is also frequently applied to Pascal programs, which are generally regarded as very readable.

Example 6

When developing large programs, we normally want to see a good many statements on one screen of, say, 25 lines, or on one printed page. It is therefore a good idea to write a rather short if-statement on one line, as is done in:

```
if (x > y) {w = x; x = y; y = w;}
```

This form is as readable as the equivalent form in Example 1, which was written on five lines.

Let us use this example for a brief discussion about where to insert semicolons. In C++, a semicolon at the end of a statement is part of that statement. Not every statement ends with a semicolon: its final character may also be a closing brace (}). This explains why a closing brace of a statement is never followed by a semicolon but may be preceded by one.

The null statement

If somewhere a statement is required but we feel no need to write one, it is permissible to write only a semicolon, which is then called a *null statement*. For example, the first semicolon in the following if-statement represents a null statement:

```
if (a < b) ; else x = 123;
```

We must not omit this semicolon, because the keyword *else* must be preceded by a statement. It goes without saying that the following if-statement has the same effect as the previous one but is much clearer:

```
if (a >= b) x = 123;
```

A more interesting application of the null statement follows in the next section.

2.5 Iteration Statements

There are three types of *iteration statements*, which are informally also known as *loops*:

While-statement:

```
while (condition) statement
```

Do-statement:

```
do statement while (expression);
```

For-statement:

```
for (for-init-statement  condition; expression) statement
```

To see how they work, let us use all three of them for the same purpose, namely to compute the sum

$$s = 1 + 2 + ... + n$$

without using the equality $s = \frac{1}{2} n(n + 1)$. Supposing that s, n, and i have been declared as integer variables, we can compute s as follows:

With a while-statement:

```
s = 0; i = 1;
while (i <= n)
{   s += i;   ++i;
}
```

With a do-statement (to be used here only if $n > 0$):

```
s = 0; i = 1;
do
{   s += i;
    ++i;
}  while (i <= n);
```

With a for-statement:

```
s = 0;
for (i=1; i<=n; ++i) s += i;
```

Figure 2.2(a) illustrates both the first and the third solutions (with *while* and *for*, respectively), while Figure 2.2(b) shows how the second solution (with *do ... while*) works.

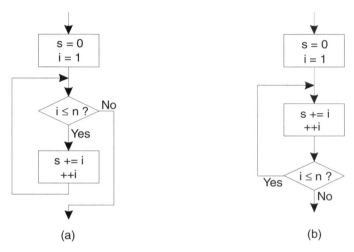

(a)   (b)

Figure 2.2. Loops: (a) while-statement and for-statement; (b) do-statement

In all three solutions, the process of repeatedly increasing both s by i and i by 1 continues as long as the test $i \leq n$ succeeds. In the while-statement this test is done at the beginning of the loop, before s is increased. This is an important point, because n may be 0 (or negative). In that case the eventual value of s will be equal to 0. Incidentally, people often write i++ instead of ++i in for- and while-statements such as those above. Which form is used is irrelevant in these cases.

In the do-statement, on the other hand, that test takes place after the inner part of the loop has been executed. The first time, s is increased by i regardless of the value of n. So if n is zero, s will be equal to 1, which is undesirable. We should therefore use the do-statement (also called do-while-loop) only if we know that n is positive. The inner part of a do-while-loop is always executed at least once, but the inner part of a while-statement may not be executed at all.

In the general form

```
for (for-init-statement  condition; expression) statement
```

of the for-statement, the for-init-statement may be the null statement (as we will see in a moment) and both the *condition* and the *expression* are optional (that is, they can be absent). If they are present, the effect of this for-statement is best described by means of the following, equivalent form with while:

```
for-init-statement
while (condition)
{  statement
   expression;
}
```

(Actually there is an exception to this equivalence, as we will see when discussing the continue-statement in the next section.)

The for-init-statement can be either an *expression statement* (that is, a semicolon possibly preceded by an expression) or a *simple declaration*. In either case, it ends with a semicolon, as these three examples illustrate:

```
;
i = 0;
int i = 0;
```

In the first example, the for-init-statement consists only of a semicolon, so it is in fact a null statement. Both the first and the second examples are expression statements, while the third is a simple declaration.

If, in the above general form of the for-statement, we omit the *condition* or the *expression*, the semicolon occurring between them must be present. For example, the for-init-statement appears as the null statement and the *expression* is omitted in the following (very contrived) fragment:

```
a = b = 1; x = 0;
for ( ; x < 1000; ) x += (a += b++);
```

We can replace the second of these two lines with the following, equivalent (and equally contrived) while-statement:

```
while (x < 1000) x += (a += b++);
```

(As we will see in Section 3.5, the parentheses surrounding a += b++ are superfluous in these fragments.) There would be an endless loop if, in the for-statement, we also omitted the *condition*. With the break-statement, to be discussed in the next section, it will be possible to write a for-statement that terminates normally even though the condition is omitted.

We frequently use a running variable, which is initialized by the for-init-statement, tested in the condition, and updated in the expression, as is done in

```
for (int i=0; i<n; ++i) ...
```

but this is by no means necessary. For example, we might replace our last example of a for-statement with the following, possibly confusing but equivalent fragment:

```
b = 1; x = 0;
for (a=1; x<1000; ++b) x += (a += b);
```

It should also be noted that the *condition* in the while- and for-statements can contain simple variable declarations with initialization, in the same way as with if-statements. For example, the following fragment is correct (and produces –3 –2 –1 as output):

```
int j = 0;
while (int m = j-3)
{   cout << m << " ";
    ++j;
}
```

This loop terminates because *m* will eventually be equal to zero (or *false*).

Producing a table

Let us now turn to a complete program. It will produce a table with two columns *x* and *f*(*x*), where

$$f(x) = x^2 + x + 1/x$$

We want *x* to run from 2.0 to 4.0, with step 0.2, as shown in the following table, which is the output we want:

```
x               f(x)

2.0      6.5000000000
2.2      7.4945454545
2.4      8.5766666667
2.6      9.7446153846
2.8     10.9971428571
3.0     12.3333333333
3.2     13.7525000000
3.4     15.2541176471
3.6     16.8377777778
3.8     18.5031578947
4.0     20.2500000000
```

The following program solves this problem:

```
// table.cpp: This program produces a table.
#include <iostream>
#include <iomanip>
using namespace std;

int main()
{   cout << " x              f(x)\n\n";
    cout << fixed;
```

```
for (int i=20; i<=40; i+=2)
{  double x = i/10.0;
   cout << setw(3) << setprecision(1)
        << x << " "
        << setw(15) << setprecision(10)
        << x * x + x + 1/x << endl;
}
return 0;
}
```

Note the use of the manipulator *setw* in this program, to specify the width of the number in question. (If more positions are required than specified by *setw*, as many positions are used as are needed.)

The C++ language does *not* require the 'running variable' in a for-statement to have integer type, so it seems more natural to use a floating-point variable instead of the *int* variable *i* for this purpose, as is done in

```
for (double x=2.0; x<=4.0; x+=0.2)
```

However, this would not be correct. Floating-point values are only approximated: the values actually stored in memory may slightly differ from the theoretically correct values. In this example, this may not really affect the final digits in the above table, but yet there may be something wrong. The condition $x <= 4.0$ in the for-statement says that this statement is to terminate as soon as x is greater than 4. Now the problem here with the floating-point variable x is that this variable may be slightly greater than 4 at the moment when it should be exactly equal to 4. If this happens (which is really the case with, for example, Visual C++), the last line of the above table is omitted. In our program *table.cpp*, there is no such problem, because rounding errors do not apply to the integer running variable *i*. It is true that the problem in the above modified for-loop can easily be remedied by writing, for example, 4.1 instead of 4.0 in the condition, but it is always wise to use integer running variables. In this way we avoid cumulating rounding errors. This example shows that besides knowledge of the C++ language itself we should also have some idea about how numbers are stored inside the computer.

2.6 Break, Continue, Goto, Switch

The break-statement

The execution of a loop terminates immediately if the following statement is executed in its inner part:

```
break;
```

If this break-statement occurs inside some nested loops, only the innermost enclosing loop is terminated. Here is a program which demonstrates this statement:

```
// break.cpp: Demonstration of the break-statement.
#include <iostream>
using namespace std;

int main()
{   double s = 0, x;
    cout << "Enter numbers, separated by blanks.\n";
    cout <<
    "They are added up as long as they are positive.\n\n";
    for (;;)
    {   cin >> x;
        if (x <= 0) break;
        s += x;
    }
    cout << "Sum of the positive numbers that have "
            "been read: " << s << endl;
    return 0;
}
```

The interesting point about this program is that the test for the termination of the loop is placed neither at the beginning nor at the end but in the middle of the loop. This is a very natural thing to do: we can test a number only after reading it, so inside the loop reading x should precede the test. On the other hand, if the loop is not terminated, s is to be increased by x, so it is logical to write s += x; after the test. In Section 3.2 we will discuss loops with the test in the middle once again. Instead of

```
for (;;)
```

we might have written

```
while(1)
```

But for the break-statement, we would have endless loops in both cases.

The continue-statement

The continue-statement looks similar to the break-statement, but it works essentially differently. We write it (inside a loop) as

```
continue;
```

Normally the continue-statement is executed conditionally, as in

```
while (...)
{   xxx
    if (condition) continue;
    yyy
}
```

where ..., *xxx*, *yyy* stand for valid program text. The meaning of this loop is given by the following, equivalent form:

```
while (...)
{   xxx
    if (!(condition))
    {   yyy
    }
}
```

The continue-statement causes an immediate jump to the test for continuation of the (smallest enclosing) loop. Note that in the former fragment we have only one brace pair, whereas there are two in the latter. This shows that continue-statements can reduce the number of nested compound statements.

With *continue* in the for-statement, the running variable is updated in the normal way. More precisely, we can replace the form

```
for (for-init-statement  condition1; expression) statement
{   xxx
    if (condition2) continue;
    yyy
}
```

with the following while-construction, which is equivalent to it. Note that the *expression* is evaluated even if the fragment *yyy* is skipped:

```
for-init-statement
while (condition1)
{   xxx
    if (!(condition2))
    {   yyy
    }
    expression;
}
```

The goto-statement

As we have seen, continue-statements can sometimes be used to reduce the number of nested compound statements: with many nested brace pairs it is not always easy to see which closing brace belongs to a given opening brace, especially if (in large programs) they are very far apart. However, in most cases it is the other way round: properly indented nested compound statements make a program considerably more readable than programs written in the style of 'unstructured' languages, such as assembly languages, where jump or branch instructions are frequently used. C++ programmers can use something similar, namely the *goto-statement*. Its use is not recommended.

Let us consider two programs, *even1.cpp* and *even2.cpp*, one without and the other with goto-statements. They solve the same problem: integers are read from the keyboard, and the sum of those which are even is computed. Odd integers are ignored; the integer –1 signals the end of the input data. These two programs are equivalent, but the style of *even2.cpp* is old-fashioned. Its readability is not as good as that of *even1.cpp*, because we cannot immediately see its loop structure. Program *even2.cpp* may not be a striking example of bad readability, because it is very short and simple. However, programs with goto-statements become far less readable if they grow larger and more complicated. Curiously enough, the trouble with the goto-statement is that we can do too much with it: we can use it to jump to positions where we should not jump to. The higher-level control constructs for loops and conditional execution are more restricted and therefore safer.

```cpp
// even1.cpp: Solution without goto-statements.
#include <iostream>
using namespace std;

int main()
{   int x, s = 0;
    cout << "Enter positive integers, followed by -1:\n";
    for (;;)
    {   cin >> x;                   // Read x.
        if (x == -1) break;         // Exit if x is -1.
        if (x % 2 == 0) s += x;     // Use x only if it is even.
    }
    cout << "Sum of even integers: " << s << endl;
    return 0;
}
```

```cpp
// even2.cpp: Solution with goto-statements.
#include <iostream>
using namespace std;

int main()
{   int x, s = 0;
    cout << "Enter positive integers, followed by -1:\n";
11: cin >> x;                       // Read x.
    if (x == -1) goto 12;           // Exit if x is -1.
    if (x % 2 == 0) s += x;         // Use x only if it is even.
    goto 11;                        // Back to start of loop.
12: cout << "Sum of even integers: " << s << endl;
    return 0;
}
```

The switch-statement

The switch-statement can be regarded as a (very restricted and therefore innocent) kind of goto-statement. The place we jump to depends on the value of an integer expression. Its general form is

```cpp
switch (condition) statement
```

with one or more so-called *case-labels* in the statement. The condition must be of integral
type (that is, *int* or a related type, such as *char* or *short*), of an enumeration type, or of a
class type which can be converted to integral or enumeration type by a conversion function
(as we will discuss in Section 6.7). It follows that the condition must not be of floating-
point type.

In the following example, the variable *y* is increased by 1 if *x* is equal to one of the
integers that occur in the case-labels, and left unchanged otherwise:

```
switch (x) case 100: case 150: case 170: case 195: y++;
```

The switch-statement is more often used in a somewhat different way, as the following
example demonstrates. It shows another application of the break-statement, which may be
used not only in loops but also in switch-statements:

```
switch (letter)
{ case 'N': case 'n': cout << "New York\n"; break;
  case 'L': case 'l': cout << "London\n"; break;
  case 'A': case 'a': cout << "Amsterdam\n"; break;
  default: cout << "Somewhere else\n"; break;
}
```

For example, let us assume *letter* to be equal to '*L*' (or '*l*'). Then a jump to the statement
that prints *London* takes place. The break-statement that follows causes immediate exit
from the switch-statement. Without it, *Amsterdam* would also have been printed. If *letter*
is not equal to one of the letters in the case-labels, a jump to the default-label takes place,
so that *Somewhere else* is printed. If the line starting with *default* had been omitted,
nothing would have been printed in that case. Only one default-label is allowed. The
values in the case-labels must be constant expressions of type *int* (or of some related type)
and they must all be different. Note that the colon after case-labels may be followed by any
number of statements, which need not be enclosed in braces. New C++ programmers who
use switch-statements often forget to insert break-statements, and are then surprised that
the computer does more than they expect.

2.7 Simple Declarations

In C++ declarations are statements. As indicated below, simple declaration such as those
we have seen so far begin with a *specifier sequence* (see also Section 2.2), which is
followed by a *declarator list*, terminated by a semicolon.

specifier sequence	*declarator list*	*semicolon*
`const unsigned long int`	`xx = 123L, yy = 456L`	`;`

The technical terms *sequence* and *list* are often used in the C++ Standard. As this example
illustrates, the elements of a list are separated by commas, while this is not the case with a

sequence. Here *const*, *unsigned*, *long*, and *int* are specifiers, while $xx = 123L$ and $yy = 456L$ are declarators. The order of the specifiers in a specifier sequence is arbitrary. Although the following looks very unusual, it is a correct declaration, equivalent to the above one:

```
int unsigned const long xx = 123L, yy = 456L;
```

Note that the variables *xx* and *yy* must be initialized here because of the *const* specifier. These variables are said to have a *const-qualified* type; that is, they are in fact constants.

Exercises

2.1* Write a program to read a sequence of positive integers and to display the greatest of these. Use a negative integer to signal the end of the input data.

2.2* Write a program that reads a sequence of positive real numbers and computes their average. A negative number signals the end of the input data.

2.3* Write a program that reads an integer (into a variable of type *int*) and computes the sum of its final two decimal digits.

2.4* Write a program that reads 20 integers and counts how often a larger integer is immediately followed by a smaller one.

2.5* Write a program to read 10 integers and to find the second smallest of them.

2.6* When three numbers are given, it may or may not be possible to use them as the lengths of the sides of a triangle. Write a program to find this out for three real numbers read from the keyboard. If such a triangle exists, examine if it has an obtuse or a right angle.

2.7* With a positive integer *s* read from the keyboard, find all sequences of two or more consecutive integers whose sum is equal to *s*. For example, if *s* is 15, there are exactly three solutions:

```
1   2   3   4   5
4   5   6
7   8
```

2.8* Write a program that reads the (small) positive integers *n* and *k*, and uses these to display a board of $n \times n$ squares, similar to a chessboard. The white squares are blank and the black ones consist of $k \times k$ asterisks (*). As with a chessboard, there must be a black square in the lower-left corner.

2.9*   Write a program that reads a sequence of 20 integers to determine the smallest and the largest of them as well as the positions of these two elements in the sequence. In case they occur more than once, find the position of the first occurrence of the smallest number and that of the last occurrence of the largest number.

2.10*   Write a program that reads n, followed by the n^2 integers:

$$a_{11}, a_{12}, ..., a_{1n}$$
$$a_{21}, a_{22}, ..., a_{2n}$$
$$...$$
$$a_{n1}, a_{n2}, ..., a_{nn}$$

most of which are zero. Compute the maximum distance of a nonzero element to the main diagonal; in other words, compute the largest absolute value $|i - j|$ for which a_{ij} is nonzero. To compute the absolute value of an *int* value k, use *abs(k)*, for which you need the header *<cstdlib>*.

3

More Operators

3.1 Conditional Expressions

Besides the conditional statement (beginning with *if*) there is also the *conditional expression*, in which the two characters ? and : are used instead of the keywords *if* and *else*. It has the following form:

```
logical-expression ? expressionA : expressionB
```

Actually, these three expressions are subject to certain restrictions, to be discussed at the end of Section 3.6. To determine the value of this whole conditional expression, the *logical-expression* is evaluated first. Its purpose is similar to that of the parenthesized condition after *if* in a conditional statement, and its type must be *bool* (or integral, so that it can be converted to *bool*). If its value is *true*, *expressionA* is evaluated; otherwise, *expressionB* is evaluated. In other words, on the basis of the *logical-expression* a choice is made between *expressionA* and *expressionB*, and the value of the chosen expression is taken as the value of the whole conditional expression. The conditional statement and the conditional expression are different not only in their appearance but also in the way they are used; that is, they are used in different contexts. A conditional expression, possibly surrounded by parentheses, can occur in any expression; a conditional statement cannot. Here is an example in which a conditional expression is used in this way:

```
z = 3 * (a < b ? a + 1 : b - 1) + 2;
```

If we used a conditional statement we would have to write

```
    if (a < b) z = 3 * (a + 1) + 2; else z = 3 * (b - 1) + 2;
```

or, introducing the temporary variable t,

```
    if (a < b) t = a + 1; else t = b - 1;
    z = 3 * t + 2;
```

The form with the conditional expression is more efficient than these two program fragments with conditional statements. Conditional expressions are also useful as arguments of functions, which we will discuss in Chapter 4. Another example is the short form

```
    cout << "The greater of a and b is " << (a > b ? a : b);
```

instead of

```
    cout << "The greater of a and b is ";
    if (a > b) cout << a; else cout << b;
```

As we will see in Section 3.6, the parentheses enclosing the conditional expression are necessary in this example. Here is a third example of using a conditional expression:

```
    cout << (u == v ? "Equal" : "Unequal");
```

Now that we have seen so many cases in which a conditional expression is to be preferred to a conditional statement, you may wonder if there are also cases in which we need or prefer the latter. This is indeed the case. First, we should bear in mind that in a conditional statement the 'else part' may be absent, whereas in a conditional expression there must always be a colon, followed by an expression. For example, the effect of the conditional statement

```
    if (a < b) c = 0;
```

cannot be obtained with a conditional expression, unless we write something that is both contrived and inefficient, such as

```
    c = (a < b ? 0 : c);
```

or

```
    a < b ? (c = 0) : 0;
```

Second, the statements that are part of a conditional statement can be quite complex; for example, they can be compound statements in which loops occur. In such cases we cannot use conditional expressions. The conditional statement is therefore by no means a superfluous language element.

3.2 The Comma Operator

Two expressions, separated by a comma operator, as indicated in

```
expression1, expression2
```

form a new expression. The two expressions are evaluated in the given order, and the value of the whole expression is equal to that of *expression2*. This language construct is useful only if *expression1* does something more than just yielding a value (since that value is ignored). Here is an example in which this is the case:

```
// sum1: Solution based on comma operator.
s = 0;
while (cin >> i, i > 0)
    s += i;
```

This program fragment computes the sum of positive integers entered on the keyboard and followed by an integer that is zero or negative. It uses the expression

```
cin >> i, i > 0
```

The interesting point about *sum1* is that the expression *cin >> i* occurs as part of the condition of the while-statement, although its purpose is not to test for loop continuation. The comma operator is needed here, because we want another expression, *i > 0*, for this test. Note that the test is done between two actions that are also in the loop. This is shown in Figure 3.1, which also applies to program fragment *sum2*. This fragment is another way of writing a loop with the test in the middle, and is based on the break-statement (see Section 2.6).

```
// sum2: Solution based on the break-statement.
s = 0;
for ( ; ; )
{   cin >> i;
    if (i <= 0) break;
    s += i;
}
```

We now see that in C++ (and in C) we have at least two ways of programming a loop with the test in the middle. If we had none, we would probably have used the following solution to the same problem:

```
// sum3: Solution without comma-expression or break.
s = 0;
cin >> i;
while (i > 0)
{   s += i;
    cin >> i);
}
```

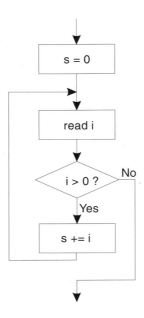

Figure 3.1. Loop with test in the middle

Version *sum*3 does not correspond to Figure 3.1. A flow diagram for it would have two boxes for *read i*, one outside and one inside the loop. As a solution to our summation problem, *sum*3 is less natural than *sum*1 and *sum*2.

Signaling the end of numerical input data

In our last example, the integer sequence read from the keyboard was terminated by a nonpositive integer. We often want to use some other means to signal the end of the input data, such as, for example, entering the word *END*. The following solution to this problem again uses the comma operator:

```
// sum4: Reading as many numbers as possible.
s = 0;
while (cin >> i, !cin.fail())
    s += i;
```

Now suppose that, after encountering some nonnumeric end-of-data signal, say, the word *END*, we want to read some more numbers. Then the first thing we have to do is to clear an error flag, by writing

```
cin.clear();
```

It is then necessary to skip all those nonnumeric characters (such as the three letters *E*, *N*, *D*). Assuming that the user, after entering these characters, presses the Enter key, we could try to skip the characters in question as follows:

```
char ch;
do cin >> ch; while (ch != '\n');    // Incorrect!
```

However, this does not work, because each time *cin >> ch* is executed all leading white-space characters are skipped. When we are reading numbers, this is normally what we want, but this time we want to read only one character at a time, even if the character read is a white-space character, such as '\n'. Fortunately, this more literal way of reading one character is also possible. All we have to do is replace *cin >> ch* with *cin.get(ch)*. Thus our program fragment that skips all characters until a newline character has been read should read

```
do cin.get(ch); while (ch != '\n'); // Correct.
```

The curious form *cin.get(ch)* will be discussed in detail in Chapters 6 and 10. This type of function call is introduced here so that we can use it in exercises.

The fragment *sum*4 was shown as another example of using the comma operator. Actually, this operator was not really necessary here, since we can replace

```
while (cin >> i, !cin.fail())
```

with

```
while (cin >> i)
```

as we will discuss in Chapter 10.

More than one comma

If we use more than two expressions separated by commas, the comma operator behaves like some other operators in this regard. For example,

```
x = a + b, y = x + 1, z = x + y
```

simply means

```
(x = a + b, y = x + 1), z = x + y
```

so here we have again one expression, followed by a comma operator, followed by another expression. This is similar to $u + v + w$, meaning $(u + v) + w$.

Potentially confusing situations

Since the comma character is used not only as an operator but also for other purposes, we must be more precise than we have been so far to avoid confusion. We therefore distinguish between *expressions* and *assignment-expressions*, the former being a generalization of the latter. Assignment operators, such as = and +=, are followed by an *assignment-expression*. An expression (not an *assignment-expression*) can consist of several *assignment-expression*s separated by commas. If we write, for example,

```
x = 5.1, 6.2       // expression
```

the above discussion helps to understand the meaning of this expression. Since the portion "5.1, 6.2" is not an *assignment-expression*, we cannot interpret the above expression as

```
x = (5.1, 6.2)       // ???
```

On the other hand, a comma operator allows its operands to be assignments, so that the interpretation

```
(x = 5.1), 6.2       // !!!
```

is possible. Since it is the only possibility, this must be the correct way of reading the original expression. If you wonder in what context such strange expressions can possibly occur in programs, you may find this example helpful (even though the statement is very clumsy):

```
y = (x = 5.1, 6.2);     // x = 5.1, y = 6.2
```

It should be noted that the technical term *assignment-expression*, when used formally, is slightly misleading, since it denotes any expiation except those that consist of two operands separated by a comma, and it does not necessarily involve any assignment at all. We will often use the simpler term *expression* instead. For example, 'expressions' used as function arguments (to be discussed in detail in Chapter 4) must actually be *assignment-expression*s, so that the function call

```
f(x, y)
```

will be interpreted as one with two arguments, *x* and *y*. If a function argument could really be any expression, the compiler might mistake

```
x, y
```

as a single expression (containing the comma operator). This interpretation is technically prevented by allowing only *assignment-expression*s as function arguments. However, since *x* and *y* do not really assign anything, and since it is unlikely that humans will make such mistakes, we prefer the simpler term *expression* in informal discussions.

3.3 Bit Manipulation

We can apply the following bit-manipulation operators to integer operands:

&	Bitwise AND
|	Bitwise OR
^	Bitwise XOR (exclusive OR)
~	Inversion of all bits
<<	Shift left
>>	Shift right

(Note that we have already used the operators << and >> for other purposes, namely for stream input and output. Likewise, the single ampersand (&), used here for bitwise *AND* is also used as the unary *address-of* operator (to be discussed in Section 4.3). This is quite normal in C++: the meaning of an operator token is clear only if we know the number and the types of the operands.)

The term *bitwise*, used above, means that the operation in question applies to all pairs of bits in the same positions. This will be clear from the examples that follow. Let us assume *sizeof(int)* to be 2, so that type *int* takes 16 bits. These days this is rather unrealistic, but it will be clear how to modify these examples for *int* values of 32 bits.

The operator & gives a 1 in a bit position of the result only if the two bits of the operands in the same position are also 1. For example, we can find the value of 0x3A6B & 0x00F0 as follows:

```
0x3A6B              = 0011 1010 0110 1011
0x00F0              = 0000 0000 1111 0000
—————————————————————————————————————————— &
0x3A6B & 0x00F0 = 0000 0000 0110 0000 = 0x0060
```

As this example shows, we can use the operator & to extract some bits from a whole machine word. Counting the bits from right to left, starting at 0, we have extracted the bits 4, 5, 6, 7 in this example. In the result they have the same values as these bits in the first operand, 0x3A6B; this is so because bits 4, 5, 6, 7 in the second operand (called a *mask*) are 1 and all others are 0. For example, by writing

```
int i = 0x3A6B, j;
j = i & 0xF0;
```

we select the bits (0110) in the positions 4, 5, 6, 7 of variable *i* and copy them into variable *j*, where they will occur in the same positions. All other bits of *j* will be zero.

We have an analogous situation with |. This operator gives 0 for all positions in which the two corresponding operand bits are 0, as the following example shows:

```
0x3A6B              = 0011 1010 0110 1011
0x00F0              = 0000 0000 1111 0000
                    ─────────────────────── |
0x3A6B | 0x00F0 =   0011 1010 1111 1011 = 0x3AFB
```

This illustrates that we can use the operator | to set some bits (that is, to make them equal to 1) and leave the others unaltered.

The operator ^ gives 1 for all positions in which the two corresponding operand bits are different, and it gives 0 if they are equal:

```
0x3A6B              = 0011 1010 0110 1011
0x00F0              = 0000 0000 1111 0000
                    ─────────────────────── ^
0x3A6B ^ 0x00F0 =   0011 1010 1001 1011 = 0x3A9B
```

We can see that ^ inverts the selected bits and leaves the others unaltered.

With the operator ~ each bit in the result is the inverse of the corresponding bit of its operand. It has only one operand, that is, it is a unary operator. Here is an example:

```
 0x3A6B = 0011 1010 0110 1011
~0x3A6B = 1100 0101 1001 0100 = 0xC594
```

We can use both operators & and ~ if we want to reset some bits, that is, if we want to copy all bits, except for some selected positions which are to be set to zero. For example, after the execution of

```
int i = 0x3A6B, j;
j = i & ~0xF0;
```

the bits of j will be equal to those of i, except for those in the positions 4, 5, 6, 7, which will be zero. Remember, the mask ~$0xF0$ is equal to $0xFF...F0F$, where the numbers of leading hexadecimal digits F is determined by the word length. In other words, we write ~$0xF0$ instead of $0xFF0F$ if $sizeof(int) = 2$, and instead of $0xFFFFFF0F$ if $sizeof(int) = 4$. The expression ~$0xF0$ is clearly to be preferred for reasons of portability.

With << the result is obtained by shifting the first operand as many positions to the left as the second operand specifies. We lose bits on the left, and zero bits are inserted on the right, as the following example shows:

```
0x63B7          = 0110 0011 1011 0111
0x63B7 << 4 =   0011 1011 0111 0000 = 0x3B70
```

We can shift to the right in a similar way by using >>:

```
0x63B7          = 0110 0011 1011 0111
0x63B7 >> 4 =   0000 0110 0011 1011 = 0x063B
```

Here the leftmost bit of the first operand is 0. Unfortunately, things are not so easy if that bit happens to be 1. If the type of the first operand is *unsigned int* (or *unsigned short int* or *unsigned long int*), it is guaranteed that zeros will be shifted into the word on the left-hand side. This is also the case if the first operand has type *int* (or *long int* or *short int*) and its leftmost bit is 0, as is the case in the above example. In the remaining case, with an *int* (or *short int* or *long int*) operand the leftmost bit of which is 1, the result is system dependent: with most computers, the leftmost bit, regarded as a 'sign bit,' will shift into the word on the left-hand side, but zeros may be used instead. If the first operand is a hexadecimal constant, as in the above example, we are certain that zeros are inserted on the left, because such a constant is taken as unsigned. In practice, however, we normally use variables rather than constants; if we want zeros to be inserted on the left, we should use the *unsigned* specifier for such variables.

Bit operations combined with assignments

Not only the arithmetic operators +, −, *, /, and %, but also the bit operators &, |, ^, <<, and >> can be combined with assignment, which gives the following new operators:

```
&=    |=    ^=    <<=    >>=
```

For example, we can shift the contents of the int variable *i* one bit to the left by writing

```
i <<= 1;
```

instead of

```
i = i << 1;
```

(As we will see in Section 3.6, << has higher precedence than =.)

Output and input of hexadecimal numbers

Now that we are frequently using hexadecimal constants, it is useful to know how to use hexadecimal constants in input operations and how to produce them in output. The word *hex*, used in the same way as *endl*, is all that is required. Both these word are referred to as *manipulators*. There is another manipulator, *dec*, to revert to the decimal number system. Here is an example:

```
// hexadec.cpp: Hexadecimal and decimal input and output.
#include <iostream>
using namespace std;

int main()
{   cout << "Enter a hexadecimal integer x and a "
            "decimal integer y:\n";
    int x, y;
    cin >> hex >> x >> dec >> y;
```

```
    cout << "0x" << hex << x << " = " << dec << x << endl;
    int s = x + y;
    cout << "Their sum (hexadecimal): " << hex << s << endl;
    cout << "Their sum (decimal):      " << dec << s << endl;
    return 0;
}
```

The following demonstration will be helpful to understand this program:

```
Enter a hexadecimal integer x and a decimal integer y:
1f   10
0x1f = 31
Their sum (hexadecimal): 29
Their sum (decimal):      41
```

In the input, we might have entered the hexadecimal number $0x1f$ in a different format, such as $0x1F$, $0X1f$, or simply $1F$.

3.4 Simple Arrays

Each variable used so far corresponds to only one number (or one character). With many programming problems we want to use sequences of numbers (or other objects), the elements of which have the same name and are distinguished by an integer 0, 1, 2, 3, ... We can do this by using *arrays*. Here we will only deal with the most elementary aspects of arrays; they will be discussed in more detail in Chapter 5. The array declaration

```
int a[100];
```

specifies that *a* has type 'array of 100 *int*,' and it enables us to use the following array elements:

```
a[0], a[1], ..., a[99]
```

The constant 100 in the declaration says that there are a hundred array elements, but the final element is $a[99]$, not $a[100]$. In this example the elements of the array have type *int*, as indicated in the declaration. This may be any other type instead. When using array elements, we can write any integer expression between the square brackets, as is done, for example, in the statement

```
k = 50 * a[3 * i + j/2] - 1;
```

provided that the expression $3 * i + j/2$ has a nonnegative value that is less than 100. The value denoted between brackets is called a *subscript*. It must have type *int* (or *unsigned int*), no matter what the array-element type is. This example also illustrates that array elements can be used in the same way as the simple variables we have been using so far.

In the declaration, the dimension 100 is only given as an example, but we must always write array dimensions as constants, or, in general, as *constant expressions*. For example, since *n* has a const-qualified type in the following example, the declaration of the array *a* that follows is correct:

```
const int n = 100;
int a[3 * n + 1];
```

The following program uses an array *a* to store 30 integers read from the keyboard, which are then printed in the reverse order:

```
// lifo.cpp: This program reads 30 integers and prints them
//              in the reverse order (Last In, First Out).
#include <iostream>
#include <iomanip>
using namespace std;

int main()
{   const int n = 30;
    int i, a[n];
    cout << "Enter " << n << " integers:\n";
    for (i=0; i<n; ++i)
       cin >> a[i];
    cout << "\nThe same integers, in reverse order:\n";
    for (i=0; i<n; ++i)
       cout << setw(6) << a[n-i-1]
            << (i % 10 == 9 ? '\n' : ' ');
    return 0;
}
```

As for *setw*, occurring in this program, recall that we have also used this in Section 2.5. Notice the conditional expression

```
i % 10 == 9 ? '\n' : ' '
```

whose value is a space character in most cases but is a newline character when *i* is equal to 9, 19, or 29. In this way, the output will show three lines of ten integers each. (In the input the integers may be distributed over several lines any way the user likes.)

Initializing an array

We can initialize an array by writing a list of constant expressions, separated by commas, surrounded by braces and preceded by =, as the following example shows:

```
int a[4] = {34, 22};  // All four elements initialized.
int b[4];             // No elements initialized.
```

Any trailing elements for which we do not specify values are set to zero, so the values of $a[0]$, $a[1]$, $a[2]$, and $a[3]$ are 34, 22, 0, and 0, respectively. This applies only if we initialize at least one element: array b is not initialized. There is a special, very convenient facility for initializing character arrays:

```
char name[20] = "Tim"; // "Tim" instead of {'T','i','m','\0'}
```

Here we use the string literal "*Tim*"; recall that we have already discussed string literals in Section 1.5. We will discuss the initialization of arrays in more detail in Sections 4.5 and 5.4.

3.5 Associativity

With operators of equal precedence, such as + and −, we have to take the *associativity* of these operators into account. Let us discuss this by means of an example. It is obvious that the expression

```
a - b + c - d
```

is equivalent to the first of the following two expressions:

```
((a - b) + c) - d                    a - (b + (c - d))
```

This is expressed in a technical way by saying that the operators + and − (which have the same precedence) are *left-associative*. We see that this phrase means that the expression in question is equivalent to one in which pairs of parentheses have been inserted so that it is clear how the operands group together and in such a way that all open parentheses are placed at the beginning. Each operator always associates in the same way: it is either left-associative or right-associative. This characteristic of an operator is called its *associativity*. Remember that the concept of associativity is relevant only if the same operator occurs more than once in an expression or if several operators with the same precedence occur in it.

Since most operators, like + and −, are left-associative, the most efficient way of discussing associativity is to focus on the exceptions. Only the following operators are right-associative:

(i)   All unary operators (with only one operand).
(ii)   The operator ?:, used in conditional expressions.
(iii)   The assignment operators =, +=, −=, *=, /=, %=, &=, |=, ^=, <<=, >>=

All other operators are left-associative. Here is a (not very practical) example of (i):

```
- ! 0
```

Since – and ! are used here as unary operators, they are right-associative, so when inserting imaginary parentheses we must start on the right, which gives –(!0). Because !0 is equivalent to !*false*, its value is *true* or 1, so that –!0 is equal to –1.

As for (ii), here is an example, which without any explanation may not be clear:

```
a < b ? x : c == d ? y : z
```

Since the operator ?: is right-associative (and because this operator has lower precedence than the others in this expression, as we will see in the next section), we should read this as

```
a < b ? x : (c == d ? y : z)
```

Let us illustrate rule (iii) by means of a complete program:

```cpp
// assign.cpp: Assignment operators.
#include <iostream>
using namespace std;

int main()
{   int i = 20, j = 10, k, l, m;
    k = l = i += j += m = 1;
    cout << "m=" << m << "   j=" << j << "   i=" << i
         << "   l=" << l << "   k=" << k << endl;
    return 0;
}
```

Since all operators in $k = l = i += j += m = 1$; are right-associative, imaginary parentheses should start on the right, which gives

```
k = (l = (i += (j += (m = 1))));
```

We may, in fact, write this statement instead of the corresponding statement without parentheses. Whether or not we do this, the output is as follows:

```
m=1   j=11   i=31   l=31   k=31
```

An operator's associativity does not determine the order in which its operands are evaluated. It is particularly important to be aware of this if we are tempted to write something like

```
k = (++i) * (5 + i);   // Wrong
```

Which operand of this multiplication is evaluated first is undefined. For example, if i is initially zero, k may be assigned the value $1 \times 5 = 5$ or $1 \times 6 = 6$. Here is a more complicated example:

```
a[i+=3] = (b[i+=4] = (c[i+=5] = (i+=6))); // Wrong
```

We must not assume that i += 6 is performed first and i += 3 last. If we omit all parentheses ( ) here, its meaning is exactly the same. In either form the effect of this statement is undefined. In general, if any assignment occurs in an expression, the variable which is given a value should not occur once again in that expression. If it does, the effect is undefined.

The only operators for which the order of evaluation is defined are &&, ||, ?: and the comma operator (,).

Sequence points

In the C++ Standard, the notion of *sequence points* has been introduced to indicate points in the execution sequence that are guaranteed to be reached in a fixed order. If a variable is modified in an expression between two successive sequence points, there should not be more than one occurrence of it in that expression. The expression $k = (++i) * (5 + i)$, shown above, is executed between two successive sequence points, and the variable i is modified in it and also occurs twice. This expression therefore violates the rule just mentioned. There is a sequence point at the completion of each 'full expression' (which is an expression that is not a subexpression of another expression) but there is also one at the completion of the subexpression a in the following expressions:

```
a && b
a || b
a ? b : c
a, b
```

For example, there is nothing wrong with the expressions

```
(++i) && (5 + i)
(++i), (5 + i)
```

although, as we have seen, their effect would be undefined if we used the multiplication operator (*) instead of the logical-and (&&) or the comma (,) operator in them.

3.6 Precedence of Operators and Grammar Rules

For most binary operators, you can find their precedence in the following list. Operators on the same line have the same precedence; otherwise, the operators in this list occur in descending order of precedence:

```
*    /    %
+    -
<<   >>
<    <=   >    >=
==   !=
```

```
&
^
|
&&
||
=   +=   -=   *=   /=   %=   |=   ^=   <<=   >>=
,
```

This simple list is easy to use in most practical cases, but it does not cover all operators and there are some situations that require a different, more technical approach, based on *grammar rules*, which will be the subject of the remaining part of this section.

In accordance with the above list, we have already seen in Section 3.2 that the comma operator has lower precedence than assignment operators. We used the notions *expression* and *assignment-expression* to demonstrate that in

```
x = 5.1, 6.2
```

the comma operator (,) has a looser binding than the assignment operator (=). The expression in question consists of two assignment expressions, separated by a comma operator. In general, when reading complicated expression, we begin by looking for the operator with the loosest binding, that is, with the lowest precedence.

As the above second operand (that is, the literal 6.2) demonstrates, an *assignment-expression* need not necessarily be an assignment in the usual sense of the word. To indicate that an expression consists of one or more *assignment-expressions*, separated by a comma operator, we will use the following notation:

> *expression*:   (Example: `cin >> x, ++x, 5 * x`)
>   *assignment-expression* ⌊ , *assignment-expression* ... ⌋

The special bracket pair ⌊ ⌋ indicates that what it contains is optional, and ... expresses that the preceding part may be repeated. In other words, we read this formal notation as follows: an expression consists of an *assignment-expression*, possibly followed by a comma, which, if present, must be followed by another *assignment-expression*; then another comma and an *assignment-expression* may follow, and so on. Rules such as this one, usually expressed by formal notations such as the one above, are known as *grammar rules*. The example at the end of the line does not belong to the grammar rule; it goes without saying that not every expression is similar to the given example. Here the example illustrates that several comma operators may occur. Instead we could have used just the literal 123, which is also an expression. However, this example 123 is not typical of *expression* in that it also satisfies the definition of the notions that follow (from *assignment-expression* up to *primary-expression*), while the given one (containing two commas) does not. This principle of using examples that are typical of the notion in question is also applied in the grammar rules that follow.

This grammar rule for *expression* would be very clear if we knew what we may substitute for *assignment-expression*. This notion is therefore syntactically defined similarly:

assignment-expression: (Example: `x = a < b ? a : b`)
⌊ *logical-or-expression* = ... ⌋ *conditional-expression*

where = denotes one of the following operators:
= += −= *= /= %= >>= <<= &= ^= |=

In other words, an *assignment-expression* consists of a *conditional-expression*, possibly preceded by one or more *logical-or-expressions*, each immediately followed by an assignment operator, such as = or +=.

conditional-expression: (Example: `a < b ? a : b`)
logical-or-expression ⌊ ? *expression* : *assignment-expression* ⌋

As this grammar rule expresses, a conditional-expression need not contain a question mark (?), but if it does, it must also contain a colon (:). Surprisingly, any expression may occur between these two characters and an assignment may follow the colon. For example, this is a correct conditional-expression, and it should be interpreted as the line that follows it:

```
a < b ? cin >> x, x + 1 : x = 0
a < b ? (cin >> x, x + 1) : (x = 0)
```

Since a *conditional-expression* contains a *logical-or-expression* and may also contain an *expression* and an *assignment-expression*, the precedence rules for the operator ?: are too complicated to be expressed in a simple table of all operators listed in decreasing (or increasing) order of precedence. This is why we are using more formal grammar rules here. We now proceed with the *logical-or-expression*:

logical-or-expression: (Example: `x < 0 && y == 0 || x > 5`)
logical-and-expression ⌊ || *logical-and-expression* ...⌋

This is again a very simple rule, stating that a logical-or-expression consists of a logical-and-expression, possibly followed by the operator ||, which, if present, must be followed by another logical-and-expression. As the ellipses (...) indicate, this may be followed by another operator ||, and so on.

The rule for the *logical-and-expression* is similar and so are some rules that follow. It will by now be clear that the operators introduced in successive rules of this simple kind occur in order of increasing precedence. For example, && occurring in the following rule has higher precedence than || or the previous rule.

logical-and-expression: (Example: `x < 0 && y == 0`)
inclusive-or-expression ⌊ && *inclusive-or-expression* ...⌋

inclusive-or-expression: (Example: `b | 0xFF`)
exclusive-or-expression ⌊ | *exclusive-or-expression* ...⌋

exclusive-or-expression:
   and-expression ⌊ ^ *and-expression* ... ⌋
(Example: **b ^ 0xFF**)

and-expression:
   equality-expression ⌊ & *equality-expression* ... ⌋
(Example: **b & 0xFF**)

equality-expression:
   relational-expression ⌊ == *relational-expression* ... ⌋
where == may be replaced with !=
(Example: **x == 0**)

The last rule may cause confusion, as the following example of a *equality-expression* illustrates:

   a == b != c

First, it should be clear that we have to read this as follows:

   (a == b) != c

This form prepares us for the second hurdle: it is the truth value of $a == b$ (that is, *true* or *false*) that is compared with c. Since *true* and *false* are implicitly converted to 1 and 0, if necessary, the variable c may be of arithmetic type, but it is *not* compared with b.

relational-expression:
   shift-expression ⌊ < *shift-expression* ... ⌋
where < denotes one of the operators < > <= >=
(Example: **a >= b**)

shift-expression:
   additive-expression ⌊ << *additive-expression* ... ⌋
where << may be replaced with >>
(Example: **b >> 3**)

additive-expression:
   multiplicative-expression ⌊ + *multiplicative-expression* ... ⌋
where + may be replaced with −
(Example: **a * b + c**)

multiplicative-expression:
   pm-expression ⌊ * *pm-expression* ... ⌋
where * denotes one of the operators * / %
(Example: **a * b**)

So far, the operators we have used were familiar to us. This will be different with some that follow. The following rule is about pointers to class members (hence the prefix *pm*), to be discussed in Section 6.14, but listed here for the sake of completeness:

pm-expression: (Example: `p .* length`)
   cast-expression ⌊ .* *cast-expression* ... ⌋

where .* may be replaced with –>*

cast-expression: (Example: `(float)(int)'A'`)
   ⌊(*type-id*) (*type-id*) ... ⌋ *unary-expression*

where *type-id* denotes a type

Unlike the previous grammar rules, some of those which remain to be discussed are more complex in that there are several alternatives, each of which takes a separate line. The set of grammar rules we are dealing with is intended to discuss the precedence of operators, not to discuss all possible expressions of the C++ language. To avoid confusion by listing a great many notions, we will from now on be less formal, omitting some alternatives to be discussed later, and writing <*other alternatives*> to indicate this omission:

unary-expression: (Example: `++k`)
   postfix-expression
   ++ *cast-expression*
   `sizeof` *unary-expression*
   `sizeof` (*type-id*)
   <other alternatives>
where ++ denotes one of   ++   ––   *   &   +   –   !   ~

postfix-expression: (Example: `a[i]++`)
   primary-expression ⌊ ... (see below) ⌋
   <other alternatives>

A *postfix-expression* can begin with a *primary-expression*, possibly followed by several constructs, of which we mention only three:

-   a pair of square brackets containing an expression
-   a pair of parentheses, possibly containing an *expression-list*
-   the operator ++ or ––

There may be several of these, so besides simple forms such as

```
a[i]
f(x, y, z)
```

more complicated ones such as those below are also possible:

```
b[i][j](x)++
g()[i](j)
```

The syntactic definition of an *expression-list* (occurring in the above discussion of *postfix-expression*) is very simple, but we must not confuse it with a single expression that contains comma operators. In an *expression-list* the commas are not operators but separators:

expression-list: (Example: `x + y, x - y, 0`)
  assignment-expression ⌊ , *assignment-expression* ⌋

Finally, we have

primary-expression: (Example: `x`)
  literal
  identifier
  (*expression*)
  <other alternatives>

An example

In Section 5.12, we will discuss an expression of the form

```
*a[i]
```

and we will then have to decide to which of the following expressions this is equivalent:

```
*(a[i])
(*a)[i]
```

Although it takes a lot of energy to verify that the grammar rules admit (only) the first interpretation, this can be done, as we will now show. In the above rules we find that a *unary-expression* can consist of an asterisk followed by a *cast-expression*. Thus *a[i] is a *unary-expression* if a[i] is a *cast-expression*. This happens to be the case, since a *cast-expression* can consist of a *unary-expression*, which in turn can consist of a *postfix-expression*, which can have the following form:

***primary-expression*[*expression*]**

Since, as we have just seen, *a[i] can be interpreted (or *parsed*, as one usually says) as an asterisk followed by a cast-expression, it can be read as *(a[i]). The grammar would be ambiguous if *a[i] could also be parsed as (*a)[i]. The impossibility of this interpretation follows from the rule for *postfix-expression*. As we have just seen, this says that an expression surrounded by square brackets can only be preceded by a *primary-expression*, for which *a does not qualify. Summarizing, we find that the given expression *a[i] can only be parsed as

`* cast-expression`

so that

    `*a[i]`   should be read as   `*(a[i])`

Grammar rules are very important for language experts and compiler builders. Fortunately, ordinary application programmers will need them only occasionally, especially when reading unfamiliar code written by others. Since examples of valid constructs are much easier to remember, we normally prefer these to grammar rules.

3.7 Arithmetic Conversions and Casts

In Section 2.1 we dealt with the arithmetic operators +, –, *, /, and %. We will now discuss in more detail how the type of the expression

    `operand1    operator    operand2`

(in which *operator* is one of the five operators just mentioned) depends on the types of *operand*1 and *operand*2. Now that we are familiar with associativity and precedence of operators, it will be clear that this general form applies not only to very simple expressions, such as $a + b$, but also to more complicated ones, such as

    `a * b - c * d - e * f`

According to Sections 3.5 and 3.6 we should read this as

    `((a * b) - (c * d)) - (e * f)`

This has indeed the general form just shown, with $((a * b) - (c * d))$ as *operand*1, and $(e * f)$ as *operand*2.

The precise rules to find the type of an expression may seem rather complicated, but fortunately we will seldom need them, because they have been devised in such a way that the type in question is just what we intuitively expect. If you think the following discussion tedious, don't worry. It is included here because it is important to know that every arithmetic expression has a type that can be derived from those of its operands, and this book might be considered incomplete if it did not show how this can be done.

First, integral promotion may take place: any operands that have type *char*, *short int* (both in their signed and unsigned varieties), or an enumerator type are promoted to type *int* if this type can represent all the values of the original type. If not, the original type is converted to *unsigned int*.

Type conversion (to be discussed below) is now applied to the operands to ensure that their types will be the same. The common type thus obtained is then used as the type of the result. This operand type conversion is done by applying at most one of the seven rules listed below. These rules are to be considered in the given order, and only one of them is to be applied; as soon as the two operands have the same type, any remaining rules are ignored. For brevity, the phrase 'an operand is converted to a given type' will include the case that this operand already has that type. For example, rule 1 includes the case that both operands are *long double*:

1. If either operand is *long double*, the other is converted to this type.
2. If either operand is *double*, the other is converted to this type.
3. If either operand is *float*, the other is converted to this type.
4. If either operand is *unsigned long int*, the other is converted to this type.
5. If either operand is *long int* and the other is *unsigned int*, the *unsigned int* operand is converted to *long int*, provided that *long int* can represent all the values of *unsigned int*. If that is not the case, both operands are converted to *unsigned long int*.
6. If either operand is *long int*, the other is converted to this type.
7. If either operand is *unsigned int*, the other is converted to this type.

Note that very often none of these rules applies because both operands have type *int* (possibly due to integral promotion, discussed earlier in this section).

The types *signed char* and *unsigned char*

Besides type *char*, we have the types *signed char* and *unsigned char*. In C++, these are three distinct types. If we use *char* variables only to store real characters, the distinction is not important, because these use only seven bits so that the 'sign bit' is zero; in other words, the normal characters have positive values between 0 and 127. Things are different if we assign other values, such as, for example, '\xFF' to a *char* variable. In this case we had better write *signed char* or *unsigned char*, instead of just *char*, to avoid machine dependence. The implementation specifies whether the high-order bit of a plain *char* object is treated as a sign bit. Although formally *char* is distinct from both *signed char* and *unsigned char*, it behaves as one of these two types in the following program, the output of which is system dependent:

```
// signedch.cpp: This program finds out whether the leftmost
//               bit of type char is a sign bit.
#include <iostream>
using namespace std;

int main()
{   signed char s_ch = '\xFF';
    unsigned char u_ch = '\xFF';
    char ch = '\xFF'; // Binary: s_ch = u_ch = ch = 11111111
    int s, u, i;
    s = s_ch; // From signed char to int
    u = u_ch; // From unsigned char to int
    i = ch;    // From char to int (system dependent)
    cout << "For this C++ implementation, type char has " <<
    ( i == s ? "a sign bit.\n" :
      i == u ? "no sign bit.\n" :
      "not been implemented correctly.\n"
    );
    return 0;
}
```

Assuming that type *int* takes 32 bits, we can write the binary representations of *s* and *u*, along with their values, as follows in two's complement notation:

```
s = 11111111 11111111 11111111 11111111 = -1     (= s_ch)
u = 00000000 00000000 00000000 11111111 = 255    (= u_ch)
```

The value of *i*, on the other hand, is system dependent. It is equal to either *s* or *u*. Note that the values of *s_ch*, *u_ch*, and *ch* are a matter of interpretation: they have the same internal representation, namely 11111111. The difference between signed and unsigned character types becomes apparent only after converting these types to type int. In program *signedch.cpp* this is done by using assignments. As discussed in this section, conversion to type *int* (that is, integral promotion) also takes place in expressions, such as in *s_ch* + 1 and *u_ch* + 1; the values of these expressions are 0 and 256, respectively, despite the fact that *s_ch* and *u_ch* are represented by identical bit strings.

You may think this discussion about signed and unsigned characters rather theoretical and perhaps even useless. However, character variables are in practice used not only for normal characters but also for any byte values and for very short integers. Especially in the latter case it is very important for the keyword *char* to be preceded by either *signed* or *unsigned*.

Signed and unsigned integers

Program *beware.cpp* shows that we should be very careful with comparing *int* and *unsigned int* values. Before we look at such comparisons, note that we can use the expression ~0x1 (or ~1) to obtain a word with all 1-bits except for the bit at the extreme right, which is 0. With 16-bit words, we could write 0xFFFE, but then we would have to write 0xFFFFFFFE with 32-bit words. The ~ operator provides a convenient and portable way of padding with 1-bits at the left.

```
// beware.cpp: Can a negative value be equal to a
//             positive one?
#include <iostream>
using namespace std;

int main()
{   unsigned u = ~0x1; // u = 0xF...FE
    int i = u;         // i = -2 (same bit pattern as u)
    if (i == u) cout << "i == u\n";
    if (i < 0) cout << "i < 0\n";
    if (u > 0) cout << "u > 0\n";
    return 0;
}
```

This program produces the following curious output:

```
i == u
i < 0
u > 0
```

Although *i* and *u* have the same internal representation, they have different types. In the comparison *i* == *u*, conversion of *i* from *int* to *unsigned int* takes place, according to point 7 at the beginning of this section. Such a conversion does not alter the bit pattern of *i* so both operands now have the same large positive value ($2^n - 2$). Since *i* is equal to –2, the test *i* < 0 clearly gives the answer *true*. To evaluate *u* > 0, we have an *unsigned int* operand *u* and an *int* operand 0 again, so point 7, just mentioned, is applied here to the second operand, 0. This does not alter the value of 0, so the test *u* > 0 also succeeds. Incidentally, we could also have found this simply by observing that any nonzero unsigned value is positive.

Simple cast expressions

Forced type conversion can be achieved by means of a special operator, the *cast*. Traditionally, this was written in a rather simple way. For example, if the variable *n* is of type *int* and we want to write an expression of type *float* and with a value equal to *n* we could write either of the following:

```
(float)n
float(n)
```

These two forms are now deprecated, which means that we are discouraged to use them. Instead, the following form is recommended:

```
static_cast<float>(n)
```

We normally use *static_cast*; besides this, we will briefly discuss *const_cast* (in Section 5.3) and *dynamic_cast* (in Section 6.12). There is also the low-level, more dangerous *reinterpret_cast*, which we can use for implementation-dependent activities, such as converting integer values to pointers and vice versa, but which we should avoid if we can.

Static casts are useful for many purposes; one is to convert a signed type to the corresponding unsigned type or vice versa. Let us use our example about signed and unsigned characters once again. If we write

```
signed char s_ch = '\0xFF';
int i;
i = static cast<unsigned char>(s_ch);
```

the value of *i* will be 255, while it would be –1 if we had omitted the cast, writing simply *i* = *s_ch*.

A very useful application of the cast is a division operation that, although applied to integers, is to yield a real quotient. For example, in

```
int i = 14, j = 3;
float x, y;
x = i/j;
y = static_cast<float>(i)/static_cast<float>(j);
```

we have $x = 4.0$ and $y = 4.666...$. According to the conversion rules discussed in this section, we could have omitted one of the two casts in the last statement. For example,

```
y = static_cast<float>(i)/j;   // y = 4.666...
```

would also have been correct. By contrast, the following statement performs integer division (with integer 4 as its result!) before the cast is applied:

```
y = static_cast<float>(i/j);   // y = 4.0
```

In the last example, the result would have been the same if we had omitted the cast, since conversion is performed automatically if an integer value (4) is assigned to a floating-point variable (y).

A conversion can really alter a value, as is the case in

```
int i;
float x = -6.9F;
i = x;
```

Here i is given the value –6. Using a cast is highly recommended here, not to make the computer do some additional work for us, but rather for the sake of documentation. Using a cast by writing

```
i = static_cast<int>(x);
```

instead of the above assignment $i = x$, we can see more clearly that i is obtained by truncating x. The presence of this cast does not make any difference in regard to the code generated by the compiler.

3.8 Lvalues and Rvalues

Let us consider *assignment-expression*s of the following form

```
E1 = E2
```

In most cases $E1$ will be the name of a variable, but it can also be a quite complex expression, as we will see in a moment. An expression that may occur as a left operand of an assignment is called a *modifiable lvalue*. To simplify our discussion, we will simply use the term *lvalue* when we actually mean *modifiable lvalue*. It will be clear that none of the following expressions is an lvalue:

```
3 * 5
i + 1
"ABC"
```

Such expression, which can appear as right-hand (but not left-hand) sides of assignments, are referred to as *rvalues*. The most obvious kinds of lvalues are names of simple variables and array elements. If an lvalue is surrounded by parentheses, it remains an lvalue. For example, after

```
int i, j, a[100], b[100];
```

the following three expressions are lvalues because they can appear as the left-hand sides of assignments:

```
i
a[3 * i + j]
(i)
```

It goes without saying that these expression, although being lvalues, can also appear as right-hand sides of assignments. Whenever an lvalue appears in a context where an rvalue is expected, the lvalue is converted to an rvalue.

In Chapter 5 we will see that the name of an array is not an lvalue, so with the above declaration of *a* and *b* we cannot write

```
a = b;    // Error
```

By contrast, the following is a valid assignment statement, which assigns zero to the smaller of the variables *i* and *j* and leaves the other unchanged:

```
(i < j ? i : j) = 0;
```

In general, the conditional expression

```
logical-expression ? expressionA : expressionB
```

is an lvalue only if *expressionA* and *expressionB* are of the same type and are both lvalues. The result of a static cast, as used in the following example, is not an lvalue, so this is not correct:

```
int x;
static_cast<double>(x) = 3.14;    // Error
```

A comma-expression is an lvalue if its right operand is:

```
(i = 1, j) = 2;     // Equivalent to i = 1; j = 2;
```

Each of the assignment operators =, +=, −=, *=, /=, %=, &=, |=, ^=, <<=, >>= requires an lvalue as its left operand. The resulting expression is an lvalue. However, using such lvalues as is done in the following example is unwise:

```
int i;
(i = 2) = 3;        // '= 2' makes no sense.
(i += 5) = -i;      // Result undefined.
```

Assigning the value 2 to *i* makes no sense here because this value is immediately overwritten by 3. The result of the third line is undefined. As we have seen in Section 3.5, we should not use a variable more than once in an expression if this expression modifies the variable (except for certain expressions containing &&, ||, ?: or ,).

The expressions *E*1 and *E*2 must be lvalues in ++*E*1 and *E*2++. Curiously enough, ++*E*1 is an lvalue but *E*2++ is not. (Remember, ++*E* is equivalent to *E*+=1, which, as we have seen, is also an lvalue.) This is illustrated by the following example:

```
int i, j;
i = 0; j = ++ ++i;   // j = i = 2
i = 0; j = i++ ++;   // Error
```

It is strongly recommended to use a blank space in expressions such as ++ ++*i*, but if we do not, the meaning is the same. Sequences of more than two successive plus signs not separated by blank space are sometimes very difficult to interpret. For example, if we write

```
i+++j
```

it may at first not be clear how to choose between *i*++ + *j* and *i* + ++*j*. In cases such as this, the compiler processes as many characters as can possibly be combined into one *operator token*, such as ++. In this example, there are two possible choices for a token that follows *i*, namely ++ and +. Since ++ is a longer sequence than just +, it is the right choice, so the above expression means the same as

```
i++ + j
```

Note that taking the longest possible sequence must be applied even if this choice makes the rest invalid. For example, in

```
i ++ j     // invalid
```

the sequence ++ is taken as one operator, which makes this form invalid, even though taking both +-characters as separate operators would have made it valid. Writing a space character between both +characters would have led to the following valid form:

```
i + +j     // valid
```

It will now be clear that we must not insert blank spaces in a character sequence, such as ++, &&, <=, that forms a single token

Exercises

3.1 Read in a sequence of integers, followed by a nonnumeric character. Determine the largest of these and how many times this largest integer occurs in the sequence.

3.2* A sequence of positive integers is to be read from the keyboard, followed by a nonnumeric character. For each of the factors 2, 3, and 5, count how many of the integers that are read are multiples of that factor.

3.3* A sequence of real numbers, followed by a nonnumeric character, is to be read from the keyboard. Compute the sum of the 1st, 3rd, 6th, 10th, 15th, 21st, ... elements of this sequence.

3.4 Read in a sequence of integers (some of which may be equal). Count how many distinct integers are given. You may assume that there will be no more than 20 (although the sequence length is unlimited).

3.5 Read in a sequence of integers. From each integer, its least significant six bits are taken, which form a small integer (less than 64). The program is to produce a table with all small integers obtained in this way, along with their frequencies.

3.6 Write a program which reads a date given as three positive integers (month, day, year), as, for example,

```
12 31 1990
```

Your program is to compute the day number of this date, counted from January 1st of that year. So in the given example, that day number would be 365. Take into account that the year may be a leap year. This is the case if the given year number is a multiple of 4 but not a multiple of 100. There is one exception: it is also a leap year if it is a multiple of 400.

3.7 Show that by means of bit operations you can store four nonnegative integers, each less than 16, into an *short int* variable x. Write a program which first reads four such integers, a_0, a_1, a_2, a_3, and stores them into the variable x. Then the user is asked to enter an integer i $(0 \leq i \leq 3)$ to find a_i (in x) and to print its value.

3.8 Show how you can efficiently multiply an integer that is read from the keyboard (and that is not too large) by 100, without using the operator *. Use the operators << and +.

3.9   Read a hexadecimal integer from the keyboard (using the *hex* manipulator). In its binary representation, we number the bits 0, 1, ..., starting on the right. Swap the following bits, and print the result as a hexadecimal integer:

        bit 0 and bit 7,
        bit 1 and bit 6,
        bit 2 and bit 5,
        bit 3 and bit 4.

3.10   As Exercise 3.9, but now the bits 0 to 7 are to be rotated one position to the left (instead of being swapped):

        bit 0 moves to bit 1;
        the original bit 1 moves to bit 2;

           ...

        the original bit 6 moves to bit 7;
        the original bit 7 moves to bit 0.

3.11   Read in the number sequence

$$n, x, a_n, a_{n-1}, ..., a_1, a_0$$

to compute

$$y = a_n x^n + a_{n-1} x^{n-1} + ... + a_1 x + a_0$$

by means of Horner's method. This means that, for example, with $n = 3$, the following identity is used

$$a_3 x^3 + a_2 x^2 + a_1 x + a_0 \equiv \{(a_3 x + a_2)x + a_1\}x + a_0$$

With values of n other than 3 the method works analogously. Use type *double* for all numbers except for n, which is an integer.

3.12*   A sequence of ten integers is to be read from the keyboard. Search this sequence for the first element that is equal to the tenth, and print the position of that first element. (If all elements are equal, that position is 1; if they are all distinct, it is 10.)

3.13   Write a program that sorts the real numbers a_0, a_1, ..., a_{n-1}, read from the keyboard, using the straight selection sorting method. It is given that n will be no greater than 25, so the n real numbers can be placed in an array of that size. First, search the sequence for its smallest element and exchange this with a_0. Then, deal with the remaining sequence, starting with a_1, in the same way, and so on. When, finally, there is a remaining sequence of length 1, all elements in the array are in increasing order and can be printed. (Sorting should in practice not be done in this way, but rather by means of the sort algorithm, to be discussed in Chapter 9.)

3.14* Write a program which reads 25 positive integers a_0, ..., a_{24}, which are absolute frequencies. Show these in a graphical form known as a histogram. This should consist of 25 vertical bars, the jth bar ($0 \leq j < 25$) being a column of a_j letters I. The lower endpoints of all bars are to appear on the same horizontal line.

3.15* Write a program which reads a sequence of integers, followed by a nonnumeric character, and counts how often each of the integers 0, 1, ..., 15 occurs in this sequence. Print the result in a table.

3.16* Write a program that reads a positive integer n (not greater than 25), to print a table of n lines and n columns, which has the following form:

```
1  1  1   . . .   1
1  2  2   . . .   2
1  2  3   . . .   3
.  .  .            .
.  .  .            .
.  .  .            .
1  2  3   . . .   n
```

3.17* Write a program that reads a sample of n real values x_i, followed by a nonnumeric character. The following numbers, used in statistics to characterize certain properties of the sample, are to be computed:

a. The mean value: $(\Sigma\, x_i)/n$
b. The variance: $\{(\Sigma\, x_i^2) - (\Sigma\, x_i)^2/n\}/(n - 1)$
c. The range: largest value – smallest value

($\Sigma\, x_i$ is the sum of all x_i; $\Sigma\, x_i^2$ is the sum of all x_i^2.)

4

Functions and Program Structure

4.1 Function Definitions and Declarations; Recursion

In mathematics functions are abstract notions. By contrast, they consist of concrete program text in C and C++. In some other languages a distinction is made between functions on the one hand and procedures or subroutines on the other. In C++ we use the term function for both purposes.

Let us begin by considering a function *fun* with four parameters, x, y, i, and j, where x and y have type *float*, and i and j have type *int*. We will define this function in such a way that *fun*(x, y, i, j) is equal to

$$\frac{x - y}{i - j}$$

if $i \neq j$. If $i = j$, we cannot compute this quotient because in a division the denominator must not be zero. In that case, *fun* is to return the value 10^{20}, preceded by the sign of the numerator $x - y$, unless this is also zero: if that happens, *fun* is to return the value 0. Program *fdemo*1.*cpp* shows how this can be done. It consists of two functions, *fun* and *main*:

```
// fdemo1.cpp: Demonstration program with a function.
#include <iostream>
using namespace std;
```

```
float fun(float x, float y, int i, int j)
{  float a = x - y;
   int b = i - j;
   return b != 0 ? a/b :
      a > 0 ? +1e20F :
      a < 0 ? -1e20F : 0.0F;
}

int main()
{  int ii, jj;
   float xx, yy;
   cout <<
   "Enter two real numbers followed by two integers:\n";
   cin >> xx >> yy >> ii >> jj;
   cout << "Value returned by function: "
        << fun(xx, yy, ii, jj) << endl;
   return 0;
}
```

An expression such as

```
fun(xx, yy, ii, jj)
```

near the end of the program, is referred to as a *function call*, or simply a *call*, while *xx*, *yy*, *ii*, and *jj* are the *arguments* used in this call. A function call implies the execution of the actions described by the function, after which the program is resumed at the position immediately after the call. The variables *x*, *y*, *i*, and *j*, occurring on the program line

```
float fun(float x, float y, int i, int j)
```

are referred to as the *parameters* of the function *fun*. Their initial values are those of the corresponding arguments used in calls to this function. In our program there is only the call shown above, so that the initial values of *x*, *y*, *i*, and *j* are *xx*, *yy*, *ii*, and *jj*, respectively. The variables *a* and *b* are called *local variables*, since they do not exist outside the function. Parameters behave like local variables in this regard. There would be no problem whatsoever if the names *x*, *y*, *i*, *j*, *a*, and *b* were used in the *main* function for other purposes. In particular, the argument names *xx*, *yy*, *ii*, and *jj* were deliberately chosen differently from the parameter names *x*, *y*, *i*, and *j* because they will normally be different in more realistic programs, but the program would also have been correct if, in the *main* function, we had consistently written *x* instead of *xx*, and so on.

A return statement of the form

```
return expression;
```

causes a jump back to the calling function (*main* in our example), with the evaluated expression as the return value. In *fdemo*1.*cpp* we have used a rather complicated conditional expression in the return statement.

Here is a demonstration of this program, which computes 80.0/16 = 5.0:

```
Enter two real numbers followed by two integers:
100.5 20.5
20 4
Value returned by function: 5
```

In program *fdemo1.cpp* the function *fun* is called only once, but there may be more. When the compiler processes a call of a function, it must already have processed either the definition of that function (that is, that function itself) or a *declaration* of it, such as the one below:

```
float fun(float x, float y, int i, int j);
```

As this example shows, a function declaration provides information about the function's parameters and its return value. The following program is very similar to the previous one, but the order of functions *main* and *fun* is different:

```
// fdemo2.cpp: The function fun, called in main, is declared
//             before and defined after main.
#include <iostream>
using namespace std;

float fun(float x, float y, int i, int j); // declaration

int main()
{   int ii, jj;
    float xx, yy;
    cout <<
    "Enter two real numbers followed by two integers:\n";
    cin >> xx >> yy >> ii >> jj;
    cout << "Value returned by function: "
         << fun(xx, yy, ii, jj) << endl;
    return 0;
}

float fun(float x, float y, int i, int j) // definition
{   float a = x - y;
    int b = i - j;
    return b != 0 ? a/b :
        a > 0 ? +1e20 :
        a < 0 ? -1e20 : 0.0;
}
```

Since the function *fun* is used before it is defined, there is a declaration at the beginning of the program. It is also possible to declare (but not define) a function inside another function. In this example, the (one-line) declaration of *fun* could have been written, for example, after the declaration of *xx* and *yy*. Yet another way of declaring *fun* is by combining this declaration with those of *float* variables. In other words, in program *fdemo2.cpp* we can omit the one-line declaration of *fun*, just before the function *main*, provided we replace the first three lines of *main* with either

```
int main()
{  int ii, jj;
   float xx, yy;
   float fun(float x, float y, int i, int j);
```

or

```
int main()
{  int ii, jj;
   float xx, yy, fun(float x, float y, int i, int j);
```

However, we must bear in mind that declaring *fun* within *main* makes this declaration valid only in *main*, while declaring it 'globally' (that is, not inside any function) makes such a declaration valid until the end of the program file. While a function definition may occur only once, a function can be declared as often as we like.

The parameter names may be absent in the declaration (not in the definition) of a function. For example, *fun* can also be declared as follows:

```
float fun(float, float, int, int);
```

However, we prefer writing these parameter names, because, in more realistic programs, they often indicate what they are about, so that they make the program easier to understand.

A function definition also counts as a function declaration. In our first program, *fdemo1.cpp*, the definition of *fun* before *main* implies that *fun* is defined before it is called, so that no separate declaration is needed. (Note, however, that if we have two functions *f* and *g*, which, under certain conditions, call each other, we need a special declaration for one of them.)

Function arguments need not be simple variables: they can also be more complex expressions. (As discussed in Section 3.2, the kind of expression that is allowed as an argument is technically referred to as *assignment-expression*, so, for obvious reasons, it must not consist of two operands separated by a comma operator.) For example, we can write

```
float result = fun(xx + 1, 2 * yy, ii + 2, jj - 1);
```

In this case the parameters x, y, i, and j will be assigned the values of $xx + 1$, $2 * yy$, $ii + 2$, and $jj - 1$, respectively. The order in which the arguments are evaluated is undefined. In the above example that order is irrelevant, but the following example is different in this regard:

```
float result = fun(xx, yy, ++i, i + 3);   // Wrong
```

Here the value of *i* is changed when the third argument is evaluated, and *i* is also used in the fourth argument. The order in which the third and the fourth arguments are evaluated is undefined, which means that in evaluating *i* + 3 either the increased or the original value of *i* is used.

Recursion

Calls to functions can also occur in functions other than *main*. For example, we may call a function *f* in a function *g*, which in turn is called in the function *main*. A call to function *f* may occur even in function *f* itself. If this is the case, we say that we are using *recursion* and the function *f* is said to be *recursive*. For example the function *f* in the following program is recursive because there is a call to *f* in this function *f* itself:

```
// recurs.cpp: Recursion.
#include <iostream>
using namespace std;

int f(int n)
{   int x = n - 1, y;
    if (n <= 1)
        y = 1;
    else
        y = n * f(x);
    return y;
}

int main()
{   cout << f(3) << endl;
    return 0;
}
```

The call *f*(3) in the *main* function gives rise to the computation of

```
3 * f(2)
```

where *f*(2) is equal to

```
2 * f(1)
```

and, finally,

```
f(1) = 1
```

so we have

```
f(3) = 3 * f(2) = 3 * 2 * f(1) = 3 * 2 * 1 = 6
```

In general, the function *f* computes *n*-factorial, written as *n*!, where

$$n! = n \times (n-1) \times (n-2) \times ... \times 2 \times 1$$

The local variables x and y are created for each call of the function f, even if there is still a previous call that has not yet completed. We could have written a shorter, equivalent function f, using a conditional expression:

```cpp
int f(int n){return n <=1 ? 1 : n * f(n - 1);}
```

or a version that is not recursive at all:

```cpp
int f(int n)
{  int y = 1;
   for (int i=2; i<=n; ++i)
      y *= i;
   return y;
}
```

Unlike this example, there are applications in which recursion is really useful and difficult to avoid. Recursion may be *indirect*, which means that a function calls itself via some other functions. For example, function f may call function g, which calls function h, and, depending on some condition, this function h calls f.

4.2 Keyword *void*, Global Variables, Namespaces

Functions not returning a value

The function *fun* of Section 4.1 returns a *float* value, as the keyword *float* at the beginning of the function shows. Instead, functions may return values of other types, or no value at all. Instead of a normal type *keyword*, such as *float*, we write *void* at the beginning of functions that do not return values, as the following program illustrates:

```cpp
// prmax3.cpp: A function that prints the maximum of three
//             integers.
#include <iostream>
using namespace std;

void prmax3(int x, int y, int z)
{  if (y > x) x = y;
   if (z > x) x = z;
   cout << "The maximum of these three is: " << x << endl;
}

int main()
{  int i, j, k;
   cout << "Enter three integers: ";
   cin >> i >> j >> k;
   prmax3(i, j, k);
   return 0;
}
```

Note that *prmax*3 does not contain a return statement. If we like we may write

```
return;
```

at the end of this function, but this would be superfluous and very unusual, since a function, when its end is reached, returns to its caller anyway. Yet this simple form of the return statement may be useful if it is executed conditionally and is followed by other statements, as in

```
void test(int x)
{  if (x < 0) return;
   ...
}
```

The parameter *x* of *prmax*3 is used as a local variable. Although the value of *x* is altered, this alteration will not affect the corresponding argument *i*. (If we wanted to alter *i* in this way, a different approach would be required, as we will see in Section 4.3.)

Functions without parameters

A function need not have any parameters. Program *nopar.cpp* contains a function that has none. The task of this function is to read a real number and to return this number. As mentioned in Section 3.2, we can use the value of *cin.fail*() to check whether a read attempt has failed. So far, we have usually omitted such checks about the correctness of the input data, but in practice it is wise to include them. In a large program, we may want to read input data at a great many places; it would then be rather tedious if we had to include such a check each time we wanted to read a number. Instead, we can write a function of our own to perform the following tasks:

1. Try to read a real number from the keyboard.
2. Check if this number is valid, and if so, return it.
3. Upon entry of any invalid characters, skip these until the end of the line is reached, ask the user to retry and go back to step 1.

The following program shows how this can be done.

```
// nopar.cpp: Using a function without parameters.
#include <iostream>
using namespace std;

double readreal()
{  double x;
   char ch;
   for (;;)
   {  cin >> x;
      if (!cin.fail())        // See Section 3.2
         break;
```

```
        cin.clear();              // See Section 3.2
        do ch = cin.get(); while (ch != '\n');
        // Rest of incorrect line has now been skipped.
        cout << "Incorrect. Enter a number:\n";
    }
    return x;
}

int main()
{   double xx;
    float x;
    cout << "Enter a real number: ";
    xx = readreal();
    cout << "Another one, please: ";
    x = readreal();
    cout << "The following numbers have been read: "
        << xx << " " << x << endl;
    return 0;
}
```

Apart from its use for functions that do not return a value (as in program *prmax*3), the word *void* may also be used to indicate that a function has no parameters. For example, the following two lines are equivalent:

```
double readreal(void)
double readreal()
```

A function that returns a value may also be called as one that does not. For example, if we want to skip three numbers in the input, ignoring their values, we can use our function *readreal* as follows:

```
readreal(); readreal(); readreal();
```

The *main* function

In view of the word *int* at the beginning of

```
int main()
```

it is logical that a *main* function should return an *int* value, which explains the following statement, which we usually write at the end of that function:

```
return 0;
```

For example, with MS-DOS, the return value, such as 0 here, can be used in a batch file as an error level. We therefore replace 0 with a different value, such as 1, if we want to terminate program execution in the case of a run-time error. If we omit the return-statement in the *main* function, some current compilers produce warnings or error messages such as:

```
Function should return a value.
```

Curiously enough, despite the word *int* at its beginning, a *main* function need not contain a return statement. According to the C++ Standard, if control reaches the end of *main* without encountering a return statement, the effect is that of executing

```
return 0;
```

To avoid the compiler warnings and error messages just mentioned, these apparently superfluous return statements are still present in the *main* functions in this book.

Global variables

The variables that we use in a function can be either *local* or *global*. They are said to be *local* if they are declared and used only in that function. As a rule, we use local variables, unless this has serious drawbacks. Global variables are declared outside functions, at the same level as functions are defined. Here is a very simple (and therefore unrealistic) example:

```
// globvar.cpp: A global variable.
#include <iostream>
using namespace std;
int i;

void print_i()
{   cout << i << endl;
}

int main()
{   i = 123;
    print_i();
    return 0;
}
```

Because we have declared *i* prior to both *print_i* and *main*, we can use this variable in both functions. Note that function *print_i* does not have parameters, nor does it return a value. Although, in principle, functions like this can do all kinds of useful work, this programming style is not recommended. We should be very careful with functions that have *side effects*, that is, functions that change the values of global variables. For example, if we had assigned a new value to *i* in function *print_i*, the call *print_i( )* would have been confusing, because the function name does not suggest any side effects: we expect *i* still to have the value 123 after the call.

As we will see in Section 4.6, it makes sense to distinguish between the terms *declaration* and *definition* (and between the corresponding verbs *to declare* and *to define*) for variables in the same way as we have done for functions. Every definition is also a declaration, but the reverse is not true. For example, in program *globvar.cpp* we can replace the function *print_i* with this version:

```
void print_i()
{   extern int i;
    cout << i << endl;
}
```

Here

```
extern int i;
```

is a declaration that is not a definition. Such declarations do not really introduce new variables; they only announce the use of variables defined elsewhere. A definition of a variable can occur only once and can initialize that variable. By contrast, a declaration of a variable that is not a definition can occur as often as we like and cannot be combined with initialization. In this second version of *print_i*, this declaration of *i* is superfluous because the definition of *i* occurs in the same program file. This will be different in Section 4.6, in which we will discuss programs that consist of more than one file.

The scope-resolution operator ::

C++ enables us to use a global variable even in a function in which another variable with the same name is defined. We can indicate that the global variable is meant by writing the scope-resolution operator :: in front of the variable name, as the following program illustrates:

```
#include <iostream>
using namespace std;
int i = 1;

int main()
{   int i = 2;
    cout << ::i << endl;   // Output: 1 (global variable)
    cout << i << endl;     // Output: 2 (local variable)
    return 0;
}
```

Namespaces

Especially if our program consists of more than one file (as we will discuss in Section 4.6), we must be careful to avoid *name clashes*. The *namespace* concept can be very helpful in this regard. We have already discussed some aspect of namespaces in Section 1.2. In the following program, there are two global variables *i*, which do not clash because they are in distinct namespaces *A* and *B*. We can tell these variables apart by using their fully qualified names *A*::i and *B*::i, as has been done here in the *main* function:

```
// namespace.cpp: The namespace concept.
#include <iostream>
using namespace std;

namespace A
{   int i = 10;
}

namespace B
{   int i = 20;
}

void fA()
{   using namespace A;
    cout << "In fA:    "
         <<   A::i << " " << B::i << " "
         << i << endl;    // In namespace A, i is A::i.
}

void fB()
{   using namespace B;
    cout << "In fB:    "
         << A::i << " " << B::i << " "
         << i << endl;    // In namespace B, i is B::i.
}

int main()
{   fA(); fB();
    cout << "In main: " << A::i << " " << B::i << endl;
    return 0;
}
```

This program produces the following output:

```
In fA:    10 20 10
In fB:    10 20 20
In main: 10 20
```

If a function contains the *using-directive*

```
using namespace A;
```

then for any name, such as *i*, occurring in that function after that declaration, the compiler first checks if there is a name *A::i*. If this is not the case, it looks for an unqualified name *i*. The functions *fA* and *fB* differ in that the former uses namespace *A* and the latter namespace *B*. Writing just *i* therefore means the same as *A::i* in *fA* and *B::i* in *fB*. Since there is no using-directive for *A* or *B* in the *main* function, here the use of just *i* is not allowed.

If a name *i* belongs to a namespace *A* we can use *i* only by indicating in one of the following three ways that this name belongs to *A*:

1. Instead of just *i*, we write the following form each time we use this name:

   ```
   A::i
   ```

2. We write the following using-declaration, after which, in the scope of this declaration, we can simply write *i* instead of *A::i*:

   ```
   using A::i;
   ```

3. We write the following using-directive, after which, in the scope of this directive, we can simply write *i* instead of *A::i*:

   ```
   using namespace A;
   ```

As for the relative merits of these three solutions, the first is the clearest and most direct, although this notation may look tedious if *i* occurs very often and (instead of *A*) a long namespace name is used. The second solution is more attractive in this regard since, after this using-declaration, we simply write *i* each time we need this name. The third solution is rather radical in that we need to write very little program code but we cannot always clearly see which of the names used in the code that follows belongs to namespace *A*. If the name *i* is used for different purposes, the using-directive may be confusing, as the following example illustrates:

```
// confuse.cpp: Confusing because of two variables i.
#include <iostream>
namespace A {int i = 10;};

int main()
{   int i = 20;
    using namespace A;
    std::cout << i << std::endl; // Output: 20
    return 0;
}
```

In this example the using-directive should be interpreted as 'the name *A::i* is available as if it had been defined as a global variable *i*.' Since there is a local variable *i* here, this hides any global name *i*. In other words, a using-directive does not add a name to the local scope. This is different with a using-declaration. If we replace the using-directive in the above program with the using-declaration

```
using A::i;
```

the compiler will produce an error message because this using-declaration causes a multiple declaration of *i*, which is similar to defining, say, an *int* and a *float* variable *i* in the *main* function. On the other hand, the following program is correct:

```
// addtoloc.cpp: A::i is added to the local scope of main.
#include <iostream>
namespace A { int i = 10; };
int i = 20;

int main()
{  using A::i;
   std::cout << i << std::endl; // Output: 10
   return 0;
}
```

The using-declaration in the *main* function adds *A::i* to the local scope. This program would be incorrect if we replaced this using-declaration with the using-directive

```
using namespace A;
```

because it would then be unclear which *i* was to be used in the output statement. We could then make this clear by replacing this output statement with either

```
std::cout << A::i << std::endl; // Output: 10
```

or

```
std::cout << ::i << std::endl; // Output: 20
```

4.3 Altering Variables via Parameters

So far, function parameters could be regarded as local variables, which obtain their initial values from the corresponding arguments. This principle does not enable us, for example, to write a function that exchanges the values of two variables, passed to it as arguments. If we try to do this as follows:

```
void swap0(int x, int y)  // Error
{  int temp = x;
   x = y; y = temp;
}
```

then, with two int variables *i* and *j*, the call

```
swap0(i, j)
```

will not have the desired effect. Although, inside *swap0*, the values of *x* and *y* are exchanged, the arguments *i* and *j* are used only once, namely to give the parameters *x* and *y* their initial values. After exchanging these, the new values of *x* and *y* are not passed back to *i* and *j*. The principle of parameter passing used here is technically known as *call by value*.

Still, we can achieve our goal, and in C++ this can even be done in two ways. The first is specific to C++ and is based on what is referred to as *call by reference parameter passing*, or simply *reference parameters*. The second is the one C programmers are familiar with; it is based on using addresses and *pointers*. We will now discuss these two methods.

Reference parameters and reference variables

Here is a solution to our swapping problem; it is based on using the reference parameters *x* and *y*, and the parameter-passing method used is known as *call by reference*:

```
void swap1(int &x, int &y)
{  int temp = x;
   x = y; y = temp;
}
```

Note the use of the ampersand &. When used for parameters as above, it indicates that not only the value of the arguments but also their addresses are passed to the function. The variables *x* and *y* are no longer local variables but rather alternative notations for the arguments, such as *i* and *j* in the call

```
swap1(i, j);
```

It will be clear that the arguments of *swap*1 must be lvalues (see Section 3.8), so *i* + 1 instead of *i* would not be allowed.

The idea of reference parameters, as used in *swap*1, will be easier to understand if we also discuss reference variables in general, outside the context of function calls. In the following program, *x* is a reference variable; it is not really an independent, new variable but rather an alternative way of accessing *i*:

```
// refvar.cpp: Demonstration of a reference variable.
#include <iostream>
using namespace std;

int main()
{  int i, &x = i;
   i = 2; x *= 100;
   cout << "The value of i is now " << i << ".\n";
   cout << "Using x, we also find i = " << x << ".\n";
   return 0;
}
```

The most remarkable point of this program is that *x* *= 100 actually multiplies *i* by 100. Then the new value of *i* is printed. The output is

```
The value of i is now 200.
Using x, we also find i = 200.
```

In contrast to other variables, reference variables must be initialized so we cannot write

```
int &x;   // Error.
```

After the initialized declaration of x in program *refvar.cpp*, any assignment to x means an assignment to i. It is not possible to change this connection of x and i, so we cannot link x with a variable other than i later.

In function *swap*1, when called with i as its first argument, the relationship between x and i is the same as it is in program *refvar.cpp*. There is only a difference in notation: the formal parameters x and y are related to the arguments i and j by the call *swap*1(i, j) as would be the case after

```
int &x = i, &y = j;
```

Addresses and pointers

The C language does not offer the call by reference parameter-passing facility we have been discussing for C++. Yet we can write a function in C to swap the values of two variables (as well as other functions that alter the values of variables via their parameters). This method is also available in C++, and it is certainly worthwhile to be familiar with it. It is based on supplying addresses as arguments and on two unary operators, each taking an operand that follows the operator:

Operator	*Meaning*
&	The address of the object given by the operand
*	The object that has the address given by the operand

An address is a number permanently associated with a memory location. As * is the inverse operator of &, the expression *&*i* is just a complicated way of writing i. We are normally interested only in the value of a variable, not in its address; that is, we are not interested in where a variable is located in memory. Yet it sometimes makes sense to use the operator &, as is done in the following function call:

```
swap2(&i, &j);
```

From this call and from the fact that arguments supply the corresponding parameters with initial values, it follows that the parameters of *swap*2 must be variables whose values are addresses. Such variables are called *pointers*. If these pointer parameters are p and q, the values of p and q are addresses of certain locations, and we must write *p and *q to denote the contents of these locations. As we are dealing with addresses of *int* variables, *p and *q have type *int*, which explains why p and q are declared as

```
int *p, int *q
```

in the following function definition, which is the solution to our swapping problem:

```
void swap2(int *p, int *q)
{   int temp = *p;
    *p = *q; *q = temp;
}
```

Remember, in each call to *swap2* we must not forget to supply addresses as arguments, as we have done in the call *swap2(&i, &j)*. During execution of the function *swap2* the situation is as shown in Figure 4.1. Remember, the pointers *p* and *q* cease to exist after the completion of the function call.

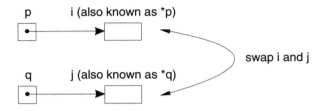

Figure 4.1. Use of pointers p and q to swap i and j

This function *swap2* can interchange the values of any two *int* objects. Let us, for example, consider the case that these are elements of array *a*, declared as

```
int a[100];
```

If we want to interchange the values of the first and the final elements, we can write

```
swap2(&a[0], &a[99]);
```

We will discuss pointers in more detail in Section 5.3.

4.4 Types of Arguments and Return Values

Argument types

Function arguments are automatically converted to the required parameter types, if this is possible. If it is not, an error message is given. For example, the call *f*(5) in the following program is correct, even though 5 has type *int* and *f* has a *float* parameter. This call is in fact equivalent to *f*(5.0*F*), and the output of this program is 26.

```
// argconv.cpp: Argument conversion from int to float.
#include <iostream>
using namespace std;
```

```
float f(float x)
{  return x * x + 1;
}

int main()
{  cout << f(5) << endl;
   return 0;
}
```

The conversion from the argument 5 to *float*, the type of parameter *x*, is possible because such a conversion is also possible in a declaration with initialization:

```
float x = 5;
```

This is a general rule: any conversions from argument types to parameter types are similar to similar conversions that may take place in initializations; if the latter is possible, so is the former, and vice versa. With the above function *f*, the call to *f* in the following main function is incorrect:

```
int main()
{  float t = 5;
   cout << f(&t);    // Error
   return 0;
}
```

The address argument &*t* is incompatible with the *float* parameter *x*. The error made here is analogous to the one in the initialization

```
float x = &t;    // Error
```

where both *x* and *t* have type *float*. The compiler will not accept these constructions.

Types of return values

The conversion rules for initialization also apply to return statements. An example is

```
int g(double x, double y)
{  return x * x - y * y + 1;
}
```

Although the keyword *int* at the beginning of this function promises that *g* will return an integer, the expression in the return statement has type *double*. The compiler will accept this, and perform the same conversion as it does when compiling the following initialization, where *i* has type *int*:

```
int i = x * x - y * y + 1;
```

In either case truncation takes place, so 7.9, for example, is converted to 7. As discussed in Section 3.7, a cast is to be recommended in this assignment statement, so that we may see more clearly what actually happens. The same applies to the return statement: although not required by the compiler, the cast in the following version of the return statement is very welcome as a reminder that, because of conversion from *double* to *int*, the values before and after conversion may be different:

```
return static_cast<int>(x * x - y * y + 1);
```

4.5 More about Initialization

It is often convenient to initialize variables, that is, to give values to them as we declare them. We have already done this several times, but we have not yet discussed all aspects of this subject. When initializing variables, we should bear in mind the following rules:

(i)   Variables can be initialized only when memory locations are assigned to them.
(ii) In the absence of explicit initialization, the initial value 0 is assigned to all variables that are *global* or *static*.

As we already know, the term *global* in (ii) refers to variables that are declared outside functions. The new term *static* is used for all variables in the declaration of which the keyword *static* is used. Global and static variables have in common that their memory locations are permanent, whereas nonstatic, local variables are assigned memory locations temporarily, on a 'stack.' As the latter variables are automatically assigned memory locations when the functions in which they are declared are entered, they are called *automatic* variables, and we may use the keyword *auto* for them. Memory for automatic variables is released when the functions in which they are declared are left. According to rule (i), static variables local to a function are initialized only the first time this function is called.

For example, in the following program the variable *i* is set to 1 only once. The first call prints that value and increments *i*. The second call is more interesting in that *i* is not initialized once again: it still has its last value, 2, because the keyword static causes its memory space to be permanent. In other words, the variable *i* keeps its value between two successive calls to the function *f* (which is by no means the case with nonstatic local variables). Consequently, this program prints the values 1 and 2:

```
// statvar.cpp: A local static variable.
#include <iostream>
using namespace std;

void f()
{   static int i = 1;
    cout << i++ << endl;
}
```

```
int main()
{   f(); f();
    return 0;
}
```

If we had separated the declaration and the assignment (by writing *static int i*; *i* = 1; instead of *static int i* = 1;) the value 1 would have printed twice, as it would have been if we had simply omitted the keyword *static*.

According to rule (ii), the declaration

```
static int i;
```

is equivalent to

```
static int i = 0;
```

We have not yet discussed why static variables might be useful. A simple, but interesting application of a local static variable is its use as a 'flag' that indicates whether a function is called for the first time. Sometimes we want some special action to take place during the first call. Here is a very simple example, which you can easily replace with a more practical one yourself:

```
void f()
{   static bool firsttime = true;
    if (firsttime)
    {   cout <<
        "This is printed only the first time f is called.\n";
        firsttime = false;
    }
    cout << "This is printed each time f is called.\n";
}
```

If a recursive function contains a static variable, there is only one version of this variable, which is shared by all recursive calls. Recall that this is different with normal local variables, as mentioned in Section 4.1.

We can also initialize arrays, by writing their initial values within a pair of braces. Again, the rules (i) and (ii) apply. There must not be more initial values between the braces than there are array elements. If there are fewer (but at least one!), the trailing elements are initialized to 0. For example, with

```
float a[100] = {23, 41.5};
```

we have

```
a[0] = 23; a[1] = 41.5; a[2] = ... = a[99] = 0.
```

If, for an initialized array, we omit the array length, the number of initial values is taken as that length, as, for example, in

```
int b[] = {95, 34, 72};
```

which is equivalent to

```
int b[3] = {95, 34, 72};
```

So far, we have been writing (numerical) initial values as literals, which is allowed for any variable that is initialized. We can generalize this as follows. First, we may write constant expressions (such as 123 * 4 – 3 * 30) whenever numerical literals are allowed. For simple automatic variables, we can go further than that and initialize them with any expression of a suitable type. But remember, global and static variables (with permanent memory) and arrays may only be initialized with constant expressions. These rules are easy to remember if we bear in mind that initialization can take place only when memory space is allocated. For variables with permanent memory space, this is before the program is executed, so values computed at run time cannot be used for the initialization of such variables.

If we want to initialize arrays of characters, we can write a list of character constants between braces, as is done in

```
char str[16] = {'C', 'h', 'a', 'r', 'l', 'e', 's', ' ',
                'D', 'i', 'c', 'k', 'e', 'n', 's'};
```

Although the initialization list consist of only 15 character constants, we give array *str* the value 16 to accommodate a trailing null character ('\0'). We need not write this null character at the end of the list because in a partially initialized array all remaining elements are set to zero, and for character constants zero means the null character.

However, the above way of initializing is very tedious for long strings, as in this example. Fortunately, we may use a string literal instead of the above list of character literals surrounded by braces. In other words, we can abbreviate the declaration just given by

```
char str[16] = "Charles Dickens";
```

If we had omitted 16 here, array *str* would still have had length 16 because that is the number of bytes used for the given string literal (including the null character). If, instead of 16, we specify a larger number, all trailing unused elements of *str* would contain the null character '\0'. We cannot replace 16 with a smaller value in this example because there must be room for a trailing null character, which will be added automatically. The following example illustrates this more clearly:

```
char s[3] = "ABC";    // Incorrect: no room for trailing '\0'
char t[4] = "ABC";    // Correct
char u[8] = "ABC";    // Correct
```

We will discuss arrays of characters (or C-style strings) in Section 5.4.

Default arguments

A simple but nice facility in C++ is the possibility of supplying a function with fewer arguments than there are parameters. All we have to do is supply the parameters with default argument values, which we write in the same way as when initializing normal variables. Once a parameter is initialized, any subsequent parameters must also be initialized. For example, with a function *f* of the form

```
void f(int i, float x = 0, char ch = 'A')
{ ...
}
```

we may, if we like, omit either only the third argument or both the second and the third arguments, so that the following calls are allowed:

```
f(5, 1.23, 'E');
f(5, 1.23);          // Equivalent to f(5, 1.23, 'A');
f(5);                // Equivalent to f(5, 0, 'A');
```

If function *f* is not only defined, but also separately declared, any default argument values may be specified only once, either in the declaration or in the definition, but not in both. For example, we may write

```
void f(int i, float x = 0, char ch = 'A'); // Declaration
...
void f(int i, float x, char ch)            // Definition
{ ...
}
```

We must not insert = 0 and = 'A' in this definition because default values were already given in the declaration.

4.6 Separate Compilation and Unnamed Namespaces

Large C++ programs are preferably split up into several program files, also called *modules* or *translation units*. This is important in view of maintenance: any future program changes should preferably affect only a few modules of limited size. The modules of a program are compiled separately and linked together later by a so-called *linker*, as Figure 4.2 illustrates.

ith programs consisting of several modules, we normally also use a header file of our own. This header file is used by the compiler, not by the linker. We will discuss this by means of a simple example. In a *main* function, located in the program file *mainfile.cpp*, we want to call a function *f*, defined in another file, *funcfile.cpp*. Only these two files are compiled and the resulting object files are linked. For example, with Visual C++ this can be done by adding these two files (and no others) to a 'project.' Alternatively, we can use the following command to compile and link both files, resulting in the executable file *mainfile.exe*:

```
cl mainfile.cpp funcfile.cpp
```

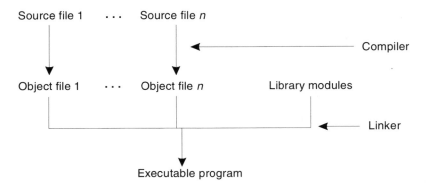

Figure 4.2. Separate compilation

In *funcfile.cpp*, we want to use a global variable, *counter*, to count how many times the function *f* is called. This variable should be global to the file *funcfile.cpp*, but inaccessible in *mainfile.cpp*. Computing *f* as $f(x) = k * x + n$, we want to assign values to both *k* and *n* before the calls to *f* are executed. Just to compare two ways of doing this, we do this differently for *n* and for *k*, as we will discuss in a moment. Here is the header file *func.h*, in which the functions *setk*, *f*, and *getcounter* are declared:

```
// func.h: Header used in mainfile.cpp and funcfile.cpp.
void setk(int kk);
int f(int x);
int getcounter();
```

The following program 'includes' this header file, which means that there is a line starting with #*include*, followed by the file name *func.h* enclosed by string quotes ("). Because of these string quotes, the compiler first looks for this file in the current directory. If it cannot find it there, it also looks in standard directories for headers, as if we had written *<func.h>* instead of "*func.h*":

```
// mainfile.cpp: Demonstration of separate compilation.
//    The file funcfile.cpp should be linked.
#include <iostream>
#include "func.h"
using namespace std;

int main()
{   extern int n;
    n = 10;
    setk(5);
    cout << "f(2) = " << f(2) << endl;
    cout << "f(3) = " << f(3) << endl;
    cout << "Function f was called " << getcounter()
         << " times.\n";
    return 0;
}
```

The functions *setk*, *f*, and *getcounter* are defined in the following file, which is the first file in this book that does not contain a *main* function and that, unlike header files, will be compiled as an independent unit (hence the name *translation unit*):

```
// funfile.cpp: Definitions of functions setk, f, and
//              getcounter.
#include "func.h"
int n;

namespace
{   int k;
    int counter = 0;
}

void setk(int kk){k = kk;}

int f(int x)
{   counter++;
    return k * x + n;
}

int getcounter(){return counter;}
```

Since $k = 5$, $n = 10$, and we are computing $f(x) = kx + n$, the output of this program is as shown below:

```
f(2) = 20
f(3) = 25
Function f was called 2 times.
```

As the variable *n* illustrates, it is technically possible to define a variable in one file, and, after declaring it by means of the word *extern*, using it in another file. Here *n* is explicitly assigned the value 10 in *mainfile.cpp* and is then used in *funfile.cpp*. This way of dealing with global variables is not recommended. It is much better to use a variable that is global in only one file, as is the case with *k* and *counter*, defined in the file *funfile.cpp*. Access to these variables can be achieved by using special functions. In *mainfile.cpp* the function *setk* assigns a value to *k*, while *getcounter* retrieves the value of *counter*. The modern way of making global variables inaccessible outside the file in which they are defined is by defining them in an *unnamed namespace*, as is done in

```
namespace
{   int k;
    int counter = 0;
}
```

Unlike *n*, the names *k* and *counter* cannot be made accessible in the file *mainfile.cpp* by writing

```
extern int k, counter;
k = 5;
counter = 0;
```

If we try to do this, we obtain an error message, such as

```
unresolved external symbol
```

Before namespaces were introduced in C++ the word *static* was used for variables such as *k* and *counter* in this example, so that it was usual to write

```
static int k, counter = 0;
```

This use of *static* is now deprecated, and using an unnamed namespace is recommended instead. Incidentally, both here and in the original program, it is not really necessary to set *counter* equal to zero by initializing this variable, since global variables are implicitly initialized to zero.

Functions, too, can be made inaccessible in other files by using unnamed namespaces. Let us illustrate this by making the program even more academic than it already is. We could write

```
namespace
{   int k;
    int counter = 0;
    int sum(int a, int b){return a + b;}
}
```

in the file *funcfile.cpp* to define the function *sum* that is accessible in this file, enabling us to use the statement

```
return sum(k * x, n);
```

in the function *f*. Because the function *sum* belongs to an unnamed namespace, it is not accessible in other program files.

The advantage of limiting the scope of a name to only one program file is that the same name may be used for other purposes in other files belonging to the same program. Realistic programs usually consist of more than two files, which are also more complex than what we have seen here. This way of avoiding 'pollution of the global namespace' by using unnamed namespaces is then very useful.

As a rule, we prefer local variables to global ones. If it is really necessary or desirable for some variables to be global, we preferably limit their scope to the file in which they are defined. As we know, all C++ functions are global: we cannot define a function inside another function. However, as we have seen, we can restrict their scope to the file in which they occur, which makes them 'less global' than other functions. When you are writing a module of a large program, you are strongly recommended to use this notion of unnamed namespaces for the definition of every function and of every global variable that is used only in that module.

4.7 Some Mathematical Standard Functions

When developing science and engineering applications we often use some well-known mathematical functions, which are available in the standard library. We can include their declarations in our program by writing

```
#include <cmath>
```

in which case the line

```
using namespace std;
```

must also be present. Formerly, we did not use this using directive and, instead of the above #*include* line, we wrote

```
#include <math.h>
```

which is still possible. Except for some rather technical functions (to be discussed in Section 11.6), the declarations of these mathematical functions are listed below, along with some information which will probably be sufficient for those who want to use them. Remember, thanks to our #*include* line, we need not actually write these declarations in our programs:

`double cos(double x);`	$\cos x$ (x in radians)
`double sin(double x);`	$\sin x$
`double tan(double x);`	$\tan x$
`double exp(double x);`	$\exp x$
`double log(double x);`	$\ln x$ (natural logarithm)
`double log10(double x);`	$\log x$ (base 10)
`double pow(double x, double y);`	x^y
`double sqrt(double x);`	$\sqrt{x}$
`double floor(double x);`	*floor*$(4.9) = 4.0$, *floor*$(-1.4) = -2$ etc.
`double ceil(double x);`	*ceil*$(8.1) = 9.0$ etc.
`double fabs(double x);`	$|x|$
`double acos(double x);`	arccos x
`double asin(double x);`	arcsin x
`double atan(double x);`	arctan x, range $(-\pi/2, \pi/2)$
`double atan2(double y, double x);`	see explanation below
`double cosh(double x);`	$\cosh x$
`double sinh(double x);`	$\sinh x$
`double tanh(double x);`	$\tanh x$

Besides the function *fabs*, to be used for floating-point expressions, there are also the functions *abs* for type *int* and *labs* for type *long int*. These are declared in the header

<cstdlib> (or *<stdlib.h>*) as we will see in Section 11.9. These three functions should not be confused. The function *fabs* is too slow for *int* values, and, more seriously, *abs* converts floating values to *int*:

```
float x = abs(-4.56);    // x = 4.0
float y = fabs(-4.56);   // y = 4.56
```

The function *atan2* comes in very handy if, in the *xy*-plane, a point P(*x*, *y*), not coinciding with the origin O, is given and we want to know the (positive or negative) angle φ between OP and the positive *x*-axis, as shown in Figure 4.3. This angle φ is equal to *atan*(*y*/*x*) if *x* is positive. However, the latter expression is undefined for zero *x* and is different from φ for negative *x*. There are no such problems with the function *atan2*, which takes *y* and *x*, in that order, as individual parameters. We should therefore use the expression *atan2*(*y*, *x*) instead of *atan*(*y*/*x*) for this purpose. For any *x* and *y* (not both zero), *atan2*(*y*, *x*) is defined as the angle φ that satisfies

$$\cos \varphi = \frac{x}{\sqrt{x^2 + y^2}} \qquad \sin\varphi = \frac{y}{\sqrt{x^2 + y^2}} \qquad -\pi < \varphi \leq \pi$$

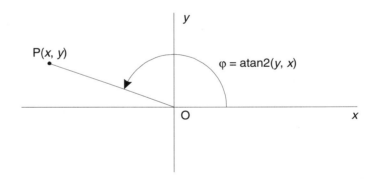

Figure 4.3. The **atan2** *function*

4.8 Function Overloading

Unlike C, the C++ language allows us to define two or more functions with the same name, provided that their numbers of parameters or their parameter types differ. For example, we can write the following two output functions for numbers:

```
void writenum(int i)      // Function 1
{ cout << setw(10) << i;
}
```

```
void writenum(float x)    // Function 2
{  cout << setw(12) << setprecision(3) << x;
}
```

After these function definitions, a call of the form

```
writenum(expression);
```

will call function 1 if expression has type *int* and function 2 if it has floating-point type. These two functions *writenum* are distinguished by their parameter types. Here is an example in which the distinction is made on the basis of the number of parameters:

```
double f(float x)
{  ...
}

double f(float x, float y)
{  ...
}
```

It is not required for both functions *f* to return values of the same type, as is the case here. Note, however, that functions with the same name but different return types must also be different in the number or types of their parameters. For example, the following would be incorrect:

```
int g(int n)
{  ...
}

float g(int n)  // Error: again only one int parameter.
{  ...
}
```

Defining several functions with the same name is technically known as *overloading*. (In Section 6.6 we will see that not only functions but also operators can be overloaded.)

Type-safe linkage

You may wonder how the linker can distinguish between several functions with the same name, differing only in the types of their parameters. After all, with separate compilation, it is possible for one module to call a function, say, *f*, with an *int* argument, while there are two definitions of *f* in other modules, one with an *int* and one with a *float* parameter. This problem is solved by *name mangling*: the function name *f* is appended with coded information about its parameters, and this information is supplied to the linker. This convention provides a very safe way of linking program modules together, hence its name *type-safe linkage*. We can benefit from it even if we do not apply function overloading at all. Suppose that in one module we use a function *f*, which we declare in this module as follows:

```
void f(int i);
```

Suppose also that there is a function *f*, which has the following form:

```
void f(float x)
{  ...
}
```

This definition happens to be in a module other than the declaration just shown. If we had been programming in C, we would have had a serious problem, not detected by the compiler and the linker. In C++, however, the linker will detect this error.

4.9 References as Return Values

In Section 4.3 we discussed reference parameters. The return value can also be a reference, as is the case with the function *maxim* in the following program:

```
//reffun.cpp: Reference as return value.
#include <iostream>
using namespace std;

int &maxim(int &x, int &y)
{  return (x > y ? x : y);
}

int main()
{  int a = 23, b = 15;
   cout << "a = " << a << "  b = " << b << endl;
   // First call to maxim:
   cout << "The larger of these is " << maxim(a, b)
        << endl;
   // Second call to maxim:
   maxim(a, b) = 0;  // A function call as left-hand side!
   cout <<
   "The larger of a and b is set to 0. Thus we now have \n";
   cout << "a = " << a << "  b = " << b << endl;
   return 0;
}
```

This program shows two calls of the function *maxim*. The first is only to compute the maximum of *a* and *b*, which could also have been done if the three occurrences of the ampersand & in the first line of *maxim* had been omitted. The second call in the statement

```
maxim(a, b) = 0;
```

is more interesting. In some other languages we cannot write a function call as the left-hand side of an assignment statement. In C++ this is possible because of the reference concept in this language, which enables us to write functions that return lvalues (see Section 3.8). Function *maxim* does not return (only) the value of one of its arguments, but rather this argument itself. It is essential here that the arguments are variables and that we use & in the declaration of the parameters *x* and *y*.

The output of demonstration program *reffun.cpp* is as follows:

```
a = 23   b = 15
The larger of these is 23
The larger of a and b is set to 0. Thus we now have
a = 0   b = 15
```

Warning

If a function returns a reference, it is essential for the variable in question to exist after the function call. We must therefore not try to return a local variable of a function as a reference. The following function is therefore not correct:

```
int &incorrect()
{  int x = 123;
   return x;     // Error due to & in the first line.
}
```

4.10 Reference Parameters and *const*

In Section 4.3 we introduced reference parameters as a means to modify the corresponding arguments. There is another useful aspect of reference parameters that we should not overlook, namely that these parameters prevent the argument values from being copied. This aspect is not interesting with primitive types, such as *int*, since copying an *int* object is as efficient as copying its address. However, it is important with objects that are more complex, as we will discuss in Chapter 6. In the meantime, we can use the type *string* (see Section 1.6) as an example. Since *string* objects can contain strings of different sizes, it will be clear that their implementation is rather complex and that copying a string object may take more time than copying its address. Now suppose that we want to write a function that takes a *string* argument. If we wrote

```
void f(string s)        // (1)
```

the arguments used in calls to *f* would be copied. To avoid this waste of time, we could write

```
void f(string &s)       // (2)
```

This is more efficient, but, unlike (1), it enables the function *f* to modify the corresponding argument. In many practical cases, such a modification of the argument is not required and it is then desirable to indicate this clearly. This is done by also using the word *const*, in the following way:

```
void f(const string &s)   // (3)
```

This is very often the preferred way of declaring a string parameter, and we frequently use this principle for complex types other than *string* as well. This third form is also useful if the corresponding string is not a modifiable lvalue. For example, because of the word *const* used below for the string *t*, the call *f(t)* is invalid in combination with the above line (2):

```
const string t = "ABCDEFGHIJKLMNOPQRSTUVWXYZ";
f(t); // Const argument not allowed in combination with (2)
```

This call to *f* agrees with both function headings (1) and (3), of which (3) is preferred for reasons of efficiency.

4.11 Inline Functions

Calling a (normal) function causes a jump to the function code to be executed; later, a jump back to the calling function (such as, for example, *main*) will take place. Also, any arguments have to be passed to the function, and a return value has to be passed back to the calling function. If the function contains very little code and is to be called very frequently, it may make sense to use the keyword *inline* at the beginning of its declaration (and its definition). By doing this, we ask the compiler to implement the function in question by inline code, as if we had actually written the code to be executed, instead of writing a call to a function that contains such code. For example, suppose that we often want to compute

$$1 + 2 + ... + n = \frac{1}{2}n(n + 1)$$

as a function of *n*, and that, for esthetic reasons, we want to write this each time as a function call, although we would rather not call a real function for reasons of efficiency. We then write

```
inline int sum(int n) {return n * (n + 1) / 2;}
```

We can later call it as a normal function, although the compiler will try to implement it as inline code. For example, writing

```
y = 1.0 / sum(k + 1);
```

is then equivalent to something like

```
{int t; y = 1.0 / (t = k + 1, t * (t + 1) / 2);}
```

Note that the argument value $k + 1$ is computed only once.

4.12 Some Preprocessor Facilities

Macros

Inline functions are new in C++. In C we can use *macros* for the same purpose. As these are also available in C++ and are widely used, we will pay some attention to them as well, even though in C++ inline functions are to be preferred. In the case of our previous example, we could write

```
#define sum(n) ((n) * ((n) + 1) / 2)
```

This is a macro definition. Macro calls have the same form as function calls, so this macro, too, can be used as follows:

```
y = 1.0 / sum(k + 1);
```

Macro calls are expanded before the actual compilation process takes place. In this example, the resulting expanded statement will be

```
y = 1.0 / ((k + 1) * ((k + 1) + 1) / 2);
```

Between the first slash and the semicolon, we find the macro expansion. It consists of the form $((n) * ((n) + 1) / 2)$, found in the macro definition, in which all occurrences of the parameter n have been replaced with the argument $k + 1$. It will now be clear why there are so many parentheses in the above macro definition. If we had written

```
#define sum(n) n * (n + 1) / 2
```

then $y = 1.0 / sum(k + 1)$; would have been expanded as

```
y = 1.0 / k + 1 * (k + 1 + 1) / 2;
```

which is seriously wrong. Note that the above macro is less efficient than the inline function *sum* of the previous section, because in our example it computes $k + 1$ twice.

Macros can have any number of parameters. Here is a very simple macro, which has no parameters at all:

```
#define LENGTH 100
```

After this, we can write the symbolic constant *LENGTH* instead of 100.

Conditional compilation

We can instruct the preprocessor to compile a program fragment (A) only if a certain condition is met; if not, there can be another fragment (B) that is to be compiled instead. This can be done as follows:

```
#if constant expression
    Program fragment A
#else
    Program fragment B
#endif
```

Note that this is a preprocessor statement, not a normal conditional statement: it is executed during compilation time, not during execution time. We always write *#if* at its beginning and *#endif* at its end. The line *#else* (and program fragment B) is optional. The condition after *#if* must be a constant expression so that it can be evaluated by the compiler. If its value is nonzero, the compiler compiles program fragment A; otherwise it compiles program fragment B, if present.

Conditional compilation is interesting especially in combination with the use of header files. For example, if *MAX* is a symbolic constant defined (as a macro without parameters) in the header file *a.h*, we can write

```
#include "a.h"
#define LENGTH 100

#if LENGTH < MAX
    ...   // Program fragment A
#endif
```

Whether or not program fragment A is compiled depends on how *MAX* is defined in the header file *a.h*.

Preprocessor statements for conditional compilation may be nested. However, instead of doing this, we can often use a special construction with *#elif*, as, for example,

```
#if LENGTH < 100
    ... // Fragment A
#elif LENGTH < 1000
    ... // Fragment B
#else
    ... // Fragment C
#endif
```

As its name suggests, *#elif* is a combination of *#else* and *#if*, but it does not require an *#endif* (as would *#if*). This example is equivalent to the following, with two *#if*s and therefore also with two *#endif*s:

```
#if LENGTH < 100
   ... // Fragment A
#else
   #if LENGTH < 1000
      ... // Fragment B
   #else
      ... // Fragment C
   #endif
#endif
```

With conditional compilation we can make the compiler temporarily ignore a portion of our program. We sometimes want to do this during program development. Most people would insert the comment tokens (/* and */) for this purpose, but this will cause a problem if the program fragment that is to be ignored already contains comment, because comments must not be nested. In that case we can simply use a line with *#if* 0 at the beginning and one with *#endif* at the end (instead of /* and */). For example, the second and the third of the following lines are ignored by the compiler, and the comment on the second line causes no problems:

```
#if 0
   i = 123;  /* Some comment */
   j = i + 1;
#endif
```

Tests about names being known

The preprocessor can check whether or not a name has been defined, as the following example shows:

```
#if !defined(PI)
#define PI 3.14159265358979
#endif
```

Only if *PI* has not been defined will the second line be processed; if *PI* has already been defined, this line is ignored. This prevents any problems with conflicting definitions of *PI*: we may define symbolic constants more than once, but such multiple definitions must be identical. Therefore the above conditional definition of the constant *PI* is useful if (a) we do not know whether this constant has been defined in a header file that we are using and (b) we do not know the precision used in such a definition, if any.

In combination with *defined*(...), we can use the logical operators !, ||, and &&. These operators cannot be used in combination with the older alternative forms *#ifdef* and *#ifndef*:

`#ifdef name`	is equivalent to	`#if defined(name)`
`#ifndef name`	is equivalent to	`#if !defined(name)`

If we want to cancel the effect of

```
#define name text
```

we can 'undefine' *name* by writing

```
#undef name
```

Thus, to be complete, we should say that the operator *defined* and the preprocessor directives *#ifdef* and *#ifndef* apply to names defined with *#define*, in so far as these names have not been undefined by means of *#undef*.

It is not an error to use *#undef* for a name that has not been defined at all, so we may use it to cancel any previous definition of a name without being sure that there is one.

Making the compiler display error messages of our own

We can use a line starting with *#error* to make the compiler display an error message of our own. This is useful especially in connection with conditional compilation and with special information in header files. For example, suppose that we have various versions of a certain header file (say, *myfile.h*), and we want to check that its correct version (say, version B) is included. If in that header file the version number is defined as

```
#define V_B
```

(in which the replacement text is allowed to be absent) we can perform this check as follows:

```
#include "myfile.h"
#if !defined(V_B)
#error You should use Version B of myfile.h!
#endif
```

If we use a version of *myfile.h* that does not contain the definition of *V_B*, the compiler will display the error message given on the *#error* line, after which compilation terminates.

Pragmas

Although we prefer to restrict ourselves to language elements accepted by any C++ compiler, it may sometimes be necessary or desirable to deviate from this principle and to use facilities that depend on a particular compiler and on a particular machine. For such system-dependent facilities, lines of the form

```
#pragma ...
```

can be used. The three dots in this line denote some piece of text that causes the compiler, if it recognizes that text, to perform certain actions. Most applications of #pragma are rather technical. For example, it may be possible to write *#pragma inline* to insert inline assembly code in our programs. You might find further details in the reference manual of your C++ compiler.

Exercises

In the following exercises, whenever you are asked to write a function, this should be a general one; you should also demonstrate this function by a program that need *not* be general. In at least one of these exercises, use distinct modules for the *main* module and the function to practice the principle of separate compilation (or 'modular programming').

4.1 Write the function *rectangle(w, h, outline)*, to display a rectangle of asterisks (*). The *int* parameters w and h are the width and the height of the rectangle, expressed in numbers of asterisks. If the *bool* parameter *outline* is *true*, only the outline of the rectangle is to appear. If it is *false*, a solid rectangle of $w \times h$ asterisks is required.

4.2 Write the function *digitsum(n)*, which computes and returns the sum of the decimal digits of the integer parameter n.

4.3* Write a program that reads a decimal digit d and displays a table with two columns: one for positive integers x, less than 100, and one for their squares x^2. Only those lines in which the digit d occurs in both x and x^2 are to be displayed. For example, if d is equal to 2, the table will contain the line

    82   6724

since $82^2 = 6724$ and 2 occurs both in 82 and in 6724.

4.4 Write the function *sort4*, which has four parameters. If the integer variables a, b, c, and d are available and have been assigned values, we want to write

```
sort4(a, b, c, d);
```

to sort these four variables, so that after this call we have

$a \leq b \leq c \leq d$

Write also a version *sort4p* based on pointers, in the style of C. The following call to this function accomplishes the above task:

```
sort4p(&a, &b, &c, &d);
```

4.5* Write a program that reads a positive integer and writes it as a product of prime factors. For example, we have $120 = 2 \times 2 \times 2 \times 3 \times 5$.

4.6 In the following program, the function f is recursive (see Section 4.1). This program reads the integer k from the keyboard. With successive values $k = 0, 1, 2, ..., 5$, investigate (first without and then with the computer) what the output of this program will be.

```
// recfun.cpp: Demonstration of a recursive function.
#include <iostream>
using namespace std;

void f(int n)
{  if (n > 0)
   {  f(n-2); cout << n << " "; f(n-1);
   }
}

int main()
{  int k;
   cout << "Enter k: "; cin >> k;
   cout << "Output:\n";
   f(k);
   cout << endl;
   return 0;
}
```

4.7   Write the function $gcd(x, y)$ which computes the greatest common divisor of the
       integers x and y. These two integers are nonnegative and not both equal to zero.
       Use Euclid's algorithm, according to which we can write (using the C++ operator
       %):

$$gcd(x, y) \;=\; \begin{cases} x & \text{if } y = 0 \\ gcd(y, x\%y) & \text{if } y \neq 0 \end{cases}$$

       Write a C++ function gcd that is recursive and therefore closely related to this
       formulation of Euclid's algorithm. Write also a nonrecursive version, $gcd1$.

4.8*   Write a program to solve the problem known as the Towers of Hanoi. There are
       three pegs, A, B, C, on which disks with holes in their centers can be placed. These
       disks all have different diameters. A larger disk must never be placed on top of a
       smaller one. There are n disks, numbered 1, 2, ..., n from the smallest to the largest.
       Initially all these disks, in the right order, are on peg A, so that pegs B and C are
       empty. The problem is to move all disks, one by one, from peg A to peg C, never
       placing a larger disk on a smaller one; peg B may be used as auxiliary. Write a
       program that reads n and displays the solution to this problem. For example, if
       $n = 2$, we want the following output:

```
Disk 1 from peg A to peg B.
Disk 2 from peg A to peg C.
Disk 1 from peg B to peg C.
```

4.9   Write the macro $max2(x, y)$; its value (that is, the value of its expansion) is equal to
       the greater of x and y. Use $max2$ to write another macro, $max3(x, y, z)$, the value of
       which is the greatest of x, y, and z. Solve this problem also by means of inline
       functions. Which solution do you prefer and why?

4.10 Write a function declared as

```
unsigned char bcd(int n);
```

This function has the task of building a byte (of eight bits) containing the least significant two decimal digits of the argument, n, in the format known as *binary coded decimal*, and returning this byte. For example, if n is equal to 12345, the rightmost decimal digits, 4 and 5, are written 0100 and 0101 in four bits, so in this case the byte to be returned is represented by the bit sequence 0100 0101.

4.11* Write a program which reads the three real numbers a, b, and c, to compute the real numbers x_1 and x_2 that satisfy the quadratic equation $ax^2 + bx + c = 0$, if such real numbers exist.

4.12* A sequence of 20 integers is to be read from the keyboard. For each pair of successive integers in this sequence, compute the absolute value of their difference. The largest of these absolute values is to be printed.

4.13* Write a program to approximate the value of x (between $\pi/2$ and π) that satisfies the following equation:

$$\sin x - x/2 = 0$$

Use the Newton–Raphson method (also known as the Newton method), which is a well-known numerical method for solving equations of the form $f(x) = 0$. Starting with some value x_0 as an approximation of the solution x, you repeatedly replace the approximation x_n with a better one, x_{n+1}, which is computed as:

$$x_{n+1} = x_n - f(x_n)/f'(x_n)$$

In our case we have $f(x) = \sin x - x/2$ and $f'(x) = \cos x - 1/2$. You can use, for example, $x_0 = 3$ as a start value. Find a termination condition yourself. The Newton–Raphson method can be explained as follows. We begin by drawing the tangent to the graph of f at point $(x_0, f(x_0))$, to find the point where this tangent intersects the x-axis. The x-coordinate of this new point is x_1. Then x_2 is derived from x_1 in the same way as x_1 has been derived from x_0, and so on.

4.14* A ladder has a given length L. It is placed against a wall, and touches a box, which is a cube with height 1, as shown in Figure 4.4. Compute the distance x between the box and the bottom of the ladder.

4.15* Both a real number x and an integer n are to be read from the keyboard. Compute the following sum, which is an approximation of the mathematical expression e^x (e = 2.718281828459... ; $n! = 1 \times 2 \times \ldots \times n$):

$$1 + x + \frac{x^2}{2!} + \frac{x^3}{3!} + \ldots + \frac{x^n}{n!}$$

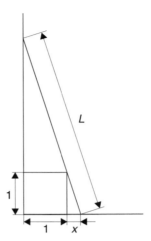

Figure 4.4. Ladder and box

4.16* We can write 8/35 = 1/(4 + 3/8). Applying the same process to 3/8, we obtain 8/35 = 1/{4 + 1/(2 + 2/3)}. We proceed in this way until the final plus sign is followed by the numerator 1. In our example, this is the case after another step, which gives 8/35 = 1/[4 + 1/{2 + 1/(1 + 1/2)}]. We can represent such an expression, called a *continued fraction*, by listing all integers that occur in it except for all numerators 1. In this example we obtain 4, 2, 1, 2. Write a program which reads two positive integers *a* and *b* and computes the sequence representing the continued fraction for *a*/*b*.

4.17* Write a program which reads the positive integers a_1, a_2, ..., a_n to find all pairs (i, j) (with $i < j$) for which the greatest common divisor of a_i and a_j is equal to 1.

4.18* With a given integer *n*, compute the *n*th element F_n of the Fibonacci sequence, which is defined as follows:

$$F_0 = 0$$
$$F_1 = 1$$
$$F_n = F_{n-1} + F_{n-2} \quad (n \geq 2)$$

For reasons of efficiency, do not use recursion. For some large values of *n*, also compare the quotient F_n/F_{n-1} with the following number:

$$\tau = 2 \cos 36° = (1 + \sqrt{5})/2 = 1.6180339887...$$

(Verify the fact that the sequence

$$..., \tau^{-2}, \tau^{-1}, 1, \tau, \tau^2, ...$$

is similar to the Fibonacci sequence in that the sum of any two successive elements is equal to the next element in the sequence.)

5

Arrays, Pointers, and Strings

5.1 Address Arithmetic

This section is more important than it may seem at first sight. Although its title might suggest it to be about some technical subject that ordinary programmers could safely ignore, the rest of this chapter, and in fact a considerable portion of the C++ language, is based upon it.

In Section 4.3 we discussed expressions such as &x, the values of which are addresses. There are other kinds of expressions, which when evaluated also yield addresses. One of these is the name of an array, written without brackets. The address obtained in this way is that of the first element of the array in question. For example, after the declaration

```
char s[50];
```

we can use s, not followed by [...], as shorthand for &($s[0]$), which, incidentally, we may write as &$s[0]$.

Another expression whose value is an address is $s + i$, where i is an integer. In this case the address is that of $s[i]$, so we have the following equivalent expressions (with ≡ meaning 'is equivalent to').

```
s        ≡      &s[0]
s + i    ≡      &s[i]
```

This notation may look a bit complicated, but it is simply based on the situation shown in Figure 5.1.

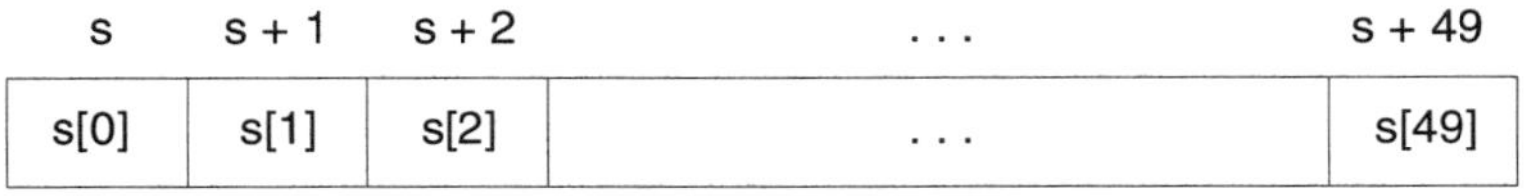

s	s + 1	s + 2		. . .		s + 49
s[0]	s[1]	s[2]		. . .		s[49]

Figure 5.1. Elements of array s *and their addresses*

If you wrote a program in assembly language and you wanted to use an array of 50 bytes, you would use a name, such as *s*, for its start address. The addresses of the allocated bytes would be *s*, *s* + 1, ..., *s* + 49. It would then be very natural to denote these bytes themselves as *s*[0], *s*[1], ..., *s*[49], and that is what we are doing in C and C++.

In our example, the addresses (yielded by the expressions) *s* and *s* + *i* lie *i* bytes apart. A byte is used here as a unit only because *s* is a *char* array, that is, because each element takes one byte. In general, address arithmetic takes into account the size of the object the address of which is given, and uses that size as a unit of memory space. This makes address arithmetic more convenient and more useful than it would otherwise have been. (It also illustrates that, unlike assembly language, C and C++ are high-level languages.) For example, let us use *int* array *a*, declared as

```
int a[10];
```

In this case the addresses *a* and *a* + *i* lie *i* integers (not *i* bytes) apart. Fortunately, the equivalence

```
a + i      ≡      &a[i]
```

also holds for this *int* array *a* and, in fact, for any array. For example, the following two calls to the function *swap2*, discussed in Section 4.3, are equivalent:

```
swap2(&a[0], &a[9]);
swap2(a, a + 9);
```

Besides the *address-of* operator &, there is also the indirection operator *, as we have seen in Section 4.3. We use it to denote an object whose address is given. Now that we know which addresses are represented by *a* and *a* + *i*, it will be clear why, in the following, the expressions on the left are equivalent to those on the right:

```
*a         ≡      a[0]
*(a + i)   ≡      a[i]
```

For example, the following two lines are equivalent:

```
for (i=0; i<10; ++i) cout << a[i] << " ";
for (i=0; i<10; ++i) cout << *(a + i) << " ";
```

It is also possible to subtract an integer from an address, as is done in

```
&a[9] - 3
```

Recalling that &a[9] can be written as $a + 9$, we see that this subtraction gives $a + 6$, which can be written as &a[6]. We can also subtract an address from another address, as in

```
&a[9] - &a[6]
```

Rewriting this as

```
(a+9) - (a+6)
```

makes it evident that the result is 3. Other arithmetic operations on addresses are not allowed. For example, we cannot compute the sum of two addresses.

Suppose that p and q denote the addresses of two elements of the same array. We now want to find some address between p and q, preferably the one in the middle. If p and q were subscript values, we might think that we should write $(p + q)/2$ but we cannot use this expression because it would involve two illegal address operations (addition and division). The way to obtain the desired value is by writing

```
p + (q - p)/2
```

Here all operations are legal, for $q - p$ has integer type, and so has $(q - p)/2$, which may therefore be added to p.

5.2 Function Arguments and Arrays

It follows from the previous section that we have access to all elements of an array if we are given its start address. There is therefore no need in C++ (or in C) for any special parameter-passing mechanism for arrays. Instead of the array itself, we use the address of its first element as an argument; in the function that is called we can compute the addresses of the other elements by means of address arithmetic. Provided we use it accurately, this principle is very convenient. The fact that the name of an array denotes its starting address makes array arguments very simple. The following program demonstrates a function that finds the smallest element of a given integer array:

```
// minimum.cpp: Finding the smallest element of an
//               integer array.
#include <iostream>
using namespace std;
```

```
int minimum(const int *a, int n)
{  int small = *a;
   for (int i=1; i<n; ++i)
      if (*(a+i) < small) small = *(a+i);
   return small;
}

int main()
{  int table[10];
   cout << "Enter 10 integers: \n";
   for (int i=0; i<10; ++i)
      cin >> table[i];
   cout << "\nThe minimum of these values is "
        << minimum(table, 10) << endl;
   return 0;
}
```

Recalling Section 4.3, we know that

```
const int *a, ...
```

in the first line of function *minimum* implies that *a* is a *pointer*, which denotes the address of an integer. The word *const* indicates that the function *minimum* will not modify any data through this pointer. If we omit this word *const*, the programs works as well, but its use is strongly recommended in cases like this. The corresponding argument, *table*, is the address of *table*[0], so the following two calls are equivalent:

```
minimum(&table[0], 10)
minimum(table, 10)
```

The above version of the function *minimum* makes it very clear that address arithmetic is applied. As an alternative, we can write a version that does not do this to the same extent but may, on the other hand, be considered more readable because it uses conventional array notation. In the last section we have seen that we may replace $a[i]$ with $*(a + i)$. These two expressions are really equivalent: we can also replace the latter with the former, which leads to

```
int minimum(const int *a, int n)
{  int small = a[0];
   for (int i=1; i<n; ++i)
      if (a[i] < small) small = a[i];
   return small;
}
```

We can emphasize the array nature of *a* even more by replacing the first line of this function with

```
int minimum(const int a[], int n)
```

Note that the array length is omitted in *a*[ ], which reflects the fact that the corresponding argument array can have any length.

Although not demonstrated here, it is also possible to alter the array elements in question instead of only using their values, provided we omit the *const* qualifier. Any assignment to *a*[*i*] or to *(a + i)* implies the modification of array *table* in the *main* function.

5.3 Pointers

If we declare

```
int *p, n=5, k;
```

then *p* is a pointer variable, or *pointer*, for short. We use pointers to store addresses, as we use arithmetic variables to store numbers. For example, we can place the address of *n* in *p* by writing

```
p = &n;
```

In this example, **p* denotes an object (of type *int*) in memory. Immediately after this assignment statement, this object happens to be the *int* variable *n*. After storing the address of *n* in *p* in this way, and as long as we do not assign another address to *p*, we can regard **p* as just another expression for *n*. If we proceed with

```
k = *p;
```

the value of *k* will therefore be 5, as if we had written

```
k = n;
```

The process of obtaining this value 5 using *p* is known as *dereferencing*, and the unary operator * in **p* is sometimes called a *dereferencing operator*. You should be very careful in distinguishing between the expressions *p* and **p*. Since *p* is of type *pointer-to-int*, we can assign addresses of *int* objects to it; by contrast, we can assign *int* values to **p* because this expression has type *int*. Because *p* points to the *int* variable *n*, the following statement assigns 6 to *n*:

```
*p = 6;
```

This way of changing an object through a pointer is not possible if the word *const* is used in the *specifier sequence* (see Section 2.7) of a declaration, as is the case in

```
const int *q;
```

or, equivalently,

```
int const *q;
```

After either of these declarations, we can assign a value to *q* but not to the object pointed to by *q* (and therefore denoted as **q*), as the comments in the following statements indicate:

```
q = &n;     // OK
*q = 6;     // Wrong
```

This use of the word *const* in a specifier should not be confused with that in the declarator list, as, for example, in

```
int *const r = &n, *const s = &k, *t;
```

Here the declarator consist only of the word *int*, while there are the following three declarators:

```
*const r = &n
*const s = &k
*t
```

Because of the way *const* is used here for the pointers *r* and *s*, these pointers themselves cannot be modified (so that initialization is really required) but it is possible to modify the objects they point to:

```
r = &k;     // Wrong
*r = 123;   // OK
```

The word *const* occurs more frequently in a specifier than in a declarator, that is, it is usually the object pointed to (not the pointer itself) that we want to prevent from being modified. Examples of such pointers are the pointer *q* in the example above and the parameter *a* occurring in the program line

```
int minimum(const int *a, int n)
```

discussed in Section 5.2. Let us refer to such pointers as *const pointers*. The following version minimum (equivalent to that of Section 5.2) shows the use of another const pointer, *p*:

```
int minimum(const int *a, int n)
{   int small = *a;
    for (const int* p=a+1; p<a+n; ++p)
       if (*p < small) small = *p;
    return small;
}
```

Initially, *p* is assigned the value *a* + 1, that is, the address of *a*[1]. This is shown in Figure 5.2, where it is assumed that *minimum* has again been invoked by the following call

```
minimum(table, 10)
```

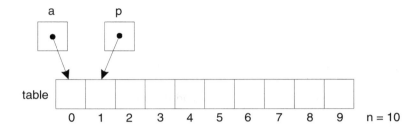

Figure 5.2. Situation immediately after **p = a + 1**

By repeatedly incrementing *p*, we move each time to the next element, until *p* is equal to *a* + *n*. Then *p* is equal to the address of the memory location that follows the final element, *table*[*n* − 1]. Incidentally, this example shows that the less-than operator < can be applied to addresses (which is also the case with the operators >, <=, >=, ==, and !=.)

In some cases, the use of the word *const*, although recommended, is not essential as far as the compiler is concerned. This is different in the program line

```
for (const int* p=a+1; p<a+n; ++p)
```

Here we cannot omit *const* because we must not assign a const pointer such as *a* or an expression such as *a* + 1 to a non-const pointer. If this were allowed, it would be possible to use a const pointer in a sneaky way to modify the data to which it points. In the following example, this is (unsuccessfully) tried by letting *p* point to the same object as *a*, that is, to the variable *n*. Since assigning something directly to *∗a* is not possible, it should not be possible to do this indirectly either. Such an indirect assignment is indeed made impossible because it is forbidden to assign *a* to *p* in this fragment:

```
int n = 5;
const int *a;
int *p;
a = &n;

// Here is an (unsuccessful) attempt to modify *a,
// which should not be done because a is a const pointer:

p = a;     // Not allowed, so this attempt fails!
*p = 6;
```

Casting away *const*ness

In the above discussion it was suggested that const pointers cannot be assigned to non-const pointers. Actually this is true only as far as implicit conversions are concerned. There is special kind of cast to perform such conversions, and those from const references to non-const references. It will be clear that this is a dangerous thing to do, and the result of it is in most cases undefined. However, there are special situations in which such conversions are absolutely safe. Let us demonstrate this with an extremely simple example. Suppose we want to use the expression

```
maxim(a, b)
```

for the greater of the *int* variables *a* and *b*, and this must be done in such a way that we can write, for example,

```
maxim(a, b) = 0;
```

We have already solved this problem in program *reffun.cpp* of Section 4.9, in which this statement occurs. The function *maxim* of that program is repeated below:

```
// First maxim function:
int &maxim(int &x, int &y)
{  return (x > y ? x : y);
}
```

However, there is one thing that is impossible with this function. Since its parameters are non-const references, the arguments must not be const variables, so that we cannot write

```
const int c = 7, d = 8;
t = maxim(c, d);
```

We now want to make this possible as well. The principle of overloading enables us to define a second function *maxim* with *const int* parameters, which solves this problem. Let us try to do this by benefiting from the *maxim* function that we already have. In other words, we demand that this second *maxim* function contains a call to the first. Because this example is extremely simple, this is not really worthwhile here, but it may be in other cases. The following complete program contains both the above (first) function *maxim* and a second based on the first:

```
// constcast.cpp: An application of const_cast.
#include <iostream>
using namespace std;

// First function maxim:
int &maxim(int &x, int &y)
{  return (x > y ? x : y);
}
```

```
// Second function maxim:
inline const int &maxim(const int &x, const int &y)
{  return maxim(const_cast<int &>(x), const_cast<int &>(y));
}

int main()
{  int a = 5, b = 6, t;
   maxim(a, b) = 0;
   // Assign 0 to the larger of a and b, that is, to b.
   const int c = 7, d = 8;
   t = maxim(c, d);
   // Assign the larger of c and d, that is 8, to t.
   cout << b << " " << t << endl; // 0 8
   return 0;
}
```

Because of the use of *const_cast* in the second *maxim* function, the call to *maxim* in its return statement contains non-const references to *x* and *y* and will therefore invoke the first *maxim* function, which has non-const parameters. Note that besides two explicit conversions from const to non-const, there is also an implicit conversion the other way: the expression following the word *return* is a non-const reference, but the function returns a *const* reference. The word *inline* at the very beginning is not essential, but it was added to make this function faster. In fact, it makes the statement

```
t = maxim(c, d);
```

about as efficient as the following one, which we might have used if we had defined only the first *maxim* function:

```
t = maxim(const_cast<int &>(c), const_cast<int &>(d));
```

Another application of a pointer

Suppose that we know that the *int* variable *i* is equal to 1, 2, or 3. There are also three float variables, *x*, *y*, and *z*. It is required to assign a number that is read from the keyboard to *x* if *i* = 1, to *y* if *i* = 2, or to *z* if *i* = 3. Then that *float* variable is to be divided by 5, and, finally, the resulting value must be displayed. It is required that the other two *float* variables remain unaltered. The use of a pointer enables us to decide only once which of the variables *x*, *y*, or *z* is to be used and to program all this in very compact code:

```
float x, y, z, *p;
int i;
...
p = (i == 1 ? &x : (i == 2 ? &y : &z));
                              // Assign &x, &y, or &z to p
cin >> *p;                    // Read x, y, or z
cout << (*p /= 5);            // Divide x, y, or z by 5
                              // and show the result.
```

The importance of assigning values to pointers

After declaring a pointer, say *p*, we must not use *p before assigning a value to *p*. In other words, we can use *p only if *p* has a well-defined value. The following program violates this rule:

```
int main()
{   char *p, ch;
    *p = 'A';       // Error
    return 0;
}
```

This error is very serious because (with an undefined value of *p*) the expression *p occurs as the left-hand side of an assignment. The undefined value of *p* is used as an address, and the contents of this address are altered. This may destroy some important piece of information in memory. A tricky aspect of this is that you may get away with it on one machine and run into all kinds of trouble on another. In this example, it is very easy to correct it by inserting the statement

```
p = &ch;
```

before

```
*p = 'A';
```

After this correction, the latter statement has the effect of assigning the value 'A' to the variable *ch*.

We can use a pointer as an array, but, again, this is possible only after we have given it a suitable value. If it is a function parameter, such an initial value is automatically provided for by the corresponding argument, but for other pointer variables we have to take care of this ourselves, as is done in the following program:

```
int main()
{   char s[10], *p;
    p = s;
    p[9] = 'A';
    return 0;
}
```

In this program, the declaration of *s* allocates a block of ten bytes for it. By contrast, only one location (for an address) is allocated by declaring *p*, and its initial value is undefined. By executing the statement

```
p = s;
```

the address of $s[0]$ is assigned to p, after which we can use $p[0]$, $p[1]$, ..., $p[9]$ in the same way as $s[0]$, $s[1]$, ..., $s[9]$: the variables $p[i]$ and $s[i]$ denote the same memory location. If the statement just shown had been omitted, the statement

```
p[9] = 'A';
```

would have been incorrect and as dangerous as the assignment of 'A' to *p, discussed in our previous example.

Although we can use $p[i]$ and $s[i]$ in the same way, p and s have different types:

p	has type *pointer to char*
s	has type *array of* 10 *char*

This has several consequences. First, we can assign values to p, not to s. This is logical because p is a variable, while the array name s has a fixed value, the start address of the array. Second, the *sizeof* operator gives different values for p and s:

sizeof(p) = number of bytes for an address (2 or 4 for most machines);
sizeof(s) = 10 * *sizeof*(*char*) = 10

Pointer conversion and void-pointers

We sometimes feel a need for a general kind of pointer, to which we can assign the address of any object, irrespective of its type. Suppose we declare i and p_char as follows:

```
int i;
char *p_char;
```

Since the address of an integer has the same internal format as the address of a character, you may wonder if the following statement is allowed:

```
p_char = &i;            // Error
```

This is not the case. The expression &i has type pointer-to-int, while p_char is of type pointer-to-char. In an assignment statement such as this one, these two types are incompatible, which means that a straightforward conversion from the former to the latter type is not possible. However, if we insist, we can do it by using yet another kind of cast:

```
p_char = reinterpret_cast<char *> (&i); // Not recommended
```

As we will see in a moment, we can do better than using a character pointer here. But let us first have a look at the old way of doing this:

```
p_char = (char *)&i;    // Still possible, but deprecated
```

Note the asterisk in (*char* *), indicating that &i is to be converted to type pointer-to-char, not to type *char*.

Fortunately, we need not use pointer-to-char as a general pointer type, but we can instead use *void-pointers*, also known as *generic pointers*. For example, we can declare the void-pointer *p_void* as follows:

```
void *p_void;
```

We do not need a cast to assign the address of an object of any type to *p_void*. Using variables of the same types as above, we can therefore write the following without a cast:

```
p_void = &i;          // From pointer-to-int to pointer-to-void
```

For the opposite conversion, that is, from a void-pointer to a normal pointer, a cast is required, as the following statement illustrates:

```
p_char = static_cast<char *>(p_void);
```

Generic pointers may also be used in comparisons. For example, here is a valid and an invalid comparison:

```
int *p_int;
char *p_char;
void *p_void;
...
if (p_char == p_int) ...  // Error
if (p_void == p_int) ...  // OK
```

Address arithmetic must not be applied to void-pointers. After all, the value of *p_void* can be the address of any type, so, if *p_void* + 1 were to yield an address, it would not be clear how many bytes this address should lie apart from the address stored in *p_void*. Therefore *p_void* + 1 is not a valid expression.

Typedef declarations

For any type, no matter how complicated, there is a way to introduce a new identifier, denoting this type. We do this by writing the keyword *typedef*, followed by a normal declaration. Here is a very simple example:

```
typedef double real;
```

If we had omitted the word *typedef*, the identifier *real* would have been a variable of type *double*. By writing *typedef* here, we make this identifier *real* denote the type of that variable instead of the variable itself. In other words, the above line makes the name *real* synonymous with *double*, so we can now write, for example,

```
real x, y;
```

instead of

```
double x, y;
```

Here is a more interesting example:

```
typedef int *ptr;
```

To know what this means, we compare it with the form obtained by omitting the word *typedef*: the name *ptr* would then be a variable of type pointer-to-int. Consequently, the above line makes *ptr* denote this type, pointer-to-int. It therefore enables us to write

```
ptr p;
```

with the same meaning as

```
int *p;
```

A slightly different notation

Since we must be able to read programs written by others, it is worthwhile to consider also a slightly different way of writing pointer declarations. White-space characters are in most cases not significant, so instead of our last declaration we can also write

```
int* p;
```

Having the blank after the asterisk instead of before it seems to be an improvement, because this blank clearly separates the pointer type *int** (to be read as *pointer-to-int*) from the pointer variable *p*. Unfortunately, regarding the notation *int** as a pointer type is confusing if we declare more than one variable, as in

```
int* p, q;
```

If *int** were really equivalent to a single type identifier such as *ptr*, both *p* and *q* would be pointers. However, this is not the case. Instead of being a pointer, *q* is an *int* variable: the asterisk applies only to *p*, not to *q*. This is expressed more clearly by the equivalent declaration

```
int *p, q;
```

Another, more formal argument in favor of the notation *int *p* instead of *int* p* is that it more clearly reflects the C++ grammar. For example, in

```
int *p, k, a[100], *r;
```

there is a specifier sequence consisting only of the word *int*, followed by a (comma-separated list) of the declarators *p, k, a[100], and *r, and terminated by a semicolon. This makes it logical to combine the asterisk with the variable in question, not with the specifier *int*.

Initialization of pointers

The way we initialize pointers deserves our special attention. For example, we can write

```
int i, a[10], *p = &i, *q = a;
```

You should be aware that &*i* is the initial value used for *p*, not for **p*. Similarly, the start address of array *a*, that is, the address of *a*[0] is the initial value used for *q*, not for **q*.

5.4 C-style Strings and the Standard *string* Type

String literals, as introduced in Section 1.5, are in fact arrays of characters, although they differ from normal arrays in that they do not have names. For many years, the usual way of dealing with 'string variables' was by using normal character arrays. Since C++ inherited such strings from C, we now refer to them as *C-style strings*. Besides these, there are now also standard strings, of type *string*, which are much more convenient to use. We have already seen such strings in action in the program *twolines.cpp* of Section 1.6. The following two lines illustrate the difference between C-style and standard strings:

```
char editor[8] = "Gaynor";        // C-style string
string assistant = "Katrina";     // Standard string
```

Some inconvenient aspects of C-style strings is that we have to specify some array length and that this length must include room for a trailing null character '\0'. In the above array *editor* six positions are used for the letters of the name *Gaynor*, but this is followed by the null character, so that seven of the eight available positions are used. It follows that we can also use this array for the name *Katrina* (which requires 7 + 1 = 8 positions) but not for the name *Rosemary* (which would require an array length of at least 8 + 1 = 9). There are no such problems with the modern standard *string* type, which we therefore prefer in most situations.

Since we are not yet in a position to understand exactly how standard strings are implemented, they may at the moment look mysterious and magical, but this will not deter us from using them. This is also true for the way we can sort arrays of strings. To achieve this, we use *sort*, which is a standard *function template* or *algorithm*. Although we will not discuss templates and algorithms in detail until Chapters 7 and 9, respectively, we use the algorithm *sort* here because it is similar to a normal function and very easy to use. The following program shows how to sort an array of five strings:

```
// strings.cpp: Sorting an array of strings
#include <iostream>
#include <string>
#include <algorithm>
using namespace std;

int main()
{  const int n = 5;
   string a[n];
   cout << "  Enter five lines of text:\n";
   int i;
   for (i=0; i<n; ++i)
      getline(cin, a[i]);
   sort(a, a + n);
   cout << "  Output in alphabetic order:\n";
   for (i=0; i<n; ++i)
      cout << a[i] << endl;
   return 0;
}
```

Here is a demonstration of this program:

```
  Enter five lines of text:
algorithms
data structures
programs
languages
computers
  Output in alphabetic order:
algorithms
computers
data structures
languages
programs
```

If variable *s* is of type *string*, we may replace

```
getline(cin, s);
```

with

```
getline(cin, s, '\n');
```

with exactly the same meaning. The final argument in the second call denotes the character that should signal the end of the input. This character is read but not stored in *s*. The statement

```
cin >> s;
```

is syntactically correct, but the way it works is different. First, it skips any leading white-space characters (spaces, tabs and newline characters), after which it reads data only until the first white-space character. For example, if the user enters *data structures*, only the first word, *data*, is read by this statement.

5.5 String Constructors and String Assignment

Although the standard *string* type is easy to use, it is based on the notions of *class* and *template*, which are more advanced than most subjects discussed so far. As we will see in Section 6.2, a *constructor* is a function that creates a (possibly complicated) object. Each time we declare a string, such a constructor is called to create the string in question and to initialize it. If we write

```
string s, t;
```

a constructor is called twice, to create the objects *s* and *t* and to set them equal to the empty string. Instead, we could have declared *s* and *t* as follows, with the same effect:

```
string s(""), t("");
```

If we write

```
string str("Fernanda Naylor");
```

we obtain the string object *str*, in which the string "*Fernanda Naylor*" is stored. We could have achieved the same effect by using an assignment in the following way:

```
string str;
str = "Fernanda Naylor";
```

In this assignment the right-hand side is of type *array of* 16 *char*, while the variable *str* is of type *string*. Fortunately, this is not a problem thanks to implicit conversion.

The above functional notation in the declaration with initialization of *str* reflects the function aspect of the constructor that is used, so that we prefer it to the following declaration, which is also allowed:

```
string str = "Fernanda Naylor";
```

If we like, we can also use a functional notation for the initialization of simple standard types. For example, the following declarations are equivalent:

```
int n(123);
int n = 123;
```

There are several *string* constructors. Using the above *string* variable *str*, we could write

```
string surname(str, 9);  // surname = "Naylor"
```

Here the string *surname* is initialized with the string "*Naylor*", because this string starts at position 9 of *str*. As with arrays, we count the positions from zero, so position 0 of *str* contains *F* and position 9 contains *N*.

If we want to declare a new string, which initially should be equal to an existing one (but may later be assigned a different value) we can use a given string as an argument, as is done in

```
string another(surname); // another = "Naylor"
```

Yet another constructor is available, which we use to form a string that consist of many occurrences of the same character. For example, if we want a string *s* consisting of twenty asterisks, we can write

```
string s(20, '*');
```

In the above examples constructors were used in declarations. It is also possible to use a constructor to create an object somewhere in the middle of an expression. The following program shows that we use this constructor to display such a line of twenty asterisks, without declaring any string variable:

```
// lines.cpp:
#include <iostream>
#include <string>
using namespace std;

int main()
{  cout << string(20, '*')  // Output: ********************
          << endl;
   return 0;
}
```

This example reflects more clearly than the others that a constructor is a function.

There is also a string member function *assign* which accepts a repetition factor. The term *member function* reflects the way such functions are used. For example, the name *assign* follows a dot, which in turn follows the name *s* of a string object in this fragment:

```
string s("PQR");
s.assign(8, 'A');
```

As a result, the string *s* will obtain the value "*AAAAAAAA*", which overwrites the old value "*PQR*". According to the principle of overloading (see Section 4.8) there can be several string member functions with the name *assign*. First, we can write

```
s.assign("John");
```

which is not very spectacular because its effect is the same as that of

```
s = "John";
```

More interestingly, we can extract a substring of a given string *t* and assign it to *s*, as the following fragment shows:

```
string t("ABCDEFGHIJ");
s.assign(t, 4, 2);       // s = "EF"
```

With this function *assign*, the three parameters denote the source string, the start position and the length of the substring. Since counting starts at position 0, the substring of length 2 and starting at position 4 in "*ABCDEFGHIJ*" is the string "*EF*".

5.6 C-style Strings and Conversion

As we discussed in Section 5.4, a C-style string is an array of characters, containing the characters that we want to store, followed by a null character. In the following example, *a* and *b* are C-style strings:

```
char a[10] = "Jim", b[8] = "";
```

After this declaration, we have

```
a[0] = 'J'   a[1] = 'i'   a[2] = 'm'   a[3] = '\0'
b[0] = '\0'
```

There are many standard library functions that accept such C-style strings as arguments. An example of these is *strlen*, declared in the header <*string*>, which determines the logical length by counting how many characters precede the terminating null character, or, equivalently, it returns the position of that null character. For example, *strlen*("*Jim*") is equal to 3. Using the above example, we have

```
strlen(a) = 3
strlen(b) = 0
```

We should not confuse this logical length with the (physical) array length, obtained by *sizeof*. Here we have

```
sizeof(a) = 10
sizeof(b) = 8
```

If *strlen* were not a standard library function, it would be easy to write one ourselves, as the following version shows. As we have seen in Section 5.1, the expression *s*[*n*], used here, is equivalent to *(s + n)*:

```
int strlen(const char *s)
{   int n = 0;
    while (s[n] != '\0')
        n++;
    return n;
}
```

If, in the above example, we want to copy the contents of array *a* to array *b*, we cannot do this by writing

```
b = a;      // Wrong
```

because the expressions *a* and *b* represent the start addresses, which we cannot modify, so that the above statement is syntactically incorrect. Note that, for the same reason, the following is not a correct assignment either:

```
b = "Jim";   // Wrong
```

while

```
char b[8]  = "Jim";
```

is correct because this is not an assignment but an initialization.

To assign string *a* to *b*, the following attempt, although syntactically correct, does not have the desired effect:

```
*b = *a;
```

This would be equivalent to

```
b[0]  = a[0];
```

which is not what we want. The right way to copy *a* to *b* is

```
strcpy(b, a);
```

This function *strcpy* returns a value (ignored in the above statement) which is the address of *b*[0] in this example. As we did with *strlen*, we will have a look at our own version of *strcpy*, although we will never use it because it is immediately available as a standard library function:

```
char *strcpy(char *s, const char *t)
{   int i = 0;
    for (;;)
    {   s[i] = t[i];
        if (s[i] == '\0') break;
        i++;
    }
    return s;
}
```

Comparing two C-style strings *a* and *b* cannot be done by writing expressions such as

```
a == b
a < b
```

since such comparisons would apply to addresses, not to sequences of characters. To compare these sequences we use the function *strcmp*. The value of

```
strcmp(a, b)
```

is of type *int* and

- negative if the logical string *a* alphabetically precedes the logical string *b*
- zero if the logical strings *a* and *b* are equal
- positive if the logical string *a* alphabetically follows the logical string *b*

The term *logical string* is used here to emphasize that any characters following the null character are not used in the comparison. Actually, the comparison process may terminate before a null character is found in either string. For example, to determine that *"Jack"* alphabetically precedes *"Jim"*, only the first two characters need to be compared. This is the way our own version of *strcmp* works:

```
int strcmp(const char *s, const char *t)
{   int i = 0;
    while (s[i] == t[i])
    {   if (s[i] == '\0') return 0;
        i++;
    }
    return s[i] - t[i];
}
```

For each of the above definitions of the functions *strlen*, *strcpy*, and *strcmp*, it is an instructive exercise to write other, equivalent versions.

As arguments of the functions just mentioned we can use not only arrays of characters but any expressions (of type *char*) that evaluate to a sensible address. For example, after

```
char str[20] = "John Brown";
```

we can replace "*Brown*" with "*Violet*" in the array *str* by writing

```
strcpy(str + 5, "Violet");
```

where *str* + 5, or equivalently, &*str*[5], is the address that contains the *B* of *Brown*, which is to be replaced with the *V* of *Violet*.

Since the C-style string is a low-level concept, the programmer is fully responsible for seeing to it that no array bounds are exceeded. In this example of array *str* an array length of 11 instead of 20 would just have been sufficient to store the string "*John Brown*", but the above call to *strcpy* would then have been a serious error because, in view of the terminating null character, at least a length of 12 is required to store the resulting string "*John Violet*". Programmers who make such serious errors will not receive help from the compiler, but their programs may crash when they are executed.

The standard type *string* is more pleasant to work with in this regard. With these modern *string* objects, we can use the string member function, *c_str*, to obtain the C-style string that is stored in a *string* object, as this fragment shows:

```
string s;
s = "James Stuart";   // allowed because s is of type 'string'
char cs[30];
strcpy(cs, s.c_str());
```

The last statement has the same effect as

```
strcpy(cs, "James Stuart");
```

So much about converting standard strings to C-style strings. The reverse conversions can simply be done by using a *string* constructor that accepts a C-style string as its argument. Besides, we can use implicit conversion, as this fragment shows:

```
char a[10] = "John";
string s, t;
s = string(a);   // Explicit call to constructor
t = a;           // Implicit call to constructor
```

Since a string literal is a C-style string, implicit conversion also applies in

```
string s;
s = "Peter";
```

in which the last line is equivalent to

```
s = string("Peter");
```

Incidentally, if the array in question need not to be longer that what is required in the initialization, we can omit the number of elements. For example, the following two declarations are equivalent:

```
char s[5] = "Mary";
char s[] = "Mary";
```

In both cases the array length will be 5 so that the four letters of the name and the terminating null character can be stored. Note that, in the definition of an array, we can omit the array length only if we initialize that array.

Using pointers instead of arrays

In the above examples we have stored C-style strings in arrays. Instead, we had better use a pointer if the C-style string in question remains unchanged. For example, if we often want to use the literal "C++ *for Programmers*" in our program, we can write

```
const char *title = "C++ for Programmers";
```

Because the literal in question occurs in our program, it is stored somewhere in memory. After the above declaration the pointer *title* will contain the start address of that area of memory, so we can use it, for example, as follows:

```
cout << title << endl;
```

Instead of the above declaration, we might write

```
const char titleArray[] = "C++ for Programmers";
```

However, in this case the string will be duplicated, since apart from being stored somewhere in memory, as just mentioned, it will now also be stored in the array *titleArray*. It will now be clear that the declaration of the pointer *title* is to be preferred because it is more economical.

5.7 Type *string*: Length, Copy, and Compare

In the previous section we discussed the functions *strlen*, *strcpy*, and *strcmp* for C-style strings. We will now deal with their counterparts for standard strings. Suppose we have declared

```
string s("ABCDEFGH");
```

Then we can inquire the length of string *s* by using the string member function *length*, which has no parameters, so the following expression is equal to 8:

```
s.length()
```

Every string length is less than the constant

```
string::npos
```

so this expression, which we will use shortly, represents a very large number.

As we already know, copying one string into another is simply done by means of an assignment, as is done in

```
string s("ABC"), t;
t = s;
```

We can also easily copy a C-style string to a standard string, by explicit or implicit use of a constructor, as this fragment shows:

```
char *name = "ABC";
string s;
s = string(name);   // or simply by s = name;
```

As for copying in the opposite direction, from a standard string to a C-style string, we have already seen that this can be done by using the (old) standard library function *strcpy* and the string member function *c_str*, as is done in

```
string s("ABCDEFGH");
char cs[20];
strcpy(cs, s.c_str());
```

This copying from *s* to *cs* can also be done by using a string member function. Instead of the last line, we can write the following two statements:

```
s.copy(cs, string::npos);   // Copy from s to cs
cs[s.length()] = '\0';
```

The second argument of the function *copy* is the number of characters to be copied or a very large number to indicate that as many characters as possible are to be copied. We could have achieved the same effect by writing, for example, 10000 instead of *string::npos*. Since *copy* does not write a trailing null character, we have to do this ourselves if this character is required, as the above assignment statement shows.

If we like, we can specify a number of characters that is smaller than *string::npos*. In that case the indicated number of characters are copied, unless the end of the string is reached earlier (as is the case when *string::npos* is used). For example, with the above string *s* and character array *cs*, the effect of the following statements is as the comment indicates:

```
s.copy(cs, 3);
cs[3] = '\0';                   // cs now contains "ABC"
```

It is also possible to supply *copy* with a third argument, the start position in the given string *s*. Here is an example in which this version of *copy* is used:

```
s.copy(cs, string::npos, 2);
cs[s.length() - 2] = '\0';      // cs now contains "CDEFGH"
```

The easiest way of comparing standard strings (but not C-style strings) is by using the following well-known operators:

```
<    >    <=    >=    ==    !=
```

With two standard strings *s* and *t*, we had better not use these operators if we want a test with three possible outcomes and if, at the same time, speed is at stake. For example, by executing the fragment

```
if (s < t)
    ...
else
if (s > t)
    ...
else
    ...  // s == t
```

the strings *s* and *t* are compared twice, that is, both character sequences are traversed twice until a difference is encountered. If we replace this fragment with the following, there is only one such traversal of character sequences:

```
int c = s.compare(t);
if (c < 0)
    ...  // s < t
else
if (c > 0)
    ...  // s > t
else
    ...  // s == t
```

Note that *compare* is similar to *strcmp* (see Section 5.6) in that it returns a negative value for 'less than,' a positive value for 'greater than,' and zero for 'equal to.'

There is a special version of *compare* to compare a standard string with a C-style string. If *s* is a standard string and *cs* a C-style string, writing

```
int c = s.compare(cs);          // Efficient
```

is more efficient than first converting *cs* to a standard string and then doing the comparison in this way:

```
int c = s.compare(string(cs));  // Inefficient
```

There are also versions of *compare* that enable us to specify the start positions and to limit the number of characters that are compared. In the most flexible version, we specify the start positions of both strings and also the maximum number of characters to be compared for each of the standard strings *s* and *t*:

```
c = s.compare(s_startpos, ns, t, t_startpos, nt);
```

Here the number of characters that are compared is the smaller of *ns* and *nt*, unless the end of a string is reached prematurely. (Specifying both arguments *ns* and *nt* may look silly, but remember that they need not be literals. If they are variable expressions, the above call may be convenient in that it need not be preceded by a test to determine which is smaller.)

The following version is simpler, in that only the start position of *s* and the maximum number of characters to be compared are specified:

```
c = s.compare(s_startpos, n, t);
```

There is also a similar version for a C-style string instead of the standard string *t*, but without a start-position argument for this C-style string, since such a position can be specified by using address arithmetic. The following fragment illustrates this. It compares at most *ns* characters of the standard string *s* with at most *ncs* characters of the C-style string *cs*, starting at the positions *s_startpos* and *cs_startpos*, respectively:

```
string s(...);
char *cs = ...;
int s_startpos = ..., cs_startpos = ..., ns = ..., ncs = ...;
c = compare(s_startpos, ns, cs + cs_startpos, ncs);
```

5.8 Type *string*: Append, Insert, and Concatenate

To append a string, we can use the operator +=, as this example shows:

```
string s("ABC"), t("pq");
s += t;                     // s = "ABCpq"
```

Instead of the last statement we could have written the following one, which is hardly an improvement:

```
s.append(t);
```

There are more interesting versions of *append*. In each case, the complete string *s* is extended, so that the extra arguments apply to the string *t* in this example:

```
string s("ABC"), t("pqrstuvwxyz");
int startpos = 3, n = 2;
s.append(t, startpos, n);   // s = "ABCst"
```

It is also possible to use a C-style string, as is done here:

```
string s("ABC");
char *cs = "pqrstuvwxyz");
int n = 2;
s.append(cs, n);            // s = "ABCpq"
```

Finally, we can use a sequence of the same character, using a repetition factor as the first argument:

```
string s("ABC");
s.append(5, 'z');              // s = "ABCzzzzz"
```

If we use the member function *insert*, we have to specify a position in the target string. The entire string supplied as an argument is inserted in the following example:

```
string s("AB"), t("defg");
int insertpos = 1;
s.insert(insertpos, t);     // s = "AdefgB"
```

The version of *insert* used in the following fragment takes two additional arguments: a start position for the string that is copied and the (maximum) number of characters to be copied:

```
string s("AB"), t("defghijklmnop");
int insertpos = 1, t_startpos = 2, n = 3;
s.insert(insertpos, t, t_startpos, n);   // s = "AfghB"
```

There is also a similar version for a C-style string instead of the standard string *t*, but without a start-position argument for this C-style string, since such a position can be specified by using address arithmetic, as this example illustrates:

```
string s("AB");
const char *cs = "defghijklmnop";
int insertpos = 1, cs_startpos = 2, n = 3;
s.insert(insertpos, cs + cs_startpos, n);   // s = "AfghB"
```

Subscripting standard strings

Surprisingly, we can use the subscript operator [ ] to specify individual characters of a *string* object. Here is an example of this very convenient facility:

```
string s("ABCDEFG"), t("abcdefg");
s[1] = t[2];   // Now s = "AcCDEFG"
```

This is possible because the C++ class concept enables us to define our own operators. We should be aware that standard strings are not arrays. This is reflected by the impossibility of replacing the last statement with the following one, which would be correct if *s* and *t* were arrays:

```
*(s + 1) = *(t + 2);   // Incorrect
```

The operator +

Concatenation of strings to build a new one is done by using the binary operator +. At most one of the operands may be a C-style string or a single character, as the following examples show:

```
string s = "ABC", t = "defgh", result;
char *cs = "ijklm";
char ch = '$';
result = s + t;      // "ABCdefgh"
result = s + cs;     // "ABCijklm"
result = cs + s;     // "ijklmABC"
result = s + ch;     // "ABC$"
result = ch + s;     // "$ABC"
```

5.9 Type *string*: Search, Substring, and Swap

We use the member function *find* to search a string *s* for another (usually, shorter) string *t*. This function returns the start position of (the first occurrence of) *t* in *s*, or *string::npos* if *s* does not contain any substring *t*. There is a special version that accepts a C-style string instead of a standard string as an argument, and another one that accepts a single character as an argument. If we want to search the string *s* not from the beginning but from some other position, we can specify that position as a second argument, which is zero by default. Here are some examples:

```
string s("ABcdEFGHcdKLM"), t("cd");
unsigned int i;
i = s.find(t);        // i = 2
i = s.find(t, 3);     // i = 8
i = s.find("cd", 3);  // i = 8
i = s.find('c', 3);   // i = 8
i = s.find('Q');      // i = string::npos
```

To search the string *s* in the reverse direction, we write *rfind* instead of *find*. For example, with the above strings *s* and *t*, we have

```
i = s.rfind(t);       // i = 8
```

The string member function *substr* enables us to select a portion of a string by supplying the position and the length or the desired substring. The following example demonstrates this:

```
string s("ABCdeFGHIJKL"), t;
t = s.substr(3, 2);   // t = "de"
```

There is a string member function *swap* to exchange two strings. This function is very efficient because it does not really move the character sequences themselves but rather internal pointers that are stored in *string* objects and that point to these sequences. For example, after

```
string s("John"), t("Rosemary");
s.swap(t);   // or, equivalently, t.swap(s);
```

we have

```
s = "Rosemary", t = "John"
```

5.10 Type *string*: Input and Output

As we have discussed in Section 5.4, we can read an entire line from the keyboard by writing one of the following statements (with identical effect):

```
getline(cin, s, '\n');
getline(cin, s);
```

We have also seen that

```
cin >> s;
```

should be used if we want to read a single word. As for output, we can simply use

```
cout << s;
```

if we want only the string *s*, without any extra spaces, in the output. However, suppose we want to display a table with a column of strings followed by a column of numbers. It will then normally be required to align these strings left and the numbers right, as this example shows:

```
John         9
George     100
Jim         24
```

The following program shows how we can do this, using the manipulators *left* and *right* in addition to *setw* to specify the width, both for strings and numbers. The output of this program is the above table of three lines:

```
// align.cpp: Align strings.
#include <string>
#include <iostream>
#include <iomanip>
using namespace std;
```

```
int main()
{  string names[3] = {"John", "George", "Jim"};
   int ages[3] = {9, 100, 24};
   for (int i=0; i<3; ++i)
      cout << setw(10) << left << names[i]
           << setw(3)  << right << ages[i] << endl;
   return 0;
}
```

5.11 Multi-dimensional Arrays

We can regard a table or matrix as an array whose elements are again arrays. The notation for such a table element is in accordance with this. We write

```
table[i][j]
```

to denote the element in the *i*th row and the *j*th column of the two-dimensional array table (where, as usual, we count from 0). If we want *table* to have 20 rows and 5 columns, and elements of type *float*, for example, we declare

```
float table[20][5];
```

If you are familiar with Pascal, you must be on your guard not to make the mistake of writing *table*[*i, j*] instead of *table*[*i*][*j*]. Since

```
i, j
```

is a comma expression whose value is the same as that of *j*, the expression *table*[*i, j*] would be equivalent to *table*[*j*].

Initialization

In Section 4.5 we saw how to initialize a one-dimensional array. We can easily extend this to two-dimensional ones. Suppose that we want the *int* array *a* to have two rows and three columns with the following initial values:

```
60 30 50
20 80 40
```

We can write either of the following two lines to achieve this:

```
int a[2][3] = {{60, 30, 50}, {20, 80, 40}};
int a[2][3] = {60, 30, 50, 20, 80, 40};
```

The first of these two lines clearly shows that there are two rows and three columns. This is less clear on the second line, which is also allowed.

In the program *align.cpp* of the previous section, we have initialized an array of standard strings. Since a simple C-style string is an array of characters, it will be no surprise that we can use a two-dimensional array of characters as an array of C-style strings. The following example shows both an initialization of an array of C-style strings and the way these strings can be used:

```
char namelist[3][30] = {"Johnson", "Peterson", "Jacobson"};
for (int i=0; i<3; ++i)
   cout << namelist[i] << endl;
```

The array *namelist* consists of three rows, each containing 30 elements of type *char*, so we have

```
sizeof(namelist) = 90
```

These rows follow one another in memory. For example, the element *namelist*[1][0] immediately follows the element *namelist*[0][29].

5.12 Arrays of Pointers and Pointers to Arrays

A two-dimensional array, as we have just been discussing, is not the only way of dealing with an array of C-style strings. Instead, we may consider using an array of pointers, as the following variant of the above fragment shows:

```
char *namelistptrs[3] = {"Johnson", "Peterson", "Jacobson"};
for (int i=0; i<3; ++i)
   cout << namelistptrs[i] << endl;
```

In this fragment, *namelistptrs* is an array of pointers, so that there is only a (normal) array of three elements. The three character sequences for the names *Johnson*, *Peterson* and *Jacobson*, each followed by a null character, may be located anywhere in memory, the only requirement being that the three pointers in the array *namelistptrs* point to these sequences. If each pointer takes four bytes (which is very reasonable with 32-bit machine architecture), we have

```
sizeof(namelistptrs) = 12
```

The notation *char *namelistptr*[3] helps us to remember that *namelistptr* is an array of pointers. First, we have seen at the end of Section 3.6 that the expression **namelistptr*[i] must be read as *(*namelistptr*[i]). The way *namelistptr* is declared suggests that this expression is of type *char*, which implies that *namelistptr*[i] (without a leading asterisk) is of type *pointer-to-char*. Since each element of the array *namelistptr* is a pointer, this array itself is clearly an array of pointers.

A pointer to an array

Not only an object of an elementary type, such as *int*, but also an array object can be pointed to. In the following program, *p* is a pointer that can point to an *int* array of length 5:

```
// ptrarray.cpp: Pointer to array.
#include <iostream>
using namespace std;

int main()
{   int a[5], (*p)[5];
    p = &a;
    (*p)[3] = 123;
    cout << (*p)[3] << endl;
    return 0;
}
```

The way *p* is defined suggests that (*p)[i] is of type *int*. This implies that *p* (without [i]) is an array of *int* elements, so that *p* must be a pointer to such an array. The parentheses surrounding *p* are necessary when a square bracket ([) follows, because otherwise the binding between *p* and, for example, [3], would be stronger than that between * and *p*.

The following variation of the above program shows how we should declare a pointer to an array in a parameter list:

```
// parfun.cpp: Pointer to array as function parameter.
#include <iostream>
using namespace std;

void f(int (*q)[5])
{   (*q)[3] = 123;
}

int main()
{   int a[5];
    int (*p)[5];
    p = &a;
    f(p);
    cout << (*p)[3] << endl; // Output: 123
    return 0;
}
```

Note that the declaration of the parameter *q* in the function *f* is similar to that of the variable *p* in the *main* function.

As we have seen in Section 5.1, the expressions *a[i]* and *(a + i)* are equivalent. The former is more natural if *a* is an array, the latter if *a* is a pointer, but in either case we can replace one with the other if we like. The same principle applies to the following program, where we have a table (or matrix) consisting of two rows, each row being a one-dimensional array of three *int* elements:

```
// parray.cpp: Pointer to array that is element of
//               another array.
#include <iostream>
using namespace std;

int main()
{   int i, j, a[2][3] = {{8, 3, 6}, {5, 7, 0}}, (*p)[3];
    p = a;
    for (i=0; i<2; ++i)
    {   for (j=0; j<3; ++j)
            cout << p[i][j] << " ";
        cout << endl;
    }
    cout << sizeof(a)/sizeof(int)
         << " elements in array a.\n";
    cout << sizeof(*p)/sizeof(int)
         << " elements in each row.\n";
    return 0;
}
```

The variable p in this program is a pointer to a one-dimensional array of three *int* elements. In other words, while a is an array of two rows, p is a pointer to a row. The statement

```
p = a;
```

which, as usual, could also be written as

```
p = &a[0]
```

assigns the address of the first row to p. The following four expressions are then equivalent:

```
a[i][j]
(*(a + i))[j]
p[i][j]
(*(p + i))[j]
```

Rather arbitrarily, the third of these was used in program *parray.cpp*. Note that $p + 1$ denotes the address of the second row (p being equal to the address of the first row).

Since p is a pointer to a row, the expression *p (also known as $p[0]$) denotes a complete row. Because a row consists of elements of type *int*, the number of elements in each row is equal to

```
sizeof(*p)/sizeof(int)
```

This is confirmed by the fourth of the following output lines, produced by the program:

```
8  3  6
5  7  0
6 elements in array a.
3 elements in each row.
```

Note that in expressions such as $(*(p + i))[j]$ the outer parentheses ( ) are necessary, as follows from our discussion at the end of Section 3.6. If we wrote $*(p + i)[j]$, this would mean $*((p + i)[j])$, which is not what we want here.

In the above program and discussion we have retained array notation, using $[j]$, in all expressions denoting individual elements of array a. If we wanted, we could also have used pointer notation instead of array brackets here: $*((*(p + i)) + j)$ would be a very inconvenient but nevertheless valid form for $(*(p + i))[j]$, which in turn is an inconvenient form for $p[i][j]$. This equivalence also hold if we replace the pointer name p with the array name a.

Multi-dimensional arrays as parameters of functions

Let us return to the example of the beginning of Section 5.11, a table of three rows and five columns, defined as

```
float table[20][5];
```

If we want to use *table* as an argument of a function, say, f, this function may begin as follows:

```
int f(float t[][5])
```

The first dimension (20) of parameter t may be omitted; the second (5) (and any further dimensions) must be present. Remember that inside function f it must be possible to compute the address of each element $table[i][j]$. Since the elements of a two-dimensional array are stored row by row, the element $table[i][j]$ is stored at position $5i + j$ (with $table[0][0]$ being stored at position 0). For example, element $table[2][3]$, that is, the element in row 2 and column 3, lies at position $5 \times 2 + 3 = 13$, as you can see below:

	Col. 0	Col. 1	Col. 2	Col. 3	Col. 4
Row 0	0	1	2	3	4
Row 1	5	6	7	8	9
Row 2	10	11	12	13	14
...	...	...	...	...	...
Row 19	95	96	97	98	99

It will now be clear that the value 5 must be available to the compiler when it is compiling function f.

Instead of the above line, we can write

```
int f(float (*t)[5])
```

This is similar to what we discussed at the end of Section 5.2, where we could use either of the following lines as the beginning of function *minimum*:

```
int minimum(int a[], int n)
int minimum(int *a, int n)
```

With this *minimum* function, *a* points to the first element of an array of *int* values, and *a*[0] (equivalent to **a*) is of type *int*. Analogously, *t* points to the first element of an array of rows, each row consisting of five *float* values, and *t*[0] (or **t*) is the first row. The first element of this first row is *t*[0][0], for which we can also write (**t*)[0].

5.13 Program Parameters

The *main* function of a program can have parameters, which, not surprisingly, are known as *program parameters*. The idea is that the user, when starting the program, can supply arguments, in the form of character strings. The program can detect how many arguments are supplied and then use them. Program *progparm.cpp* will make this clear:

```
// progparm.cpp: Demonstration of using program parameters.
#include <iostream>
using namespace std;

int main(int argc, char *argv[])
{   cout << "argc     = " << argc << endl;
    for (int i=1; i<argc; ++i)
        cout << "argv[" << i << "] = " << argv[i] << endl;
    return 0;
}
```

To run this program, we enter a command line consisting of the program name followed by a number of *program arguments*, written as character sequences and separated by space characters, as, for example, in

```
progparm ABC DEFG HIJKL
```

(Users of the integrated development environment of Visual C++ can specify program arguments by using the *Project | Settings* and the *Debug* tab.) With the above program arguments, the program produces the following output:

```
argc     = 4
argv[1] = ABC
argv[2] = DEFG
argv[3] = HIJKL
```

The parameter *argc* is equal to the number of program arguments if we regard the program name also as a program argument. This name, in the form of the complete path name of the executable program, such as C:*pr**progparm.exe*, will be available through *argv*[0]. The array elements *argv*[1], ..., *argv*[*argc* − 1] are pointers to the program arguments proper, as Figure 5.3 illustrates.

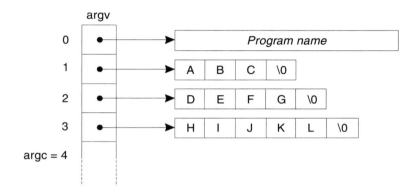

Figure 5.3. Program parameters

Each of the pointers *argv*[*i*] (*i* = 0, 1, ..., *argc* − 1) points to a C-style string. Here we have, for example,

```
argv[1][0] = 'A'
argv[1][1] = 'B'
argv[1][2] = 'C'
argv[1][3] = '\0'
```

As this example illustrates, the number of arguments is arbitrary, but we gain access to them by means of exactly two program parameters, traditionally named *argc* and *argv*, as abbreviations of *argument count* and *argument vector*. Their types must be as they are here.

The concept of program parameters enables us to write programs that are similar to conventional operating-system commands. For example, we can now regard the MS-DOS command

```
copy a:aaa.txt b:bbb.txt
```

as the command to execute a program named *copy* with *a:aaa.txt* and *b:bbb.txt* as program arguments.

5.14 In-memory Format Conversion

Sometimes we want to convert strings to numerical values, as, for example, when a number is entered on the keyboard. In the latter case, a numerical value, say, of type *double*, is constructed on the basis of the individual characters that are entered. For example,

```
1.2e-3
```

is a valid representation for a certain number, which can also be represented by other character sequences, such as 0.0012 and 12*e*–4. We now want to convert such a representation of a number to the number itself, without doing any input operation. Since such a conversion is done in memory, we sometimes use the term *in-memory format conversion* for the subject under discussion. Using the standard *string* type, we can realize this by means of an object of type *istringstream* and the header *<sstream>*, as the first part of the following program shows:

```cpp
// convdemo.cpp: In-memory format conversion
#include <iostream>
#include <sstream>
#include <iomanip>
#include <string>
using namespace std;

int main()
{   // From string s to numerical value x:
    string s("1.2e-3");
    istringstream istr(s);
    double x;
    istr >> x;                  // x = 0.0012
    cout << x << endl;
    // From numerical value y to string t:
    double y = 10.3456789;
    ostringstream ostr;
    ostr << fixed << setw(8) << setprecision(3) << y;
    string t = ostr.str();   // t = "  10.346"
    cout << t << endl;
    return 0;
}
```

After supplying the string *s* to an *istringstream* constructor by writing

```cpp
istringstream istr(s);
```

we can 'read' the desired value from the *istringstream* object *istr* that we have just declared. This is done with the same notation as that for a real input operation:

```
istr >> x;
```

The second part of program *convdemo.cpp* shows the opposite conversion. This time we are given a numerical value and we want to produce a string identical to what we would obtain if we performed real output. After

```
double y = 10.3456789;
ostringstream ostr;
ostr << fixed << setw(8) << setprecision(3) << y;
```

the desired string is stored inside the *ostringstream* object *ostr*. To retrieve it, we simply write

```
string t = ostr.str();        // t = "  10.346"
```

Because of the use of the manipulators *fixed*, *setw*, and *setprecision*, the resulting string *t* represents the value *y* in fixed-point notation, as a string of eight positions, with three positions after the decimal point.

The subject of in-memory format was introduced here so we can make use of it, but it would be more logical to discuss it after Chapters 6 (Classes and Objects) and 10 (Stream I/O). We will therefore briefly revisit this subject in Section 10.7.

5.15 Pointers to Functions

Like data, functions are stored in memory and have start addresses. In most languages we perform operations on data only, not on functions, but in C++ (and in C) we can assign the start addresses of functions to pointers. Later, such a function can be called in an indirect way, namely by means of a pointer whose value is equal to the start address of the function in question. For example, if we declare

```
float (*p)(int i, int j);
```

we can assign the start address of the function

```
float example(int i, int j)
{  return 3.14159 * i + j;
}
```

to the pointer *p* by writing

```
p = &example;
```

Unlike most other situations, the ampersand may be omitted here, so the following statement is equivalent to the last one:

```
p = example;
```

After this assignment, we can write the following function call:

```
(*p)(12, 34)
```

The asterisk may be omitted here, and it goes without saying that then the parentheses are no longer required either, so we may write the function call as

```
p(12, 34)
```

The effect of each of these calls is the same as that of

```
example(12, 34)
```

Suppose we are writing a large program at the beginning of which we want to choose one of several functions. The chosen function is then to be called a great many times. By using a pointer, the choice has to be made only once: after assigning (the address of) the selected function to a pointer, we can later call it through that pointer.

Pointers to functions also enable us to pass a function as an argument to another function. We will use a very simple example: once you understand the principle, you will be able to write more interesting applications of it yourself. Suppose that we want to write a general function to compute the sum of some values, say,

$$f(1) + f(2) + ... + f(n) \tag{5.1}$$

for any function f with return type *double* and with one *int* argument. Our general summation function, say, *funsum*, takes two arguments: n, the number of terms in the sum (5.1), and f, the function to be used. To show that *funsum* is really a general function, we will call it twice, and compute the sum of

$$reciprocal(k) = 1.0/k \qquad (k = 1, 2, 3, 4, 5)$$
$$square(k) = k^2 \qquad (k = 1, 2, 3)$$

The following program shows how this can be done:

```
// pfun.cpp: A function with a function as its argument.
#include <iostream>
using namespace std;

double funsum(int n, double (*f)(int k))
{   double s = 0;
    int i;
    for (i=1; i<=n; ++i) s += (*f)(i);
    return s;
}
```

```
double reciprocal(int k)
{   return 1.0/k;
}

double square(int k)
{   return static_cast<double>(k) * k;
}

int main()
{   cout << "Sum of five reciprocals: "
         << funsum(5, &reciprocal) << endl;
    cout << "Sum of three squares: "
         << funsum(3, &square) << endl;
    return 0;
}
```

This program computes the two sums

$1 + 1.0/2 + 1.0/3 + 1.0/4 + 1.0/5$
$1.0 + 4.0 + 9.0$

the answers of which appear in the following output of the program:

```
Sum of five reciprocals: 2.28333
Sum of three squares: 14
```

5.16 Dynamic Memory Allocation

It is possible to allocate memory at the very moment we need it and to release it when we do not need it any longer. The facilities for *dynamic memory allocation* that are available for this purpose are to be used with caution. In many cases it is better to let standard library routines do this for us. For example, if we write

```
string s, t;
...
s = t + string(100, '=');
```

new memory is allocated for the string that is built here and then assigned to *s*. This allocation is done in a safe way, in that, first, the amount of memory allocated is sufficient to store the string in question, and, second, this memory will be correctly released when the block in which string *s* is declared is left. In Chapter 9, we will discuss some other advanced facilities, such as *vector*, which also allocate and release memory in a reliable way. To *implement* such facilities, one has to program at a lower level, as most programmers frequently had to do when the type *string* and similar facilities were not yet included in the standard. We will now discuss this lower-level approach in more detail.

To create a single object of type *T* in newly allocated memory, pointed to by the pointer *p*, we can write

```
T *p = new T;
```

or, equivalently,

```
T *p;
p = new T;
```

In the latter fragment, some other actions may be performed between the declaration of the pointer *p* and its use. This type *T* can be a primitive type, such as *int*, or a user-defined one, as we will discuss in the next chapter.

It is possible to specify an initial value for the created object, writing, for example,

```
p = new T(123);
```

where 123 is assumed to be such a suitable initial value. (As we will see in the next chapter, this way of using *new* will call a constructor if *T* is a class type.)

To destroy the object pointed to by *p*, and to release the memory it takes, we write

```
delete p;
```

Here is a very simple (and therefore very impractical) example, with *int* substituted for *T*:

```
// newint.cpp: A very simple use of new and delete.
#include <iostream>
using namespace std;

int main()
{   int *p = new int(123);
    cout << ++*p << endl;    // Output: 124
    delete p;
    return 0;
}
```

Instead of the first statement in the *main* function, we could have written

```
int *p = new int;
*p = 123;
```

or

```
int *p;
p = new int;
*p = 123;
```

with the same effect.

Besides allocating and releasing memory for a single object, we can do this for an array of objects. We then use a pair of square brackets [ ] both with *new* and *delete*:

```
int n;
...      // Assign some (positive) value to n
T *a = new T[n];
...      // Use a[0], a[1], ..., a[n - 1], all of type T
delete[] a;
```

Note that the number of objects (not necessarily the number of bytes) must be supplied within square brackets with the above use of *new*, while an empty pair of such brackets is used here with *delete*. The following program puts this into practice. It asks the user to enter some integer *n*, after which *n* numbers (of type *float*) are to be entered. These numbers are stored in a dynamically allocated array, and then printed in the reverse order. Finally, the allocated memory is released:

```
// newarray.cpp: A dynamically allocated array.
#include <iostream>
using namespace std;

int main()
{  int i, n;
   cout << "Enter the sequence length n: ";
   cin >> n;
   float *a = new float[n];
   cout << "Enter n numbers: \n";
   for (i=0; i<n; ++i)
      cin >> a[i];
   cout << "Here are the same numbers in reverse order:\n";
   for (i=n-1; i>=0; --i)
      cout << a[i] << endl;
   delete[] a;
   return 0;
}
```

Remember, there is an essential distinction between parentheses and square brackets in the examples we have been using:

```
int *p = new int(123);    // 123 is an initial value
float *a = new float[n];  // n is a sequence length
```

The operator *new* with placement syntax

There is a special version of the operator *new*, briefly referred to as *placement new*, which enables us to indicate the position in memory where memory is to be used. For example, we can use a large *char* array for this purpose, writing

```
char a[1000];
int *p;
p = new (a) int;
```

This indicates that the start address of the array *a* is to be used to allocate memory for an *int* object, the address of which is to be assigned to the pointer *p*. Apparently, this is not a great achievement, because we can also realize the effect of the last statement by using the keyword *reinterpret_cast* (see Sections 3.7 and 5.3) as follows:

```
p = reinterpret_cast<int*>(a);   // Not recommended
```

However, it is possible to go a step further by overloading the operator *new*. We will not discuss operator overloading in detail until Section 6.6, but already apply it here to the operator *new*. We do this by defining a function named *operator new*. Let us demonstrate this by using a *char* array *a* as above, but by defining an operator *new* which computes the position of the first free array element each time it is used. We store this position in the static pointer *pFree*. As we have discussed in Section 4.5, local static variables keep their values between successive function calls and are initialized only once, so, in the following program, *pFree* is equal to *p*, that is, to the start address of *a*, only the first time the operator *new* is used:

```
// newplace.cpp: The operator new with placement syntax.
#include <iostream>
using namespace std;

void *operator new(unsigned int nbytes, char *p)
{  static char *pFree = p;
      // Because of 'static', pFree is initialized only once.
   cout << "nbytes = " << nbytes << endl;
      // Output inserted to show what happens.
   void *p1 = pFree;
   pFree += nbytes;
   return p1;
}

int main()
{  int *pInt;
   double *pDouble;
   char a[1000];
   pInt = new (a) int;
   *pInt = 123;
   pDouble = new (a) double;
   *pDouble = 4.56;
   // Use a hacker's tool to show that array a contains the
   // values 123 and 4.56:
   int *pI = reinterpret_cast<int*>(a);
   double *pD = reinterpret_cast<double*>(a + sizeof(int));
   if (*pI == 123 && *pD == 4.56)
      cout << "Array a used to store 123 and 4.56\n";
   return 0;
}
```

The first parameter, *nbytes*, of the function *operator new* is equal to the number of bytes required for memory allocation (its type *size_t* being synonymous with *unsigned int*). Here this number is 4 for type *int* and 8 for type *double*, as the following output shows:

```
nbytes = 4
nbytes = 8
Array a used to store 123 and 4.56
```

In other words, if we write

```
new (a) T
```

then *nbytes* is equal to *sizeof(T)*.

The second parameter, *p*, is equal to the argument *a*, occurring here in the two statements that use this operator *new*. Note that, since *pFree* is *static*, this argument *a* is used only in the first of these statements. This implies that the program also works properly if we replace

```
pDouble = new (a) double;
```

with

```
pDouble = new (a + 9999) double;
```

It goes without saying that the use of *new* in this program should *not* be followed by any use of the *delete* operator, since memory allocation is done here only by using the array *a*, which will automatically be released when the function *main* is completed.

Exercises

5.1* Use the type *string* in a program which reads a line of text and displays its reverse.

5.2* Solve Exercise 5.1 without using type *string*.

5.3 Write the *bool* function *reverse(s, t)* which examines the strings *s* and *t* to see if one of these is the reverse of the other. The value to be returned is *true* if this is the case and *false* if it is not.

5.4* Write a program that reads a sequence of 20 integers and, for each element of this sequence, counts how many smaller elements follow in the sequence.

5.5 Write a program that merges two sequences of integers. First, the integers $a_0, ..., a_9$ are read. This sequence is monotonic nondecreasing, which means that $i < j$ implies $a_i \leq a_j$. Then the sequence $b_0, ..., b_9$ is read, which is also monotonic nondecreasing. Finally, the 20 integers read are printed as one monotonic nondecreasing sequence.

5.6   Write the program *parsort.cpp*, which takes three program arguments and prints them in alphabetic order. For example, the command line

```
parsort John Albert Jack
```

causes the following lines to be displayed:

```
Albert
Jack
John
```

5.7   Write a program that reads lines of text from the keyboard and prints only the longest of these lines.

5.8*   Read a positive integer n from the keyboard and print the first $n + 1$ lines of Pascal's triangle. This triangle consists of lines of integers. Starting at the top, these lines are numbered 0, 1, ..., n, and there are $i + 1$ integers on line i. Each line starts and ends with integer 1. Except for all these integers 1, each integer in the triangle is computed as the sum of the two nearest integers on the line immediately above it. For example, with $n = 8$, Pascal's triangle is as shown below:

```
                                1
                            1       1
                        1       2       1
                    1       3       3       1
                1       4       6       4       1
            1       5      10      10       5       1
        1       6      15      20      15       6       1
    1       7      21      35      35      21       7       1
1       8      28      56      70      56      28       8       1
```

As you may know, the integers on line n, in the given order, are the coefficients a_n, a_{n-1}, ..., a_1, a_0 that occur in the right-hand side of

$$(x + 1)^n = a_n x^n + a_{n-1} x^{n-1} + ... + a_1 x + a_0$$

5.9   Predict the output produced by the following statements. Use your computer to see if your predictions are correct.

a.   `cout << "ABCDEFG"[3] << endl;`
b.   `cout << "ABCDEFG" + 3 << endl;`
c.   `cout << "\nABCDEFG" + 3 << endl;`
d.   `cout << ("GFEDCBA" + 1)[3] << endl;`
e.   `cout << "GFEDCBA"[1] - 'F' << endl;`
f.   `cout << &("ABCDEFG"[2]) << endl;`
g.   `cout << *"ABCDEFG" << endl;`

Classes and Objects

6.1 The Word *struct*

If we simply want to group some data, not necessarily of the same type, together in a record, or *structure*, we can use the keyword *struct*, as the following example shows:

```
struct Article {
   int code;
   float weight, length;
};
```

After this, *Article* is a new type, often referred to as a *class type* or *class*, as we will see in the next section. Using the variables *x* and *y* of this class, we can write, for example,

```
Article x, y;
x.code = 123;
x.weight = 12.3F;
x.length = 150.7F;
```

The parts *code*, *weight*, and *length* are referred to as *data members*, or simply *members*, of *Article*. Note that a member name is separated from the variable name, or, in general, from the expression that represents the class object, by a dot.

An object of a class type can be initialized in the same way as an array, so instead of the last four program lines we could have written

```
Article x = {123, 12.3F, 150.7F}, y;
```

If we want *y* to be a copy of *x*, we can simply write

```
y = x;
```

As we have seen in Section 5.16, it is possible to generate objects dynamically, using the *new* operator. Here we could write

```
Article *p = new Article;
```

The object that we gain access to via the pointer *p* is denoted by the expression **p*, and the *code* member of this object can be written as the left-hand side of the following assignment:

```
(*p).code = 456;
```

It follows from Section 3.6 that the dot has a stronger binding than the asterisk, so that the parentheses in this statement are really necessary. Fortunately, there is different, and more convenient, notation available. Instead of the above statement, we can write the following one, which has exactly the same meaning:

```
p->code = 456;
```

If we apply *sizeof* to a class type, the value we obtain will be at least equal to the sum of the data members, but it may be rounded up to a multiple of, say, four bytes. In other words, class objects may contain some unused space. For example, with Visual C++, we have

```
sizeof(Article) = sizeof(int) + 2 * sizeof(float) = 12
```

as we would expect, but with

```
struct Other
{   int i;
    char ch;
};
```

we find

```
sizeof(Other) = 8
```

which might at first surprise us, since

```
sizeof(int) + sizeof(char) = 4 + 1 = 5
```

6.2 A Constructor and Other Member Functions

The use of the word *struct* in Section 6.1 is very similar to that in the C language. In C++ it is also possible to provide a structure with functions, known as *member functions* and to distinguish between public and private members. If this is done, the word *class* is normally used instead of *struct*. Suppose we want to use a type *Person*, consisting of three data members: a name, a year of birth and an indication for male or female. Now consider the following file *person.h*, which contains a *class definition* (for historical reasons also referred to as a *class declaration*) for this new type:

```
// person.h: Header for the class Person.
#include <string>
#include <iostream>
#include <iomanip>
using namespace std;

class Person {
public:
   Person(const string &s = "", int yr = 0, bool m = true)
   {  name = s;
      yearOfBirth = yr;
      male = m;
   }

   void setName(const string &s){name = s;}
   void setYear(int yr){yearOfBirth = yr;}
   void setMF(bool m){male = m;}

   const string &getName()const
   {  return name;
   }
   int getAgeAtEnd2000()const
   {  return 2000 - yearOfBirth;
   }
   void print()const
   {  cout << setw(10) << left << name
           << setw(4) << right << getAgeAtEnd2000()
           << (male ? " (M)" : " (F)") << endl;
   }
private:
   string name;
   int yearOfBirth;
   bool male;
};
```

This class contains only three data members, *name*, *yearOfBirth*, and *male*, which are private, as the keyword *private*, followed by a colon, indicates. The latter means that we cannot directly access them other than from function members. All member functions are made public. There is a function *getName* to retrieve the name of a person. To demonstrate that there need not be similar functions for all private data members, such functions are omitted for *yearOfBirth* and *male*. Since these members are private, they are inaccessible in unrelated functions outside this class, but still accessible in member functions, in which we use them, as the functions *getAgeAtEnd*2000 and *print* show.

There are two ways of storing data in a *Person* object. The first is by using a constructor, that is, a function with the same name as the class. A constructor does not return any value, nor is there the word *void* at its beginning. It is called whenever a *Person* object is created. In the program *persdemo.cpp* below, this way of storing data is used for object *a*. Alternatively, we use the member functions *setName*, *setYear*, and *setMF* for this purpose. Supplying initial values to the constructor can be omitted here because all three arguments of the *Person* constructor are default arguments. The following program shows how the class *Person* can be used:

```cpp
// persdemo.cpp: Demonstration of class Person.
#include <string>
#include <iostream>
#include "person.h"
using namespace std;

int main()
{  Person a("Mary", 1980, false), b;
   b.setName("John");
   b.setYear(1975);
   b.setMF(true);
   string s = a.getName();
   cout << s << endl;     // Mary
   b.print();             // John          25 (M)
   return 0;
}
```

Instead of the line

```cpp
#include "person.h"
```

we might have written the class definition as this occurs in the file *person.h*, but the use of such a header file is very customary in realistic programs, because it enables us to use the same class definition easily in other program files, as we will see in Section 6.4.

The word *const* as used in, for example,

```cpp
void print()const
```

indicates that the function in question will not modify any data members. It will now be clear why *const* is used in a similar way in the functions *getName* and *getAgeAtEnd*2000, but not in *setName*, *setYear*, and *setMF*.

Let us now return to the *Person* constructor, which is repeated below:

```
Person(const string &s = "", int yr = 0, bool m = true)
{  name = s;
   yearOfBirth = yr;
   male = m;
}
```

Instead of specifying default values for all three parameters, we might have defined a second constructor, without any parameters. In other words, we may replace the first line of the constructor with

```
Person(const string &s, int yr, bool m)
```

provided we add the following, second constructor:

```
Person(){name = " "; yearOfBirth = 0; male = true;}
```

If we do this, only two ways of defining *Person* objects are possible: specifying three values (as we did for variable *a* in program *persdemo.cpp*) and specifying no values at all (as we did for variable *b*). This is different to the original version of the constructor, in which there are three default parameters, since this also allows us to write, for example,

```
Person x("Jim", 1960);
```

Here only the default value (*true*) for the third parameter is used.

The words *class*, *struct*, *public*, and *private*

C++ programmers normally use the word *struct* only for very simple classes, which contain no function members and in which all data members are public. In all other cases the word *class* is more popular. However, as far as the compiler (and the C++ standard) is concerned, there is only a very subtle distinction in the meanings of the words *class* and *struct*:

- With *struct* all members are public by default.
- With *class* all members are private by default.

For example, the definition

```
struct Article {
   int code;
   float weight, length;
};
```

discussed in Section 6.1, could also be written as follows, without altering its meaning:

```
class Article {
public:
    int code;
    float weight, length;
};
```

Conversely, since all members of the class *Person* are preceded by one of the words *public* and *private*, it would not make any difference if, in the file *person.h*, we replaced the word *class* with the word *struct*.

Since members are private by default if the word *class* is used, we could start with the private members without necessarily using the word private, *writing*, for example,

```
class Person {
    string name;
    int yearOfBirth;
    bool male;
public:
    ...
};
```

Except for very simple cases, such as discussed in Section 6.1, it is more customary now to start with the public members and to use the word *class* rather than *struct*.

The word *this*

If we write

```
b.print();
```

as we did in the program *persdemo.cpp*, then, when we focus on the function *print* related to this call, we refer to *b* as *the object for which the function is called*. Since *print* can also be called for objects other than *b*, we cannot use the name *b* in this function if we want to refer to this object. In member functions such as *print* in the class *Person*, there is therefore always a pointer named *this* available, which points to the object for which the function was called. As we have seen in Section 6.1, the operator –> is available to denote data members of a class object if a pointer to that object is given. The same applies to function members. Bearing this in mind, it follows that we can write the function *print* of the class *Person* as follows, if we like:

```
void print()const
{   cout << setw(10) << left << this->name
         << setw(4) << right << this->getAgeAtEnd2000()
         << (this->male ? " (M)" : " (F)") << endl;
}
```

In this version of *print*, the pointer *this* is used for the data members *name* and *male* and for the function member *getAgeAtEnd*2000. In this example, we do not really benefit from the word *this*, but this will be different in other situations (as we will see in Sections 6.4 and 6.9).

6.3 Constructor Initializers

In the previous section we have used assignments in the *Person* constructor to give data members their proper values. There is an alternative way of writing this constructor, known as a *constructor initializer*, which looks rather peculiar at first:

```
Person(const string &s = "", int yr = 0, bool m = true)
     :name(s), yearOfBirth(yr), male(m){ }
```

Between the closing parenthesis of the parameter list and the opening curly brace of the function body, we place a colon, followed by a list of the data members to be initialized, each followed by the initial value to be used between parentheses. In the current example, both solutions can be used, but only the latter one would be allowed if the data members had the *const* qualifier or if they were references. After all, const and reference variables must be initialized and cannot be given values by assignments. Since such const and reference member variables occur in the following program, we really need a constructor initializer here:

```
// initcons.cpp: A constructor using the
//                 initialization syntax.
#include <iostream>
using namespace std;

class TestInit {
public:
   TestInit(int i, float &x): ii(i), xx(x){}
   void print()const{cout << ii << " " << xx << endl;}
private:
   const int ii;
   float &xx;
};

int main()
{  float y = 8.5F;
   TestInit t(2, y);
   t.print();         // 2 8.5
   return 0;
}
```

Recall that normal const and reference variables must be initialized in their definitions. This is not the case if such variables are class members, since here we write

```
const int ii;
float &xx;
```

These variables must be initialized in the *TestInit* constructor in the way shown in this fragment:

```
: ii(i), xx(x)
```

This indicates that *i* is to be used as the initial value of *ii*, and *x* as that of *xx*. The compiler would not accept the following version of the *TestInit* constructor:

```
TestInit(int i, float &x)
{  ii = i;    // Assignment invalid because ii is const
   xx = x;    // Assignment invalid because xx is a reference
}
```

Remember, the special syntax we have been discussing in this section applies only to constructors, not to other member functions, as the term *constructor initializer* suggests.

6.4 Member Functions Defined Outside a Class

Member functions are sometimes rather large. Instead of defining them completely inside the class, it is often desirable to do this outside it, preferably even in a different program file. In this way, the header file remains reasonably small, so we can quickly understand what the class in question is supposed to do, without knowing in detail how everything is implemented. Let us demonstrate this by a program that we can use to compute the number of days between two dates of the same non-leap year. The user can enter the day and month numbers for each date, after which the algebraic difference between the second and the first date is displayed. Let us start with a demonstration of this program:

```
Enter day and month numbers of date 1:   1  1
Enter day and month numbers of date 2:  31 12
Difference in a non-leap year: 364 days
```

Since the user has entered the first and the last day of a non-leap year, the second date falls 364 days after the first, as the above output shows. Based on the class *DateDM*, to be discussed in a moment, the application program for this computation is shown below:

```
// datetest.cpp: An application of class DateDM.
//               The file dateDM.cpp must be linked.
#include <iostream>
#include "dateDM.h"
using namespace std;

int main()
{  int d, m;
   cout << "Enter day and month numbers of date 1: ";
   cin >> d >> m;
   DateDM date1(d, m);
   cout << "Enter day and month numbers of date 2: ";
   cin >> d >> m;
   DateDM date2(d, m);
```

```
    cout << "Difference in a non-leap year: "
        << date1.difference(date2) << " days\n";
    return 0;
}
```

As you can see, all we need of class *DateDM* is a constructor, which accepts both a day and a month number, and a member function *difference* that takes a second *DateDM* object as an argument. The following header file shows that only these two functions are public in the class:

```
// dateDM.h: Header file for date,
//     restricted to day and month.
//     Both are dates of a non-leap year.
class DateDM {
public:
    DateDM(int d = 1, int m = 1);
    int difference(const DateDM &date)const;
private:
    int day, month;
};
```

In this header file, the *DateDM* constructor and the function *difference* are only declared, not defined. Note the two occurrences of the word *const* in the declaration of *difference*. The first *const* indicates that the argument will not be modified by this function, even though, for reasons of efficiency, we are dealing with a reference parameter. This should not be confused with the word *const* at the end of the line, which says that this function will not modify any data members of the 'object for which it is called.' We obviously need two dates in this *difference* function, as the call

```
    date1.difference(date2)
```

shows. As we know, the object *date1* is referred to as 'the object for which the function *difference* is called,' while the object *date2* is supplied as an argument. Thanks to the two words *const* just mentioned, we know that *difference* will change neither object.

We obtain the difference of two dates by computing the absolute day numbers, each ranging from 1 through 365, for the two given dates, and then subtract the first from the second. Although the user enters month numbers m in the range 1, ..., 12, we will use array index values $i = m - 1$, which obviously lie in the range 0, ..., 11. With a given number m of a month, the number of days preceding that month will be stored in *precedingDays*[$m - 1$], where *precedingDays* is an array of 12 integer elements, which we compute using another array, *calendar*, containing the number of days for each month. More precisely, *calendar*[$m - 1$] is the number of days in month m. Starting with *precedingDays*[0] = 0 (since no days of the current year precede January 1st) and using successive values i (= $m - 1$) = 1, 2, ..., 11 for the months February, March, ..., December, we have

```
    precedingDays[i] = precedingDays[i-1] + calendar[i-1];
```

For example, when $i = 1$, this statement computes the number of days that precede February 1st as the number of days that precede January 1st, increased by 31, the number of days in January.

This array *calendar* is also useful to check the validity of day numbers entered by the user. Such checks are done in the *DateDM* constructor, as the following implementation files shows:

```cpp
// dateDM.cpp: Implementation of class DateDM.
#include <iostream>
#include "dateDM.h"
using namespace std;

namespace {
int calendar[] =
    {31, 28, 31, 30, 31, 30, 31, 31, 30, 31, 30, 31};
}

DateDM::DateDM(int d, int m)
{   if (m < 1 || m > 12)
    {   cout <<
            "Invalid month number. Value 1 used instead.\n";
        m = 1;
    }
    if (d < 1 || d > calendar[m-1])
    {   cout << "Invalid day number. Value 1 used instead.\n";
        d = 1;
    }
    day = d;
    month = m;
}

int DateDM::difference(const DateDM &date2)const
{   int precedingDays[12];
    precedingDays[0] = 0;    // 0 for January, etc.
    for (int i=1; i<12; ++i)
        precedingDays[i] = precedingDays[i-1] + calendar[i-1];
    int dayNr1 = precedingDays[month-1] + day,
        dayNr2 = precedingDays[date2.month-1] + date2.day;
    return dayNr2 - dayNr1;
}
```

By writing only the program line

```cpp
#include "dateDM.h"
```

at the beginning, we benefit from the fact that the class *DateDM* is defined in a header file.

Recall that we discussed both separate compilation and unnamed namespaces in Section 4.6. It follows that the name *calendar* is deliberately made unknown in other program files.

For each member function defined outside the class, we must clearly indicate that it belongs to the class *DateDM*, by inserting the prefix

```
DateDM::
```

just before the function name, as is done here in the following two program lines:

```
DateDM::DateDM(int d, int m)
int DateDM::difference(const DateDM &date2)const
```

The function *difference* shows that besides the private data members of the object for which the function is called, those of the object supplied as an argument are also accessible.

Although not used here, default values are specified for the parameters of the *DateDM* constructor in the file *dateDM.h*. Parameter default values occurring in the declaration of a function inside a class must not occur in the declaration of the function outside the class. We therefore write *int d*, *int m*, instead of *int d = 0*, *int m = 0*, in the definition of the *DateDM*, as the first of the two program lines above shows.

Program files used in realistic software projects

In this example we have used two program files with the extension *.cpp*, which are quite different:

- *datetest.cpp*, an *application* of the class *DateDM*
- *DateDM.cpp*, the *implementation* of this class

In each of these files the following header-file is included:

- *DateDM.h*, the *interface* of this class

This division of a program into application, implementation, and interface files is somewhat tedious for small demonstration programs such as most programs in this book. However, it is very useful and common for large, realistic programs. Such programs may even consist of more than three files: one application file, containing the *main* function, and both an interface and an implementation file for each (nontrivial) class that is used.

The word *this* used to tell parameters from data members

In the *DateDM* constructor we named the parameters *d* and *m* because the (clearer) names *day* and *month* were already in use as class members. If we like, we can use the names *day* and *month* also for the parameters, provided we address those class members as *this–>day* and *this–>month*, as the following version of the *DateDM* constructor shows:

```
DateDM::DateDM(int day, int month)
{  if (month < 1 || month > 12)
   {  cout <<
         "Invalid month number. Value 1 used instead.\n";
      month = 1;
   }
   if (day < 1 || day > calendar[month-1])
   {  cout << "Invalid day number. Value 1 used instead.\n";
      day = 1;
   }
   this->day = day;
   this->month = month;
}
```

All occurrences of *day* and *month* in this function denote the parameters, except for the left-hand sides of the following two statements at the end, in which the class members *day* and *month* obtain the current values of the parameters with the same names:

```
this->day = day;
this->month = month;
```

6.5 More about Constructors

Suppose that the object *dateA* of class *DateDM* (of the last section) is available and that we want to create the object *dateB*, equal to *dateA*. First, we can achieve this by means of initialization, writing

```
DateDM dateB(dateA);
```

or

```
DateDM dateB = dateA;
```

As we will see in Section 6.9, a *default copy constructor* is used in these cases. Second, we can use assignment, writing

```
DateDM dateB;
dateB = dateA;
```

As we will discuss in Section 6.8, the first of these lines invokes a *default constructor*. We must not replace this line with

```
DateDM dateB();    // Wrong: this is something different!
```

At first, this looks very reasonable, since we are calling a default constructor, that is, a function, without using any arguments, and we have seen in Section 4.2 that function calls always contain parentheses, even if there are no arguments. However, the designer of C++ (that is, Bjarne Stroustrup) could not use this empty parentheses pair in calls to constructors such as the one above, because the last program line has the syntactical form

```
name anothername();
```

which is already in use for the declaration (without a definition) of a function that has no parameters. For example, if we want to declare the function *readreal* of Section 4.2 without defining it, we would write

```
double readreal();
```

which has the same structure as the above wrong program line with the long comment. It will now be clear that this wrong line indeed means something very different, namely the declaration of a function *dateB* which has no parameters.

Class objects can be passed to functions as arguments. In most cases we use const reference parameters in such situations. For example, we can write

```
void printDifference(const DateDM &dat1, const DateDM &dat2)
{   cout << "Difference in a non-leap year: "
         << dat1.difference(dat2) << " days\n";
}
```

in the file *datetest.cpp* just before the function *main* and then replace the second last statement of that function with the following call, to make the program behave in exactly the same way as the original version:

```
printDifference(date1, date2);
```

So much for passing class objects as arguments. We can also return such an object as a function value. For example, we can replace the program *datetest.cpp* of Section 6.4 with the following version, which contains a function that returns a *DateDM* object:

```
// datetst.cpp: An application of class DateDM.
//              The file dateDM.cpp must be linked.
#include <iostream>
#include "dateDM.h"
using namespace std;

DateDM readDate(int i)
{   int d, m;
    cout << "Enter day and month numbers of date "
         << i << ": ";
    cin >> d >> m;
    return DateDM(d, m);
}
```

```
int main()
{  DateDM date1 = readDate(1),
          date2 = readDate(2);
   cout << "Difference in a non-leap year: "
        << date1.difference(date2) << " days\n";
   return 0;
}
```

As this program shows, a constructor can also be used in contexts other than variable declarations. At the end of the function *readDate*, we could have written

```
DateDM date(d, m);
return date;
```

but the single statement

```
return DateDM(d, m);
```

in the program is obviously to be preferred.

So much for some basic facts about constructors. We will discuss this important subject in more detail in Sections 6.8 and 6.9.

6.6 Operator Overloading and Friend Functions

In Section 4.8, when discussing function overloading, we saw that, to identify a function, not only its name but also the types and number of its arguments are required. The situation is similar with operators. For example, the division operator / performs integer arithmetic if its two operands have integer type, and floating-point arithmetic if at least one of its operands has floating-point type. C++ also enables us to overload operators ourselves. (Incidentally, this was already possible in Algol 68, back in 1968, so it is not a unique concept of C++.) Operator overloading in C++ is restricted to the following character sequences, which are also in use as standard operators:

```
new   delete   new[]   delete[]
+     -     *     /     %     ^     &     |     ~
!     =     <     >     +=    -=    *=    /=    %=
^=    &=    |=    <<    >>    <<=   >>=   ==    !=
<=    >=    &&    ||    ++    --    ,     ->*   ->
()    []
```

For example, we cannot introduce a dollar sign as an operator. The precedence of our own operators is the same as that of the standard operators with the same notation. For example, if we define our own operators + and *, the precedence of * will be higher than that of +.

To discuss operator overloading, we will use the type *vec* to work with simple vectors in the sense of mathematics and physics. (As we have already seen in Section 1.7, the term *vector* in C++ is more often used for a different purpose, which is why we will use the shorter name *vec* for this type of our own.) With two given (mathematical) vectors

```
u = (xu, yu)
v = (xv, yv)
```

we can compute their sum

```
s = (xs, ys)
```

as follows:

```
xs = xu + xv
ys = yu + yv
```

Figure 6.1 illustrates this for the vectors $u = (3, 1)$, $v = (1, 2)$, which have $s = (4, 3)$ as their sum vector.

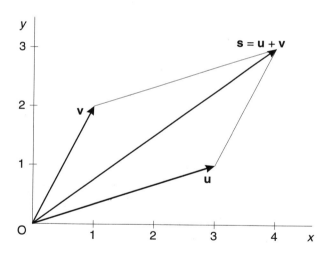

Figure 6.1. Sum of two vectors

We will now overload the addition operator +, so that we can also use it for *vec* objects. For example, we will be able to write

```
s = u + v;
```

where *s*, *u*, and *v* are variables of type *vec*. At the same time, we overload the output operator << so that this, too, can be used for *vec* objects. The following program shows how this can be done:

```cpp
// operator.cpp: Overloaded + and << operators.
#include <iostream>
using namespace std;

class vec {
public:
   vec(float xx = 0, float yy = 0): x(xx), y(yy) {}
   void printvec(ostream &os)const
   {  os << "(" << x << ", " << y << ")";
   }
   vec operator+(const vec &b)const
   {  return vec(x + b.x, y + b.y);
   }
private:
   float x, y;
};

ostream &operator<<(ostream &os, const vec &v)
{  v.printvec(os);
   return os;
}

int main()
{  vec u(3, 1), v(1, 2), s;
   s = u + v;      // This is our own operator +
   cout << "The sum of (3, 1) and (1, 2) is "
        << s       // This is our own operator <<
        << endl;
   return 0;
}
```

As this program shows, we can define a plus operator of our own by means of a function whose name consists of the keyword *operator* followed by +. The same applies for other operators, such as the program shows for <<. In this program the statement

```cpp
s = u + v;
```

is simply another way of writing

```cpp
s = u.operator+(v);
```

Although we are dealing with a binary operator (which requires two operands), the function *operator+* has only one parameter, which is the second operand, *v*. This is typical for operator functions that are implemented as member functions. The first operand, *u*, is the object for which this member function is called. This asymmetric behavior is also found in the function definition, as this statement shows:

```cpp
return vec(x + b.x, y + b.y);
```

Here *x* and *y* belong to the object (*u*) for which the function is called, while *b.x* and *b.y* belong to the second operand (*v*). In this return statement, a *vec* object is created by calling a constructor, which is similar to what we did in program *datetst.cpp*, at the end of Section 6.4. So much for the function *operator+*.

The situation is different with the other operator that is overloaded in this program. The function *operator<<* is a normal function, not a member function. We cannot define it as a member of the class *vec* because the first operator is not of type *vec*. The statement

```
cout << s;
```

(which we could have used in the program) is an abbreviated form of

```
operator<<(cout, s);
```

and *not* of

```
cout.operator<<(s);
```

To understand all this, we must know that *cout* is an object of the type *ostream*, which is a standard class. Both *cout* and *ostream* are immediately available if we use the header *<iostream>* in our program. The latter statement would be possible only if the standard class ostream contained a function *operator<<* that takes a *vec* object as an argument. This is clearly not the case and neither can we add one ourselves (unless we were prepared to modify standard headers). It will now be clear why we have not defined the function *operator<<* as a member function, but as a normal function, shown once again below:

```
ostream &operator<<(ostream &os, const vec &v)
{  v.printvec(os);
   return os;
}
```

As we will discuss in Chapter 10, the first operand of an output operator << need not necessarily be *cout*, but can also be other stream objects. By using the parameter *os* instead of the standard object *cout*, we make this function *operator<<* also applicable to file output. You may wonder why we have not written the simpler version

```
void operator<<(ostream &os, const vec &v){v.printvec(os);}
```

If we had, the statement

```
cout << s;
```

would still be possible, but the following one would not:

```
cout << s << endl;
```

Here it is required that the expression *cout* << *s* returns a reference to an *ostream* object, so that this expression can act as the left operand of the second operator << in this output statement. For this reason, the *operator<<* is always defined as a function that returns a reference to an *ostream* object.

Since the function *operator<<* is not a member function of the class *vec*, it has no access to the private data members of this class, so we cannot directly use the *x* and *y* members. In the program *operator.cpp* this problem is solved by using the public function *printvec*, which performs the actual output operations. Alternatively, we could have defined the following two public member functions in the class *vec*:

```
float getx(){return x;}
float gety(){return y;}
```

If we had done this, we could have omitted the function *printvec* and have defined the function *operator<<* as follows:

```
ostream &operator<<(ostream &os, const vec &v)
{   os << "(" << v.getx() << ", " << v.gety() << ")";
    return os;
}
```

Incidentally, once these functions *getx* and *gety* are available, we might also consider the idea of defining the function *operator+* as a non-member function. We could write it as follows outside the class *vec*, while at the same time removing the member function *operator+*:

```
vec operator+(const vec &a, const vec &b)
{   return vec(a.getx() + b.getx(), a.gety() + b.gety());
}
```

Friend functions

There is still another solution to the problem of non-member functions in which we want to use private data (or function) members of a class. It is possible to give such a function the right to access those members, by declaring it inside the class using the word *friend* at its very beginning. However, remember that this does not turn it into a member function. Here we could have inserted the following line inside the class *vec*:

```
friend ostream &operator<<(ostream &os, const vec &v);
```

Since the words *public* and *private* do not apply to declarations of friend functions, we may write this line anywhere in the class *vec* (as long as we do not place it inside another function). After this, the definition of *operator<<* outside the class can be written as follows:

```
ostream &operator<<(ostream &os, const vec &v)
{   os << "(" << x << ", " << y << ")";
    return os;
}
```

Finally, it is also possible to define this function, preceded by the word *friend*, inside the class instead of just its declaration. Again, that does not turn it into a member function, as follows from the number of parameters.

Remember:

- A function that defines a binary operator has one parameter if it is a member function.
- A function that defines a binary operator has two parameters if it is a non-member function.

In other words, the number of parameters is one less than the number of operands in the case of a member function, while these numbers are equal in the case of a non-member function.

Since *friend* functions gain access to private class members, which is against the idea of 'data *hiding*', we try to avoid them if this can be done easily.

Defining unary operators

The above discussion about the number of parameters being either equal to or one less than the number of operands also applies to unary operators (with only one operand), of which we will see an example in a moment:

- A function that defines a unary operator has no parameters if it is a member function.
- A function that defines a unary operator has one parameter if it is a non-member function.

Suppose that with a given vector *v* we want to compute the opposite vector *w*, for which the normal mathematical notation is –*w*. For example, if *v* = (2, –5) then *w* = –*v* = (–2, 5). It would be nice if we could write this in our program as

```
w = -v;
```

by defining a function *operator–* of our own. This can be done in two ways:

1. By adding the following public member function to the class *vec*:

```
vec operator-(){return vec(-x, -y);}
```

The above statement to compute *w* would then be an abbreviated form of this one:

```
w = v.operator-();
```

2. By defining a non-member function, either as a friend function or by using the
   functions *getx* and *gety*, discussed above. In the latter case, this function operator–
   would read as follows:

```
vec operator-(const vec &v)
{   return vec(-v.getx(), -v.gety());
}
```

Note that –*v.getx*( ) should be read as –(*v.getx*( )).

Only member functions allowed for some operators

The assignment operator = can only be overloaded by member functions, and the same
applies to the operators [] (for subscripting), () (for function calls), and –> (see Section
6.1).

Increment and decrement operators

Since we can use the operator ++ both as a pre-increment and as a post-increment operator
(as in ++*a* and *a*++, respectively), it is not immediately clear which applies if we define an
operator++ function. This problem is resolved as follows. If we do not take any special
measure, the prefix operator applies. The following fragment illustrates this. It also shows
that this prefix *operator*++ function can be a member or a non-member function, as we
choose:

```
class X {
public:
   X &operator++(){...}              // Member function
   ...
};
Y &operator++(Y &x){...}            // Non-member function
...
X a;
Y b;
f(++a); // This means f(a.operator++());   (prefix operator)
f(++b); // This means f(operator++(b));    (prefix operator)
```

So much for the prefix increment operator. The postfix increment operator is distinguished
from this by an extra parameter, which is of type *int* and equal to zero. The following
fragment and the comments illustrate this, again both for a member and for a non-member
function:

```
class X {
public:
   X operator++(int dummy){...}    // Member function
   ...
};
```

```
Y operator++(Y &y, int dummy){...} // Non-member function
...
X a;
Y b;
f(a++); // This means f(a.operator++(0)); (postfix operator)
f(b++); // This means f(operator++(b, 0)); (postfix operator)
```

Note that prefix operators return references, while postfix operators do not. Accordingly, ++*a* is an lvalue, but *a*++ is not, as was mentioned in Section 3.8.

Overloaded prefix and postfix decrement operators (−−) are similar to what we have been discussing for increment operators.

6.7 Operators, Conversion, and the Word *explicit*

We will now discuss another program to discuss some problems related to conversion. Let us use a class for integers modulo 24, with three operators of our own: + for addition, << for output and >> for input. With modulo arithmetic all integers are reduced to some range, which in our case consists of the numbers 0, 1, 2, ..., 23. In principle, this reduction could be done by adding or subtracting a multiple of 24 to the given number. For example,

$$241 \text{ modulo } 24 = 1$$

If the given number is nonnegative we can simply use the operator %, which gives the remainder after integer division. This operator does not immediately give the desired answer if we start with a negative number, as we will see shortly.

Our program will first perform the addition 23 + 5 modulo 24 and then ask the user to enter two integers. Each of these is reduced to modulo 24 numbers (resulting in one of the integers 0, 1, 2, ..., 23), after which their sum modulo 24 is computed and displayed:

```
// mod24.cpp: Modulo 24 addition.
#include <iostream>
using namespace std;

class mod24 {
public:
   mod24(int x = 0)
   {  t = x % 24;
      if (t < 0) t += 24;
   }
   int getvalue()const{return t;}
private:
   int t; // t = 0, 1, 2, ..., 23
};
```

```
mod24 operator+(const mod24 &a, const mod24 &b)
{  return mod24(a.getvalue() + b.getvalue());
}

ostream &operator<<(ostream &os, const mod24 &x)
{  os << x.getvalue();
   return os;
}

istream &operator>>(istream &is, mod24 &x)
{  int y;
   is >> y;
   x = mod24(y);
   return is;
}

int main()
{  mod24 x(23), y(5);
   cout << "23 + 5 modulo 24 = " << x + y << endl;
   cout << "Same result:       " << x + 5 << endl;
   cout << "Same result:       " << 23 + y << endl;
   cout << "Different result:  " << 23 + 5 << endl;
   cout << "Enter two integers: ";
   cin >> x >> y;
   cout << "Taken modulo 24, they are equal to "
        << x << " and " << y << endl;
   cout << "x + y modulo 24 =  " << x + y << endl;
   return 0;
}
```

If we compute, for example,

```
64 % 24 = 16
```

we immediately obtain the desired answer 64 modulo 24 = 16. However, if we start with a negative number, say, −29, the computation

```
-29 % 24
```

is implementation-dependent (see also Section 2.1) and may not immediately give what we want. Since the result of the real division −29.0/24.0 lies between −1 and −2, the value obtained by the integer division −29/24 will be equal either to −1 or (less likely), to −2, with corresponding values

```
-29 % 24 = -29 - 24 * (-1) = -5
```

or

```
-29 % 24 = -29 - 24 * (-2) = 19
```

Since the latter, nonnegative, result 19 is desired as the value of *t*, we write

```
if (t < 0) t += 24;
```

in the *mod*24 constructor, which, in the (likely) case of the initial result –5, also gives the desired value, computed as –5 + 24 = 19. You can check the correctness of this result 19 by observing

- that it lies in the required range from 0 to 23, and
- that the difference 19 – (–29) = 48 is a multiple of 24

We pay special attention to the cases in which one of the two operands of the addition that we perform is of type *mod*24 and the other is of type *int*. With *x* and *y* of type *mod*24, we therefore compute not only *x* + *y*, but also *x* + 5 and 23 + *y*, using our own *operator+* function. It goes without saying that the addition 23 + 5 does not invoke this function but uses the built-in addition operator. Here is a demonstration of the program:

```
23 + 5 modulo 24 = 4
Same result:      4
Same result:      4
Different result:  28
Enter two integers: 64 -29
Taken modulo 24, they are equal to x = 16 and y = 19
x + y modulo 24 =   11
```

If you find the last two of these lines difficult, the following may be helpful:

$$64 \text{ modulo } 24 = 16 \text{ (because } 64 = 2 \times 24 + 16)$$
$$-29 \text{ modulo } 24 = 19 \text{ (because } -29 = (-2) \times 24 + 19; \text{ see also the discussion above)}$$
$$16 + 19 = 35$$
$$35 \text{ modulo } 24 = 11$$

You may have noticed that the function *operator+* is not defined as a member function of the class *mod*24. If it were, the expression *x* + *y* would have been equivalent to

```
x.operator+(y)
```

which is correct only if *x* is an object of class *mod*24. The expression

```
23 + y
```

would then not have been accepted, since this would have been equivalent to the incorrect form

```
23.operator+(y)
```

This makes no sense because 23 is not a class object and it will not be converted to one in this position. By contrast, with the operator definition

```
mod24 operator+(const mod24 &a, const mod24 &b)
{  return mod24(a.getvalue() + b.getvalue());
}
```

used in the program, the expression $x + y$ is equivalent to the function call

```
operator+(23, y)
```

Since y is of type *mod*24, and since there is an *operator+* function that takes two *mod*24 arguments, the compiler will try to convert the *int* expression 23 to type *mod*24. Thanks to our *mod*24 constructor, which accepts an *int* argument, such a conversion is indeed possible, so the above function call is correct.

This *implicit conversion*, made possible by the constructor, is also performed in other situations, such as in the assignment that occurs in the following fragment:

```
mod24 x;
x = 60;           // Implicit conversion from int to mod24
cout << x << endl; // Output: 12 (since 60 modulo 24 = 12)
```

We could have made the conversion explicit by replacing the second of these three lines with one of the following ones:

```
x = mod24(60);            // Explicit call to constructor
x = static_cast<mod24)(60);  // Cast
```

The word *explicit*

In this example, the advantages of explicit calls to the constructor are not clear. However, there may be cases in which one wants to make implicit conversion by a certain constructor impossible, so that the programmer is forced to use explicit conversion. This can be realized, simply by inserting the word *explicit* at the beginning of the constructor. In other words, if we replace the first line of our *mod*24 constructor with

```
explicit mod24(int x = 0)
```

we would have to change the *main* function as well, replacing, for example,

```
x + 5
```

with one of these expressions:

```
x + mod24(5)
x + static_cast<mod24>(5)
```

and replacing 23 + *y* similarly.

So far we have taken for granted that the following two ways of initializing variables are equivalent, but there is a difference, as the comments indicate:

```
mod24 x(23), y(5);    // Correct
mod24 x = 23, y = 5; // Wrong if constructor is explicit
```

It is instructive to compare this second line with the following (rather clumsy) one, which also contains equal signs, but in which the constructor calls are explicit:

```
mod24 x = mod24(23), y = mod24(5);   // Correct
```

With a constructor that takes an *int* argument and begins with the word *explicit*, this last line and the first of the above pair of lines are correct because the calls to this constructor are explicit. On the other hand, the second of the above line pair is wrong (as the comment indicates) because it expresses implicit conversion from *int* to *mod24*.

A similar distinction applies to the following ways of initializing the array *a*:

```
mod24 a[3] = {mod24(10), mod24(20), mod24(30)};
                        // Correct
mod24 a[3] = {4, 18, 10};
                        // Wrong if constructor is explicit
                        // but otherwise correct.
```

A different solution: two special *operator+* functions

Suppose we want to maintain the word *explicit* at the beginning of the *mod24* constructor but nevertheless use expressions such as *x* + 5 and 23 + *y*. A simple and straightforward solution to this problem is adding two special *operator+* functions for these purposes. All we have to do in the program *mod24.cpp* is to insert the following functions, in addition to the one that is already there:

```
mod24 operator+(const mod24 &a, int b)
{  return mod24(a.getvalue() + b);
}

mod24 operator+(int a, const mod24 &b)
{  return mod24(a + b.getvalue());
}
```

For each of the following expressions a different function will now be used:

```
x + y
x + 5
23 + y
```

Conversion member functions

So far, we have discussed conversions from a primitive type to a class type, such as that from *int* to *mod*24. If the inverse conversion is required, we can use a *conversion member function*, which consists of a public member function that begins with the words *operator* and *int* and that has no parameters. In our class *mod*24 we might write this function as follows:

```
operator int()const {return t;}
```

By doing this, *mod*24 objects are implicitly converted to *int* if this is required. For example, with objects *x* and *y* of type *mod*24, this *operator int* function enables us to write the following statements in the *main* function:

```
int i = x;        // x is converted to int
int j = x * y;    // Both x and y are converted to int
int k = 3 * y;
i = y;            // y is converted to int
```

With only one function *operator+* , as in the original program *mod*24.*cpp*, we cannot write mixed expressions such as in

```
int k = 3 + y;
```

since it would now not be clear which of the two possibilities applies: (1) converting the first operand from *int* to *mod*24 so that our own *operator+* function is used, or (2) converting the second operand from *mod*24 to *int* so that the standard operator + applies. In other words, the situation is ambiguous. Here, at last, it really makes sense to make the *mod*24 constructor explicit. If we replace its first line with

```
explicit mod24(int x = 0)
```

then only the above possibility (2) remains, since (1) is based on an implicit conversion that cannot take place.

If there are also the two extra *operator+* functions, discussed above with *x* + 5 and 23 + *y* as examples, then these are taken because they do not require any conversion at all. (In this case it does not make any difference whether the word *explicit* is used for the constructor.) Apparently, if there are several possibilities with regard to choosing an operator function but only one is very straightforward, this one is taken and the situation is *not* ambiguous. Incidentally, this principle is not restricted to overloaded operators, but it applies to overloading in general.

In Section 10.4 we will use a conversion member function belonging to the standard class *istream* and declared as follows:

```
operator void*()const;
```

This function can convert an input stream to a void-pointer.

6.8 Destructor and Default Constructor

Let us now consider a class *row*, which has two data members:

- A pointer *ptr*, pointing to a sequence of integers.
- An integer *len*, which is the length of that sequence.

Figure 6.2 shows two objects, *r* and *s*, of such a class type, along with two sequences of three and five integers, respectively.

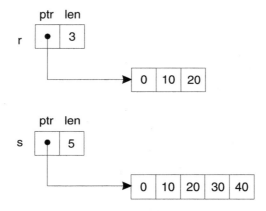

Figure 6.2. Variable-length sequences

If *ptr* and *len*, mentioned above, were the only members of the class *row*, so that this class did not contain any constructors or other member functions, the declaration on the second line of the function

```
void tworows()
{   row r, s;
    ...
}
```

would not create any integer sequences such as shown in Figure 6.2. In order to allocate memory space for these, we could insert

```
r.ptr = new int[3]; r.len = 3;
s.ptr = new int[5]; s.len = 5;
```

in this function. When leaving the above function *tworows*, memory space would automatically be released for *r* and *s*, but not for the two integer sequences pointed to. It would therefore be necessary to insert

```
    delete[] r.ptr;
    delete[] s.ptr;
```

at the end of function *tworows*. All of this would be very inconvenient and a potential source of programming errors. It would be much better if we could arrange for all required memory space to be automatically allocated and released. Since we are familiar with the notion of *constructor*, we can use this to allocate memory when the object is created. Fortunately, it is also possible to define a member function that is called automatically when the object is destroyed. We use this function, referred to as a *destructor*, to release the memory space allocated by a constructor. The name of a destructor consists of the character ~, followed by the name of the class. In our example this name is therefore *~row*. The following program shows further details:

```
// rows0.cpp: A class with a pointer, preliminary version.
#include <iostream>
#include <string>
using namespace std;

class row {
public:
    row(int n = 3)
    {  len = n; ptr = new int[n];
       for (int i=0; i<n; ++i) ptr[i] = 10 * i;
    }
    ~row() {delete[] ptr;}
    void printrow(const string &str)const
    {  cout << str;
       for (int i=0; i<len; ++i) cout << ptr[i] << ' ';
       cout << endl;
    }
private:
    int *ptr, len;
};

void tworows()
{  row r, s(5);
   r.printrow("r: ");
   s.printrow("s: ");
}

int main()
{  tworows();
   return 0;
}
```

The class *row* has not only the data members *ptr* and *len* but also the function members *row*( ), *~row*( ), and *printrow*( ). Like a constructor, a destructor does not return a value and it does not begin with the word *void*. A class can have several constructors but at most one destructor. For the objects *r* and *s* of the class *row*, the destructor *~row*( ) is automatically called when these objects cease to exist. In the function *tworows*( ), both the constructor *row*( ) and the destructor *~row*( ) are called twice: the constructor is called when *r* and *s* are created in their declarations, and the destructor on return from *tworows* to *main*. Thanks to these calls, memory for the integer sequences is automatically allocated and released in the same way as it is for the (smaller) objects *r* and *s*.

In this example, the *row* constructor has a default argument 3, which applies to *r*, since no argument is given for it in the declaration

```
row r, s(5);
```

For *s*, however, the argument 5 is used. As a result of this declaration, the constructor *row*( ) is executed twice, first with the default argument 3 for *r* and then with argument 5 for *s*. As discussed in Section 6.5, we must not replace *r* with *r*( ) in the above declaration.

Instead of providing the *row* constructor with a default argument, we could have used two distinct constructors, one with a parameter and one without. In other words, we could have written the two constructors

```
row(int n)
{  len = n; ptr = new int[n];
   for (int i=0; i<n; ++i) ptr[i] = 10 * i;
}
row()
{  len = 3; ptr = new int[3];
   for (int i=0; i<3; ++i) ptr[i] = 10 * i;
}
```

instead of the single *row* constructor in program *rows0.cpp*. Then the above definitions of *r* (without an argument) and *s* (with argument 5) would have had the same effect as they have in the program.

Default constructor

A constructor without parameters or with only default parameters is called a *default constructor*, but we also use this term differently. If we have a class that has no constructor at all, we say that a call to a default constructor takes place whenever an object of that class is created. In other words, there are two kinds of default constructor: (1) parameterless constructors, or constructors with only default parameters, of our own, and (2) fictitious ones for classes which do not contain any (visible) constructors. A declaration such as

```
Myclass r;
```

is allowed only if *Myclass* has a default constructor. It follows that this declaration is not allowed, for example, if there is exactly one *Myclass* constructor with one parameter which is not a default parameter. If we remove this constructor, the class is said to have a default constructor, so that the above declaration becomes valid.

As discussed in Section 6.3, we could have used the special initialization syntax instead of assignment in the *row* constructor of program *rows0.cpp*, writing

```
row(int n = 3): len(n), ptr(new int[n])
{  for (int i=0; i<n; ++i) ptr[i] = 10 * i;
}
```

A warning

The above discussion of classes that contain pointers is in a sense incomplete. It does not enable you to write correct realistic programs, in which objects of such classes are copied, as we will see in the next section.

Class declarations that are not definitions and nested classes

Suppose that a class *A* contains a member of type 'pointer to class *B*'. It is then not necessary that the definition of class *B* precedes that of *A*, because the amount of memory required for this pointer member does not depend on the data members of *B*. On the other hand, we have to indicate that *B* is really some class. This is done by writing a class declaration that is not a definition, as the following fragment shows:

```
class B;      // Declaration of B

class A {     // Definition of A
   ...
   B *p;      // Pointer to B used before definition of B
   ...
};

class B {     // Definition of B
   ...
};
```

In this fragment we cannot insert

```
B b;
```

in class *A* because *b* is not a pointer, so that this definition of the member *b* is allowed only after that of the class *B*. In other words, we can solve this problem by defining *B* before *A*.

If *B* is used only inside class *A*, it is a very good idea to define *B* inside *A*, so that these two classes are 'nested.' Although this is not necessary, we may as well then combine the definitions of the class *B* and variables such as *b* and *p*, as the following fragment shows:

```
class A {
   ...
   class B {
      ...
   } b, *p;
   ...
};
```

Class objects and *sizeof*

We should be very careful with using the operator *sizeof* for classes that contain pointers. The problem is that the number of bytes found by means of *sizeof* includes such pointers but not the data pointed to (see Figure 6.2). For example, suppose that we write

```
row r(1000);
```

Although this implies that a row of 1000 integers is created, the value of

```
sizeof(r)
```

is typically equal to only 8. This is because only the memory shown in Figure 6.2 on the left is taken into account, not the memory that is dynamically allocated. The same principle applies to the important standard class *string*. For example, after

```
string s("This is an example of a string"), t;
```

the values of *sizeof*(s) and *sizeof*(t) will be the same with most implementations. With Visual C++ we have

```
sizeof(s) = sizeof(t) = 16
```

6.9 Copying a Class Object

A class object that contains a pointer to dynamically allocated memory can be copied in two ways. If, as often is the case, a class contains only member functions and simple data members (which are not classes themselves), copying is by default done 'bitwise': all members, including pointers, are copied literally. We call the result a *shallow copy*; the contents of the memory area pointed to are not copied, and the copied pointer is identical to the original one. This way of copying is illustrated in Figure 6.3(a). Second, we can copy that memory area as well, using newly allocated memory for it. The result is referred to as a *deep copy*. As Figure 6.3(b) shows, the pointer of the deep copy differs from the original one.

A shallow copy and its original object share the area pointed to, while a deep copy has such an area of its own. The distinction between these two copying methods is particularly important if the memory area in question is allocated by a constructor and deleted by a destructor. What we then need is deep copies. If shallow copies were made, applying the destructor to both the original object and the copy would result in deleting the shared area twice, which is illegal and will usually cause the program to crash.

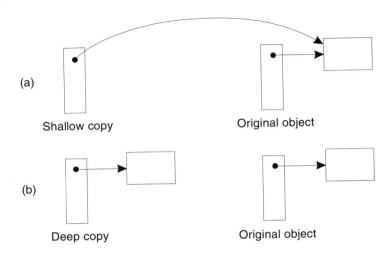

(a)

Shallow copy   Original object

(b)

Deep copy   Original object

Figure 6.3. Two kinds of copies: (a) shallow copy; (b) deep copy

Copy constructors

Copying an object occurs more frequently than you may expect. For example, in

```
mytype x(123), y(x);  // or mytype x = 123, y = x;
```

the object *x* is copied into object *y*. Also, in a call to the following function *f*, the argument is copied into parameter *w*:

```
mytype f(mytype w)
{   mytype z;
    ...
    return z;
}
```

If we use call by reference instead, writing *mytype f(const mytype &w)*, the argument in a call to *f* would not be copied. In the above function *f*, copying occurs once again in the return statement. Unfortunately, we cannot prevent this by returning a reference (inserting an ampersand just before the function name *f*), because we must not return a reference to a local variable.

For all copying operations other than by assignment, a special constructor, known as a *copy constructor* is used. If we want to write this ourselves for the class *mytype*, it would start as follows:

```
mytype(const mytype &v)
```

This constructor has the task of specifying how copying is to be done. The class name *mytype* is used here both as a function name and as a parameter name. Remember also that a copy constructor always has a reference parameter, as the ampersand indicates. The keyword *const* indicates that the copy constructor will not change the value of the argument. How copy constructors can be defined will be demonstrated shortly in a complete program.

If we do not supply a class with a copy constructor, it is still possible to copy class objects because a *default copy constructor* is then used. Recall that we used a default copy constructor in Section 6.5, writing

```
DateDM dateB(dateA);
```

which is similar to

```
mytype y(x);
```

If the class in question does not contain any pointers to dynamically allocated memory, a default copy constructor is just what we want, so we had better not write a copy constructor ourselves in this case. If there are such pointers, a default copy would generate a shallow copy, which we prevent by supplying our own copy constructor, to be used instead of the default one.

Copying by assignment operators

It goes without saying that copying also takes place in assignments, such as in the second line of

```
mytype x(123), y;
y = x;
```

However, this example of copying is essentially different from the previous ones, because here the equal sign is an operator. Although initialization and assignment look very much the same, they are distinct language constructs. To prevent shallow copying taking place in assignments, we have to define a *copy assignment operator*, which (for the class *mytype*) begins as follows:

```
mytype &operator=(const mytype &v)
```

The overloaded copy assignment operator (=) must specify how a deep copy is to be made. (The word *copy* at the beginning of the term *copy assignment operator* is used to distinguish this assignment operator = from others, such as +=.) As mentioned in Section 6.6, assignment operators can only be defined as member functions. If we define such a member function for a class of which *x* and *y* are objects, then the expression

```
x = y
```

is equivalent to the following one:

```
x.operator=(y)
```

Copying demonstrated by an example

Our class *row* in the program *rows0.cpp*, discussed in the previous section, did not contain a copy constructor and an *operator=* function. It is now time to add these to that program, and we may as well define all member functions outside the class *row*. To demonstrate that *row* can now be copied, the way we use the class *row* here is different from that in the previous section, as the following program shows:

```cpp
// rows.cpp: A class with a pointer.
#include <iostream>
#include <string>

using namespace std;

class row {
public:
    row(int n = 3);              // Default constructor
    row(const row &r);           // Copy constructor
    ~row();                      // Destructor
    row &operator=(const row &r);   // Copy assignment operator
    void printrow(const string &str)const;
private:
    int *ptr, len;
};

row::row(int n)                  // default = 3 not repeated here
{  len = n; ptr = new int[n];
   for (int i=0; i<n; ++i) ptr[i] = 10 * i;
}


row::row(const row &r)           // Copy constructor
{  len = r.len;
   ptr = new int[len];
   for (int i=0; i<len; ++i) ptr[i] = r.ptr[i];
}


row::~row() {delete[] ptr;}      // Destructor

row &row::operator=(const row &r) // Copy assignment operator
{  if (&r != this)
   {  delete[] ptr;
      len = r.len;
      ptr = new int[len];
      for (int i=0; i<len; ++i) ptr[i] = r.ptr[i];
   }
   return *this;
}
```

```
void row::printrow(const string &str)const
{  cout << str;
   for (int i=0; i<len; ++i) cout << ptr[i] << ' ';
   cout << endl;
}

int main()
{  row r, s(5), t(s);
   r = s;
   r.printrow("r: ");
   s.printrow("s: ");
   t.printrow("t: ");
   return 0;
}
```

The way the variable *t* is initialized requires a copy operator, because what we need is a deep copy of *s*. Similarly, assigning *s* to *r* requires a copy assignment operator. The copy constructor in this program is not difficult: on the basis of the argument *r* a new, identical object is generated. The copy assignment operator is more tricky:

```
row &row::operator=(const row &r) // Copy assignment operator
{  if (&r != this)
   {  delete[] ptr;
      len = r.len;
      ptr = new int[len];
      for (int i=0; i<len; ++i) ptr[i] = r.ptr[i];
   }
   return *this;
}
```

In case you are puzzled by the beginning of this function, note that the first word *row* and the first ampersand indicate that this function returns a reference to a *row* object, as might have been clearer if we had begun this function as follows:

```
row& row::operator=
```

The function would have been even clearer if this beginning had been written

```
void row::operator=
```

while at the same time the return statement had been omitted. In that case there would not have been any problem with the use of the class *row* in the current version of the program, but a statement of the form

```
t = s = r;
```

would then not have been allowed. With the class as defined in the program, such a statement is permitted, since the assignment *s* = *r* returns a reference to the object *s* which can successively be used for the assignment of a value to the variable *t*. In general, this return value is a reference to the object for which the function is called. Since *this*, discussed in Section 6.2, is a pointer to this object, this object itself is denoted by *this, which explains the statement

```
return *this;
```

at the end of the function.

This pointer *this* also occurs in the test

```
if (&r != this)
```

at the beginning of the function. This is a test to see if *r*, that is, the right-hand side of the assignment, happens to be the same object as that for which the function is called, that is, the left-hand side. We actually test whether the addresses of these two object are equal (or rather, unequal). Suppose someone writes

```
r = r;
```

Although it highly unlikely that we would ever write such a statement, we will not make this impossible. If we omitted the above test, the statement

```
delete[] ptr;
```

which is intended to release the dynamic array belonging to the left-hand-side object because we no longer need this, would be executed also in the assignment *r = r*. However, this must not happen, because in this special case the dynamic array just mentioned also belongs to the right-hand-side object, which is still needed to copy the data from. We could solve the problem in a different way by executing this delete operation after copying, as the following version shows:

```
row &row::operator=(const row &r) // Copy assignment operator
{   len = r.len;              // Second version, not recommended
    int *ptr0 = ptr;
    ptr = new int[len];
    for (int i=0; i<len; ++i) ptr[i] = r.ptr[i];
    delete[] ptr0;
    return *this;
}
```

The fact that this function does some superfluous work in the case of *r = r* is not a serious problem because this case is very far-fetched. This version is nevertheless slightly inferior to the original one because it is less economical with memory in the case of normal assignments. Since a new array is already allocated for the left-hand side before the old one is released, the amount of memory that is temporarily in use will be much more than is required if these dynamic arrays are very large. We therefore prefer the original version, which contains an if-statement to deal with the special case mentioned.

Remembering to provide a copy constructor and a copy assignment operator for classes such as *row* is particularly important because the compiler does not give any help if we omit these two functions. For example, in the program *rows0.cpp* of the previous section, each of the following lines, when inserted in the function *tworows* just before the first call to *printrow*, may cause the program to crash:

```
row t(s);    // Requires copy constructor
r = s;       // Requires copy assignment operator
```

Since the program *rows0.cpp* contains neither a copy constructor nor a copy assignment operator, shallow copies are made on each of these two lines. As follows from Figure 6.3 (a), there will then be only one dynamic array, referred to by pointers in the objects *r*, *s*, and *t*. Then later the destructor *~row*, when called for these objects, will release this dynamic array three times, which is a very nasty error.

Disabling default copy constructor and copy assignment operator

If we do not want to provide a copy constructor and a copy assignment operator for a class because we do not intend to copy objects of this class at all, it is wise to write such functions with an empty body but making them private. The compiler will then spot any attempt to make such copies and produce error messages. For example, if in the program *rows.cpp* we omit the definitions of the copy constructor and the copy assignment operator outside the class *row* and we define this class as

```
class row {          // Objects of this class cannot be copied
public:
   row(int n = 3);                 // Default constructor
   row(const row &r);              // Copy constructor
   ~row();                         // Destructor
   void printrow(const string &str)const;
private:
   void operator=(const row &r){} // Copy assignment operator
   row(const row &r){}            // Copy constructor
   int *ptr, len;
};
```

then the following program lines in the *main* function will result in two error messages:

```
row r, s(5), t(s);  // Illegal (copy constructor private)
r = s;              // Illegal (assignment operator private)
```

First, the declaration of *t* requires a copy constructor, which is inaccessible because it is preceded by the word *private*. Second, the assignment *r = s* requires an assignment operator, which is also inaccessible. If we omitted the copy constructor and the copy assignment operator altogether, the default versions of them would be used, so that the last two program lines would compile successfully, but then the program would probably crash during execution, as we discussed a short while ago.

Memberwise copying

At the beginning of this section, we restricted our discussion to classes that have no other classes as their members. If classes do have other classes as their members, the default copying method is not exactly 'bitwise,' but what is called *memberwise*. Suppose that class C has a member class M and that an object of class C is to be copied. Obviously, copying this object implies copying its M member. If C has no user-defined copy constructor, but its member M has, this copy constructor of M is called in the process of copying the M member. All members of C that are not classes are copied bitwise.

6.10 Inheritance

Suppose we have defined a certain class type B, and we want a new one, D, consisting of all members of class B and some additional members besides. Instead of copying the members of B in our program, we can then simply refer to B in the declaration of D. The new class D is said to be *derived from* the original class B, which is referred to as the *base class* of D. We say that a derived class *inherits* the members of its base class. Any object of the derived type D is at the same time an object of the base type B, while the reverse is not true. In some other languages, such as Java, the terms *superclass* and *subclass* are used instead of base and derived classes.

For example, let us consider the class *Shape* for two-dimensional geometrical objects, defined as follows:

```
class Shape {
public:
    Shape(double x = 0, double y = 0): xC(x), yC(y){}
    void printcenter()const
    {  cout << xC << " " << yC << endl;
    }
protected:
    double xC, yC;
};
```

The data members xC and yC are the coordinates of the center of a *Shape* object. As for the new keyword *protected*, we will discuss this shortly. We can do very little with this class type, nor does it give any information about what kind of objects it will be used for. We now want to use two types of very specific shapes, namely circles and squares, and we will derive the classes for these objects from *Shape*, as Figure 6.4 illustrates:

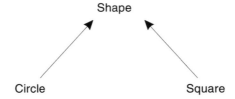

Figure 6.4. Base class and two derived classes

As usual, a circle is characterized by its center and its radius. As for a square, let us represent it by its center and one of its four vertices (or corner points). Since we will compute the areas of this circle and this square, let us first deal with a little elementary mathematics. As you probably know, the area of a circle with radius r is computed as follows:

Area of circle $= \pi r^2$

As for the square, we have to compute its area on the basis of its center $C(x_C, y_C)$ and one of its vertices, say, $P(x_P, y_P)$, as Figure 6.5 illustrates.

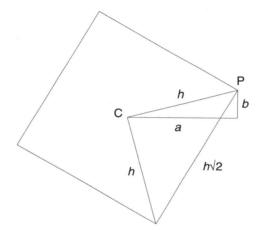

Figure 6.5. Square with given center C and corner point P

Let us denote the distance between these two points by h. We can compute this distance using

$h^2 = a^2 + b^2$

where

$a^2 = (x_P - x_C)^2$
$b^2 = (y_P - y_C)^2$

Since each edge of the square is equal to $h\sqrt{2}$, we find

Area of square $= (h\sqrt{2})^2 = 2h^2 = 2(a^2 + b^2)$

We can now benefit from our class *Shape* by defining the derived classes *Circle* and *Square* as shown in the following complete program:

```cpp
// derived.cpp: Classes Circle and Square derived from
//              class Shape.
#include <iostream>
using namespace std;

class Shape {
public:
   Shape(double x = 0, double y = 0): xC(x), yC(y){}
   void printcenter()const
   { cout << xC << " " << yC << endl;
   }
protected:
   double xC, yC;
};

const double pi = 3.1415926535897932;

class Circle: public Shape {
public:
   Circle(double xC, double yC, double r)
   :Shape(xC, yC)
   { radius = r;
   }
   double area()const {return pi * radius * radius;}
private:
   double radius;
};

class Square: public Shape {
public:
   Square(double xC, double yC, double xP, double yP)
   :Shape(xC, yC)
   { this->xP = xP;
      this->yP = yP;
   }
   double area()const
   { double a = xP - xC, b = yP - yC;
      return 2 * (a * a + b * b); // See Figure 6.5
   }
private:
   double xP, yP;
};

int main()
{ double xCircle = 2, yCircle = 2.5, radius = 2;
   Circle circle(xCircle, yCircle, radius);
   cout << "Center of circle: "; circle.printcenter();
   cout << "Radius: " << radius << endl;
   cout << "Area of circle:   " << circle.area() << endl
        << endl;
```

```
        double xCsquare = 3, yCsquare = 3.5,
            xP = 4.37, yP = 3.85;
        Square square(xCsquare, yCsquare, xP, yP);
        cout << "Center of square: "; square.printcenter();
        cout << "xP = " << xP << "  yP = " << yP << endl;
        cout << "Area of square:   " << square.area() << endl;
        return 0;
    }
```

In the definition of each of the classes *Circle* and *Square*, the first line shows the name of the base class *Shape*. The two derived classes *Circle* and *Square* are to be regarded as extensions of their base class *Shape*. Any *Circle* or *Square* object is also a *Shape* object. The keyword *public* as used in

```
    class Circle: public Shape {
```

specifies that all public members of the base class *Shape* are also public members of the derived class *Circle*. Class *Circle* is therefore said to be *publicly derived* from class *Shape*. For example, we can write

```
    Circle circle(xCircle, yCircle, radius);
    circle.printcenter();
```

Although *printcenter* does not occur directly in the declaration of class *Circle*, it is nevertheless one of its public member functions because it is a public member of class *Shape* from which class *Circle* has been publicly derived. Another point to be noted is the use of *xC* and *yC* in the *area* member function of class *Square*. These are protected members of the base class *Shape*, as the keyword *protected* indicates. Protected members are similar to private ones. The only difference is that a derived class has access to the protected members, not to the private members, of its base class.

User-defined copy assignment operators

If a copy assignment operator is defined as a member function (*operator*=) of a base class, it is not inherited by any derived class. This is because a copy assignment operator (creating a shallow copy) is implicitly declared for any class in which we do not write one ourselves. As discussed in the previous section, the distinction between shallow and deep copies is relevant only for classes that contain pointers to dynamically created memory. Implicit copy assignment operators are therefore sufficient in the classes *Shape*, *Circle*, and *Square*, so that we need not define such operators of our own here.

Constructors and destructors of derived and base classes

The derived classes *Circle* and *Square* can be regarded as extensions of their base class *Shape*. When an object of, for example, type *Square* is created, as is done by the above declaration of the variable *square*, the constructor of the base class *Shape* is called first; then that of *Square* is called. Conversely, when an object of a derived class is destroyed, destructors, if any, are called in the reverse order: first that of the derived class and then that of the base class.

We can pass arguments from the constructor in a derived class to the constructor of its base class. As we normally do this to initialize data members of the base class, the way we write this down is in the form of a constructor initializer, also discussed in Section 6.3. In the constructors of both *Circle* and *Square*, this initializer is

```
:Shape(xC, yC)
```

Since the *Shape* constructor has default arguments, this initializer is not obligatory here. If we omit it, the constructor of *Shape* is called with its default argument values 0. The initializer would really have been required if there had been no default arguments, that is, if in the constructor

```
Shape(double x = 0, double y = 0): xC(x), yC(y){}
```

(see the beginning of this section) we had omitted the two occurrences of $= 0$. In our example the values of xC and yC, as supplied to the derived class, are passed to the constructor of the base class *Shape*, and stored as the members xC and yC of this class.

Because of the way we use the classes *Circle* and *Square* in the *main* function, the program *derived.cpp* produces the following output:

```
Center of circle: 2 2.5
Radius: 2
Area of circle:    12.5664

Center of square: 3 3.5
xP = 4.37   yP = 3.85
Area of square:    3.9988
```

Figure 6.6 shows the circle and the square that are based on the above data.

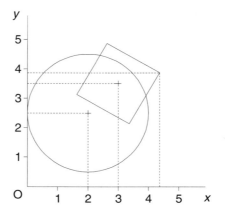

Figure 6.6. Circle and square

In the example we have been discussing, the relationship between the base class and its derived classes is illustrated by Figure 6.4. The situation can be more complicated. First, derived classes can act as base classes for other (derived) classes, so that we can build a more complex tree of classes, as shown in Figure 6.7.

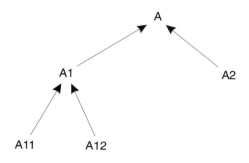

Figure 6.7. A tree of classes

Here class $A1$, although derived from class A, is the base class of $A11$ and $A12$. Second, base and derived classes need not form a tree, as we will see in a moment, when discussing multiple inheritance.

Overriding members of base classes

If a base class B and a class D derived from B contain a function with the same name and the same signature, this function of class D is said to *override* that of class B. Overriding data members is also possible. To demonstrate all this, let us use a class D containing a public *int* data member i and a function member *compute*. The base class B, from which D is derived, has similar members. Since inheritance implies an extension of the base class, there are actually two data members i in an object d of class D, as Figure 6.8 illustrates.

	B::i	(D::)i
d	6	5

Figure 6.8. An inherited data member in class D

The name i in class D overrides (or *hides*) this name of the base class B, so that i used in D means in fact $D::i$. We can nevertheless access the member i of class B in class D by using its full name $B::i$. The following program demonstrates the use of both data members i and of similar function members:

```
// ovride.cpp: The principle of overriding.
#include <iostream>
using namespace std;

class B {
public:
   int i;
   int compute()const{return i * i;}
};

class D: public B {
public:
   int i;
   int compute()const{return i + B::i;}
};

int main()
{  D d;
   d.i = 5; d.B::i = 6;
   cout << "d.compute()     = " << d.compute() << endl;
   cout << "d.B::compute() = " << d.B::compute() << endl;
   return 0;
}
```

The output of this program is shown below:

```
d.compute()     = 11
d.B::compute() = 36
```

The first value, 11, is the result of the *compute* function of class *D*. By calling this function for the object *d*, we compute the sum of the values 6 and 5, stored in this object as shown in Figure 6.8. In contrast, the value on the second line results from a call to the other *compute* function, *B::compute*, which computes $i * i$, where i is actually $B::i = 6$.

Name hiding prevented by a using-declaration

Let us again use a base class *B*, from which the class *D* is derived. If the classes *B* and *D* contain public functions with the same name, say, *f*, then *B::f* hides *D::f* even if these functions have different signatures. In the following program, *B::f* has no parameters, while *D::f* has an *int* parameter.

```
// nohiding.cpp: The principle of overriding.
#include <iostream>
using namespace std;

class B {
public:
   int f()const{return 1;}
};
```

```
class D: public B {
public:
   using B::f;
   int f(int k)const{return k;}
};

int main()
{  D d;
   cout << "d.f()  = " << d.f() << endl;
   return 0;
}
```

This programs contains two functions *f*:

```
B::f()
D::f(int)
```

Choosing the right one might seem to be a simple case of overloading, but it is not. Notice the using-declaration

```
using B::f;
```

under *public* in class *D*. This is required here to make *B::f* publicly available through class *D*. Without this using-declaration, the call *d.f*( ) in the *main* function would have resulted in an error message, such as

```
'f'  : function does not take 0 parameters
```

because there are no arguments in this call, while *D::f* has one parameter. As intended, the function *B::f* is called in the program because of the using-declaration. We could have omitted this using-declaration if, in the *main* function, we had written

```
d.B::f()
```

instead of just

```
d.f()
```

Conversion from derived to base class

If *B* is a base class from which *D* is derived, implicit conversion from *D* to *B* is possible, but, even with a cast, conversion from *B* to *D* is impossible. As for the corresponding pointer types, implicit conversion from *D** to *B** is possible, while a *static_cast* is required for the conversion from *B** to *D**. The following program illustrates all this:

```
// convdb.cpp: Conversion from derived to base class.
#include <iostream>
using namespace std;

class B {
public:
   int i;
   B(int ii = 0): i(ii){}
};

class D: public B {
public:
   float x;
   D(float xx): B(1), x(xx){}
};

int main()
{  B b(2), *pb = &b;
   D d(3.4F), *pd = &d;
   b = d;        // From derived to base: OK
   cout << "b: " << b.i << endl;
   cout << "d: " << pd->i << " " << pd->x << endl;

   pb = pd;      // Corresponding pointer types: OK
// d = b;        // Would be an error; nor is a cast possible
// pd = pb;      // Would be an error
   pd = static_cast<D*>(pb);
                 // With cast: OK (if pb points to a D object)
   cout << "After pb = pd; pd = static_cast<D*>(pb); "
           "we have\n";
   cout << "d (reached via pd): " << pd->i << " " << pd->x
        << endl;
   return 0;
}
```

The object *b* initially contains the value *i* = 2, while object *d* contains the values *i* = 1 (as specified in the constructor initializer of *D*) and *x* = 3.4. By executing

```
b = d;
```

all data members of *d* that fit into *b* are copied, which is only the value *i* = 1. This explains the first two lines of the following output:

```
b: 1
d: 1 3.4
After pb = pd; pd = static_cast<D*>(pb); we have
d (reached via pd): 1 3.4
```

The statement

```
pb = pd;
```

illustrates that it is easy and safe to make a pointer to a base class point to an object of a derived class, while the reverse is not generally true. However, now that we know that *pb* actually points to an object of type *D*, it is safe to perform this reverse operation. Since such an operation is not safe in all circumstances, we have to indicate that we know what we are doing by writing

```
pd = static_cast<D*>(pb);
```

instead of the following simpler statement, which is not allowed:

```
pd = pb;   // Incorrect
```

Because *pd* still points to *d*, we have *pd–>i* = 1 and *pd–>x* = 3.4, as the last line of the above output shows.

Class *D* contains the member *x* that does not belong to class *B*. The assignment *b* = *d* will simply omit this member *x* of *d*, since there is no room for it in *b*. Yet this is a safe operation in that it will not cause any members of *b* to be undefined. The reverse assignment, *d* = *b* is not allowed, because if it were, this member *x* would obtain some undefined value, which is clearly undesirable.

The possibility of a pointer to a base class pointing to an object of a derived class enables us to use an array of pointers that point to objects of different types. For example, if *B* is a base class of which *D*0, *D*1, and *D*2 are derived, and *d*0, *d*1, and *d*2 are objects of these three derived classes, it is possible to write

```
B *a[3];       // An array of pointers to objects of type B
a[0] = &d0;
a[1] = &d1;
a[2] = &d2;
```

This idea prepares for the notion of *polymorphism*, as we will see in Section 6.11.

There is another, important case in which a pointer to a base class actually points to an object of a derived class. Suppose the classes *D*1, *D*2, and *D*3 are derived from the base class *B*. Then we can pass objects of these three derived classes (or rather, the addresses of these objects) as arguments to the same function, writing, for example,

```
void f(const B *p){...}
...
D1 d1;
D2 d2;
D3 d3;
f(&d1); f(&d2); f(&d3);
```

The same applies to reference parameters, so that, with the above variables $d1$, $d2$, and $d3$, the following is also possible:

```
void g(const B &x){...}
...
g(d1); g(d2); g(d3);
```

Multiple inheritance

So far, it was taken for granted that each derived class should have only one base class. Actually, C++ supports *multiple inheritance*, which means that it is possible for a class to be derived from more than one base class. For example, the situation can be as shown in Figure 6.9, where the derived class *AB* has both class *A* and class *B* as its base classes.

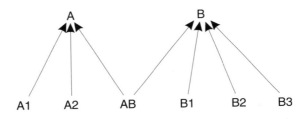

Figure 6.9. Multiple inheritance

If we want the public members of *A* and *B* to be public members of *AB*, we write the beginning to class *AB* as follows:

```
class AB: public A, public B {
    ...
}
```

If *AB* has a constructor with parameters, we can pass these to each base class as, for example, in:

```
AB(int n = 0, float x = 0, char ch = 'A')
    :A(n, ch), B(n, x)
{   ...
}
```

The creation of an object of class *AB* causes the three constructors for *A*, *B*, and *AB*, in that order, to be called.

6.11 Virtual Functions

Suppose we have declared class *ctype* as follows:

```
class ctype {
public:
    virtual void f() { ... }
    ...
};
```

The keyword *virtual* is relevant if *ctype* has derived classes, say, *ctype*1 and *ctype*2, and if we are using pointers to class objects. When using class *ctype* to define a variable of this type, as in

```
ctype v;
```

we immediately create a class object. Instead, we can only define a pointer *p* and create a class object later, as is done in

```
ctype *p;
...
p = new ctype;
```

The *ctype* object **p* created in this way is only loosely related to *p*, since *p* can also point to other *ctype* objects. Suppose that we declare the derived classes *ctype*1 and *ctype*2 as follows:

```
class ctype1: public ctype {
public:
    void f() { ... }
    ...
};

class ctype2: public ctype {
public:
    void f() { ... }
    ...
};

ctype *p;
```

We have seen in the previous section (using the assignment *pb = pd*) that implicit conversion from 'pointer to derived class' to 'pointer to base class' is possible. It follows that in the above example we can write *p = new ctype*1 and *p = new ctype*2.

The three class types *ctype*, *ctype*1, and *ctype*2 have member functions with the same name (*f*). Because of the keyword *virtual* in the base class *ctype*, function *f* is what we call a *virtual function*. This means that only during the execution of the call

```
p -> f()
```

the decision is made which of the three functions (*ctype::f*, *ctype1::f*, or *ctype2::f*) is to be called. This decision is based on the type of the object pointed to by *p*. Since the correct function is not chosen at compile time but rather at execution time, the term *late* (or *dynamic*) *binding* is used for the relationship between the pointer *p* and the function in question. If we had omitted the keyword *virtual* in the declaration of *ctype*, only the type of *p* would have been used to decide which function to use. In other words, the function *ctype::f* would have been taken, even if *p* pointed to a *ctype1* or *ctype2* object. This is not unreasonable, since, as we know, a derived type is an extension of its base type(s), so all members of a base class also belong to its derived classes. Without the keyword *virtual*, the decision about which function is to be taken is already made at compile time, so in that case we speak of *early* (or *static*) *binding*.

We now turn to a simple but complete program with pointers to base and derived classes, to see a virtual function (named *print*) in action:

```
// virtual.cpp: A virtual function in action.

#include <iostream>
using namespace std;

class animal {
public:
   virtual void print()const    // Virtual print function
   {  cout << "Unknown animal type.\n";
   }
   virtual ~animal(){} // Virtual destructor, discussed below
protected:
   int nlegs;
};

class fish: public animal {
public:
   fish(int n) {nlegs = n;}
   void print()const
   {  cout << "A fish has " << nlegs << " legs.\n";
   }
};

class bird: public animal {
public:
   bird(int n){nlegs = n;}
   void print()const
   {  cout << "A bird has " << nlegs << " legs.\n";
   }
};
```

```
class mammal: public animal {
public:
   mammal(int n){nlegs = n;}
   void print()const
   {  cout << "A mammal has " << nlegs << " legs.\n";
   }
};

int main()
{  animal *p[4];
   int i;
   p[0] = new fish(0);
   p[1] = new bird(2);
   p[2] = new mammal(4);
   p[3] = new animal;
   for (i=0; i<4; ++i) p[i]->print();
   for (i=0; i<4; ++i) delete p[i];
   return 0;
}
```

In the program line

```
for (i=0; i<4; ++i) p[i]->print();
```

the four elements of the pointer array *p* point to objects of four different class types, for each of which there is a print function. It is clearly impossible for the compiler to determine from the statement

```
p[i]->print();
```

which of the four functions *fish::print*, *bird::print*, *mammal::print*, and *animal::print* applies. Thanks to the keyword *virtual* in the base class *animal*, this choice is made at run time. Before the for-statement is executed, the *new* operator is called four times to create the objects in question. They accommodate an anonymous member for the actual class type, to enable late binding. This program produces the following output:

```
A fish has 0 legs.
A bird has 2 legs.
A mammal has 4 legs.
Unknown animal type.
```

Instead of these four lines, the text of the fourth line would have been printed four times if we had used early binding, that is, if we had omitted the keyword *virtual*.

The use of derived classes and virtual functions is often referred to as *object-oriented programming* (OOP). Using pointers of a base class type that point to objects of different derived class types, while the objects themselves contain information about their types is also known as *polymorphism*.

As for terminology, it might be mentioned that member functions are sometimes called *methods* and that calling an object's member function is referred to as *sending a message to the object*. This terminology is particularly popular with users of some OOP languages other than C++.

Implementation

Although it is not really necessary for us as programmers to bother about implementation details, it is sometimes desirable to have some idea of how things actually work inside the computer. A common way of implementing virtual functions is by using a 'virtual function table' or *vtbl*. In our last example, array element *p*[0] points to a *fish* object, while *p*[1] points to a *bird* object. As for the actual contents in memory of a class object, we normally find only data members, not function members. However, if the class in question has virtual functions, every object of that class also contains the start address of a *vtbl*. There is only one *vtbl* for a class, and the entries of this table are pointers to the member functions of that class. In our example there are two virtual functions: *print* and the destructor, which we will discuss shortly. Let us assume that the index values 0 and 1 are used for these two functions, respectively. The compiler will then convert the name *print* into the index value 0. We now consider what happens when the statements

```
p[0]->print();   // fish::print
p[1]->print();   // bird::print
```

are executed. In the first statement, the index value 0 resulting from the function name *print* leads to the first entry of the *vtbl* of class *fish*, while in the second that value 0 leads to that of class *bird*. This is possible because the object **p*[0] contains the start address of the *vtbl* of *fish*, while the object **p*[1] contains the start address of that of *bird*.

Let us now experimentally compare the sizes of the objects of two similar classes, the only difference being that one has a virtual function and the other has not. Recall that this difference may also be expressed by the terms late and early binding, respectively. In the following program the classes *late* and *early* are identical but for the keyword *virtual*:

```
// late.cpp: This program shows that a class with a virtual
//           function takes more memory than a similar class
//           in which no function is virtual.
#include <iostream>
using namespace std;

class late  {public: int i; virtual void f(){i=1;}};
class early {public: int i; void f(){i=1;}};

int main()
{   cout << "late:   " << sizeof(late) << " bytes.\n";
    cout << "early:  " << sizeof(early) << " bytes.\n";
    return 0;
}
```

The program does not do any practical work but it illustrates the point we are discussing. The following output of this program (obtained with Visual C++) shows that late binding requires an anonymous member, which is a pointer to a virtual function table, if virtual functions are implemented as we have been discussing.

```
late:    8 bytes.
early:   4 bytes.
```

This output also shows that member functions are not really stored in the class objects themselves: since the *int* member *i* of class *early* already takes four bytes, which is the size of that whole class, it follows that function *f*, although a member of the class, is not really stored in objects of this class. (If it were, much memory space would be wasted in programs with a great number of objects of the same class.)

Virtual destructors

Let us now return to the program *virtual.cpp*. As you may have noticed, there is a virtual destructor, defined as

```
virtual ~animal(){}
```

in the base class *animal* of this program. This is related to the following program line, at the end of the program:

```
for (i=0; i<4; ++i) delete p[i];
```

This loop expresses that the object to which each *p[i]* points is to be deleted. In this particular example program, all objects are the same size, but in general this need not be the case. It is then required to release exactly the memory space taken by the object in question, but the pointer type used in the *delete* statement does not give enough information about this. By supplying a virtual destructor, the type of the object itself will be used instead of the type of the base class. Therefore, whenever objects of a derived class are dynamically created, it is good practice to provide the base class with a virtual destructor. The following program is more suitable to demonstrate this than the previous ones:

```
// virtdest.cpp: A virtual destructor.
#include <iostream>
using namespace std;

class B {
public:
   virtual ~B(){}
};
```

```
class D: public B {
public:
    D(){a = new int[100000];}
    ~D(){delete[] a; cout << "Memory released!\n";}
private:
    int *a;
};

void f()
{   B *p = new D;     // Memory is allocated for 100000 integers
    delete p;  // Released again, thanks to virtual destructor
}

int main()
{   f();
    return 0;
}
```

In the function *f* an object of type *D* is dynamically created, and the pointer *p* of the base class *B* is made to point to it. Since this object contains a dynamic *int* array of length 100 000, it is important that the memory for this should be released when we do not need this object any longer. It may seem obvious that the statement

```
delete p;
```

in the function *f* takes care of this. This is indeed the case, but it is not as straightforward as it looks. First, that memory will only be released if there is a destructor for this task (as discussed in the program *rows0.cpp* in Section 6.8). As you can see in the above class *D*, the constructor of this class is accompanied by a destructor which releases the allocated memory, so all seems to be fine. However, in the above *delete*-statement, *p* is of type 'pointer-to-*B*,' and the large array just mentioned does not belong to the base class *B* but to the derived class *D*, so it is questionable whether this destructor of *D* is actually executed. Thanks to the virtual destructor in the base class *B* this is indeed the case, so that the program works properly. It would not if the word *virtual*, or the whole destructor, in *B* had been omitted. To demonstrate this clearly, the destructor of *D* produces some output, consisting of the text

```
Memory released!
```

This output does not appear if the virtual destructor or the word *virtual* in class *B* is removed.

Reusability of software

An interesting point about derived classes is that they are not specified in their base classes, nor do base classes 'know' how many derived classes there are. Consequently, we can add derived classes later, without modifying either the base class or already existing derived classes. As discussed in Section 6.4, realistic C++ software projects normally consist of interface, implementation, and application files. Now suppose we want to program a new application of some class based on existing interface and implementation files which cover almost all we want, but in which some facilities are lacking or different from what we need. With a well-designed class hierarchy of base and derived classes, it will then be possible to write interface and implementation files for a new derived class, tailored to our application, and to use these in addition to the already existing interface and implementation files, without modifying or recompiling the latter. This idea can make software more *reusable* than it was with older programming methods.

Suppressing the virtual mechanism

In program *virtual.cpp*, we have seen that

```
p[i]->print();
```

with, for example, $i = 1$, calls the print function of the derived class *bird*, not that of the base class *animal*. However, we can use the scope-resolution operator :: to suppress this mechanism enabled by the keyword *virtual*. For example, the call

```
p[1]->animal::print();
```

would cause the print function of the base class *animal* to be called, which would produce another output line

```
Unknown animal type.
```

Pure virtual functions and abstract classes

In program *virtual.cpp*, the function *print* is defined not only in the derived classes *fish*, *bird*, and *mammal*, but also in the base class *animal*, because there is also an object of this base class in this program. If we had not felt a need for this (and we had been interested only in the first three of the four output lines), it would still have been necessary to write this function (with the keyword *virtual*) in the base class, but then we could have declared the *print* in the base class as a pure virtual function by writing

```
virtual void print()const = 0;
```

If we write this in the base class *animal* of the program *virtual.cpp*, this base class is said to be an *abstract class*, which implies that it cannot be used to create objects of this class. In other words, statements such as

```
p[3] = new animal;
animal A;
```

would then be invalid. This does not make this class completely useless, because we can still derive other classes from it, as the following version of our example shows:

```cpp
// purevirt.cpp: A pure virtual function.
#include <iostream>
using namespace std;

class animal {
public:
   virtual void print()const = 0;
   virtual ~animal(){}
protected:
   int nlegs;
};

class fish: public animal {
public:
   fish(int n) {nlegs = n;}
   void print()const
   {  cout << "A fish has " << nlegs << " legs.\n";
   }
};

class bird: public animal {
public:
   bird(int n){nlegs = n;}
   void print()const
   {  cout << "A bird has " << nlegs << " legs.\n";
   }
};

class mammal: public animal {
public:
   mammal(int n){nlegs = n;}
   void print()const
   {  cout << "A mammal has " << nlegs << " legs.\n";
   }
};

int main()
{  animal *p[3];
   int i;
   p[0] = new fish(0);
   p[1] = new bird(2);
   p[2] = new mammal(4);
   for (i=0; i<3; ++i) p[i]->print();
   for (i=0; i<3; ++i) delete p[i];
   return 0;
}
```

Since *print* is now declared in the class *animal* as a pure virtual function, this class is now abstract. Consequently, the *main* function can no longer create an object of class *animal*. Making class *animal* abstract also makes it impossible to omit any of the *print* functions in the derived classes *fish*, *bird*, and *mammal*, that is, if we want to create objects of these derived class types. In general, if we derive a class *D* from the abstract class *B* and we do not provide definitions in *D* for all pure virtual functions of *B*, then this derived class *D* is in turn an abstract class; in that case we can use *D* only to derive other classes from it, not to define objects.

We have seen that making a class abstract makes its use more restricted. At first this may seem to be a disadvantage. Yet, if a class is to be used only as a base class for other classes, not to create objects of it, it is highly recommended to make it an abstract class. The compiler will then detect any accidental attempts to use the base class for creating objects, and it will also detect any missing member functions for derived classes. This is particularly interesting in the case of function parameters. For example, consider the following function:

```
function animalOutput(const animal &a)
{   cout << "Here is the output for some specific animal:\n";
    a->print();
}
```

This function is very general in that it can be called with an argument that can be an object of any class that is derived from *animal*. Since *animal* is an abstract class in which *print* is a pure virtual function, it is guaranteed that this derived class provides its own specific *print* member function, and it is this function that will be called here. If the function *print* of the base class *animal* were just a virtual function, not a pure one, there would be no obligation for the writer of the derived class just mentioned to provide it with a *print* function.

6.12 Run-time Type Information and *dynamic_cast*

A base class *B* that contains a virtual function is said to be a *polymorphic type*. As we have seen, objects of classes derived from *B* contain information about their types, which is interesting when we access such object via pointers of type *B**. Since this information is available when the program *runs* (not when it is *compiled*), it is referred to as *run-time type information* (RTTI). In Section 6.10 we saw that we can use a *static_cast* to convert from type *B** to some type *D**, where *D* is one of the classes that are derived from *B*. The expression *static_cast<D*>(p)* is correct only if the pointer *p* (of type *B**) currently points to an object of type *D*. However, if *B* is a polymorphic type, we can perform a test to see if *p* currently points to an object of type *D*. We do this by using a *dynamic_cast*. The expression

```
dynamic_cast<D*>(p)
```

is then of type *D** and equal to *p*, and otherwise it is zero. This is demonstrated by the following program, in which the classes *D* and *E* are derived from *B*:

```
// dyncast.cpp: Run-time type information and dynamic_cast.
#include <iostream>
using namespace std;

class B {
public:
   virtual int f() = 0;
};

class D: public B {
public:
   int f(){return 1;}
};

class E: public B {
public:
   int f(){return 2;}
};

int main()
{  B *p;
   D d;
   p = &d;
   if (dynamic_cast<D*>(p))
      cout << p->f() << endl;    // Output: 1
   if (dynamic_cast<E*>(p))
      cout << p->f() << endl;    // Not executed
   return 0;
}
```

Since *p* points to an object of type *D*, not of type *E*, the first of the above two casts succeeds, while the second fails, so that the program produces only the number 1 as output. If we wrote

```
E e;
p = &e;
```

just before the above two if-statements, then only the second of these would succeed and the output of the program would consist of the number 2.

The program *dyncast.cpp* contains a pure virtual function *f*. It would have made little difference if this virtual function had not been pure. For example, if we had written

```
{return 0;}
```

instead of

```
= 0;
```

in the class *B*, the program would also have been correct and its output would have been the same.

6.13 Static Class Members

Data members of a class are normally stored in every object of that class. However, if we use the keyword *static* for a class data member, there will be only one such member for the class, regardless of how many objects there are. In other words, a static class member belongs to its class type rather than to the individual objects of that type. Besides static data members, we can also use static member functions, which cannot use any data members that are specific for objects. Because of this, the *this* pointer is not available in static member functions.

Program *statmem.cpp* shows how static members can be used. The constructor of *Person* increases the static class member *count* by one each time it is called. In this way, we count how many objects of type *Person* are created:

```
// statmem.cpp: Using a static class member to
//        count how many times the constructor
//        Person() is called.
#include <iostream>
#include <string>
using namespace std;

class Person {
public:
    Person(const string &s): name(s)
    {   count++;
    }
    void print()const
    {   cout << name << endl;
    }
    static void printcount()
    {   cout << "There are " << count
            << " persons." << endl;

    }
private:
    string name;
    static int count;
};

int Person::count=0;

int main()
{   Person a("Mary"), b("Peter"), c("Charles"), *p;
    p = new Person("Kate");
    a.print(); b.print(); c.print(); p->print();
    Person::printcount();
    delete p;
    return 0;
}
```

The output of this program is as follows:

```
Mary
Peter
Charles
Kate
There are 4 persons.
```

We have to define a static class member outside the class definition, as is done here in the program line

```
int Person::count=0;
```

Since the static class member *count* is associated with the class type *Person*, not with objects of that type, we write *Person::count*, whereas we would have written, for example, *A.count* if *count* had been a nonstatic member and we had been interested in the copy of it for the object *A*. The same applies to the static member function called in the *main* function as *Person::printcount( )*. This static member function enables us to access the private static *count* member. In contrast to the *print* member function, *printcount* cannot be applied to a particular object, hence the difference in prefix in the calls *A.print( )* and *Person::printcount( )*. If we had not been able to use a static member function, it would have been necessary to make the *count* data member public and to write

```
cout << "There are " << Person::count
     << " persons." << endl;
```

instead of *Person::printcount( )* in the *main* function. The output would then have been the same as it is now.

Note the analogy between static data members and static local variables in functions. In both cases, there is only one copy of them. As was mentioned in Section 4.5, there is only one copy of a static local variable in a function, even if this function is recursive. Things are similar with a static data member of a class: there is only one copy of that member, regardless of how many objects of that class there are.

Use of member names inside classes

Suppose we have a class *Example*, which contains both a static member *s* and a nonstatic member *ns*. If, in member functions of this class, these member names are used without any prefix, then

s	is shorthand for	`Example::sm`
ns	is shorthand for	`this->ns`

For example, in the above class *Person*, we could have used the suffix *this->* for the nonstatic data member *name* and the suffix *Person::* for the static data member *count* in the member *print* and *printcount*, writing

```
void print()const
{  cout << this->name << endl;              // 'this->' added
}
static void printcount()
{  cout << "There are " << Person::count    // 'Person::' added
        << " persons." << endl;
}
```

This also applies to function members, so if we had called the above member functions in others (also belonging to the class *Person*), we might have written

```
this->print();
Person::printcount();
```

but (still occurring in *Person* member functions) the following statements would have had the same meaning:

```
print();
printcount();
```

6.14 Pointers to Class Members

In Section 5.15 we discussed pointers to functions. Unfortunately, we cannot use such pointers for functions that are class members. For example, consider the following program fragment, which defines the function *f*, the class *Example*, the pointer *p* and the variables *u*, *v*, and *w*:

```
int f(){return 123;}

class Example {
public:
    Example(int ii, int jj): i(ii), j(jj){}
    int ivalue(){return i;}
    int jvalue(){return j;}
private:
    int i, j;
};

int (*p)();
Example u(1, 2), v(3, 4), w(5, 6);
```

After writing

```
p = &f;
```

we can call the function *f* by writing (*p)( ) or even *p*( ), as we have seen in Section 5.15. Although the member function *ivalue* is very similar to the function *f*, we cannot assign it to pointer *p*. Each of the following attempts would fail:

```
p = &ivalue;          // (1) error
p = &Example::ivalue; // (2) error
p = &u.ivalue;        // (3) error
```

Attempt (1) fails because we should specify to which class *ivalue* belongs. Although (2) looks better, it is not clear at all how to use *p*. If we continued by writing *p*( ) (as an indirect call to *ivalue*), it would not be clear whether *u.i*, *v.i*, or *w.i* should be the resulting value. This explains that the C++ language does not allow (2). Finally, (3) is not correct because it is at least misleading. Since only one function *ivalue* is physically present in memory and the value of *p* can only be an address, no information about *u* is stored in *p* so we cannot expect the effect of (3) to be any different if we replace *u* with *v* or *w*.

To enable us to use pointers to class member functions, a new operator has been introduced. Instead of

```
int (*p)();
```

we should write

```
int (Example::*p)();
```

to express that *p* is intended as a pointer to a member function (without parameters and returning *int*) of the class *Example*. We can then write

```
p = &Example::ivalue;    // or: p = Example::ivalue
```

As indicated by the comment, we may write or omit the address-of operator (&) here as we like. After this assignment, we can use *p* as the second operand of a special operator, .*, as the following examples show:

```
(u.*p)()    // = u.ivalue() = u.i = 1
(v.*p)()    // = v.ivalue() = v.i = 3
(w.*p)()    // = w.ivalue() = w.i = 5
```

Instead of *ivalue*, we could use *jvalue* here, since this member function has the same type as *ivalue*. The values of those expressions would then be 2, 4, and 6.

In the above examples, the operator .* follows the variables *u*, *v*, and *w* because these variables denote class objects. In many applications we deal with class objects via pointers to those objects. Such pointers can be followed by another new operator, –>* (instead of .*). For example, if we replace

```
Example u(1, 2), v(3, 4), w(5, 6);
```

with

```
Example *p12 = new Example(1, 2),
       *p34 = new Example(3, 4),
       *p56 = new Example(5, 6);
```

we should at the same time replace

```
(u.*p)()    // = u.ivalue() = u.i = 1
(v.*p)()    // = v.ivalue() = v.i = 3
(w.*p)()    // = w.ivalue() = w.i = 5
```

with

```
(p12->*p)()   // = p12->ivalue() = p12->i = 1
(p34->*p)()   // = p34->ivalue() = p34->i = 3
(p56->*p)()   // = p56->ivalue() = p56->i = 5
```

It would be inconsistent if the new operators .* and –>* were available only for function members. They are therefore also made applicable to pointers to data members, even though normal pointers, such as *pf* in the following example, can also be used for data members:

```
class num {public: float x;} u;
float *pf;
pf = &u.x;      // pf is a normal pointer to float.
*pf = 1.23;     // Effect: u.x = 1.23
```

If we want to use a pointer to a member instead, we can write

```
class num {public: float x;} u;
float num::*pm;
pm = &num::x;   // pm is a pointer to a data member.
u.*pm = 1.23;   // Effect: u.x = 1.23
```

Comparing the above two fragments, we see that a pointer to a member enables us to delay specifying the object (*u*) until we actually use the pointer. Apparently, a pointer to a class member is not a real pointer but rather an *offset*. With a given object *u* and a pointer *pm* to a data member, the expression *u.*pm* indicates where in object *u* the member in question is to be found.

After we have seen so many program fragments, it is time to combine all we have been discussing in this section in a complete demonstration program:

```
// ptrmem.cpp: Pointers to class members.
#include <iostream>
using namespace std;
```

```
class Example {
public:
   Example(int ii, int jj): i(ii), j(jj){}
   int ivalue(){return i;}
   int jvalue(){return j;}
   int i, j;
};

int main()
{  Example u(1, 2), v(3, 4), w(5, 6), *pobject = &w;

   cout << "Pointer to function members: ";
   int (Example::*pf)();
   pf = &Example::ivalue;
   cout << (u.*pf)() << " ";     // 1
   pf = &Example::jvalue;
   cout << (v.*pf)() << " ";     // 4
   cout << (pobject->*pf)() << endl;// 6

   cout << "Pointer to data members:     ";
   int Example::*pd;
   pd = &Example::i;
   cout << u.*pd << " ";    // 1
   pd = &Example::j;
   cout << v.*pd << " ";    // 4
   cout << pobject->*pd << endl;// 6
   return 0;
}
```

The output of this program is as follows:

```
Pointer to function members: 1   4   6
Pointer to data members:     1   4   6
```

6.15 Unions and Bit Fields

This section is about two rather simple subjects that C++ has inherited from C and that logically belong to this chapter because they are related to classes.

Unions

With the class objects we have seen so far, all data members are present in memory at the same time. In other words, the amount of memory used by a normal class object is at least the sum of the amounts of memory used by its data members. In contrast to this, there is another special case of the class concept, called *union*. The notation of unions is similar to that of other classes. However, union members overlay each other. The amount of memory a union object takes is only as large as that of its largest member, which implies that there is only one member actually present at a time. For example, after writing

```
union intflo {int i; float x;} u;
```

we can use *u.i* and *u.x*, in the same way as if the above keyword *union* were replaced with *struct*. However, the members *i* and *x* share memory space, so by executing

```
u.i = 123;
u.x = 98.7;
```

the second statement destroys the value just assigned to *u.i*. In C++ the above declaration declares not only the variable *u* but also the type *intflo*. For example, we can now declare

```
intflo v;
```

Unions can be useful if we want to store only one of their members. In that case, they are more economical with memory space, especially if we use arrays of union objects. However, it is the programmer's responsibility to remember which of the members have been used. For example, the array *a* in the following program stores characters and floating-point values, in the order *char, float, char, float*, and so on:

```
// charflo.cpp: An array of unions.
#include <iostream>
using namespace std;

union charfloat {char ch; float x;};

int main()
{   const int n = 100000;
    charfloat a[n];
    for (int i=0; i<n; ++i)
    {   if (i % 2 == 0)
            a[i].ch = 'A' + i % 26;
        else
            a[i].x = 1.0F/i;
    }
    cout << "a[0].ch = " << a[0].ch << endl;
    cout << "a[1].x  = " << a[1].x << endl;
    cout << "a[2].ch = " << a[2].ch << endl;
    cout << "a[3].x  = " << a[3].x << endl;
    cout << "sizeof(a[0]) = " << sizeof(a[0]) << endl;
    return 0;
}
```

Every array element takes as much space as a *float*, which is four bytes with Visual C++, as the last line of the following output shows:

```
a[0].ch = A
a[1].x  = 1
a[2].ch = C
a[3].x  = 0.333333
sizeof(a[0]) = 4
```

If we wrote *struct charfloat* instead of *union charfloat*, every array element would take more than four bytes. (With the C++ implementation just mentioned, that number would be equal to 8 instead of 5 because there would be some unused space as discussed in Section 6.1.)

Bit Fields

Normally, the smallest unit of memory used for variables is one byte. However, it is possible for classes to have members that are smaller than one byte. As their sizes are expressed in bits, they are called *bit fields*. In the following example we have a class object *s*, with bit fields *b4*, *b1*, *b2*, consisting of 4, 1, and 2 bits, respectively. Besides, there is a *char* member *ch*:

```
struct Example {
    unsigned b4:4, b1:1, b2:2;
    char ch;
}  s;
```

Bit fields are similar to other class members, with one exception: since several of them may be located in the same byte, we cannot uniquely identify them by their addresses, and we must therefore not apply the address-of operator & to them. We can write

```
s.b4 = 7;
```

which implies that *s.b4* is a modifiable lvalue (discussed in Section 3.8), but, unlike other lvalues, it must not be preceded by the unary operator &.

6.16 Function Objects

This section is about a subject that will be very useful in Chapter 9, but that is sometimes considered confusing because it is based on several language concepts that we should all completely understand. To avoid such confusion, let us deal with these concepts one by one, before combining them.

Temporary, anonymous class objects

If a class has a default constructor (see Section 6.8), the name of that class followed by an empty pair of parentheses creates a temporary, anonymous object of this class. This is different from creating an object by using *new*, since then we obtain a pointer to the object and we ought to use *delete* later. This is not the case with the temporary object created as just mentioned and illustrated in the following program:

```cpp
// tempobj.cpp: A (not completely useless) temporary object.
#include <iostream>
using namespace std;

class Example {
public:
    void print(){cout << "Hello\n";}
};

int main()
{   Example().print();   // Output: Hello
    return 0;
}
```

If we had written the statement

```cpp
Example();
```

this would have no effect at all, but by writing

```cpp
Example().print();
```

the effect is a call to the *print* member function of the temporary *Example* object.

Before we proceed, it is worthwhile to notice the condition that the class in question should have a default constructor, and that there can be only one such constructor. The above program would also be correct if we added (only) one of the following two default constructors:

```cpp
Example()            // Default constructor
{   cout << "Object created\n";
}
Example(int i = 0) // Default constructor (because of = 0)
{   cout << "Object created with i = " << i << endl;
}
```

In contrast, the program would be incorrect, if we added the following constructor (and no others):

```cpp
Example(int i)       // Not a default constructor
{   cout << "Object created with i = " << i << endl;
}
```

As discussed in Section 6.8, the class *Example* would have no default constructor in this case.

The call-operator

Among the operators of C++ there are some that not everyone will immediately recognize as operators. One of these is a pair of parentheses, used in a function call and therefore referred to as a *call-operator*. In the same way as we can overload the plus operator by defining a function *operator+*, we define this call-operator as a function *operator*(). Let us begin with an extremely simple example:

```
// calloper.cpp: A call-operator
#include <iostream>
using namespace std;

class iprint {
public:
    void operator()(int i)const{cout << i << endl;}
};

int main()
{   iprint x;
    x(123);            // Output: 123
    iprint()(456);     // Output: 456
    return 0;
}
```

The curious beginning

```
void operator()(int i)const
```

of the call-operator definition is very logical, after all, if we compare it with, for example

```
vec operator+(const vec &b)const
```

which we wrote in Section 6.6, so the pair of parentheses in *operator*() is similar to the plus sign in *operator+*. In both cases a parenthesized parameter list follows. Since *x* is an object of the class *iprint* for which the function *operator*() with one parameter, of type *int*, is defined, we can call this function by writing

```
x(123);
```

Although *x* is a class object, its use is similar to that of a function. We can also combine this call-operator with the creation of temporary objects by using a pair of parentheses, as discussed a short while ago. Recall that a class name followed by an empty pair of parentheses creates such an object, that is, if the class in question has a default constructor. Therefore the expression

```
iprint()
```

creates such a temporary object, so that it can be used in the same way as *x*. This explains the statement

```
iprint()(456);
```

in the *main* function. Since objects such as *x* and *iprint*( ) are used in the same way as functions, they are known as *function objects*. In other words, an object of a class is a *function object* if that class satisfies two conditions:

- it has a public function *operator*( ) among its members;
- it has a default constructor.

Function object used instead of pointer to function

As we will see in Chapter 9, function objects are frequently used in STL to pass functions as arguments to other functions. In Section 5.15 we used pointers to functions to pass the functions *reciprocal* and *square* as arguments to another function, *funsum*. Recall that the latter function has two parameters, *n* and *f*, which it uses to compute the sum

$$f(1) + f(2) + \dots + f(n)$$

We demonstrated this for two cases:

$$f(k) = reciprocal(k) = 1.0/k \quad \text{with} \quad n = 5$$
$$f(k) = square(k) = k^2 \qquad \text{with} \quad n = 3$$

If it was not possible to use pointers to functions, we could still achieve about the same goal by passing function objects as arguments. We will demonstrate this by means of an example that is very similar to that of Section 5.15, so it may be helpful to have another look at that section.

Since we need two different classes, say, *reciprocal* and *square*, as arguments, we are faced with the problem of which type to use for the corresponding parameter *f* in the function *funsum*. The solution is a common abstract base class, say, *fun*, in which we declare *operator*( ) as a pure virtual function (see Section 6.11), as the following program shows:

```
// funobj.cpp: Function object used to pass functions to
//             another function.
#include <iostream>
using namespace std;

class fun {
public:
   virtual double operator()(int k)const = 0;
};
```

```
class reciprocal: public fun {
public:
   double operator()(int k)const
   {  return 1.0/k;
   }
};

class square: public fun {
public:
   double operator()(int k)const
   {  return static_cast<double>(k) * k;
   }
};

double funsum(int n, const fun &f)
{  double s = 0;
   int i;
   for (i=1; i<=n; ++i) s += f(i);
   return s;
}

int main()
{  cout << "Sum of five reciprocals: "
        << funsum(5, reciprocal()) << endl;
   cout << "Sum of three squares: "
        << funsum(3, square()) << endl;
   return 0;
}
```

In the *main* function, the second arguments *reciprocal*() and *square*() in the calls to *funsum* should not be confused with function calls. These arguments are temporary class objects, as discussed at the beginning of this section. On the other hand, the corresponding parameter *f* (of *funsum*) is used like a function in the statement

```
s += f(i);
```

which is possible because *f* is a function object.

This program is also a good example of the use of a pure virtual function. Instead of using an abstract class, we could write

```
class fun {
public:
   virtual double operator()(int k)const {return 0.0;}
};
```

but this would have three drawbacks:

- The return statement used here would be confusing, but nevertheless cannot be omitted because this function must return a value of type *double*
- Since *fun* is written only to derive other classes from it, not to create *fun* objects, we had better make the creation of such objects impossible.
- It is our intention that anyone who derives a class from *fun* should define its own *operator*( ) function. Only if *operator*( ) is a pure virtual function will the compiler insist that a writer of such a derived class does this.

Using a pure virtual function *operator*( ), as done in the program, is therefore to be preferred.

In the above example, function objects have no clear advantages over pointers to functions. This may be different in other, more advanced applications. For one thing, function objects can also contain data members, in which we can store and retrieve data computed in the *operator*( ) function.

Exercises

6.1   Write a program that reads the names and the ages of ten people, and stores these data in structures that are elements of an array. Print the average age of these people. Also, print a table of ten lines, with on each line the given data of a person, along with the (positive or negative) deviation of his or her age from the average age. Use the standard type *string* to store the names.

6.2   Write and demonstrate a very simple class *String*, similar to the class *row* discussed in Section 6.8 and 6.9 and including the two special functions that are required to copy *String* objects.

6.3*   Write a program that reads two dates of the same (non-leap) year to compute how many days the second date falls after the first. The dates are given as four-digit integers *mmdd*. For example, 1231 is the last day of the year. Print the algebraic difference: the result is negative if the first given date falls after the second. Use a class to represent both dates and to compute the desired difference.

6.4*   Write a program that reads the following integers:

$$n, l_0, u_0, l_1, u_1, ..., l_{n-1}, u_{n-1}$$

The integers l_i and u_i are the lower and upper bounds of a running variable r_i ($i = 0, 1, ..., n - 1$). Display all distinct sequences $r_1, r_2, ..., r_n$, for which $l_i \leq r_i \leq u_i$. For example, with $n = 3$, $l_0 = 5$, $u_0 = 7$, $l_1 = 2$, $u_1 = 2$, $l_2 = 8$, $u_2 = 9$, the output will be

```
5       2       8
5       2       9
6       2       8
6       2       9
7       2       8
7       2       9
```

6.5   Define a class *verylongint*, with a pointer as one of its members. This pointer points
        to a memory area in which very long integers are stored digit by digit. Besides
        constructors and a destructor, there must be functions for the operators +, *, and =,
        as well as an output operator << to display such long integers, in such a way that
        we can use this class, for example, as follows:

```
verylongint x(30000), y(20000), y1(y),
            z = "123456789012345", result;
result = x * x * x * x + y * y * y * y1 + z;
cout << result;
```

As this example illustrates, string quotes are required for integers that do not fit
into type *long int*. For integers below this limit, string quotes may be written or
omitted, as the user likes. The output to be produced by this program fragment is

```
970 123 456 789 012 345
```

(Another solution to the same problem will be required in Exercise 9.9.)

6.6*   Write a program that reads an integer n and prints all possible sequences of n bits
        in which no successive zeros occur. For example, $n = 3$ leads to

        010
        011
        101
        110
        111

7

Templates

7.1 Introduction

This chapter is about *templates*, which enable us to make our program code very general with regard to data types. Suppose, for example, that we write a function to swap the values of two *int* variables. Later, we may want a similar function for two *float* values. Templates enable us to write only one function that can be used for both purposes. Another example is a general class for, say, a binary tree. Templates provide a convenient means to write such a class without specifying the type of the data that we want to store in the nodes of the tree.

We are by now very familiar with function parameters, which represent values or objects. Templates also have parameters, but these do not represent values or objects but rather types.

7.2 Function Templates

The following program demonstrates a function template. It first exchanges the values of two *int* variables and then those of two *float* variables:

```
// ftempl.cpp: A function template for swapping the values
//             of two objects of a given, arbitrary type.
#include <iostream>
using namespace std;

template <class T>
void swapObjects(T &x, T &y){T w = x; x = y; y = w;}
```

```
int main()
{   int i = 1, j = 2;
    swapObjects(i, j);   // Now i = 2 and j = 1.
    float u = 3.4F, v = 5.6F;
    swapObjects(u, v); // Now u = 5.6 and v = 3.4.
    cout << i << " " << j << " " << u << " " << v << endl;
    return 0;
}
```

Since the sizes of *int* and *float* objects may be different, it is hard to understand that a single function should be able to perform both swapping tasks. Actually, this is not the case. Although we write only one function template here, two distinct functions will be generated, as if we had written these ourselves:

```
void swapObjects(int &x, int &y)
{   int w = x; x = y; y = w;
}
void swapObjects(float &x, float &y)
{   float w = x; x = y; y = w;
}
```

Consider this line in program *ftempl.cpp*:

```
template <class T>
```

Curiously enough, we find the keyword *class* here, even though we are not using any classes at all. Actually, we may replace *class* with the keyword *typename* here, writing

```
template <typename T>
```

which is equivalent to the previous program line.

In this example, *T* is a type parameter, which is different from a function parameter in that it denotes a type, not a value or an object. It goes without saying that the name of a type parameter need not be *T*, nor is the number of type parameters restricted to one, as we will see in a moment. However, unlike function parameter lists, template parameter lists cannot be empty. This parameter *T* is used on the second of the following lines, which looks like a normal C++ function:

```
template <class T>
void swapObjects(T &x, T &y){T w = x; x = y; y = w;}
```

Because of the first line, *swapObjects* is not a normal function but a *function template*. The function *swapObjects(int, int)* shown above is generated by the call *swapObjects(i, j)* while the function *swapObjects(float, float)* is generated by the call *swapObjects(u, v)*. If there had been another call, say, *swapObjects(m, n)* with *m* and *n* of type *int*, there would still be only two *swapObjects* functions, but there would be three if *m* and *n* in this latest call had been of type *char*, and so on. These two arguments *m* and *n* must, of course, be lvalues, and they must be of the same type.

Templates and header files

It is generally considered bad practice to write function definitions in header files. Although its appearance might at first suggest otherwise, a function template is only a model for such a definition and the compiler will not immediately convert it into executable code. Consequently, it is perfectly all right and very usual to place template definitions in header files. For example, we may use the following header file:

```
// swap.h: A header file defining the function template
//          swapObjects.
template <class T>
void swapObjects(T &x, T &y){T w = x; x = y; y = w;}
```

The following program shows how to use the above file:

```
// swapdemo.cpp: Demonstration of a function template
//               defined in the header file swap.h.
#include <iostream>
#include "swap.h"
using namespace std;

int main()
{   int i = 1, j = 2;
    swapObjects(i, j);
    float u = 3.4F, v = 5.6F;
    swapObjects(u, v);
    cout << i << " " << j << "    " << u << " " << v << endl;
        // Output: 2 1    5.6 3.4
    return 0;
}
```

Using more than one template argument

Functions templates can have more than one parameter. Each template parameter must occur as a type in the parameter list of the function, but it may appear there more than once and this latter parameter list may also contain unrelated parameters. The following program illustrates this and may be helpful to avoid confusion about these two parameter lists:

```
// ftempl2.cpp: Function templates with two parameters.
#include <iostream>
using namespace std;

template <class T, class U>
U multsum(T x, T y, U u, int n)
{   return x + y + n * u;
}

int main()
{   cout << multsum(4, 3, 0.5, 5) << endl; // Output: 9.5
    return 0;
}
```

In this program, T and U are template parameters, denoting types, while x, y, u, and n are function parameters. The type U is also used for the return value. It will be clear that the program computes the sum $4 + 3 + 5 \times 0.5 = 9.5$. Because of the arguments in the call to *multsum*, type *int* will be substituted for T and *double* for U.

Explicit template arguments

Instead of using the function argument types to decide which types are to be substituted for the template parameters, it is also possible to provide these types explicitly as a template argument list between angular brackets ($<>$) and immediately following the function name. In the above example, we could have written the following call to *multsum* in the *main* function:

```
multsum<int, double>(4, 3, 0.5, 5)
```

In this call, the part *<int, double>* indicates that *int* is to be substituted for T and *double* for U, regardless of the types of the function arguments (4, 2, 0.5, and 5 in this example). In some situations this way of specifying the template arguments is necessary or at least very useful. Suppose, for example, that we have to compute $x = a^n$, where n is a nonnegative integer. We will not use a template parameter for the exponent n, since this should always be *int*. On the other hand, besides the type for the base a the type of the result x should be specified as a template argument. Now the problem with this result type is that it need not necessarily be the same as the base type and we do not like the idea of adding another function parameter just to indicate what the result type should be. The calls to the function template *power* in the *main* function below shows that explicit template arguments are very useful in this case:

```
// powers.cpp: Two power functions resulting from a template.
#include <iostream>
using namespace std;

template <class basetype, class resulttype>
resulttype power(basetype a, int n)
{   resulttype x = 1;
    for (int i=1; i<=n; ++i)
       x *= a;
    return x;
}

int main()
{   cout << power<int, long>(10, 9) << endl;
    cout << power<double, double>(10, 30) << endl;
    return 0;
}
```

In the first call, the base type is *int* and the result type is *long*, so that we have at least a 32 bit result, even if type *int* is only 16 bit. (It is guaranteed that *long* takes at least 32 bits and that *int* takes at least 16 bits.) In the second call, the base and result types are *double*. It is no problem that we write the *int* argument 10, since this is converted to type *double*, as the first explicit template argument specifies. The output of this program is shown below:

```
1000000000
1e+030
```

The example below is slightly different from the previous ones in that the template parameter *T* does not occur literally as the type of one of the function parameters, since the latter is *const T** instead of *T*:

```
// ptrpar.cpp: Template parameter used for pointer.
#include <iostream>
using namespace std;

template <class T>
T arraysum(const T *p, int n)
{   T s = 0;
    for (int i=0; i<n; ++i)
        s += p[i];
    return s;
}

int main()
{   int a[] = {1, 2, 3};
    double b[] = {4.5, 6.7};
    cout << arraysum(a, 3) << endl;   // Output: 6
    cout << arraysum(b, 2) << endl;   // Output: 11.2
    return 0;
}
```

7.3 Class Templates

If we have two or more classes that are almost identical, it will often be desirable to generalize them in the same way as with function templates: instead of several, almost identical classes we write a single *class template*, which is a model for the actual class definitions. For example, suppose that we want to use a type *vec* for vectors (in the mathematical sense) in the same way as we did in Section 6.6, but this time we want to use two vector types: one with *int* and the other with *float* coordinates *x* and *y*. Since operations such as vector addition are done in the same way, it would be awkward if we had to write two almost identical classes. The following program shows how to use a class template for this purpose:

```
// cltempl.cpp: A class template.
#include <iostream>
using namespace std;
```

```
template <class T>
class vec {
public:
    vec(T xx = 0, T yy = 0): x(xx), y(yy) {}
    void printvec(ostream &os)const
    {  os << "(" << x << ", " << y << ")";
    }
    vec<T> operator+(const vec<T> &b)const
    {  return vec<T>(x + b.x, y + b.y);
    }
private:
    T x, y;
};

template <class T>
ostream &operator<<(ostream &os, const vec<T> &v)
{  v.printvec(os);
    return os;
}

int main()
{   vec<int> uInt(1, 2), vInt(3, 4), sInt;
    vec<float> uFloat(1.1F, 2.2F), vFloat(3.3F, 4.4F), sFloat;
    sInt = uInt + vInt;
    sFloat = uFloat + vFloat;
    cout << sInt << endl;
    cout << sFloat << endl;
    return 0;
}
```

This program computes the vector sums

$(1, 2) + (3, 4) = (4, 6)$
$(1.1, 2.2) + (3.3, 4.4) = (4.4, 6.6)$

which explains this output:

```
(4, 6)
(4.4, 6.6)
```

Like a function template, discussed in the previous section, a class template begins with

```
template < template parameter list >
```

which here has the form

```
template <class T>
```

The idea is that the actual type to be used for *T* will be specified later. In the template-declaration, we write *T* to denote this type. We use the notation *vec<T>* to indicate that *vec* is not a complete class name but that an additional type *T* is required. In other words, *vec* is a parameterized type with *T* as its parameter. Note that the suffix *<T>* is also added to the identifier *vec* in the member functions of this class template, except for the constructor, whose name is simply *vec*. In this example, *T* is actually a placeholder for either *int* or *float*, as you can see in the *main* function. Here we use the types *vec<int>* and *vec<float>*, in which *int* and *float* are the type arguments that will be substituted for the type parameter *T*.

The template parameter list, mentioned above, can consist of more than one item, each of which is either a type-parameter, that is, the keyword *class* followed by an identifier, or a non-type parameter, such as *int n*. Non-type template parameters can have integer, enumeration or pointer types. In particular, these parameters cannot have floating-point or string types. For example, only the first of the following three lines is correct:

```
template <int n>       // Correct
template <float x>     // Incorrect
template <string s>    // Incorrect
```

The first of the above lines, with the template parameter list consisting only of a non-type *int* parameter *n*, also occurs in the following fragment:

```
template <int n>
class floatsequence {
    ...
    float r[n];
};
```

We can now use, for example, sequence *a* of 100 *float* values and sequence *b* of 200 *float* values as follows:

```
floatsequence<100> a;
floatsequence<200> b;
```

This might seem similar to writing

```
float a[100], b[200];
```

but here we have no class, so we cannot benefit from member functions, derivation and so on. It makes more sense to compare the *floatsequence* variables *a* and *b* with variables of the same names defined below:

```
class floatseq {
public:
    floatseq(int n): p(new float[n]), len(n){}
    ~floatseq(){delete[] p;}
    ...
private:
    float *p;
    int len;
};
```

```
floatseq a(100);
floatseq b(200);
```

The main difference between the types *floatsequence* and *floatseq* is the way memory is allocated; it depends on your application and your computer system which is to be preferred. It should also be noted that in *floatseq* we can replace 100 and 200 with any *int* expressions, while we can use only constant expressions for these values in our *float-sequence* example.

Non-type template parameters are more interesting if we combine them with type-parameters, as this example shows:

```
template <class T, int n, class S>
class sequence
{  ...
};
```

In this case, we must use template class names that match this template argument list. In other words, we must supply a type, a constant expression of type *int*, and another type, in that order. An example of such a template class name is

```
sequence <int, 100, long>
```

Default template parameters

Like functions, templates can have default parameters. For example, suppose that, in the example we have just seen, the third argument is often the same as the first. Also, the second argument might be equal to some fixed value, say, 5. We can then replace the first line of the class template definition with the following one:

```
template <class T, int n = 5, class S = T>
```

To demonstrate this in a complete program, let us use a class template for three number sequences:

- four *int* values (1, 3, 5, 7)
- three *float* values (0.3, 0.4, 0.5)
- five *double* values (1.0, 1.1, 1.2, 1.3, 1.4)

There will be a member function *sum* to compute the sum of all elements of the sequence. The first template argument denotes the type of the sequence elements, the second the sequence length, and the third the type of sum. The following program shows the complete class template and the way it can be used to generate the above three sequences and to compute the sums:

```
// sequence.cpp: A class template with three arguments.
#include <iostream>
using namespace std;
```

```
template <class T, int n = 5, class S = T>
class sequence {
public:
    sequence(T start, T incr);
    S sum();
private:
    T r[n];
};

template <class T, int n, class S>
sequence<T, n, S>::sequence(T start, T incr)
{   for (int i=0; i<n; ++i) r[i] = start + i * incr;
}

template <class T, int n, class S>
S sequence<T, n, S>::sum()
{   S s = 0;
    for (int i=0; i<n; ++i) s += r[i];
    return s;
}

int main()
{   sequence<int, 4, long> a_int(1, 2);        // 4 elements
    sequence<float, 3> a_float(0.3F, 0.1F); // 3 elements
    sequence<double> a_double(1.0, 0.1);    // 5 elements
    cout << a_int.sum() << " "        // 16
         << a_float.sum() << " "      // 1.2
         << a_double.sum() << endl;   // 6
    return 0;
}
```

By substituting the template arguments, or their default values, we see that the statement

```
T r[n];
```

in the class template actually leads to the following three array declarations for *a_int*, *a_float*, and *a_double*, respectively:

```
int r[4];
float r[3];
double r[5];
```

The two constructor arguments (which we should not confuse with the template arguments) are the start and increment values of the sequences. The line

```
sequence<int, 4, long> a_int(1, 2);
```

indicates that the sequence *a_int* will consist of four *int* elements and a sum of type *long* and that the first sequence element will be 1 while there will be a difference of 2 between two successive sequence elements, giving the sequence 1, 3, 5, 7. Since three template arguments are supplied, the default values of the template parameters are not used here. This is different, for example, with the program line

```
sequence<float, 3> a_float(0.3F, 0.1F);
```

in which the third template argument is omitted. Here the third template argument is taken equal to the first (*float*) because of the default template parameter specified as *class S = T* in

```
template <class T, int n = 5, class S = T>
```

near the top of the program.

As indicated by comments, the output of the program consists of three sums, computed as follows:

$$1 + 3 + 5 + 7 = 16$$
$$0.3 + 0.4 + 0.5 = 1.2$$
$$1.0 + 1.1 + 1.2 + 1.3 + 1.4 = 6$$

7.4 Type *string* Revisited

Our discussion of strings in Chapters 1 and 5 was somewhat simplified in that we ignored the fact that type *string* is actually defined as follows:

```
typedef basic_string<char> string;
```

In other words, *string* is a class resulting from the class template *basic_string* by providing this with the template argument *char*. This template *basic_string* is also applicable to arguments other than *char*, as the following program demonstrates:

```
// istring.cpp: The template basic_string applied to
//                     integers.
#include <string>
#include <iostream>
using namespace std;

typedef basic_string<int> istring; // int instead of char!

int main()
{  istring s;
   s += 123;
   s += 98;
   s += 45;
   for (int i=0; i<s.length(); ++i)
      cout << s[i] << endl;
   return 0;
}
```

This program uses a string of integers instead of a character string, which is far more usual. Initially, this 'integer string' *s* is empty. Then three elements are added by using the operator +=, which we should not confuse with one for arithmetic addition. Instead, it is similar to the operator used in, for example:

```
string str;
str += 'A';
```

In other words, the *istring* type, defined in the program *istring.cpp*, is similar to an array to which we can add as many elements as we like, and the output of this program is as follows:

```
123
98
45
```

As we have seen in Section 1.7 (and as we will discuss in greater detail in Chapter 9), there is another class template, *vector*, which will be used more frequently as a kind of flexible array. A possibly more useful application of the template *basic_string* is that with *wchar_t* as a template argument:

```
typedef basic_string<wchar_t> wstring;
```

The type *wchar_t*, introduced to represent 'wide characters,' takes more than eight bits so that more than 256 distinct characters can be represented. The corresponding string type is *wstring*.

7.5 Complex Numbers

There is a standard class template *complex*, which is very interesting for some mathematically skilled programmers and electrical engineers who use complex numbers in their computations. If you are not familiar with complex numbers at all, you are advised to ignore this section.

Let us start our brief discussion of this subject with an example. The following program uses the type *complex<double>* to solve the quadratic equation

$$ax^2 + bx + c = 0$$

where *a*, *b*, and *c* are arbitrary complex numbers (provided $a \neq 0$):

```
// quadeq.cpp: Solving a quadratic equation with
//             complex numbers.
#include <iostream>
#include <complex>
using namespace std;
```

```
int main()
{   complex<double> a, aa, b, c, D, sqrtD, x1, x2;
    cout <<
        "Enter the complex numbers a (nonzero), b, and c:\n";
    cin >> a >> b >> c;
    if (a == 0.0)
    {   cout << "a must be nonzero.\n";
        return 1;
    }
    D = b * b - 4.0 * a * c;
    sqrtD = sqrt(D);
    aa = 2.0 * a;
    x1 = (-b + sqrtD)/aa;
    x2 = (-b - sqrtD)/aa;
    cout << "Solution (complex):\n"
        << x1 << " " << x2 << endl;
    return 0;
}
```

Both in the output, and, if desired, in the input, complex numbers are written as pairs of real numbers, separated by a comma and surrounded by parentheses. For example, (1.0,2.5) represents the complex number $1 + 2.5i$ (also known as $1 + 2.5j$).

To see program *quadeq.cpp* in action, let us begin with the equation

$$x^2 + 1 = 0$$

In this case we have $a = 1$, $b = 0$, and $c = 1$, so the coefficients happen to be real numbers. Instead of entering these as number pairs, we can simply write literals in the usual form, as this demonstration shows:

```
Enter the complex numbers a (nonzero), b, and c:
1 0 1
Solution (complex):
(0,1) (0,-1)
```

The two roots (that is, the two numbers forming the solution) of the given equation are the imaginary numbers i and $-i$, since both i^2 and $(-i)^2$ are equal to -1.

Let us now use the equation

$$ix^2 - 1 = 0$$

as a second example. Here we have $a = i$, $b = 0$, and $c = -1$. Since the coefficient a is i, which is not a real number, we have to write this value as the number pair (0,1):

```
Enter the complex numbers a (nonzero), b, and c:
(0, 1) 0 -1
Solution (complex):
(0.707107,-0.707107)  (-0.707107,0.707107)
```

Apparently, the roots are

$$x_1 = 0.5\sqrt{2}(1-i) \quad = \cos(-45°) + i\sin(-45°)$$
$$x_2 = 0.5\sqrt{2}(-1+i) = \cos 135° + i\sin 135°$$

To check these results, we compute their squares, finding

$$x_1^2 = \cos -90° + i\sin -90° = -i$$
$$x_2^2 = \cos 270° + i\sin 270° = -i.$$

Substituting the computed values x_1 and x_2 in the given equation $ix^2 - 1 = 0$, we obtain

$$i \times (-i) - 1 = 0$$

so that the computed x_1 and x_2 are indeed the roots of this equation.

Finally, we use an example with real coefficients and real roots:

$$2x^2 - x - 6 = 0$$

Since we can also write this equation as

$$(x-2)(2x+3) = 0$$

we immediately see that 2 and –1.5 are the roots to be computed. In view of the generality of the program, it displays these real roots as the number pairs (2, 0) and (–1.5, 0), as the following demonstration shows:

```
Enter the complex numbers a (nonzero), b, and c:
2 -1 -6
Solution (complex):
(2,0) (-1.5,0)
```

Since *complex* is a template in C++, we can specify the base type, used for the real and imaginary parts, as a template argument. Besides *double*, used in our example, the types *float* and *long double* are also reasonable candidates for this base type.

For a given complex value $a + bi$, we can obtain the real and imaginary parts a and b by using the parameterless member functions *real* and *imag*. With type *complex<double>*, these functions would return a value of type *double*. There is a constructor with two default parameters of the base type and with zero as default value. The available operators are listed below:

$$= \quad += \quad *= \quad /= \quad + \quad - \quad * \quad / \quad == \quad !=$$

There are also some useful (nonmember) functions. In our description of them, the complex number z is related to the real numbers a, b, ρ (= *rho*), and θ (= *theta*) as follows:

$$z = a + bi = \rho(\cos\theta + i\sin\theta)$$

These functions are listed below:

real(*z*)	*a*, the real part of *z*
imag(*z*)	*b*, the imaginary part of *z*
conj(*z*)	*a* – *bi*, the conjugated value of *z*
polar(*rho, theta*)	$z = \rho(\cos\theta + i\sin\theta)$
abs(*z*)	$\rho = \sqrt{a^2 + b^2}$
arg(*z*)	$\theta = \text{atan2}(b, a)$ (see Section 4.7 for *atan2*)
norm(*z*)	$\rho^2 = a^2 + b^2$

sin(*z*), *cos*(*z*), *sinh*(*z*), *cosh*(*z*), *tan*(*z*), *tanh*(*z*), *sqrt*(*z*), *exp*(*z*), *log*(*z*), *log*10(*z*)

Finally, there are four functions *pow* for exponentiation, where $pow(a, b) = a^b$ and where the possible types of *a* and *b* will be clear from the following fragment:

```
double x;
complex<double> z, z1;
int n;
// The following expressions are now possible for
// exponentiation:
// pow(z, n), pow(z, x), pow(z, z1) and pow(x, z)
```

Exercises

7.1*   Write and demonstrate the function template *displaysorted*3, which can be used to display three values for which the operator < is defined in ascending order. In the following fragment it is first used for three *double* values and then for three strings:

```
double x = 3.4, y = 7.5, z = 1.2;
string s("John"), t("Peter"), u("Nicholas");
displaysorted3(x, y, z);
displaysorted3(s, t, u);
```

This should produce the following output:

```
1.2 3.4 7.5
John Nicholas Peter
```

7.2   Turn the class *row* of Section 6.9 into a class template, so that it can be used not only for integers but also for other objects.

8

Exception Handling

8.1 Errors and Exceptions

When we are writing large and complicated programs, one of the most difficult subjects is dealing adequately with errors that occur due to special circumstances. Examples of these are:

- Memory exhaustion.
- An input file cannot be opened.
- Division by zero due to incorrect input data.

In example programs, which we want to be easy-to-read, we sometimes omit checks to detect such errors. For example, in this book we have often seen code to read numbers from the keyboard, or to allocate memory by using *new*, without checking if such attempts succeed. In practice such checks are highly recommended. If we have decided to write them in our programs, the question arises what to do if such tests fail. It would be best if, possibly assisted by the user, we could solve the problem and continue program execution. Sometimes this is too complicated and we prefer terminating the program by calling the *exit* function (see Section 11.9).

What is exception handling?

We often use the term *exception handling* when we actually mean *error handling*. The former is a generalization of the latter. In other words, every run-time error is an exception, but there are exceptions which we need not regard as an error. For example, if we try to assign a value greater than 255 to a char variable, only the eight least significant bits of that

value will be used. By calling this situation an exception, we avoid any discussion whether
or not it should be considered an error. We may define exception handling as dealing with
run-time errors and other exceptional situations .

Exception handling: where?

Besides thinking about what action to take in the case of an error, we must also discuss
where to perform such an action. Suppose we have a *main* function which calls function
compute, which in turn calls function *detail*. There are three levels in this example:

- *main*, the highest level;
- *compute*, the medium level;
- *detail*, the lowest level.

It may be desirable to react in *main* to an error occurring in *detail*. In general, if an error
occurs at a low level we often want to deal with this error at a higher level. In other words,
instead of

```
...
int main()
{  ... compute(...) ...
}

void compute(...)
{  ... detail(...) ...
}

void detail(...)
{  ...
   if (error) ...
   ...
}
```

we want to write something like this:

```
...
int main()
{  ...
   compute(...);
   if (error) ...
   ...
}

void compute(...)
{  ... detail(...)  ...
}

void detail(...)
{  ...
}
```

The error actually occurs in *detail*. However, since this function is invoked by a call to *compute* in the *main* function, we may as well regard this error as a failure of function *compute* and we may want to base an error message or any other action on this view. The traditional way of dealing with this problem is by letting both *detail* and *compute* return a status code, indicating success or failure. This solution may be undesirable because of its complexity or it may even be impossible. For example, we could not have used it if the above function *compute*, instead of being a *void* function, already had returned a value for a purpose other than its status. Errors may also occur in *constructors*, which, as we know, do not return values at all. All this makes a special language construct for exception handling very desirable.

8.2 Using the Keywords *try*, *catch*, and *throw*

C++ offers us a very convenient means to solve the problem discussed at the end of the last section. It is based on three new keywords, *try*, *catch*, and *throw*, which you can find in this program fragment:

```
...
void detail(...)
{  ...
   if (error) throw 123;
   ...
}
void compute(...)
{  ...  detail(...)  ...
}
int main()
{  ...
   try {compute(...);}
   catch (int i) { ... }
   ...
}
```

If an error occurs in the function *detail*, the expression *throw* 123 is executed. As a result, this function is immediately left and program execution resumes in the compound statement { ... } following *catch*(*int i*) in the *main* function. In this compound statement, we can use *i*, whose value is 123. The compound statement just mentioned is not executed if the expression *error* in the function *detail* is equal to *false*. The following program is based on the above fragment:

```
// except1.cpp: Example of exception handling
#include <iostream>
using namespace std;

void detail(int k)
{  cout << "Start of detail function.\n";
   if (k == 0) throw 123;
   cout << "End of detail function.\n";
}
```

```
void compute(int i)
{   cout << "Start of compute function.\n";
    detail(i);
    cout << "End of compute function.\n";
}

int main()
{   int x;
    cout << "Enter x (0 will throw an exception): ";
    cin >> x;
    try {compute(x);}
    catch (int i) {cout << "Exception: " << i << endl;}
    cout << "The End.\n";
    return 0;
}
```

The output of this program depends on whether or not 0 is entered as input data. Here is a demonstration in which this is the case:

```
Enter x (0 will throw an exception): 0
Start of compute function.
Start of detail function.
Exception: 123
The End.
```

Code that executes a throw-expression, such as *throw* 123, is said to *throw an exception*. As the above output shows, the functions *detail* and *compute* are not completed.

If any nonzero integer is entered, no exception is thrown and the demonstration will be similar to this one:

```
Enter x (0 will throw an exception): 1
Start of compute function.
Start of detail function.
End of detail function.
End of compute function.
The End.
```

This output shows that for nonzero *x* values all three functions are completed in the normal way and the compound statement following *catch(int i)* is skipped.

Although the keywords *try*, *catch*, and *throw* are intended for exception handling, they could be used for just another flow of control. For example, if in function *detail* we replaced == with !=, the exception would be thrown for any nonzero input value.

To use exception handling in programs of our own, we must discuss a few points in some more detail. In program *except*1.*cpp*, the line

```
catch (int i) {cout << i << endl;}
```

is called an *exception handler*, or simply, a *handler*, and a succession of at least one handler is referred to as a *handler-sequence*. A *try-block* is syntactically defined as

```
try compound-statement handler-sequence
```

It follows that

```
try {compute(x);}
catch (int i) {cout << i << endl;}
```

is an example of a try-block. Note that, according to the terminology of the C++ Standard, the part starting with *catch*, that is, the handler, belongs to the try-block. There may be several handlers in the same try-block, but at least one is required. Instead of *catch (int i)* we could have written only *catch (int)* if we do not need the value *i*. Since this *i* can only have the value 123 in this (trivial) example, we might as well have written

```
catch (int) {cout << "123\n";}
```

instead of the above handler.

The fragment

```
throw 123
```

is technically known as a *throw-expression*, and it is an expression of type *void*. As usual, we obtain a statement by appending a semicolon. When an exception is thrown, control is transferred to a handler whose try-block was most recently entered and not yet exited. If there are several handlers in this try-block, the type of the expression following the *throw* keyword determines which one is taken. Program *except2.cpp* illustrates this.

If the user enters 0, an *int* exception is thrown and the first handler is executed. If he or she enters an nonzero integer, followed by a question mark, a *char* exception is thrown and the second handler is executed. If, instead, a nonzero integer is followed by a character other than a question mark, no exception is thrown. If 0? is entered, an *int* exception is thrown because of the order of the throw expressions in this program. Once control is transferred to a handler, there is no automatic return, so throw '?' will not be executed if *i* is zero.

```
// except2.cpp: Two handlers in a try-block.
#include <iostream>
using namespace std;

int main()
{   int i;
    char ch;
    cout << "Enter an integer, followed by some "
            "nonnumeric character:\n";
    try
    {   cin >> i >> ch;
        if (i == 0) throw 0;
        if (ch == '?') throw '?';
    }
    catch (int) {cout << "Zero entered.\n";}
    catch (char) {cout << "Question mark entered.\n";}
    cout << "The End.\n";
    return 0;
}
```

A handler can only be entered by throwing the corresponding exception, so at most one handler will be executed in this example, as the following four demonstrations illustrate:

```
Enter an integer, followed by some nonnumeric character:
0!
Zero entered.
The End.

Enter an integer, followed by some nonnumeric character:
2?
Question mark entered.
The End.

Enter an integer, followed by some nonnumeric character:
1!
The End.

Enter an integer, followed by some nonnumeric character:
0?
Zero entered.
The End.
```

Try-blocks may be dynamically nested, as this example shows:

```
void h()
{   ...
    if (...) throw 1;
    if (...) throw 2.0;
    ...
}
void g()
{   try {h();}
    catch(double) {...}
}
void f()
{   try {g();}
    catch(int) {...}
    catch(double) {...}
}
```

Function *h* is called from a try-block in function *g*, which in turn is called from a try-block in function *f*. If *throw* 1 is executed in function *h*, the *int* handler in *f* is invoked because there is no *int* handler in *g*. If *throw* 2.0 is executed, however, a choice must be made between the *double* handlers in *g* and in *f*. In this case the *double* handler of *g* is taken because it is the one whose try-block was most recently entered and not yet exited.

If in function *h* an exception of any type other than *int* and *double* were thrown, there would be no matching handler. In that case a built-in function *terminate* would be called, to terminate the program.

Re-throwing an exception

With exceptions in dynamically nested functions, as in the last example, it is possible for a handler at a lower level to re-throw the exception to a handler at a higher level. For example, in the following program an exception is thrown at the lowest level, in function *h*.

```
// except3.cpp: Re-throwing an exception.
#include <iostream>
using namespace std;

void h()              // Lowest level
{   throw 0;
}

void g()              // Intermediate level
{   try {h();}
    catch(int)
    {   cout << "Catch in g\n";
        throw; // This statement re-throws the exception.
    }
}

int main()            // Highest level
{   try {g();}
    catch(int){cout << "Catch in main\n";}
    return 0;
}
```

The handler in function *g*, in which *h* is called, deals with this exception, and the handler in the function *main* would not normally be used. However, in certain circumstances it may be desirable for the handler in *g* to transfer control to the handler in *main*, so that this one can also deal with the exception in question. This is done by means of the statement

```
throw;
```

in the handler of *g*. The output of this program, listed below, clearly shows that first the handler in *g* and then the one in *main* is executed:

```
Catch in g
Catch in main
```

In more realistic programs both throw-statements (in the functions *g* and *h*) would be part of if-statements, so that their execution depends on some condition. The examples of exception handlers discussed so far are also unrealistic in that we have used simple types such as *int* and *double*, while normally class types are used for this purpose, as we will see in the next section.

8.3 Exception Classes

As we have seen in Section 6.16, the name of a class (which has a default constructor) followed by an empty pair of parentheses, such as

```
Example()
```

forms a temporary, anonymous object of that class. Incidentally, the same applies to primitive standard types, so that *int*() represents a value of type *int* (equal to zero). For example, in our previous program, *except3.cpp*, we could have written the function *h* as follows:

```
void h()              // Lowest level
{  throw int();
}
```

The following program demonstrates this principle for the simplest possible class, which has no members at all:

```
// except4.cpp: The simplest possible exception class.
#include <iostream>
using namespace std;

class MyException { };

int main()
{  try
   {  throw MyException();
   }
   catch (MyException)
   {  cout << "Exception thrown.\n"; // This text is displayed
   }
   return 0;
}
```

If a class *D* is derived from a base class *B*, any *D* object is also a *B* object. A handler with type *B* is therefore a match for a throw-expression with an object of type *D*, as the following program demonstrates:

```
// except5.cpp: Catch with base class matches throw with
//              derived class.
#include <iostream>
using namespace std;

class B { };
class D: public B { };
```

```
int main()
{   try
    {   throw D();
    }
    catch (B)
    {   cout << "Exception thrown.\n"; // This text is displayed
    }
    return 0;
}
```

A more realistic example

Instead of a default constructor, we may use a constructor that accepts some value to provide the handler with some details about the exception. The following program demonstrates this with an exception that is more realistic than what we have seen so far. It defines a class *Array* (with *int* elements and with a fixed length of 10, for simplicity) which provides a subscript operator, so that objects of this class behave like real arrays. However, subscripts are checked and rejected if they are negative or greater than the maximum index value 9:

```
// except6.cpp: Our own subscripting operator with
//               array-bounds checking.
#include <iostream>
using namespace std;

class OutOfBounds {
public:
    OutOfBounds(int ii): i(ii){}
    int indexValue(){return i;}
private:
    int i;
};

class Array {        // For int array of length 10.
public:
    int &operator[](int i)
    {   if (i < 0 || i >= 10) throw OutOfBounds(i);
        return a[i];
    }
private:
    int a[10];
};

int main()
{   Array a;
    try
    {   a[3] = 30;
        cout << "a[3] = " << a[3] << endl;
        a[100] = 1000;
        cout << "a[1000] = " << a[1000] << endl;
    }
```

```
    catch (OutOfBounds error)
    {  cout << "Subscript value " << error.indexValue()
            << " out of bounds.\n";
    }
    return 0;
}
```

As you can see in the *main* function, we try to use the expressions $a[3]$ and $a[100]$. The result of this is shown in the output of this program:

```
a[3] = 30
Subscript value 100 out of bounds.
```

The *operator*[ ] function

```
int &operator[](int i)
{  if (i < 0 || i >= 10) throw OutOfBounds(i);
   return a[i];
}
```

performs the test that we need and throws an *OutOfBounds* exception by calling the constructor of this *OutOfBounds* class. In the (anonymous) object constructed in this way the incorrect subscript value *i* is stored. This object is obtained as the variable *error* in the handler in the *main* function. The member function *indexValue* returns this incorrect index value, so that it is available in the handler.

Note the ampersand (&) in the above first line of the *operator*[ ] function. This is necessary because this function is not only to return the value of the array element in question but that element itself (that is, an lvalue) so we can use an expression such as $a[3]$ as the left-hand side of an assignment.

8.4 Error Handling with *new*

In the original version of C++, the operator *new* returned the value 0 (also known as *NULL*) if memory allocation failed. According to the C++ standard, a *bad_alloc* exception must be thrown in this case, where *bad_alloc* is a class defined in the header <*new*>. The following program tests if this actually happens, so you can use it to check if your compiler conforms to the standard in this regard:

```
// newtest1.cpp: Default exception for 'new'.
#include <iostream>
#include <climits>
#include <new>
using namespace std;

int main()
{  char *p;
```

```
    try
    {  for (;;)
        {  p = new char[INT_MAX];
           if (p == NULL)
           {  cout << "The operator new returns NULL (= 0).\n";
              cout <<
              "This is not in accordance with Standard C++.\n";
              exit(1);
           }
        }
    }
    catch (bad_alloc)
    {  cout << "A bad_alloc exception has been thrown, "
                "which is correct.\n";
    }
    return 0;
}
```

Unfortunately, not all current C++ compilers cause this program to throw a *bad_alloc* exception. For example, Visual C++ 6.0 causes this program to produce the output

```
The operator new returns NULL (= 0).
This is not in accordance with Standard C++.
```

It should be possible to use the function *set_new_handler* to specify our own new-handler. For example, if we insert the function

```
void failing()
{  cout << "Memory allocation fails." << endl;
   throw bad_alloc();
}
```

before *main* in the program *newtest1.cpp*, and we write

```
set_new_handler(failing);
```

say, just before

```
for(;;)
```

this function *failing*, known as a *new-handler* should be called.

8.5 Exception Specifications

A function defined in the usual way can throw any exception. We can restrict the exceptions that a function can throw by adding something to that function. For example, by writing

```
void f() throw(X, Y)
{   ...
}
```

the function *f* can throw only the exceptions *X* and *Y*. The suffix

```
throw(...)
```

as used here, is called an *exception-specification* and can list any number of exceptions. Only the exceptions listed can be thrown. In particular, this list can be empty. The function *g*, defined as

```
void g() throw()
{   ...
}
```

can therefore throw no exception at all. As we know, the opposite case, which enables any exception to be thrown, is obtained by omitting this suffix altogether. So the function *f* defined as

```
void f()
{   ...
}
```

can throw any exception.

Exercises

8.1*   Write and demonstrate a function which tries to read an integer from the keyboard and throws an exception if this attempt fails.

8.2   Demonstrate the principle of exception handling by means of a function that (by using the standard library function *sqrt*) computes the square root of a nonnegative real number, supplied as an argument. If a negative argument is supplied, an exception is to be thrown.

9

Introduction to STL

9.1 Access to Vectors via Iterators

We have briefly discussed some important elements of the Standard Template Library (STL) in Section 1.7. The line

```
vector<string> v;
```

of the program *introstl.cpp* of that section should now be much clearer. Providing the class template *vector* with the template argument *string*, we obtain the type *vector<string>*. The class template *vector* is said to be a *sequence container*. As we will see shortly, there are also some other sequence containers, as well as some other STL containers, known as *associative containers*. With *i* of type *int*, we used the expression

```
v[i]
```

as if *v* were an array. It will now be clear that this is possible because C++ enables us to define our own operators, including the subscripting operator, for classes. With such *operator*[ ] functions, defined in the header *<vector>*, we cannot normally replace *v*[*i*] with **(v + i)* as we can with arrays. Yet pointer notation is also possible for vectors, but instead of real pointers we use so-called *iterators*. Here is a variation of the program *introstl.cpp*, just mentioned, which behaves in the same way as the original program but which is slightly different in that it uses an iterator:

```
// itera.cpp: Iterator-based version of introstl.cpp.
#include <iostream>
#include <string>
#include <vector>
#include <algorithm>
using namespace std;

int main()
{   vector<string> v;
    cout << "Enter lines of text to be sorted,\n";
    cout << "followed by the word stop:\n";
    for (;;)
    {   string s;
        getline(cin, s);
        if (s == "stop")
            break;
        v.push_back(s);
    }
    sort(v.begin(), v.end());
    cout << "The same lines after sorting:\n";
    for (vector<string>::iterator i=v.begin(); i!=v.end(); ++i)
        cout << *i << endl;
    return 0;
}
```

In this program the original loop

```
for (int i=0; i<v.size(); ++i)
    cout << v[i] << endl;
```

has been replaced with this one:

```
for (vector<string>::iterator i=v.begin(); i!=v.end(); ++i)
    cout << *i << endl;
```

In this modified version, the variable *i* is an iterator, of type *vector<string>::iterator*. This rather complicated notation shows that the type *iterator* used here is defined within the class *vector<string>*. As this for-statement illustrates, the *vector<string>* member functions *begin* and *end* return values of this very iterator type. The notation

```
*i
```

as used here is based on an overloaded unary operator *, and it shows that iterators are very much like pointers. The similarity between iterators and pointers is also reflected by the availability of the operator –> (see Section 6.1) for iterators. For example, if we want to obtain the C-style string stored in the *string* object **i*, we can use either of the following, equivalent expressions:

```
(*i).c_str()
i->c_str()
```

The above for-statement is similar to the one in the following fragment, which displays array *a* instead of vector *v*:

```
int a[N], *p;
...
for (p=a; p != a+N; ++p)
    cout << *p << " ";
```

It is usual in mathematics to write [*a*, *b*] for the closed interval $a \le x \le b$, while we write (*a*, *b*) for the open interval $a < x < b$. This explains the notation

  [*a*, *b*)

which is often used for the interval

  $a \le x < b$

Likewise, we will sometimes write

  [*ia*, *ib*)

for the range of iterator values used for *i* in this fragment:

```
vector<int>::iterator i, ia, ib;
...
for (i = ia; i != ib; ++i) ...
```

Note that we have written

```
i != ib
```

instead of

```
i < ib
```

which we have normally used in for-loops in which *i* has the type *int*. Actually, we could also use the latter notation for iterators as long as we are dealing with vectors. In view of containers other than vector, in which iterators can be compared with != but not with <, we also use != for vectors.

Going backward

It would be very tricky to traverse the vector elements in the reverse order, using only the means we have been discussing. Fortunately, there are also *reverse iterators* for this purpose. In the program *itera.cpp*, if we like, we can traverse the elements of the vector *v* from back to front as follows:

```
vector<string>::reverse_iterator i;
for (i=v.rbegin(); i != v.rend(); ++i)
    cout << *i << endl;
```

Note that we write ++*i* here, not −−*i*.

9.2 Vectors, Lists, Deques; Container Adaptors

In program *itera.cpp* there are three lines, shown once again below, that contain the word *vector*:

```
#include <vector>
{   vector<string> v;
for (vector<string>::iterator i=v.begin(); i!=v.end(); ++i)
```

This *vector* concept provides for contiguous memory allocation, with the possibility of efficiently adding and removing elements at the back. There is also a slightly more complex container type, known as a *deque*, in which elements can also be added and removed at the front. To replace a vector with a deque in the program *itera.cpp*, all we need to do is consistently replace the word *vector* with *deque*. As shown in the program below, we can replace *push_back* with *push_front*, to demonstrate adding new elements at the front, which would not be possible with a vector. Since the elements are placed in alphabetic order by the *sort* algorithm, such a change, as implemented in the following program, does not make any difference in the way the program behaves for the user:

```
// itdeque.cpp: Using a deque instead of a vector.
#include <iostream>
#include <string>
#include <deque>
#include <algorithm>
using namespace std;

int main()
{   deque<string> v;
    cout << "Enter lines of text to be sorted,\n";
    cout << "followed by the word stop:\n";
    for (;;)
    {   string s;
        getline(cin, s);
        if (s == "stop")
            break;
        v.push_front(s);
    }
    sort(v.begin(), v.end());
    cout << "The same lines after sorting:\n";
    for (deque<string>::iterator i=v.begin(); i!=v.end(); ++i)
        cout << *i << endl;
    return 0;
}
```

There is a third sequence container, *list*, which in some respects is different from a vector and a deque. Actually, this list container is based on a doubly-linked list, which would involve a considerable amount of programming if had to do this ourselves. With STL, we can write *list* instead of *vector* or *deque*, but we also have to replace

```
sort(v.begin(), v.end());  // v is a vector or a deque
```

with

```
v.sort();                  // v is a list
```

Instead of using the *sort* algorithm, which is in fact a template function, we have to use a member function with the same name for a list.

The user will not notice any difference in the behavior of these three program versions, but the internal data representation is different. This is relevant with regard to the available operations that can be performed efficiently. Like a deque, a list allows us to use both member functions *push_back* and *push_front*. However, unlike a vector and a deque, a list enables us even to insert and delete items efficiently at any position, as Figure 9.1 indicates.

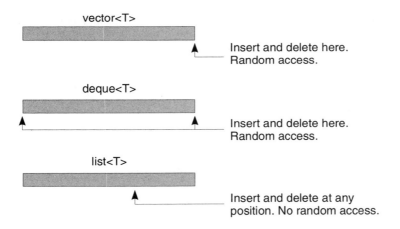

Figure 9.1. Properties of three sequence containers

In other words, we can efficiently insert and delete elements only at the end of a vector, both at the beginning and at the end of a deque, and at any position in a list. Although a vector is very limited with regard to insertions and deletions, it has the advantage of providing *random access*, as does a deque but not a list. Some examples will clarify these differences. For the sake of completeness, it should be pointed out that there is a fourth sequence container, the conventional array, defined as

```
T a[N];
```

for an array with elements of type *T*. We will demonstrate that we can successfully use STL to sort an array. In other words, STL can be useful even in programs that use only conventional arrays, not any typical STL container, as we will see in the next section.

As the following table shows, vectors, deques, and lists do not support the same set of operations:

Operation	Function	*vector*	*deque*	*list*
insert at the end	*push_back*	✓	✓	✓
delete at the end	*pop_back*	✓	✓	✓
insert at the beginning	*push_front*	-	✓	✓
delete at the beginning	*pop_front*	-	✓	✓
insert anywhere	*insert*	(✓)	(✓)	✓
delete anywhere	*erase*	(✓)	(✓)	✓
sort	*sort* (algorithm)	✓	✓	-

The entry (✓) (in parentheses) indicates that the *insert* and *erase* functions, though available for vectors and deques, are considerably slower for these containers than they are for lists. They are said to be *linear time* for vectors and deques, which means that the time they take is proportional to the length of the sequence stored in the container. By contrast, all operations indicated by ✓ (without parentheses) are *constant time*, that is, the time they require does not depend on the sequence length.

So far, we have only seen the functions *push_back* and *push_front* in action. The following program shows how to use all functions (*push_back*, *pop_back*, *push_front*, *pop_front*, *insert*, and *erase*) for insertion and deletion, listed in the above table.

```cpp
// insdel.cpp: Insertions and deletions in a list.
#include <string>
#include <iostream>
#include <list>
using namespace std;

void showlist(const string &str, const list<int> &L)
{  list<int>::const_iterator i;
   cout << str << endl << "   ";
   for (i=L.begin(); i != L.end(); ++i)
      cout << *i << " ";
   cout << endl;
}

int main()
{  list<int> L;
   int x;
   cout << "Enter positive integers, followed by 0:\n";
   while (cin >> x, x != 0)
      L.push_back(x);
   showlist("Initial list:", L);
   L.push_front(123);
   showlist("After inserting 123 at the beginning:", L);
   list<int>::iterator i = L.begin();
   L.insert(++i, 456);
   showlist(
      "After inserting 456 at the second position:", L);
   i = L.end();
   L.insert(--i, 999);
```

```
     showlist(
        "After inserting 999 just before the end:", L);
     i = L.begin(); x = *i;
     L.pop_front();
     cout << "Deleted at the beginning: " << x << endl;
     showlist("After this deletion:", L);
     i = L.end(); x = *--i;
     L.pop_back();
     cout << "Deleted at the end: " << x << endl;
     showlist("After this deletion:", L);
     i = L.begin();
     x = *++i; cout << "To be deleted: " << x << endl;
     L.erase(i);
     showlist("After this deletion (of second element):",
        L);
     return 0;
  }
```

The functions for insertion and deletion are here applied to a *list*, since this container type is the only one for which all these functions are available and efficient, as the above table indicates. Here is a demonstration of this program:

```
Enter positive integers, followed by 0:
10 20 30 0
Initial list:
  10 20 30
After inserting 123 at the beginning:
  123 10 20 30
After inserting 456 at the second position:
  123 456 10 20 30
After inserting 999 just before the end:
  123 456 10 20 999 30
Deleted at the beginning: 123
After this deletion:
  456 10 20 999 30
Deleted at the end: 30
After this deletion:
  456 10 20 999
To be deleted: 10
After this deletion (of second element):
  456 20 999
```

The type *const_iterator*, used in the following fragment, requires an explanation:

```
void showlist(const string &str, const list<int> &L)
{ list<int>::const_iterator i;
```

As discussed in Section 4.10, it is good practice to supply reference (and pointer) parameters with the word *const* in the above way if such parameters do not modify the objects referred to. Since *showlist* modifies neither the string *str* nor the list *L*, there are two occurrences of *const* in the first of these two program lines. Then on the second line we must define the variable *i* as a *const_iterator* to be able to use it for *L*. If there was no such requirement, it would be very difficult (or impossible) for the compiler to spot any attempts to modify **i*, which, after *i = L.begin*(), would be wrong because of the use of *const* in *const list<int> L*.

Erasing a subsequence

If [*i*1, *i*2) is a valid range in a vector *v*, we can erase the subsequence of *v* given by this range in the following way:

```
v.erase(i1, i2);
```

This also applies to containers other than vectors.

Container adaptors

We will now discuss some containers (stacks, queues, and priority queues) which are restricted versions of the *vector*, *deque*, and *list* sequences and referred to as *container adaptors*. In particular, iterators are not available for these containers.

Stacks

A *stack* is a data structure that admits only two operations to modify its size: *push*, to insert an element at the end, and *pop*, to delete an element at the end. In other words, a stack is based on the principle of Last In First Out (LIFO). Besides *push* and *pop*, there are also the member functions *empty* and *size*, with their usual meaning, and *top* (instead of *back*) for access to the final element.

We can represent a stack by each of the three STL sequence containers vector, deque, and list. A stack is therefore not an entirely new container type, but rather a special version of a vector, a deque, or a list, which explains the term *container adaptor*.

For example, let us use a stack to read a sequence of integers and to display them in the reverse order. Any nonnumeric character will act as a code for 'end of input.' In the following program this stack is represented by a vector, but it also works if we replace all occurrences of *vector* with *deque* or *list*. This program also demonstrates the use of the member functions *empty*, *top*, and *size*.

```
// stack1.cpp: Using a stack to read a number sequence
//      of arbitrary length and to display this sequence
//      in the reverse order.
#include <iostream>
#include <vector>
#include <stack>
using namespace std;

int main()
{   stack <int, vector<int> > S;
    int x;
```

```
    cout <<
        "Enter some integers, followed by a letter:\n";
    while (cin >> x) S.push(x);
    while (!S.empty())
    {   x = S.top();
        cout << "Size: " << S.size()
            << "      Element at the top: " << x << endl;
        S.pop();
    }
    return 0;
}
```

The *stack* template has two arguments, as this program line shows:

```
stack <int, vector<int> > S;
```

It is very important to write > >, with a blank space in the middle. If we omit this space between the two successive characters >>, the compiler will interpret these as the operator >>, as used in bit and input operations.

After some integers, entered by the user, have been pushed onto the stack, the program repeatedly displays both the stack size and the element to be popped from the stack, as this demonstration shows:

```
Enter some integers, followed by a letter:
10 20 30 A
Size: 3      Element at the top: 30
Size: 2      Element at the top: 20
Size: 1      Element at the top: 10
```

We cannot use iterators for stacks, let alone traverse them. The stack container provides the assignment operator = and comparison operators such as == and <. The operator < performs a lexicographic comparison, as the following program demonstrates:

```
// stackcmp.cpp: Stack assignments and comparisons.
#include <iostream>
#include <vector>
#include <stack>
using namespace std;

int main()
{   stack <int, vector<int> > S, T, U;
    S.push(10); S.push(20); S.push(30);
    cout << "Pushed onto S: 10 20 30\n";
    T = S;
    cout << "After T = S; we have ";
    cout << (S == T ? "S == T" : "S != T") << endl;
    U.push(10); U.push(21);
    cout << "Pushed onto U: 10 21\n";
    cout << "We now have ";
    cout << (S < U ? "S < U" : "S >= U") << endl;
    return 0;
}
```

This program produces the following output:

```
Pushed onto S: 10 20 30
After T = S; we have S == T
Pushed onto U: 10 21
We now have S < U
```

Figure 9.2 illustrates the last comparison.

Figure 9.2. Lexicographical comparison of stacks

The elements at the bottom are compared first. Since these are both 10, the second lowest elements, 20 and 21, are compared. We have $S < U$ because $20 < 21$. This is similar to the comparison of strings, where we start with the first characters instead of the elements at the bottom of the stacks.

It is interesting to note that the *top* member function returns a reference, which enables us to modify the top of a nonempty stack without performing a pop and a push operation. For example, we can simply write

```
S.top() = 15;
```

instead of

```
S.pop();
S.push(15);
```

Queues

A *queue* is a data structure in which we can insert elements at one end, the back, and remove them from the opposite end, the front. We can inspect (and modify) the elements at the front and at the back, as Figure 9.3 illustrates.

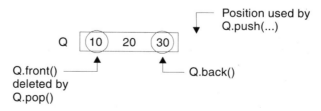

Figure 9.3. A queue

Unlike a stack, we cannot represent a queue by a vector, because this does not provide the *pop_front* operation. For example, we cannot write

```
queue <int, vector<int> > Q;   // Error
```

This line will be correct if we replace *vector* with either *deque* or *list*. The following program shows that the queue member functions *push* and *pop* work as indicated in Figure 9.3.

```
// queue.cpp: Using a queue; a demonstration of the
//            member functions push, pop, back, and front.
#include <iostream>
#include <list>
#include <queue>

using namespace std;

int main()
{   queue <int, list<int> > Q;
    Q.push(10); Q.push(20); Q.push(30);
    cout << "After pushing 10, 20 and 30:\n";
    cout << "Q.front() = " << Q.front() << endl;
    cout << "Q.back()  = " << Q.back() << endl;
    Q.pop();
    cout << "After Q.pop():\n";
    cout << "Q.front() = " << Q.front() << endl;
    return 0;
}
```

The output of this program is

```
After pushing 10, 20 and 30:
Q.front() = 10
Q.back()  = 30
After Q.pop():
Q.front() = 20
```

The queue member functions *empty* and *size* are similar to those of the stack container, and so are the assignment and comparison operators. Comparison starts at the front elements; if these are equal the next elements are compared, and so on.

Priority queues

A *priority queue* is a data structure in which, as long as it is not empty, only the largest element can be retrieved. As with stacks, the most important member functions are *push*, *pop*, and *top*. The following program uses these functions:

```cpp
// prqueue.cpp: A priority queue; a demonstration of the
//              member functions push, pop, empty, and top.
#include <iostream>
#include <vector>
#include <functional>
#include <queue>
using namespace std;

int main()
{   priority_queue <int, vector<int> > P;
    int x;
    P.push(123); P.push(51); P.push(1000); P.push(17);
    while (!P.empty())
    {   x = P.top();
        cout << "Retrieved element: " << x << endl;
        P.pop();
    }
    return 0;
}
```

This program produces the following output, in which the numbers appear in descending order:

```
Retrieved element: 1000
Retrieved element: 123
Retrieved element: 51
Retrieved element: 17
```

Since it is essential that elements can be compared, the *priority_queue* template accepts an optional third argument. Here we might replace the declaration

```cpp
priority_queue <int, vector<int> > P;
```

with the following version, without any essential difference in meaning:

```cpp
priority_queue <int, vector<int>, less<int> > P;
```

Here *less<int>* is a standard class, used to form function objects (see Section 6.16). If we want to retrieve the elements in increasing order, we simply replace *less<int>* with *greater<int>*. We can specify any ordering we like by writing a function object of our own. Let us demonstrate this by another example, in which the elements are retrieved in increasing order of the final digits of the integers stored in the priority queue:

```cpp
// lastdig.cpp: A priority queue; P.top() is the element
//              whose last digit is less than (or equal to)
//              that of the other elements.
#include <iostream>
#include <vector>
#include <queue>
using namespace std;
```

```
class CompareLastDigits {
public:
    bool operator()(int x, int y)
    {   return x % 10 > y % 10;
    }
};

int main()
{   priority_queue <int, vector<int>,
        CompareLastDigits> P;
    int x;
    P.push(123); P.push(51); P.push(1000); P.push(17);
    while (!P.empty())
    {   x = P.top();
        cout << "Retrieved element: " << x << endl;
        P.pop();
    }
    return 0;
}
```

In the output of this program, the inserted numbers 123, 51, 1000, 17 appear in ascending order of their last digits ($0 < 1 < 3 < 7$):

```
Retrieved element: 1000
Retrieved element: 51
Retrieved element: 123
Retrieved element: 17
```

Note that we really have to use a function object because the third template argument (if present) of the *priority_queue* must be a type. The identifier *CompareLastDigit* denotes such a type. The comparison

```
x % 10 > y % 10;
```

contains a greater-than character, which causes the element with the smallest final digit to be selected. This is similar to using *greater<int>* if the smallest element is to appear first.

9.3 Iterator Categories

We can apply the *sort* algorithm to arrays, to vectors, and to deques, but not to lists. By contrast, the *find* algorithm can be applied to all these four container types. (In this section, we are using the term *container* for what is actually a *sequence container*, ignoring other container types, which we will introduce in Section 9.6.) It will be clear that we only need one pass over all elements to find a given value, while efficient sorting requires random access. In both cases *iterators* are used, but the *sort* algorithm requires 'more powerful' iterators than does the *find* algorithm, used to search a container for an item. It makes sense to divide iterators into five categories, according to the operations that are defined for them. Suppose that *i* and *j* are iterators of the same type. Then the three operations

```
i == j          i != j          i = j
```

are possible, regardless of the iterator category. As for some other operations, the following table shows which apply to each iterator category. We suppose that x is a variable of the same type as the container elements in question and that n is of type *int*:

Iterator category	Operations (in addition to $i == j, i != j, i = j$)	Provided by containers	Required by typical algorithm
input	$x = {*}i$, $++i$, $i++$	all four	*find*
output	${*}i = x$, $++i$, $i++$	all four	*copy* (destination)
forward	as both input and output	all four	*replace*
bidirectional	as forward and $--i$, $i--$	all four	*reverse*
random access	as bidirectional and $i + n, i - n$, $i += n, i -= n$, $i < j, i > j, i <= j, i >= j$	*array, vector, deque* (not *list*)	*sort*

According to the second column of this table, a *forward* iterator provides all operations of *input* iterators and all those of *output* iterators. *Bidirectional* iterators provide pre- and post-decrement operations in addition to all operations provided by forward iterators. Adding yet another set of operations (+, −, +=, −=, <, >, <= and >=), we arrive at the *random-access* iterator category. Adding an integer to an iterator is possible only for random-access iterators. This operation is required, for example, by the *sort* algorithm. Since a *list* does not provide a random-access iterator, we cannot apply the *sort* algorithm to a list.

The following program, uses the *find* algorithm, just mentioned, applied to a list:

```cpp
// find1.cpp: Finding a given value in a list.
#include <iostream>
#include <list>
#include <algorithm>
using namespace std;

int main()
{   int x;
    list<int> v;
    v.push_back(2); v.push_back(5); v.push_back(8);
    cout << "Enter an integer to be found in {2, 5, 8}:\n";
    cin >> x;
    list<int>::iterator i = find(v.begin(), v.end(), x);
    if (i == v.end()) cout << "Not found.";
    else
    {   cout << "Found ";
        if (i == v.begin())
            cout << "as the first element.";
        else cout << "after " << *--i;
    }
    cout << endl;
    return 0;
}
```

As this program shows, we search the list *v* for the item *x* by writing

```
list<int>::iterator i = find(v.begin(), v.end(), x);
```

The if-statement that follows illustrates that this call to *find* returns the value *v.end()* if the item is not found. We now focus our attention to the line

```
else cout << " after " << *--i;
```

You may have wondered why we did not use the expression $*(i - 1)$ instead of $*--i$; after all, it is not clear why we should change the value of *i*. The answer is that $i - 1$ is valid only for random-access iterators, while $--i$ is also correct for bidirectional iterators. Since *v* is a list, *i* is a bidirectional iterator, for which the expression $i - 1$ is not valid. This program therefore no longer compiles if we replace $*--i$ with $*(i - 1)$.

Instead of

```
list<int> v;
v.push_back(2); v.push_back(5); v.push_back(8);
```

we could have written

```
int a[3] = {2, 5, 8};
list<int> v(a, a+3);
```

to obtain a list *v* containing the elements 2, 5, and 8, in that order. It will be clear that this is possible because the *list* class template has more than one constructor. The same holds for *vector* and *deque* containers.

As the above table shows, the less-than operator is not available for iterators provided by lists. The comments in the following fragment illustrate this:

```
// Demonstration of random-access iterators:
int a[3] = {2, 5, 8};
vector<int> v(a, a+3);
vector<int>::iterator iv = v.begin(), iv1;
iv1 = iv + 1;
bool b1 = iv < iv1;
// In the last two lines, + and < are allowed
// because iv and iv1 are random-access iterators.

// Demonstration of bidirectional iterators:
list<int> w(a, a+3);
list<int>::iterator iw = w.begin(), iw1;
iw1 = iw + 1;          // Error
bool b2 = iw < iw1;    // Error
// In the last two lines, + and < are not allowed
// because iw and iw1 are bidirectional iterators.

// By contrast, the following two lines are correct:
iw1 = iw;
bool b3 = iw == iw1;
```

Iterator category required by algorithms

Of all possible operations on iterators, the *find* algorithm only requires those which are provided by input iterators, since it needs only to 'read' sequence elements, executing, for example, the assignment $x = *i$. This is why the name *find* occurs as an example for input iterators in the column *Required by typical algorithm* of the table we have been discussing.

We can use the *copy* algorithm (also listed in that table) in the following way to copy all elements of the sequence container *v* to the container *w*, provided that *w* already contains enough elements to store all elements of *v*:

```
copy(v.begin(), v.end(), w.begin());
```

On the other hand, if new elements in *w* still have to be generated to store those to be copied from *v*, we should use an inserter (to be discussed in Section 9.10), writing

```
copy(v.begin(), v.end(), inserter(w, w.begin()));
```

Let us assume that *v* is a vector and *w* a list. To verify that this call to *copy* is in accordance with the table at the beginning of this section, observe that the destination *w* is a *list*, which provides the bidirectional iterator category. Only the output-iterator category is required for *w*, but bidirectional iterators support all output-iterator operations, so there is no problem. Since the *copy* algorithm requires only an output iterator as its third argument, it will not apply the operators --,+, -, <, <=, >=, and > to iterators referring to elements of *w*; neither will it 'read' anything from *w* by executing something like $x = *i$. The opposite operation, $*i = x$, will be executed, however, to 'write' the copied values into *w*.

Stream iterators: using *copy* for input and output

We can use the *copy* algorithm to perform output, as the following fragment illustrates:

```
const int N = 4;
int a[N] = {7, 6, 9, 2};
copy(a, a+N, ostream_iterator<int>(cout, " "));
```

We can also define an iterator variable *i* to use this as the third argument of *copy*. This is done by replacing the above call to *copy* with these two statements:

```
ostream_iterator<int> i(cout, " ");
copy(a, a+N, i);
```

In either case, the numbers 7, 6, 9, and 2 are written to *cout*, as if we had written

```
for (int* p=a; p != a+N; ++p)
   cout << *p << " ";
```

We can use the same idea for input, writing

```
istream_iterator<int, ptrdiff_t>(file)
```

where *file* is the input stream. This rather complex expression is to be used instead of, for example, *v.begin*( ), which we would use if we wanted to copy from the container *v*. If we omit *file* on the above line, we obtain the expression

```
istream_iterator<int, ptrdiff_t>()
```

to be used instead of *v.end*( ) because it denotes end-of-file. For example, suppose that we are given the file *example.txt*, with the following contents:

```
10 20 30
40 50
```

It is given that this file contains only integers (separated and possibly followed by white-space characters), but we do not know how many integers there are in the file. The following program reads the integers from this file and displays them on the screen:

```
// copyio.cpp: Using the copy algorithm for I/O.
#include <fstream>
#include <iostream>
#include <iterator>
#include <vector>
using namespace std;
typedef istream_iterator<int> istream_iter;

int main()
{   vector<int> a;
    ifstream file("example.txt");
    if (file.fail())
    {   cout << "Cannot open file example.txt.\n";
        return 1;
    }
    copy(istream_iter(file), istream_iter(),
        inserter(a, a.begin()));
    copy(a.begin(), a.end(),
        ostream_iterator<int>(cout, " "));
    cout << endl;
    return 0;
}
```

Since the program ignores the structure of the input file, its output consists of only one line:

```
10 20 30 40 50
```

Iterator operations

Recall that we can perform arithmetic operations with random-access iterators in the same way as we can with pointers, writing, for example,

```
int n, dist;
...     // i and i0 are random-access iterators
i0 = i;
i += n;
dist = i - i0;   // dist == n
```

Instead, we can use the functions *advance* and *distance*, as the following fragment shows:

```
int n, dist;
...     // i and i0 are iterators, not necessarily
        // belonging to the random-access category
i0 = i;
advance(i, n);
distance(i0, i, dist);   // dist == n
```

This works for *all* iterators, provided the value of *n* is reasonable, so that the modified value of *i* refers either to an existing element of the container in question or to the past-the-end element. If *i* is a forward iterator, *n* can only be positive. Then the above call to *advance* has the same effect as applying the ++ operator *n* times to *i*. The *advance* and *distance* operations will be executed much faster for random-access iterators than for other iterator types.

9.4 Arrays and STL Algorithms

STL algorithms, such as *sort*, can very well be applied to arrays, with normal pointers acting as iterators.

```
// sortarr.cpp: Sorting an array.
#include <iostream>
#include <algorithm>
using namespace std;

int main()
{   int a[10], x, n = 0, *p;
    cout << "Enter at most 10 positive integers, "
        "followed by 0:\n";
    while (cin >> x, x != 0 && n < 10) a[n++] = x;
    sort(a, a+n);
    cout << "After sorting: \n";
    for (p=a; p != a+n; ++p) cout << *p << " ";
    cout << endl;
    return 0;
}
```

It is important to note the similarity between the calls

```
sort(v.begin(), v.end());
```

which we use to sort the vector *v* with

```
sort(a, a+n);
```

in program *sortar.cpp*. In both calls the first argument refers to the first element of the sequence container and the second to the *past-the-end* element, that is, the position just after the final element. This is a general principle, applying not only to *sort* but to most STL algorithms. We can also apply this principle to a part, or *subsequence*, of a given sequence. For example, we can sort only *a*[3], *a*[4], *a*[5], and *a*[6] by writing

```
sort(a+3, a+7);
```

or, equivalently,

```
sort(&a[3], &a[7]);
```

as Figure 9.4 illustrates.

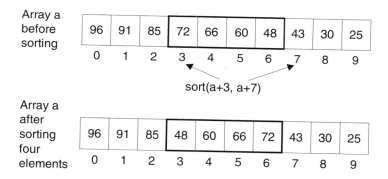

Figure 9.4. Sorting a subsequence

It may at first seem more logical to supply the address of the last element, *a*[6], instead of that of the past-the-end element, *a*[7], in this example. However, using the past-the-end element has several advantages. For example, we can now find the number of elements by a simple subtraction:

Number of elements = $7 - 3 = 4$

This convention also enables us to write the for-loop

```
for (i=3; i!=7; ++i) ...
```

if we want to do something with the sorted elements. The principle of selecting only a subsequence also applies to containers other than arrays, such as vectors. For example, if, in program *sort1.cpp*, vector *v* also contains at least seven elements, we can sort *v*[3], *v*[4], *v*[5], and *v*[6] by writing

```
vector<int>::iterator i, j;
i = v.begin() + 3;
j = v.begin() + 7;
sort(i, j);
```

or, simply,

```
sort(v.begin()+3, v.begin()+7);
```

Initialization of containers

As we have seen in Section 4.5, the definition of an array can include a list of initial values. For example, we can write

```
int a[3] = {10, 5, 7};
int b[] = {8, 13}; // equivalent to int b[2] = {8, 13};
int c[3] = {4};    // equivalent to int c[3] = {4, 0, 0};
```

Initialization is also possible for the other three types of sequence containers, as this example shows:

```
int a[3] = {10, 5, 7};
vector<int> v(a, a+3);
deque<int> w(a, a+3);
list<int> x(a, a+3);
```

Not only an array but also a vector, a deque, or a list can be used as the basis for initializing *the same* container type. For example, if we proceed with

```
vector<int> v1(v.begin(), v.end());
```

vector $v1$ will be identical with vector v, both consisting of the three *int* elements 10, 5, and 7. This example is correct because both v and $v1$ are of the same container type *vector*. By contrast, the following does not compile, because we cannot use the values of the list x to initialize the vector $v1$:

```
vector<int> v1(x.begin(), x.end());
```

It will be clear that initializing STL containers is made possible by constructors. There are also constructors that accept an integer, indicating the desired size and, optionally, a value to be used for all newly created elements. For example, we can write

```
vector<int> v(5, 8); // Five elements, all equal to 8.
```

or

```
vector<int> v(5);
```

In the latter case, the vector v has five elements, which will all be set to zero. This form may be useful if we intend to assign values to these elements later.

9.5 Special Member Functions for Lists

As we already know, an advantage of lists over vectors and deques is the possibility of inserting and deleting elements in any position in constant time, but they have the disadvantage of not providing random access. An STL list can very well be implemented as a doubly-linked list, as shown in Figure 9.5. Since the nodes of this list contain links both to the next and to the previous nodes, the operations ++ and ––, applied to iterators, will be efficient, that is, they will take constant time. By contrast, moving from a node to a node that lies *n* positions further in the list will take $O(n)$ time, which means that the computing time required for this task is linearly proportional to *n*.

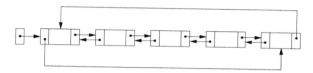

Figure 9.5. A doubly-linked list

To insert a node somewhere in the middle of the list, four pointer members of nodes have to be given appropriate values, since there must be two pointers (from its left and right neighbors) pointing to that node and two others pointing from that node to its neighbors. No other nodes have to be updated, which explains why insertion in any position is constant time. Deleting a node is equally efficient.

If nodes are inserted in a list, all iterators referring to nodes of that list remain valid, which, as we know, need not be the case with vectors and deques.

Many member functions, such as constructors and insert functions, can be used in the same way as with vectors and deques, but, as we have just been discussing, all list insertions take constant time. There is no subscripting operator [] for lists, since subscripting is associated with random-access iterators, while the list iterators are only bidirectional.

The *sort* and *unique* member functions

As we have seen in Section 9.2, the *sort* algorithm does not work with lists. Instead, there is a list member function *sort*. Another list-specific function is *unique*, which removes any consecutive duplicate elements. These two functions are declared in the class template *list* as follows:

```
void sort();
void unique();
```

The following program demonstrates both functions:

```
// list1.cpp: The list member functions sort and unique.
#include <iostream>
#include <list>
using namespace std;

void out(const char *s, const list<int> &L)
{   cout << s;
    copy(L.begin(), L.end(),
        ostream_iterator<int>(cout, " "));
    cout << endl;
}
int main()
{   list<int> L(5, 123);
    L.push_back(100);
    L.push_back(123);
    L.push_back(123);
    out("Initial contents: ", L);
    L.unique();
    out("After L.unique(): ", L);
    L.sort();
    out("After L.sort():    ", L);
    return 0;
}
```

As the output of this program shows, *unique* deals only with consecutive elements, resulting in two elements 123 in the result: one before and the other after the element 100.

```
Initial contents: 123 123 123 123 123 100 123 123
After L.unique(): 123 100 123
After L.sort():    100 123 123
```

If we had called the two member functions in the opposite order

```
L.sort(); L.unique();
```

the final result would have consisted of only two elements:

```
100 123
```

Splicing

Another list-specific operation is *splicing*, that is, moving one or more consecutive elements from one list to another, without allocating or deallocating memory for these elements. There are three *splice* member functions, which (inside the *list* class) can be declared as shown below. In the explaining comments, *L* and *M* are lists of the same type:

```
void splice(iterator position, list<T>& x);
```

If *i* is a valid iterator for *L*, the following statement inserts the contents of *M* before *i* in *L* and leaves *M* empty. This does *not* work if *L* and *M* are the same list:

```
L.splice(i, M);
```

```
void splice(iterator position, list<T>& x, iterator j);
```

If *i* is a valid iterator for *L*, and *j* likewise for *M*, the following statement removes the element to which *j* refers and inserts it before *i*. This also works if *L* and *M* are the same list:

```
L.splice(i, M, j);
```

```
void splice(iterator position, list<T>& x,
    iterator first, iterator last);
```

If *i* is a valid iterator for *L* and [*j*1, *j*2) is a valid range in *M*, the following statement removes the elements of that range and inserts them before *i* in *L*. This also works if *L* and *M* are the same list:

```
L.splice(i, M, j1, j2);
```

We will demonstrate the last *splice* function to change the list as indicated in Figure 9.6.

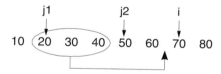

Figure 9.6. Splicing

The elements 20, 30, 40 of the sequence 10, 20, 30, 40, 50, 60, 70, 80 are moved to their new position between 60 and 70. The resulting sequence is

```
10 50 60 20 30 40 70 80
```

which is exactly the output produced by the following program:

```
// splice.cpp: Splicing.
#include <iostream>
#include <list>
using namespace std;

int main()
{   list<int> L;
    list<int>::iterator i, j1, j2, j;
    for (int k = 10; k <= 80; k += 10)
    {   L.push_back(k);
        j = L.end();
        if (k == 20) j1 = --j; else
        if (k == 50) j2 = --j; else
        if (k == 70) i = --j;
    }
    L.splice(i, L, j1, j2);
    copy(L.begin(), L.end(), ostream_iterator<int>(cout, " "));
    cout << endl;
    return 0;
}
```

Note the statement

```
i = --j;
```

(and similar ones) in this program. We cannot replace this with

```
i = j - 1;
```

because the plus and minus operators are not defined for bidirectional iterators. The $--$ operator is required here because the iterator $j = L.end()$ refers to the position just after the most recent element, added by *push_back*. Instead of this solution with three if-statements, we could have used the *find* algorithm (see Section 9.11), replacing the above rather complicated for-loop with the following fragment:

```
for (int k = 10; k <= 80; k += 10)
   L.push_back(k);
j1 = find(L.begin(), L.end(), 20);
j2 = find(L.begin(), L.end(), 50);
i = find(L.begin(), L.end(), 70);
```

This fragment is quite acceptable for the short sequence used in this program, but the solution adopted in the complete program would have been more efficient than this fragment if the sequence had been very long.

Recall that algorithms such as *find* are defined in the header *algorithm*, so that we have to write

```
#include <algorithm>
```

at the top of program that use algorithms.

The *remove* algorithm

Suppose that the list L contains the sequence {1, 4, 3, 1, 2} and that we want to remove all elements equal to 1. There is a *remove* algorithm, which performs part of this task, in the sense that it shifts all other elements to the front, retaining their relative order. In other words, the new list L then starts with the subsequence {4, 3, 2}, and the remaining elements are garbage. This *remove* algorithm returns an iterator denoting the value past-the-end of this subsequence. In order to retain only this subsequence and to delete the garbage following it, we can use the *list* member function *erase*. Incidentally, all this applies not only to lists but also to vectors and deques. The following program does just what we have been discussing. It works with a list, but it would also work if we consistently replace the word *list* with either *vector* or *deque*:

```
// removal.cpp: The remove algorithm.
#include <iostream>
#include <algorithm>
#include <list>
#include <iterator>
using namespace std;
```

```
int main()
{   int a[6] = {1, 4, 1, 3, 1, 2};
    list<int> L(a, a + 6);
    list<int>::iterator new_end =
        remove(L.begin(), L.end(), 1);
    cout << L.size() << endl;   // 6 (still garbage at the end)
    L.erase(new_end, L.end());  // Remove last three elements
    cout << L.size() << endl;   // 3 (garbage removed)
    return 0;
}
```

The list member function *remove*

If all list elements equal to a given value are to be deleted, the two-step approach, consisting of calls to the *remove* and *erase* algorithms, as we have just been discussing, is not very efficient. It is much better to use the list member function *remove* for this purpose. This function is declared inside the *list* template class as follows:

```
void remove(const T& value);
```

This function is specific for lists; it is not available as member functions of vectors and deques. The following program shows that it is quite simple to use:

```
// removemf.cpp: The list member function remove.
#include <iostream>
#include <list>
using namespace std;

void out(const char *s, const list<int> &L)
{   cout << s;
    copy(L.begin(), L.end(),
        ostream_iterator<int>(cout, " "));
    cout << endl;
}

int main()
{   int a[6] = {1, 4, 1, 3, 1, 2};
    list<int> L(a, a + 6);
    out("Initial sequence L:\n", L);
    L.remove(1);
    out("After L.remove(1):\n", L);
    return 0;
}
```

This program produces the following output:

```
Initial sequence L:
1 4 1 3 1 2
After L.remove(1):
4 3 2
```

The list member function *reverse*

The *list* container also provides a *reverse* function, declared in the class *list* as follows:

```
void reverse();
```

This member function, available only for lists, not for vectors or deques, takes advantage of the way lists are implemented. For a list *L* we therefore prefer the member-function call

```
L.reverse();
```

to the following call of the *reverse* algorithm:

```
reverse(L.begin(), L.end());
```

Note, however, that this *reverse* algorithm is also applicable to vectors, deques and even arrays.

The list member function *merge*

If two sequences are in ascending order, they can very efficiently be combined into one sequence, also in ascending order. This process is referred to as *merging*. Merging lists can be much more efficient than merging vectors or deques, since only links, not the list elements themselves, need to be copied. The *list* class contains the following declaration of a *merge* member function:

```
void merge(list<T>& x);
```

The following program demonstrates how to use this *merge* member function:

```
// lstmerge.cpp: The list member function merge.
#include <iostream>
#include <list>
using namespace std;
void out(const char *s, const list<int> &L)
{  cout << s;
   copy(L.begin(), L.end(), ostream_iterator<int>(cout, " "));
   cout << endl;
}

int main()
{  list<int> L1, L2, L3;
   list<int>::iterator new_end;
   L1.push_back(10); L1.push_back(20); L1.push_back(30);
   L2.push_back(15); L2.push_back(35);
   out("Initial sequence L1:\n", L1);
   out("Initial sequence L2:\n", L2);
   L1.merge(L2);
   out("After L1.merge(L2):\n", L1);
   return 0;
}
```

This program produces the following output:

```
Initial sequence L1:
10 20 30
Initial sequence L2:
15 35
After L1.merge(L2):
10 15 20 30 35
```

The last line shows the new list *L*1, while *L*2 is empty.

There is also a *merge* algorithm, which is not restricted to lists. It can even merge sequences stored in different container types and produce the result in yet another container type. For example, the following program merges the array *a* and the list *L* and places the result in the vector *v*:

```
// mergealg.cpp: The merge algorithm.

#include <algorithm>
#include <list>
#include <vector>
#include <iostream>

using namespace std;

int main()
{   int a[3] = {10, 20, 30};
    list<int> L;
    L.push_back(15); L.push_back(35);
    vector<int> v;

    merge(a, a + 3, L.begin(), L.end(),
        inserter(v, v.begin()));
    for (int i=0; i<v.size(); ++i)
        cout << v[i] << " ";   // 10 15 20 30 35
    cout << endl;
    return 0;
}
```

Since *merge* does not create room for the result, the fifth argument of the above call to *merge* uses an inserter, which we will discuss in Section 9.10. This would not have been necessary if we had specified a length of (at least) 5 for the vector *v*, as the following declaration of *v* and call to *merge* show:

```
vector<int> v(5);
merge(a, a + 3, L.begin(), L.end(), v.begin());
```

9.6 Introduction to Associative Containers

Besides arrays and lists, used for sequence containers (array, vector, deque and list), *balanced trees* form another classical data structure to store and retrieve data efficiently. They form the basis for another group of containers provided by STL, called (*sorted*) *associative containers*. As we have done before, we will focus on *using* these containers rather than on their implementation. There are four types: sets, multisets, maps and multimaps. Before discussing their use, let us first see how they differ.

Sets

Each element of a *set* is identical with its key, and keys are unique. Because of this, two distinct elements of a set cannot be equal. For example, a set can consist of the following elements:

```
123
124
800
950
```

Multisets

A *multiset* differs from a set only in that it can contain equal elements. For example we can have a multiset consisting of the following four elements:

```
123
123
800
950
```

Maps

Each element of a *map* has two members, known as a *key* and a *value*. No two keys of a map can be equal. For example, a map can consist of the following four elements, each having a numerical key and an alphabetic value:

```
123    John
124    Mary
800    Alexander
950    Jim
```

Multimaps

A *multimap* differs from a map in that duplicated keys are allowed. For example, here is a multimap consisting of four elements (with numerical key):

```
123    John
123    Mary
800    Alexander
950    Jim
```

In contrast to sequence containers, associative containers keep their elements sorted, regardless of the way these are inserted.

9.7 Sets and Multisets

In this section and the next, we will discuss a single, simple program for each of the four associative container types; these two sections are not complete with regard to all possible operations for these containers, but they should make their most important characteristics very clear.

Sets

Let us begin with two sets of integers. Although elements are inserted in different ways, the resulting sets are identical:

```cpp
// set2.cpp: Two identical sets, created differently.
#include <iostream>
#include <set>
using namespace std;

int main()
{   set<int> S, T;
    S.insert(10); S.insert(20); S.insert(30);
    S.insert(10);
    T.insert(20); T.insert(30); T.insert(10);
    if (S == T) cout << "Equal sets, containing:\n";
    for (set<int>::iterator i = T.begin();
        i != T.end(); ++i)
            cout << *i << " ";
    cout << endl;
    return 0;
}
```

This program gives the output

```
Equal sets, containing:
10 20 30
```

which demonstrates that the order 20, 30, 10, in which the elements of T were inserted is irrelevant; neither does set S change when the element 10 is inserted for the second time. Remember, keys are unique in sets but can be duplicated in multisets, as we will see in a moment.

Since we are using sets of integers, for which there is a standard less-than operator (<), it is not necessary to specify how set elements are to be compared. If this were the case, we could provide the *set* template with a second template argument. Here we might have written

```cpp
set<int, less<int> > S, T;
```

instead of just

```cpp
set<int> S, T;
```

Recall that we have also used this form *less<int>* when we were discussing priority queues in Section 9.2. This second template argument is superfluous in the present example, where these keys are integers, but remember, the set container can also be used with keys of user-defined types (instead of *int*). The blank space in

```
less<int> >
```

prevents confusion with the operator >>.

Although sets are not sequences, we can apply both iterators and the functions *begin* and *end* to them, as this program illustrates. These iterators are bidirectional (see Section 9.3); in other words, with iterator *i* of type *set<int, less<int> >::iterator*, the expressions ++*i*, *i*++, −−*i*, and *i*−− are valid, but *i* + *N* and *i* − *N* are not.

Multisets

The following program shows that equal keys can occur in multisets. Just for a change, let us use the *copy* function for output, as discussed in Section 9.3:

```
// multiset.cpp: Two multisets.
#include <iostream>
#include <set>
using namespace std;

int main()
{   multiset<int> S, T;
    S.insert(10); S.insert(20); S.insert(30);
    S.insert(10);
    T.insert(20); T.insert(30); T.insert(10);
    if (S == T) cout << "Equal multisets:\n"; else
                cout << "Unequal multisets:\n";
    cout << "S: ";
    copy(S.begin(), S.end(), ostream_iterator<int>(cout, " "));
    cout << endl;
    cout << "T: ";
    copy(T.begin(), T.end(), ostream_iterator<int>(cout, " "));
    cout << endl;
    return 0;
}
```

The output of this program shows that the key 10 occurs twice in the multiset *S*. Since it occurs only once in *T*, these two multisets are unequal:

```
Unequal multisets:
S: 10 10 20 30
T: 10 20 30
```

As with sets, we may have provided the multiset template with an extra template argument, writing, for example,

```
multiset<int, less<int> > S, T;
```

9.8 Maps and Multimaps

Maps

The term *associative container* becomes clear when we are dealing with maps. For example, a telephone directory associates names with numbers. With a given name, also known as a *key*, we want the corresponding number. In other words, a phone book is a mapping from names to numbers. If the name *Johnson, J.* corresponds to number 12345, STL enables us to establish a map *D* so that we can write the following statement to express the mapping shown on the second line:

```
D["Johnson, J."] = 12345;
```
"Johnson, J." $\rightarrow$ 12345

Note that this is similar to conventional arrays, such as

```
a[5] = 'Q';
```
5           $\rightarrow$ *'Q'*

In the latter case, subscript values are 0, 1, 2, ..., while this restriction no longer applies to maps. The following program shows that maps are easy to use:

```cpp
// map1.cpp: First application of a map.
#include <iostream>
#include <string>
#include <map>
using namespace std;

int main()
{   map<string, long> D;
    D["Johnson, J."]  = 12345;
    D["Smith, P."]    = 54321;
    D["Shaw, A."]     = 99999;
    D["Atherton, K."] = 11111;
    string GivenName;
    cout << "Enter a name: ";
    getline(cin, GivenName);
    if (D.find(GivenName) != D.end())
       cout << "The number is " << D[GivenName];
    else
       cout << "Not found.";
    cout << endl;
    return 0;
}
```

The declaration of the map *D* in this program contains two template arguments, the first for the type of the key and the second for the type of the value, as this statement shows:

```cpp
map<string, long> D;
```

In this case the less-than operator (<) is applied to the keys. If a different comparison operation for keys is required, we can supply one of our own, as a third template argument. For example, we could have written

```
map<string, long, compare> D;
```

provided that, before the *main* function, we had defined the following function object class:

```
class compare {
public:
   bool operator()(const string &s, const string &t)const
   {  return s < t;
   }
};
```

Since the normal less-than operator for strings is used in the above return statement, the program modified in this way would be equivalent to the original one, *map*1.*cpp*. Incidentally, a third way of achieving the same effect is using the standard function object class *less<string>*, which is similar to what we discussed for sets and multisets.

Multimaps

The following program shows that multimaps can contain equal keys:

```
// multimap.cpp: A multimap containing equal keys.
#include <iostream>
#include <string>
#include <map>
using namespace std;

typedef multimap<string, long> mmtype;

int main()
{  mmtype D;
   D.insert(mmtype::value_type("Johnson, J.", 12345));
   D.insert(mmtype::value_type("Smith, P.", 54321));
   D.insert(mmtype::value_type("Johnson, J.", 10000));
   cout << "There are " << D.size() << " elements.\n";
   return 0;
}
```

Its output is:

```
There are 3 elements.
```

It is interesting to compare this program with one in which we replace the above typedef-declaration with

```
typedef map<string, long> mmtype;
```

Because of the use of *map* instead of *multimap*, the modified program produces the following output line:

```
There are 2 elements.
```

With this map-based version, the pair (*"Johnson"*, J., 10000) overwrites (*"Johnson"*, J., 12345), while these two pairs are both stored in the original program, *multimap.cpp*.

The subscripting operator is not defined for multimaps, so we cannot insert an element by writing, for example,

```
D["Johnson, J."]  = 12345;
```

Instead, we write

```
D.insert(mmtype::value_type("Johnson, J.", 12345));
```

where *mmtype* actually means

```
multimap<string, long>
```

Since the identifier *value_type* is defined inside the *multimap* template class, the prefix *mmtype*:: preceding *value_type* is required here. The definition of this identifier *value_type* is based on the template *pair*, which we will discuss now.

As with maps, the multimap constructor accepts an optional third argument for comparisons.

9.9 Pairs and Comparisons

To do more interesting things with maps and multimaps, we need to be familiar with the *pair* template class, which is also useful for other purposes. It is defined in the header *utility*. The following program uses this class:

```
// pairs.cpp: Operations on pairs.
#include <iostream>
#include <utility>
using namespace std;

int main()
{  pair<int, double> P(123, 4.5), Q;
   Q = pair<int, double>(122, 4.5);
   cout << "P: " << P.first << " " << P.second << endl;
   cout << "Q: " << Q.first << " " << Q.second << endl;
   if (P > Q) cout << "P > Q\n";
   ++Q.first;
   cout << "After ++Q.first: ";
   if (P == Q) cout << "P == Q\n";
   return 0;
}
```

As this program illustrates, the *pair* template takes two template arguments, the types of the *pair* data members *first* and *second*. The *pair* constructor, used for *P*, takes two initial values for these data members. There is also a default constructor for a *pair*, which is used here for *Q*.

We can replace

```
Q = pair<int, double>(122, 4.5);
```

with the following statement, in which the types of the elements follow from the expressions that are supplied as the arguments of *make_pair*:

```
Q = make_pair(122, 4.5);
```

For any two pairs *P* and *Q*, the values of the expressions $P == Q$ and $P < Q$, and so on, are in accordance with the well-known lexicographical ordering, as these examples illustrate:

```
(122, 5.5) <  (123, 4.5)
(123, 4.5) <  (123, 5.5)
(123, 4.5) == (123, 4.5)
```

In program *pairs.cpp*, we initially have $P > Q$, but after increasing *Q.first* by one, *P* and *Q* become equal, as the following output of this program demonstrates:

```
P: 123 4.5
Q: 122 4.5
P > Q
After ++Q.first: P == Q
```

Comparisons

When writing comparison operators (also known as *relational operators*) for our own types, we have to define only == and <. The four remaining operators, !=, >, <=, and >= are then automatically defined by the STL in the namespace *std::rel_ops* by means of four function templates. For example, the operator != is defined in terms of the operator == as follows:

```
template <class T1, class T2>
inline bool operator!=(const T1 &x, const T2 &y)
{   return !(x == y);
}
```

The following program shows that the operators !=, >, <= and >= are available for the class *Example*, even though we have defined only the operators < and == for this class:

```
// rel_ops.cpp: Relational operators.
#include <iostream>
#include <utility>
using namespace std;
using namespace std::rel_ops;
```

```
    class Example {
    public:
        Example(int i = 0, int j = 0): a(i), b(j){}
        int a, b;
        bool operator==(const Example &y)const
        {   return a == y.a && b == y.b;
        }

        bool operator<(const Example &y)const
        {   return a < y.a || a == y.a && b < y.b;
        }
    };

    int main()
    {   Example u(1, 3), v(1, 2);
        if (u > v)   cout << "u > v\n";
        if (u >= v) cout << "u >= v\n";
        if (u != v) cout << "u != v\n";
        if (u <= v) cout << "u <= v\n";
        return 0;
    }
```

For two *Example* objects $u = (i_u, j_u)$ and $v = (i_v, j_v)$, the above *operator<* function expresses
that $u < v$ if either $i_u < j_u$ or both $i_u = j_u$ and $i_v < j_v$. This definition, together with the obvious
one of the operator ==, is sufficient for all six relational operators to be available. Since the
tests in the first three if-statements in the *main* function succeed, while that of the fourth
fails, the program produces the following output:

```
    u > v
    u >= v
    u != v
```

Instead of defining *operator==* and *operator<* as member functions, we could also have
defined them as follows, outside the class *Example*. The word *inline* (see Section 4.11) at
their beginning is not essential:

```
    inline bool operator==(const Example &x, const Example &y)
    {   return x.a == y.a && x.b == y.b;
    }

    inline bool operator<(const Example &x, const Example &y)
    {   return x.a < y.a || x.a == y.a && x.b < y.b;
    }
```

Note that the using-directive

```
    using namespace std::rel_ops;
```

is really required. The four comparison operators !=, >, <= and >= have been defined in a
special namespace, *rel_ops*, to enable us to define these operators ourselves, if we like,
without any conflicting names. We then simply omit the above namespace using-directive.

Maps revisited

Since a map contains pairs (k, d), where k is the key and d the value (or data), we can expect the *pair* template to be useful for maps. In the same way as for a sequence container, we can use an iterator i for an associative container; then $*i$ denotes a pair, *i–>first* being the key and *i–>second* the value. For example, using iterator i and the same map as in Section 9.8, we can display the entire map contents (with the keys in ascending order) by using the following for-loop:

```
map<string, long, compare>::iterator i;
for (i = D.begin(); i != D.end(); ++i)
   cout << setw(9)
        << i->second << " "
        << i->first << endl;
```

Note that in this way we display the *i–>second* before *i–>first*, so that we need not worry about how many positions to reserve for the names in output such as

```
11111 Atherton, K.
12345 Johnson, J.
99999 Shaw, A.
54321 Smith, P.
```

This format is also easier to deal with in input operations, because in this way we can read, in this order, a number, one blank space and a string ending at the end of the line. But remember, this string is the key, despite its position at the end of the line.

9.10 Function Objects and Function Adaptors

Some more examples of function objects

Function objects, introduced in Section 6.16, are sometimes considered confusing and mysterious. Since they are really useful, let us once again experiment a little with this subject without using any STL facilities. The following program shows a class *sq* that we can use to compute the square x^2 of an integer x:

```
// funobj1.cpp: A simple function object.
#include <iostream>
using namespace std;

struct sq {
   int operator()(int x)const {return x * x;}
};

int main()
{  cout << "5 * 5 = " << sq()(5) << endl; // 25
   return 0;
}
```

As discussed in Chapter 6, the keyword *struct* is frequently used instead of *class* if the class in question has only public members. Except for the default access rights (private for *class* and public for *struct*), these two keywords are equivalent.

Referring to Section 6.16, we know that the expression *sq*( ) calls the default constructor of class *sq*, so that this expression represents an object of that class. The line

```
int operator()(int x){return x * x;}
```

in this class defines the *operator*( ) in such a way that *sq*( )(5) is a valid function call, returning 25. It is important to distinguish the following expressions:

sq	a class (that is, a type), which we will refer to as a *function class*
sq( )	a function object
sq( )(5)	a function call

Function objects offer all the possibilities of normal functions, but they offer some others besides. An interesting aspect is that the classes on which they are based can be used as template arguments, as the following program demonstrates:

```
// funobj2.cpp: Function classes used as
//               template arguments.
#include <iostream>
using namespace std;

struct square {
    int operator()(int x)const {return x * x;}
};

struct cube {
    int operator()(int x)const {return x * x * x;}
};

template <class T>
class cont {
public:
    cont(int i): j(i){}
    void print()const {cout << T()(j) << endl;}
private:
    int j;
};

int main()
{   cont<square> sqobj(10);
    cont<cube> cubeobj(10);
    sqobj.print();   // Output (= area of square):    100
    cubeobj.print(); // Output (= contents of cube): 1000
    return 0;
}
```

In the *main* function of this program, the function classes *square* and *cube* act as template arguments. We may regard *cont<T>* as a very restricted container, since it can store only one integer. However, it is very general in that the type parameter *T* can be any function class whose function takes an *int* argument and returns an *int* value. In this example, these function classes are *square* and *cube*. As you can see, the *print* member function of the template class *cont* computes and displays the area of a square and the contents of a cube, respectively. Although program *funobj2.cpp* seems to be very contrived, it may be helpful in understanding more interesting programs.

The *operator*( ) functions in our above example have only one parameter, while there are two parameters in many other cases, such as with priority queues. Let us now use such functions with two parameters. We will use a template class *PairSelect*, containing a print function that prints the smaller element of the pair according to a less-than relation of our own, supplied as a template argument. Let us also supply the type of the pair elements as template arguments. The following program uses two ordering relations. They are implemented as *binary predicates*, that is, as functions that have two parameters and return a logical value. Our first binary predicate, *LessThan*, is a template, so we can use it for any data type for which the operator < is defined. The second, *CompareLastDigits*, is a normal function class, not a template, which returns *true* if the final digit of the first argument is less than that of the second, and *false* otherwise:

```
// funobj3.cpp: The operator() function is a
//              binary predicate.
#include <iostream>
using namespace std;

template <class T>
struct LessThan {
   bool operator()(const T &x, const T &y)const
   {  return x < y;
   }
};

struct CompareLastDigits {
   bool operator()(int x, int y)const
   {  return x % 10 < y % 10;
   }
};

template <class T, class Compare>
class PairSelect {
public:
   PairSelect(const T &x, const T &y): a(x), b(y){}
   void PrintSmaller()const
   {  cout << (Compare()(a, b) ? a : b) << endl;
   }
private:
   T a, b;
};
```

```
int main()
{  PairSelect<double, LessThan<double> > P(123.4, 98.7);
   P.PrintSmaller(); // Output: 98.7

   PairSelect<int, CompareLastDigits> Q(123, 98);
   Q.PrintSmaller(); // Output: 123 (because 3 < 8)
   return 0;
}
```

The program first displays the value 98.7 because this is less than the other *PairSelect* element, 123.4. Then it displays 123 because its last digit, 3, is less than the last digit of 98.

The STL template *less<T>* is very similar to the class template *LessThan<T>* of the program *funobj3.cpp*. You can find the following definition in the header *functional*:

```
template <class T>
struct less: binary_function<T, T, bool> {
   bool operator()(const T& x, const T& y) const
   { return x < y;
   }
};
```

The only difference between this STL class *less* and our class *LessThan* is that *less* is defined as a class derived from the base class *binary_function*. As we have seen in Section 6.10 (using a base class *B* and derived classes *D*1, *D*2, and *D*3 as an example), this makes it possible to write functions that have a (reference) parameter of the base class and call these with arguments of classes derived from it. Remember, there are other classes (such as *greater*) besides *less*, which are also derived from *binary_function*. We will discuss this base class *binary_function* in more detail later in this section.

This class *binary_function* is empty but for some typedef declarations, and the same applies to its unary counterpart *unary_function*. The following definitions of these classes also occur in the header *functional*:

```
template <class Arg, class Result>
struct unary_function {
   typedef Arg argument_type;
   typedef Result result_type;
};

template <class Arg1, class Arg2, class Result>
struct binary_function {
   typedef Arg1 first_argument_type;
   typedef Arg2 second_argument_type;
   typedef Result result_type;
};
```

We do not require the typedef declarations of these two base classes for our present purpose, but they are in the header *functional* for the definition of binders and negators, to be discussed in a moment.

As you may expect, the program *funobj3.cpp* also works well if we replace our own *LessThan<T>* template class with the STL template class *less<T>*. To do this, you can modify this program as follows:

1. At the top of the program, add the two lines *#include <functional>* (or *#include <algorithm >*) and *using namespace std;*.
2. Remove the definition of the class *LessThan*.
3. Replace *LessThan* with *less* in the second line of the *main* function.

Unary predicates and binders

In mathematics, we can turn a function f of two arguments into one that has only one by keeping one argument of f constant. For example, we can define function g as

$$g(x) = f(x, c)$$

where c is a constant. Now suppose we want to use the STL template *less<T>* to count how may values of an *int* array a, of say, 10 elements, are less than 100. As we will see in Section 9.11, there is a *count_if* algorithm for such tasks, but this requires a *unary predicate* rather than a binary one. A call to this algorithm for the purpose just mentioned has the following form:

```
n = count_if(a, a + 10, 'the condition a[i] < 100');
```

If we write a Boolean function for this condition, this would be a function with only one parameter. For example, we could write

```
bool ratherSmall(int x){return x < 100;}
```

Then we might write

```
n = count_if(a, a + 10, ratherSmall);
```

to determine how many elements of a are less than 100. We are here dealing with the condition

$$x < 100$$

in which only one variable occurs, so that can be regarded as a Boolean function of one argument, also known as a *unary predicate*. This condition is obviously a special case of the following expression, which we can regard as a binary predicate because of the two variables x and y:

$$x < y$$

We say that we want to *bind* the second argument of *less<T>* to the value 100. The way to do this in STL is by using a *binder*, which is a special case of a *function adaptor*. To turn a binary predicate into a unary one by binding its second argument, we use the binder *bind2nd*. In our example, the expression

```
bind2nd(less<int>(), 100)
```

is what we need to indicate that only the values less than 100 are to be counted. The following program illustrates this:

```
// binder.cpp: The bind2nd adaptor used to count how
//                   many array elements are less than 100.
#include <iostream>
#include <algorithm>
#include <functional>
using namespace std;

int main()
{   int a[10] = {800, 3, 4, 600, 5, 6, 800, 71, 100, 2},
        n;
    n = count_if(a, a + 10, bind2nd(less<int>(), 100));
    cout << n << endl; // Output: 6
    return 0;
}
```

There is also a binder *bind1st* to bind the first argument. To demonstrate this, let us replace $x < 100$ with the equivalent condition

$$100 > x$$

We can obtain this by binding the first operand y of

$$y > x$$

to the value 100. The program *binder.cpp* will therefore give exactly the same result if we replace the call to *count_if* with this one:

```
n = count_if(a, a + 10, bind1st(greater<int>(), 100));
```

Negators

Programmers frequently use the unary operator ! (not). For example, the expression

```
!(x < y)
```

is equivalent to

```
x >= y
```

The *not2* negator works in the same way for function objects that take two arguments. A negator is another kind of *function adaptor*; it is implemented as a template function that accepts a binary predicate object, such as *less<int>*( ), as an argument. We can therefore write

```
not2(less<int>())
```

instead of

```
greater_equal<int>
```

The following program demonstrates this. It sorts an array of five elements to place these in descending order:

```
// not2demo.cpp: The not2 adaptor demonstrated.
#include <iostream>
#include <algorithm>
#include <functional>
using namespace std;

int main()
{   int a[5] = {50, 30, 10, 40, 20};
    sort(a, a+5, not2(less<int>()));
    for (int i=0; i<5; ++i) cout << a[i] << " ";
    // Output: 50 40 30 20 10
    cout << endl;
    return 0;
}
```

Instead of the above call to the sort algorithm, we could have written

```
sort(a, a+5, greater_equal<int>());
```

or simply

```
sort(a, a+5, greater<int>());
```

The function adaptor *not1* takes a unary predicate object. Since the *bind1st* and *bind2nd* adaptors return a unary predicate, an expression such as

```
bind2nd(less<int>(), 100)
```

is a an acceptable argument for *not1*, as this program shows:

```
// not1demo.cpp: The not1 adaptor demonstrated.
#include <iostream>
#include <algorithm>
#include <functional>
using namespace std;
```

```
int main()
{   int a[10] = {800, 3, 4, 600, 5, 6, 800, 71, 100, 2},
      n;
    // Count how many elements are not less than 100:
    n = count_if(a, a + 10,
        not1(bind2nd(less<int>(), 100)));
    cout << n << endl; // Output: 4
    return 0;
}
```

Note that counting how many elements of the array are at least 100 could have been done by the following, simpler call to *count_if*:

```
n = count_if(a, a + 10,
    bind2nd(greater_equal<int>(), 100));
```

In either case, the output is 4, since exactly four elements (800, 600, 800, 100) of array *a* are not less than 100.

Two useful STL base classes

You may wonder why we discussed the negator *not2* by using the standard function object *less<int>*() in

```
sort(a, a+5, not2(less<int>()));
```

occurring in program *not2demo.cpp*. It seems that we might as well have started with a function object of our own, writing, for example,

```
sort(a, a+5, not2(iLessThan()));
```

where *iLessThan* is a function class defined as

```
struct iLessThan {                  // ???
bool operator()(int x, int y)const {return x < y;}
};
```

However, that would not have compiled. The *not2* adaptor requires that its argument type is a class derived from the class *binary_function* (or rather, from a specialization of the class template *binary_function*). This is easy to realize by inserting

```
: binary_function<int, int, bool>
```

immediately after the name *iLessThan* in the above definition of this class. The three template arguments *int*, *int*, and *bool* denote the types of the two arguments and of the result, which we would use if we wrote a simple function, such as

```
bool lessthan(int x, int y){return x < y;}
```

for the same purpose.

Using *binary_function<int, int, bool>* as a base class of class *iLessThan*, we obtain the following complete program, which is equivalent to *not2demo.cpp* of the previous section:

```
// not2own.cpp: The not2 adaptor applied to a function
//                    object of our own.
#include <iostream>
#include <algorithm>
#include <functional>
using namespace std;

struct iLessThan: binary_function<int, int, bool> {
bool operator()(int x, int y)const {return x < y;}
};

int main()
{   int a[5] = {50, 30, 10, 40, 20};
    sort(a, a+5, not2(iLessThan()));
    for (int i=0; i<5; ++i) cout << a[i] << " ";
    // Output: 50 40 30 20 10
    cout << endl;
    return 0;
}
```

We can also apply the *not*1 adaptor to a function object of our own. In program *not1demo.cpp* of the previous section we used *not*1 in the expression

```
not1(bind2nd(less<int>(), 100))
```

to count how many elements of an array were not less than 100. In this expression, we will replace

```
bind2nd(less<int>(), 100)
```

with the simpler form

```
LessThan100()
```

where *LessThan*100 is a class of our own, as the following complete program shows:

```
// not1own.cpp: The not1 adaptor applied to a
//                    function object of our own.
#include <iostream>
#include <algorithm>
#include <functional>
using namespace std;

struct LessThan100: unary_function<int, bool> {
bool operator()(int x)const {return x < 100;}
};
```

```
int main()
{   int a[10] = {800, 3, 4, 600, 5, 6, 800, 71, 100, 2},
        n;
    // Count how many elements are not less than 100:
    n = count_if(a, a+10, not1(LessThan100()));
    cout << n << endl; // Output: 4
    return 0;
}
```

In the above definition of the class *LessThan*100, the part

```
: unary_function<int, bool>
```

indicates that this class has (a specialization of) *unary_function* as its base class. We write *unary_function<int, bool>* because *not*1 takes a unary predicate object with a single *int* argument and returning a *bool* value.

Function objects and *transform*

STL provides the following template classes, which we can use as function objects by adding a pair of parentheses:

```
plus<T>              minus<T>
multiplies<T>        divides<T>          modulus<T>
equal_to<T>          not_equal_to<T>
greater<T>           less<T>
greater_equal<T>     less_equal<T>
logical_and<T>       logical_or<T>
negate<T>            logical_not<T>
```

To illustrate some of those we have not yet used, let us first introduce the *transform* algorithms. There are two: one for unary and one for binary operations. We use them to transform all elements of a range. For example, suppose that we want to use the elements $a[i]$ of an *int* array a to assign values $b[i] = -a[i]$ to another array, b. One way to achieve this is by a call to the *transform* algorithm for unary operations, using the *negate<T>* template, as the following program shows:

```
// negate.cpp: The transform algorithm and negate<T>.
#include <iostream>
#include <algorithm>
#include <functional>
using namespace std;

int main()
{   int a[5] = {10, 20, -18, 40, 50}, b[5];
    transform(a, a + 5, b, negate<int>());
    for (int i=0; i<5; ++i) cout << b[i] << "  ";
    // Output: -10  -20  18  -40  -50
    cout << endl;
    return 0;
}
```

The function object *logical_not<T>*( ) is very similar to *negate<T>*( ). If we write

```
transform(a, a + 5, b, logical_not<int>());
```

then the array b will be assigned the values $b[i] = !\,a[i]$. In other words (with *int* arrays a and b), each element $b[i]$ will be 0 if $a[i]$ is $\neq 0$ and it will be 1 if $a[i]$ is 0. Instead of both a source array a and a destination array b, we may use only one.

So much for the unary version of *transform*. There is also a version that uses two source sequences instead of one and accepts a binary function object. Suppose, for example, that we want to use the arrays a and b to compute the sum array s, where

$$s[i] = a[i] + b[i]$$

The following program shows the use of the *plus<int>* template to achieve this:

```
// plus.cpp: The transform algorithm and plus<T>.
#include <iostream>
#include <algorithm>
#include <functional>
using namespace std;

int main()
{   int a[5] = {10, 20, -18, 40, 50},
        b[5] = { 2,  2,   5,  3,  1}, s[5];
    transform(a, a + 5, b, s, plus<int>());
    for (int i=0; i<5; ++i) cout << s[i] << " ";
    // Output: 12   22   -13   43   51
    cout << endl;
    return 0;
}
```

Instead of a separate array s, we can use one of the source arrays a and b if we like, replacing s with either a or b in the call to *transform*.

Instead of *plus*, corresponding to +, we can use one of the other arithmetic binary function objects: *minus*, *multiplies*, *divides*, and *modulus*, for −, *, /, and %, respectively. This also applies to the binary function objects *equal_to*, *not_equal_to*, *greater*, *less*, *greater_equal*, *less_equal*, *logical_and*, and *logical_or*, corresponding to the operators ==, !=, >, <, >=, <=, &&, and ||, but these return a *bool* value, and the last two of them are normally applied to arguments that are also of type *bool*. Although this list seems impressive, it will often lack some special operation that we want to use in connection with the *transform*. In such cases we can use function objects of our own, defining a class derived from either the *binary_function* or the *unary_function* templates, as discussed in the previous section. For example, suppose that we are again given the two *int* arrays a and b and that we want to compute the array *result* as follows:

```
result[i] = a[i] + 2 * b[i]
```

(for, say, $i = 0, 1, ..., 5$). The following program shows how a class *compute*, written for this purpose, can be used:

```cpp
// compute.cpp: The transform algorithm and a
//              function object of our own.
#include <iostream>
#include <algorithm>
#include <functional>
using namespace std;
struct compute: binary_function<int, int, int> {
   int operator()(int x, int y)const{return x + 2 * y;}
};

int main()
{  int a[5] = {10, 20, -18, 40, 50},
       b[5] = { 2,  2,   5,  3,  1}, result[5];
   transform(a, a + 5, b, result, compute());
   for (int i=0; i<5; ++i) cout << result[i] << "  ";
      // Output: 14  24  -8  46  52
   cout << endl;
   return 0;
}
```

The same applies to the *transform* version that takes a unary function object. For example, if we want to replace all five elements $a[i]$ of the *int* array a with the value $1.0/(a[i] * a[i] + 1)$ (using array a as both a source and a destination), we can do this by using a class derived from the *unary_function* template, as the following program shows:

```cpp
// compute1.cpp: Replacing a[i] with 1.0/(a[i]*a[i]+1).
#include <iostream>
#include <algorithm>
#include <functional>
using namespace std;
struct compute1: unary_function<int, double> {
   double operator()(int x)const{return 1.0/(x*x + 1);}
};

int main()
{  int a[5] = {2, 0, 1, 3, 7};
   double b[5];
   transform(a, a + 5, b, compute1());
   for (int i=0; i<5; ++i) cout << b[i] << " ";
   // Output: 0.2 1 0.5 0.1 0.02
   cout << endl;
   return 0;
}
```

Iterator adaptors

There are two kinds of iterator adaptors: insert iterators and reverse iterators. In this section, we will encounter some iterator types that we have already discussed and some new ones besides.

Insert iterators

Algorithms such as *copy* will copy in insert mode if we write, for example,

```
copy(v.begin(), v.end(), inserter(w, w.begin()));
```

The *insert iterator* (or *inserter*, for short), used here as the third argument of *copy*, is very general in that we supply the position, *w.begin*( ) in this example, where insertion is to take place. If insertion (in the container *w*) is to take place at the end, we can write *w.end*( ), as this program illustrates:

```
// copy3.cpp: Copying a vector using 'inserter'.
#include <iostream>
#include <vector>
#include <list>
using namespace std;

int main()
{   int a[4] = {10, 20, 30, 40};
    vector<int> v(a, a+4);
    list<int> L(2, 123);
    copy(v.begin(), v.end(), inserter(L, L.end()));
    list<int>::iterator i;
    for (i=L.begin(); i != L.end(); ++i)
        cout << *i << " "; // Output: 123 123 10 20 30 40
    cout << endl;
    return 0;
}
```

Since inserting at the end is a very common operation, there is a special insert iterator for it, called *back_inserter*. The above program works in exactly the same way if we replace the call to the *copy* algorithm with this one:

```
copy(v.begin(), v.end(), back_inserter(L));
```

As a *back_inserter* always inserts at the back, it takes only one argument, the container.

Yet another insert iterator, *front_inserter*, works in a peculiar way: every newly inserted element is placed at the front, which has the effect that the values will occur in the reverse order. For example, if we replace the call to the *copy* algorithm in program *copy*3.*cpp* with the line

```
copy(v.begin(), v.end(), front_inserter(L));
```

then the program will produce the following output:

```
40 30 20 10 123 123
```

So far, we have been using insert iterators only as arguments of algorithms, such as *copy* and *merge*. We can also use them in other ways. For example, instead of

```
    L.push_front(111); L.push_back(999);
```

we can write

```
    *front_inserter(L) = 111; *back_inserter(L) = 999;
```

Reverse iterators

There are the following iterators for type *vector<int>*, and it goes without saying that there are similar iterators for other types, such as *list<double>*:

```
    vector<int>::iterator
    vector<int>::reverse_iterator
    vector<int>::const_iterator
    vector<int>::const_reverse_iterator
```

Recall that in Section 9.1 we used a reverse iterator in the following fragment to display all elements of vector *v* in the reverse order.

```
    vector<string>::reverse_iterator i;
    for (i=v.rbegin(); i != v.rend(); ++i)
        cout << *i << endl;
```

The *const* versions are required if the container itself has the *const* attribute, as is the case in the following program:

```
    // c_iter.cpp: const_iterator and
    //              const_reverse_iterator.
    #include <iostream>
    #include <list>
    using namespace std;

    void showlist(const list<int> &x)
    {   // Forward:
        list<int>::const_iterator i;
        for (i=x.begin(); i != x.end(); ++i)
            cout << *i << " ";
        cout << endl;    //  Output: 10 20 30
        // Backward:
        list<int>::const_reverse_iterator j;
        for (j=x.rbegin(); j != x.rend(); ++j)
            cout << *j << " ";
        cout << endl;    //  Output: 30 20 10
    }

    int main()
    {   list<int> L;
        L.push_back(10); L.push_back(20); L.push_back(30);
        showlist(L);
        return 0;
    }
```

We cannot omit the two occurrences of *const_* in the function *showlist*, unless we also omit the word *const* in the first line of this function. Since this function does not alter the list in question, it is considered good programming practice to maintain this occurrence of *const*.

Stream iterators

We have used stream iterators in Section 9.3 in connection with the *copy* algorithm. It is also possible to use these iterators in a more elementary way, and the second argument taken by an *ostream_iterator* constructor need not be a string consisting only of a space, as the following program shows:

```
// outiter.cpp: Output iterator; assignment statements
//                 reading data from a file.
#include <iostream>
#include <iterator>
using namespace std;

int main()
{   ostream_iterator<int> i(cout, "abc\n");
    *i++ = 123;
    *i++ = 456;
    cout << endl;
    return 0;
}
```

This program produces the following output:

```
123abc
456abc
```

Things are always a little bit trickier with input, because we want to be able to detect the end of the input stream. The following is a very strange solution to the problem of reading all integers from the file *num.txt*, where this is a text file containing only integers in the usual format:

```
// initer.cpp: Input iterator; assignment statements
//                 performing input from a file.
#include <iostream>
#include <fstream>
#include <iterator>
using namespace std;

int main()
{   ifstream file("num.txt");
    if (file)
    {   istream_iterator<int> i(file), eof;
        int x;
        while (i != eof)
        {   x = *i++;
            cout << x << " ";
        }
```

```
    }   else cout << "Cannot open file num.txt.";
    cout << endl;
    return 0;
}
```

For example, if the file *num.txt* consists of the two lines

```
10 20
30
```

the program will produce the following output:

```
10 20 30
```

9.11 Nonmodifying Sequence Algorithms

The algorithms discussed in this section only *inspect* sequences, without modifying them. Some of them accept an optional binary predicate, as indicated by *binpred* in the following list:

```
for_each(first, last, operation);
```

This algorithm does a given operation for each element.

```
i = find(first, last, val);
i = find_if(first, last, pred);
```

Returns the iterator value pointing to the first element in the sequence that is equal to a given value or, in the case of *find_if*, that satisfies a given predicate. The value *last* is returned if no such element is found.

```
i = find_first_of(first, last, first2, last2);
i = find_first_of(first, last, first2, last2, binpred);
```

Finds a value from the second sequence in the first, or, in the case of the second version, uses a given binary predicate instead of a test for equality.

```
i = adjacent_find(first, last);
i = adjacent_find(first, last, binpred);
```

Finds an adjacent pair of equal elements, or uses a given binary predicate instead of a test for equality.

```
n = count(first, last, val);
n = count_if(first, last, pred);
```

Counts how many elements have a given value or satisfy a given predicate.

```
b = equal(first, last, first2);
b = equal(first, last, first2, binpred);
```

True if the elements of the two sequences are pairwise equal, or pairwise satisfy a binary predicate.

```
itpair = mismatch(first, last, first2);
itpair = mismatch(first, last, first2, binpred);
```

Finds the first element (in the first sequence) for which two sequences differ, or for which a given binary predicate fails. The result is returned as a pair containing an iterator for the first and one for the second sequence, indicating the elements that do not match, if any, or, if all elements match, a pair of iterator values the first of which is equal to *last* and the second pointing to the corresponding element in the sequence that starts at *first2*.

```
i = search(first, last, first2, last2);
i = search(first, last, first2, last2, binpred);
```

The first of these two algorithms finds the first occurrence of the second sequence as a subsequence of the first. The second finds the first occurrence of a subsequence that is related to second sequence by a given binary predicate. The return value is *last* if this is not possible.

```
i = find_end(first, last, first2, last2);
i = find_end(first, last, first2, last2, binpred);
```

As the two *search* algorithms, but searching backwards (so it finds the last occurrence if several subsequences match).

```
i = search_n(first, last, n, val);
i = search_n(first, last, n, val, binpred);
```

Finds the subsequence of *n* successive elements equal to a given value or related to a given value by a binary predicate.

Thanks to the principle of overloading, there can be two algorithms with the same name, as the above list shows. The following program demonstrates both versions of the *adjacent_find* and *search_n* algorithms and only one version of the others:

```
// nonmodif.cpp: Nonmodifying algorithms.
#include <iostream>
#include <vector>
#include <functional>
#include <algorithm>
using namespace std;

void display_greater_than10(int x)
{   if (x > 10) cout << x << " ";
}

int main()
{   int a[8] = {10, 12, 7, 3, 17, 7, 7, 3};
    vector<int> v(a, a+8);
    typedef vector<int>::iterator itType;
    itType i;
```

```
    for_each(v.begin(), v.end(), display_greater_than10);
    cout << endl;                          // 12 17

    i = find(v.begin(), v.end(), 7);
    cout << i - v.begin() << endl;  // 2 (v[2] = 7)

    i = find_if(v.begin(), v.end(),
       bind2nd(greater<int>(), 13));
    cout << i - v.begin() << endl;  // 4 (v[4] > 13)

    int b[3] = {17, 7, 3};
    i = find_first_of(v.begin(), v.end(), b, b + 3);
    cout << i - v.begin() << endl;  // 2 (v[2] = 7 occurs in b)

    i = adjacent_find(v.begin(), v.end());
    cout << i - v.begin() << endl;  // 5 (v[5] = v[6])

    i = adjacent_find(v.begin(), v.end(), greater<int>());
    cout << i - v.begin() << endl;  // 1 (v[1] > v[2])

    int n = count(v.begin(), v.end(), 7);
    cout << n << endl;                     // 3 (3 occurrences of 7)

    n = count_if(v.begin(), v.end(),
       bind2nd(greater<int>(), 10));
    cout << n << endl;                     // 2 (2 elements > 10)

    bool eq = equal(v.begin(), v.end(), a);
    if (eq) cout << "v and a are equal\n";
    a[2]++;           // Now a[2] = 8 and v[2] = 7

    pair<itType, int*> itPair =
       mismatch(v.begin(), v.end(), a);
    if (itPair.first != v.end())
       cout << *itPair.first << " != "
       << *itPair.second << endl;     // 7 != 8

    a[2]--;         // Now a[2] = b[2] = 7 again.
    i = search(v.begin(), v.end(), b + 1, b + 3);
    cout << i - v.begin() << endl;  // 2 (v[2]=b[1], v[3]=b[2])

    i = find_end(v.begin(), v.end(), b + 1, b + 3);
    cout << i - v.begin() << endl;  // 6 (v[6]=b[1], v[7]=b[2])

    i = search_n(v.begin(), v.end(), 2, 7);
    cout << i - v.begin() << endl;  // 5 (v[5] = v[6] = 7)

    i = search_n(v.begin(), v.end(), 2, 10, less<int>());
    cout << i - v.begin() << endl;  // 2 (v[2] < 10, v[3] < 10)

    return 0;
}
```

Since *find_if* requires a unary predicate as its third argument, we apply the binder *bind2nd* to the standard function object *greater<int>*( ), writing

```
bind2nd(greater<int>(), 13)
```

to express 'greater than 13.' Since *v*[4] = 17 is the first element in the sequence that is greater than 13, this call to *find_if* returns an iterator value to this element. We demonstrate this by displaying the integer 4, obtained by subtracting *v.begin*( ) from this iterator value.

The second call to *search_n* searches the sequence *v* for a subsequence of length 2, consisting of elements less than 10, while the first call to this algorithm simply looks for a subsequence of length 2 consisting of elements equal to 7.

9.12 Modifying Sequence Algorithms

The algorithms of this section modify the sequence they operate upon. With those algorithms that place the result in a different sequence, we must see to it that there is room for that result in that sequence, or, alternatively, use an inserter, as discussed in Section 9.10.

```
transform(first, last, res, op);
transform(first, last, first2, res, binop);
```

The first of these algorithms applies the operation *op* to every element of the sequence [*first, last*) and writes the result in the sequence starting at *res*. As for the second, two sequences, starting at *first* and *first2*, are given. The binary operation *binop* is applied to corresponding elements of these two sequences and the resulting elements are placed in the sequence starting at *res*.

```
copy(first, last, res);
```

Copies the sequence [*first, last*) into the sequence starting at *res*, starting with the first element.

```
copy_backward(first, last, resLast);
```

Copies the sequence [*first, last*) into the sequence [*resFirst, resLast*) of the same length, starting with the last element.

```
swap(x, y);
```

Swaps the two objects *x* and *y* (of the same type, but not necessarily belonging to an STL container).

```
iter_swap(i1, i2);
```

Swaps the two sequence elements pointed to by the iterators *i*1 and *i*2.

```
swap_ranges(first, last, first2);
```

Swaps the sequence [*first, last*) with that starting at *first2*.

```
replace(first, last, val, new_val);
```
Replaces all elements that are equal to *val* with elements equal to *new_val*.

```
replace_if(first, last, pred, new_val);
```
Replaces all elements satisfying a given predicate with elements equal to *new_val*.

```
replace_copy(first, last, res, val, new_val);
```
As *replace*, but places the result in a different sequence.

```
replace_copy_if(first, last, res, pred, new_val);
```
As *replace_if*, but places the result in a difficult sequence.

```
fill(first, last, val);
```
Replaces every element with a given value.

```
fill_n(first, n, val);
```
Replaces the first *n* elements of a sequence with a given value.

```
generate(first, last, operation);
```
Replaces every element with the result of an operation.

```
generate_n(first, n, operation);
```
Replaces the first *n* elements with the result of an operation.

```
remove(first, last, val);
```
Removes all elements that have a given value.

```
remove_if(first, last, pred);
```
Removes all elements that satisfy a given predicate.

```
remove_copy(first, last, res, val);
remove_copy_if(first, last, res, pred);
```
The first algorithm removes all elements that have a given value, but places the result in a different sequence. The second removes all elements that satisfy a given predicate, but places the result in a different sequence.

```
unique(first, last);
unique(first, last, binpred);
```
Removes equal adjacent elements, or adjacent elements that satisfy a binary predicate.

```
unique_copy(first, last, res);
unique_copy(first, last, res, binpred);
```
Copies a sequence and removes equal adjacent elements, or adjacent elements that satisfy a binary predicate.

```
reverse(first, last);
reverse_copy(first, last, res);
```

> The first algorithm reverses the order of elements in the given sequence, while the second places the result in a different sequence.

```
rotate(first, middle, last);
rotate_copy(first, middle, last, res);
```

> Rotates the elements, such that the element pointed to by *middle* becomes the first element. Again, the second algorithm places the result in a different sequence.

```
random_shuffle(first, last);
random_shuffle(first, last, gen);
```

> Places the elements of a sequence in random order. The second version does this on the basis of a random number generator of our own.

```
partition(first, last, pred);
stable_partition(first, last, pred);
```

> Divides a sequence into two partitions by placing elements that match a predicate first. The second algorithm guarantees that the relative order in either partition is preserved. For example, if the record sequence {5, "*John*"}, {5, "*Peter*"}, {3, "*Mary*"} is partitioned, using the numbers as keys and with a predicate requiring the key to be less than 4, *stable_partition* guarantees that the resulting order is {3, "*Mary*"}, {5, "*John*}, {5, "*Peter*"}, with *John* preceding *Peter* because these names (with identical keys, 5) occurred in that order in the original sequence.

The following program demonstrates all these algorithms, except some that are very similar to others. For example, the algorithm *replace* is omitted because it is similar to *replace_copy*, the only difference being that the former deals with only one sequence, which is modified, while the latter leaves the given sequence unchanged but writes the resulting modified version in another sequence, *res*. In contrast to the program of the previous section, this program uses arrays, with pointers acting as iterators:

```cpp
// modif.cpp: Modifying algorithms.

#include <iostream>
#include <algorithm>
#include <functional>
#include <string>
#include <cstdlib>

using namespace std;

void show(int *first, int* last, const string s)
{  for (int* p = first; p != last; p++) cout << *p << " ";
   cout << "(" + s + ")\n";
}
```

```cpp
class twopowers {      // Used with generate and generate_n
public:
   twopowers(): i(1){}
   int operator()(){int k = i; i *= 2; return k;}
private:
   int i;
};

class myrandom {      // Used with random_shuffle
public:
   myrandom(){srand(1234567U);}
   int operator()(int n){return rand() % n;}
};

bool differingAtMostOne(int x, int y) // Used with unique_copy
{  return y - x <= 1;
}

int main()
{  int a[8] = {1, 1, 2, 2, 3, 3, 4, 4},
      b[8], res[8];
   transform(a, a + 8, b, negate<int>());
   show(b, b + 8, "transform-1"); // -1 -1 -2 -2 -3 -3 -4 -4

   transform(a, a + 8, b, res, multiplies<int>());
   show(res, res + 8, "transform-2");
                           // -1 -1 -4 -4 -9 -9 -16 -16

   copy(a, a + 8, res);
   show(res, res + 8, "copy");   // 1 1 2 2 3 3 4 4

   // To shift all elements a position to the right, in the
   // same container, use copy_backward, not copy:
   copy_backward(res, res + 7, res + 8);
   show(res, res + 8, "copy_backward"); // 1 1 1 2 2 3 3 4

   int x = 5, y = 20;
   swap(x, y);
   cout << x << " " << y << endl;      // 20 5

   iter_swap(res, res + 7); // or: swap(res[0], res[7])
   show(res, res + 8, "iter_swap"); // 4 1 1 2 2 3 3 1

   swap_ranges(a, a + 8, res);
   show(res, res + 8, "swap_ranges"); // 1 1 2 2 3 3 4 4
   swap_ranges(res, res + 8, a); // Restore old situation
   show(res, res + 8, "swap_ranges (restore)");
                           // 4 1 1 2 2 3 3 1

   replace_copy(a, a + 8, res, 3, 5);
      // Copy from a to res, but change each 3 into 5
```

```
show(res, res + 8, "replace_copy"); // 1 1 2 2 5 5 4 4

replace_copy_if(a, a + 8, res, bind2nd(less<int>(), 3), 0);
    // Copy from a to res, but change elements less than 3
    // into zero.
show(res, res + 8, "replace_copy_if"); // 0 0 0 0 3 3 4 4
// Algorithms 'replace' and 'replace_if' omitted.

fill(res, res + 8, 1);
show(res, res + 8, "fill");          // 1 1 1 1 1 1 1 1

fill_n(res, 8, 2);
show(res, res + 8, "fill_n"); // 2 2 2 2 2 2 2 2

generate(res, res + 8, twopowers());
show(res, res + 8, "generate");      // 1 2 4 8 16 32 64 128

generate_n(res, 8, twopowers());
show(res, res + 8, "generate_n");   // 1 2 4 8 16 32 64 128

int *new_end = remove_copy(a, a + 8, res, 3);
show(res, new_end, "remove_copy"); // 1 1 2 2 4 4

new_end = remove_copy_if(a, a + 8, res,
    bind2nd(less<int>(), 3));
show(res, new_end, "remove_copy_if"); // 3 3 4 4
// Algorithms 'remove' and 'remove_if' omitted.

new_end = unique_copy(a, a + 8, res);
show(res, new_end, "unique_copy-1");   // 1 2 3 4

new_end = unique_copy(a, a + 8, res, differingAtMostOne);
show(res, new_end, "unique_copy-2");     // 1 3
// Two versions of 'unique' omitted.

reverse_copy(a, a + 8, res);
show(res, res + 8, "reverse_copy");      // 4 4 3 3 2 2 1 1
// Algorithm 'reverse' omitted.

rotate_copy(a, a + 2, a + 8, res);
show(res, res + 8, "rotate_copy");       // 2 2 3 3 4 4 1 1

random_shuffle(res, res + 8);
show(res, res + 8, "random_shuffle-1");
                        // 4 3 2 3 1 1 4 2 (in my test run)

random_shuffle(a, a + 8, myrandom());
show(a, a + 8, "random_shuffle-2");
                        // 4 2 3 3 1 4 1 2 (in my test run)
```

```
new_end = partition(a, a + 8, bind2nd(less<int>(), 3));
show(a, a + 8, "partition-1");   // 2 2 1 1 3 4 3 4
cout << new_end - a << " in first partition\n";   // 4

// The algorithm stable_partition works similarly, but
// preserves the relative order within each partition.
// This can be relevant with more complex elements
// each consisting of a key and a value, and with
// duplicated keys.
return 0;
}
```

9.13 Sorting-related Algorithms

Less-than and other comparison operations

Algorithms that are related to sorting depend on a relation operation, for which we frequently use the less-than operator <. Instead, we can use the greater-than operator >, or use some other binary comparison predicate. However, we must be very careful with the latter. The chosen predicate must be similar to < with regard to the following requirements:

1. If $x < y$ and $y < z$, then $x < z$.
2. If $x < y$, then $y < x$ is false.

Note that both 1. and 2. also hold if we replace < with > but not if we replace it with <=, ==, or !=.

For each of the following algorithms, all related to sorting, there are two versions. The first is based on the operator < (that is, the built-in one for simple types such as *int* or a user-defined one for class objects). The second version takes an additional argument, which is a binary predicate to be used for comparisons instead of the operator <. For example, if we are sorting objects of type *T*, we can take *greater<T>*( ) for this extra argument to obtain the resulting sequence in descending order:

```
sort(first, last);
sort(first, last, compare);
```
    Sorts a sequence of objects.

```
stable_sort(first, last);
stable_sort(first, last, compare);
```
    As first *sort* algorithms above, but preserves the order of elements with equal keys (see also *stable_partition* in the previous section).

```
partial_sort(first, middle, last);
partial_sort(first, middle, last, compare);
```
    Sorts the sequence in such a way that the elements in the range [*first, middle*) appear as they would if we used *sort(first, last)*.

```
i = partial_sort_copy(first, last, first2, last2);
i = partial_sort_copy(first, last, first2, last2, compare);
```

Similar to *partial_sort*, but with the result in the second sequence. If the second range is smaller than the first, only the first *last2 – first2* sorted elements appear in the second sequence and the return value is equal to *last2*. In any case, the return value is an iterator indicating the end of the sorted sequence in [*first2, last2*).

```
nth_element(first, position, last);
nth_element(first, position, last, compare);
```

Re-arranges the elements such that **position* becomes the value that it would be if the entire sequence were sorted.

```
i = lower_bound(first, last, value);
i = lower_bound(first, last, value, compare);
```

With a sorted sequence [*first, last*), these algorithms find the first occurrence of a given value.

```
i = upper_bound(first, last, value);
i = upper_bound(first, last, value, compare);
```

With a sorted sequence [*first, last*), these algorithms find the position just after the last occurrence of a given value.

```
itPair = equal_range(first, last, value);
itPair = equal_range(first, last, value, compare);
```

With a sorted sequence [*first, last*), these algorithms find a subsequence of elements with a given value.

```
bool b = binary_search(first, last, value);
bool b = binary_search(first, last, value, compare);
```

These algorithms determine whether a given value occurs in a given sorted sequence.

```
i = merge(first1, last1, first2, last2, result);
i = merge(first1, last1, first2, last2, result, compare);
```

Merges two sorted sequences. For example, merging {1, 3, 8} and {4, 5, 8, 12} gives the result {1, 3, 4, 5, 8, 8, 12}. The return value *i* indicates the end of the result.

```
inplace_merge(first, middle, last);
inplace_merge(first, middle, last, compare);
```

Merges the sorted subsequences [*first, middle*) and [*middle, last*) into [*first, last*).

The following program shows how the above algorithms, or at least one version of each, can be used:

```cpp
// sortdemo.cpp: Sorting related STL algorithms.
#include <iostream>
#include <algorithm>
#include <string>
```

```
#include <functional>
#include <utility>
using namespace std;
using namespace std::rel_ops;   // See Section 9.9

class rectype {
public:
   int nr;
   string name;
   rectype(int i = 0, string str = ""): nr(i), name(str){}

   bool operator==(const rectype &y)const
   {  return nr == y.nr;
   }
   bool operator<(const rectype &y)const
   {  return nr < y.nr;
   }
};

void show(rectype *first, rectype* last)
{  for (rectype* p = first; p != last; p++)
   cout << p->nr << " " << p->name << "   ";
   cout << endl;
}

bool greaterthan(const rectype &x, const rectype &y)
{  return x > y; // or: y < x
}

int main()
{  rectype a[5] = {rectype(5, "John"),
                   rectype(5, "Peter"),
                   rectype(3, "Mary"),
                   rectype(7, "Ann"),
                   rectype(2, "Tim")};
   rectype b[5];
   copy(a, a + 5, b);
   sort(b, b + 5);
   show(b, b + 5);
   // Output: 2 Tim  3 Mary  5 John  5 Peter  7 Ann
   // (but Peter might have preceded John)

   // If preserving the order John Peter is essential,
   // use stable_sort instead of sort.
   copy(a, a + 5, b);
   //    stable_sort(b, b + 5, greater<rectype>());
   stable_sort(b, b + 5, greaterthan);  // descending
   show(b, b + 5);
   // Output: 7 Ann  5 John  5 Peter  3 Mary  2 Tim
```

```
copy(a, a + 5, b);
partial_sort(b, b + 2, b + 5);
show(b, b + 5);
// Output: 2 Tim  3 Mary  5 Peter  7 Ann  5 John
rectype *p = partial_sort_copy(a, a + 5, b, b + 2);
//  The two smallest elements of a appear in b,
//  and p points to b[2], hence:
show(b, p);
// Output: 2 Tim  3 Mary
copy(a, a + 5, b);
nth_element(b, b + 1, b + 5);
// Place b[1] where it belongs, as this output shows:
show(b + 1, b + 2);   // Output: 3 Mary

copy(a, a + 5, b);
sort(b, b + 5);
b[3] = b[2] = b[1];
// so [b+1, b+4) is a range of equal elements
rectype *first = lower_bound(b, b + 5, b[2]);
cout << "Lower bound: " << first - b << endl;
// Output: Lower bound: 1
rectype *last = upper_bound(b, b + 5, b[2]);
cout << "Upper bound: " << last - b << endl;
// Output: Upper bound: 4
pair<rectype*, rectype*> itPair =
    equal_range(b, b + 5, b[2]);
cout << "itPair: " << itPair.first - b << " "
                   << itPair.second - b << endl;
// Output: itPair: 1 4

cout << (binary_search(b, b + 5, rectype(3, "xxx")) ?
    "Found\n" : "Not found");   // only the key 3 is used.
// Output: Found

rectype c[3] = {rectype(3, "Charles"),
                rectype(4, "George"),
                rectype(6, "Bill")};
                          // Another sorted sequence
rectype d[8];
last = merge(b, b + 5, c, c + 3, d);
show(d, last);
// Output (on only line, not two):
// 2 Tim  3 Mary  3 Mary  3 Mary  3 Charles  4 George
// 6 Bill  7 Ann
copy(b, b + 5, d);
copy(c, c + 3, d + 5);  // Concatenation of b and c in d
inplace_merge(d, d + 5, d + 8);
show(d, d + 8);   // Same output as with 'merge'.
return 0;
}
```

Set operations on sorted structures

For the following algorithms, the elements in the given ranges must be sorted, either on the basis of either the operator < or a given binary predicate for comparisons. Instead of *sequence*, we will use the term *range* here, since these algorithms can be used not only for sequence containers, but also for sets and multisets:

```
bool b = includes(first1, last1, first2, last2);
bool b = includes(first1, last1, first2, last2, compare);
```

Tests if every element of the first range also occurs in the second.

```
i = set_union(first1, last1, first2, last2, result);
i = set_union(first1, last1, first2, last2, result, compare);
```

Fills the result with every element that occurs in the first or the second range (or in both). If all elements of the first range are distinct and the same is true for the second, then each element of the resulting range [*result, i*), will be unique.

```
i = set_intersection(first1, last1, first2, last2, result);
i = set_intersection(first1, last1, first2, last2, result,
        compare);
```

Fills the result with every element that occurs in both the first and the second ranges. The resulting range will be [*result, i*).

```
i = set_difference(first1, last1, first2, last2, result);
i = set_difference(first1, last1, first2, last2, result,
        compare);
```

Fills the result with those elements which occur in the first range but not in the second. The resulting range will be [*result, i*).

```
i = set_symmetric_difference(first1, last1, first2, last2,
        result);
i = set_symmetric_difference(first1, last1, first2, last2,
        result, compare);
```

Fills the result with those elements which occur in exactly one of the two given ranges.

The following program demonstrates the above algorithms, or rather, the first versions of them:

```
// setopstr.cpp: Set operations on sorted structures.
#include <iostream>
#include <string>
#include <algorithm>
using namespace std;

void show(const string &s, const int *begin,
          const int *end)
{   cout << s << " ";
    copy(begin, end, ostream_iterator<int>(cout, " "));
```

```
        cout << endl;
}

int main()
{   int a[4] = {1, 5, 7, 8}, b[3] = {2, 5, 8},
        sum[7], *pSumEnd,
        prod[4], *pProdEnd,
        dif[3], *pDifEnd,
        symdif[7], *pSymDifEnd;
    pSumEnd = set_union(a, a+4, b, b+3, sum);
    pProdEnd = set_intersection(a, a+4, b, b+3, prod);
    pDifEnd = set_difference(a, a+4, b, b+3, dif);
    pSymDifEnd = set_symmetric_difference(a, a+4, b, b+3,
        symdif);
    show("a:      ", a, a+4);
    show("b:      ", b, b+3);
    show("sum:    ", sum, pSumEnd);
    show("prod:   ", prod, pProdEnd);
    show("dif:    ", dif, pDifEnd);
    show("symdif:", symdif, pSymDifEnd);
    if (includes(a, a+4, b, b+3))
        cout << "a includes b.\n";
    else cout << "a does not include b.\n";
    if (includes(sum, pSumEnd, b, b+3))
        cout << "sum includes b.\n";
    else cout << "sum does not include b.\n";
    return 0;
}
```

This program produces the following output:

```
a:      1 5 7 8
b:      2 5 8
sum:    1 2 5 7 8
prod:   5 8
dif:    1 7
symdif: 1 2 7
a does not include b.
sum includes b.
```

Heap operations

A *heap* is a particular organization of elements in a range [*start*, *end*), where *start* and *end* are random access operators. Let us begin with the following example of a heap:

```
i ->     0  1  2  3  4  5  6  7  8  9
a[i] -> 80 70 60 40 50 45 30 25 20 10
```

In this example, and in any heap of ten elements, we have

$a[0]$ is not less than $a[1]$ and $a[2]$
$a[1]$ is not less than $a[3]$ and $a[4]$
$a[2]$ is not less than $a[5]$ and $a[6]$
$a[3]$ is not less than $a[7]$ and $a[8]$
$a[4]$ is not less than $a[9]$

In general, a container a with elements $a[0]$, $a[1]$, ..., $a[n-1]$ is said to satisfy the *heap condition* if

$$a[i] \geq a[2 * i + 1]$$
$$a[i] \geq a[2 * i + 2]$$

as far as these elements belong to the container. It follows that the first element ($a[0]$) of a heap is the largest. Heaps are useful as priority queues, discussed in Section 9.2, since there are operations to extract the first element and to insert a new element while maintaining the heap condition. Extracting the first element of an STL heap is done in two steps: we copy the first element in the usual way and then call the *pop_heap* algorithm, occurring in the following list. Again, for each algorithm of this group, there is a version that takes a binary predicate to be used instead of the operator < for comparisons:

```
push_heap(first, last);
push_heap(first, compare comp);
```
   Adds a element to the heap.

```
pop_heap(first, last);
pop_heap(first, last, compare);
```
   Removes an element from the heap.

```
make_heap(first, last);
make_heap(first, last, compare);
```
   Makes a sequence ready to be used as a heap.

```
void sort_heap(first, last);
void sort_heap(first, last, compare);
```
   Sorts the heap.

For example, using an array a of length 10 as a heap, we can write

```
x = *a; pop_heap(a, a+10);
```

or, in the case of a vector or deque v:

```
x = *v.begin(); pop_heap(v.begin(), v.end());
```

The function *pop_heap* logically removes the first element of the container and then restores the heap condition.

Similarly, we insert a new element in these two steps: we add a new element at the end of the heap and then call the *push_heap* algorithm. For example:

```
a[9] = x; push_heap(a, a+10);
```

or

```
v.push_back(x); push_heap(v.begin(), v.end());
```

The *push_heap* algorithm restores the heap condition correctly if only the final element of a heap violates it. The more powerful (but more time-consuming) function *make_heap* turns a sequential container (allowing for random access) into a heap. Finally, we can apply the *sort_heap* algorithm to a heap to obtain a sorted sequence, Note that this algorithm places the elements in ascending order, so they no longer satisfy the heap condition. The four heap algorithms just mentioned are used in the following program:

```cpp
// heapdemo.cpp: Demonstration of heap operations.
#include <iostream>
#include <string>
#include <algorithm>
using namespace std;

void show(const string &s, const int *begin,
          const int *end)
{ cout << s << endl << "   ";
  copy(begin, end, ostream_iterator<int>(cout, " "));
  cout << endl;
}

int main()
{ cout << "   ";
  for (int i=0; i<10; ++i) cout << "  " << i;
  cout << endl;
  int a[10] = {20, 50, 40, 60, 80, 10, 30, 70, 25, 45};
  show("Initial contents of a:", a, a+10);
  random_shuffle(a, a+10);
  show("After random_shuffle(a, a+10):", a, a+10);
  make_heap(a, a+10);
  show("After make_heap(a, a+10):", a, a+10);
  int x = *a;
  pop_heap(a, a+10);
  show("After x = *a and pop_heap(a, a+10):", a, a+9);
  a[9] = x;
  push_heap(a, a+10);
  show("After a[9] = x and push_heap(a, a+10):",
      a, a+10);
  sort_heap(a, a+10);
  show("After sort_heap(a, a+10):", a, a+10);
  return 0;
}
```

This program produces the following output, which illustrates our above discussion:

```
      0  1  2  3  4  5  6  7  8  9
Initial contents of a:
   20 50 40 60 80 10 30 70 25 45
After random_shuffle(a, a+10):
   80 60 20 40 30 70 25 45 10 50
After make_heap(a, a+10):
   80 60 70 45 50 20 25 40 10 30
After x = *a and pop_heap(a, a+10):
   70 60 30 45 50 20 25 40 10
After a[9] = x and push_heap(a, a+10):
   80 70 30 45 60 20 25 40 10 50
After sort_heap(a, a+10):
   10 20 25 30 40 45 50 60 70 80
```

After the call to *make_heap*, the first element is the largest, but the sequence is not completely in descending order; for example, 40 precedes 50. It is a heap, however, so that, after copying its first element (80) to the variable *x*, we can apply the *pop_heap* algorithm, to obtain a heap of only nine elements. This value 80 is then again inserted by first placing it at the end and then applying the *push_heap* algorithm to restore the heap condition. Finally, the heap is sorted by the special *sort_heap* algorithm, which benefits from the special arrangements of the elements and will therefore be faster than the general *sort* algorithm.

Minimum and maximum

If we want to find the maximum or minimum of two objects for which the less-than operator < is defined, we can use the *min* and *max* algorithms. There are also versions of *min* and *max* that take a third argument, a binary predicate for comparisons. The same applies to the algorithms *min_element* and *max_element*, which we use to find iterators pointing to the minimum and maximum values of sequences:

```
minvalue = min(a, b);
minvalue = min(a, b, compare);

maxvalue = max(a, b);
maxvalue = max(a, b, compare);

i = min_element(first, last);
i = min_element(first, last, compare);

i = max_element(first, last);
i = max_element(first, last, compare);
```

The following program demonstrates both *max*, using a special binary predicate to compare the last decimal digits of two numbers, and *min_element*, using the operator < for comparisons:

```
// minmax.cpp: The max algorithm (used with a special
//             comparison) and the min_element algorithm
//             applied to a list.

#include <iostream>
#include <algorithm>
#include <list>
using namespace std;

bool CompareLastDigit(int x, int y)
{   return x % 10 < y % 10;
}

int main()
{   int x = 123, y = 74, MaxLastDigit;
    // Out of x and y, choose the value with
    // the larger last decimal digit:
    MaxLastDigit = max(x, y, CompareLastDigit);
    cout << MaxLastDigit << endl;   // Output: 74

    int a[5] = {10, 30, 5, 40, 20};
    list<int> L;
    L.insert(L.begin(), a, a+5);
    list<int>::iterator i;
    i = min_element(L.begin(), L.end());
    cout << *i << endl;     // Output: 5
    return 0;
}
```

In this program, the call to *max* returns 74 because the last digit (4) of this value is larger than that of 123. Then *min_element* finds the element 5 (or rather, an iterator pointing to it), which is the minimum value stored in the list *L*.

Lexicographical comparison

We can compare two sequences lexicographically, that is, in the way we compare two text strings. Their first elements determine the comparison result if these are different; otherwise, we compare their second elements if any, and so on. There are two *lexicographical_compare* algorithms: one with four parameters, based on the less-than operation <, and the other taking an additional argument for comparisons:

```
bool b = lexicographical_compare(first1, last1,
                                 first2, last2);
bool b = lexicographical_compare(first1, last1,
                                 first2, last2, compare);
```

Determines which of two sequences comes first when they are lexicographically compared.

The following program demonstrates both versions:

```
// lexcomp.cpp: Lexicographical comparison.
#include <iostream>
#include <algorithm>
#include <functional>
using namespace std;

int main()
{   int a[4] = {1, 3, 8, 2},
        b[3] = {1, 3, 9};

    cout << "a: ";
    copy(a, a+4, ostream_iterator<int>(cout, " "));

    cout << "\nb: ";
    copy(b, b+3, ostream_iterator<int>(cout, " "));
    cout << endl;

    if (lexicographical_compare(a, a+4, b, b+3))
        cout << "Lexicographically, a precedes b.\n";

    if (!lexicographical_compare(a, a+4, b, b+3,
        greater<int>()))
        cout <<
        "Using the greater-than relation, we find:\n"
        "b lexicographically precedes a.\n";
    return 0;
}
```

This program produces the following output:

```
a: 1 3 8 2
b: 1 3 9
Lexicographically, a precedes b.
Using the greater-than relation, we find:
b lexicographically precedes a.
```

If the sequences are of unequal length and the shorter one occurs as the beginning of the larger, an absent element in one sequence acts as one that 'precedes' any present element in the same position of the other container. For example, {1, 2} lexicographically precedes {1, 2, –5}, regardless of the comparison operator.

Permutation generators

If we have n distinct objects, we can build $n! = 1 \times 2 \times ... \times n$ distinct sequences from them by repeated calls to *next_permutation*. Successive calls to this algorithm make these permutations appear in lexicographical order, if possible. The *bool* return value indicates whether there is still another new permutation. The sequences appear in the reverse order if we use *prev_permutation*. For both algorithms, there is also a version that takes a binary predicate for comparisons as a third argument:

```
bool b = next_permutation(first, last);
bool b = next_permutation(first, last, compare);

bool b = prev_permutation(first, last);
bool b = prev_permutation(first, last, compare);
```

The output of the following program will make this clear:

```
// permgen.cpp: Permutation generator, generating all
//              permutations of the sequence 1 2 3.

#include <iostream>
#include <algorithm>
using namespace std;

int main()
{  int a[3] = {1, 2, 3}, k;
   cout << "Six successive calls to next_permutation.\n"
      "Situation before call and value returned by "
      "call:\n";

   for (k=0; k<6; ++k)
   {  copy(a, a+3, ostream_iterator<int>(cout, " "));
      bool b = next_permutation(a, a+3);
      cout << boolalpha << b << endl;
         // As we will see in Section 10.2, b will appear
         // as true or false (not as 1 or 0) because of
         // the manipulator boolalpha.
   };
   cout <<
      "Three successive calls to prev_permutation.\n"
      "Situation before call and value returned by "
      "call:\n";
   for (k=0; k<3; ++k)
   {  copy(a, a+3, ostream_iterator<int>(cout, " "));
      bool b = prev_permutation(a, a+3);
      cout << boolalpha << b << endl;
   };
   return 0;
}
```

Starting with {1, 2, 3}, this program displays the contents of array *a* just *before* it calls the function *next_permuation*. There are six such calls. The first returns *true* and gives array *a* the contents {1, 3, 2}; the second also returns *true* and generates {2, 1, 3}, and so on. As you can see in the output below, the permutations appear in lexicographical order. When *a* = {3, 2, 1}, the sixth call to *next_permutation* returns *false* and gives *a* the original contents {1, 2, 3}. As for *prev_permutation*, this function works in the opposite way. It returns *false* when it changes {1, 2, 3} into {3, 2, 1} and *true* after transitions from {3, 2, 1} to {3, 1, 2}, from {3, 2, 1} to {2, 1, 3} and so on:

```
Six successive calls to next_permutation.
Situation before call and value returned by call:
1 2 3 true
1 3 2 true
2 1 3 true
2 3 1 true
3 1 2 true
3 2 1 false
Three successive calls to prev_permutation.
Situation before call and value returned by call:
1 2 3 false
3 2 1 true
3 1 2 true
```

Remember, there are also versions of *next_permutation* and *prev_permutation* that take an additional argument to specify a comparison operator.

9.14 Generalized Numeric Algorithms

The following program line is required for the subject of this section:

```
#include <numeric>
```

The algorithms to be discussed here are listed below.

```
result = accumulate(first, last, init);
result = accumulate(first, last, init, binary_op);
```

The first version adds the elements of a sequence to a given initial value and returns the result. Instead of the operator + to form the sum, we can specify any other binary operator, using the second version of this algorithm.

```
result = inner_product(first1, last1, first2, init);
result = inner_product(first1, last1, first2, init,
      binary_op1, binary_op2);
```

The first version computes the inner product of the two given sequences and adds this to a given initial value. The inner product of the sequences $\{a_0, a_1, ..., a_{n-1}\}$ and $\{b_0, b_1, ..., b_{n-1}\}$ is defined as $a_0b_0 + a_1b_1 + ... + a_{n-1}b_{n-1}$. Instead of additions and multiplications, used for this computation, we can apply other binary operations, provided via the *binary_op*1 and *binary_op*2 parameters, respectively, of the second version.

```
i = partial_sum(first, last, result);
i = partial_sum(first, last, result, binary_op);
```

The first version places cumulative sums of a sequence in a result sequence. For example, using the sequence $\{2, 3, 4, 8\}$, the cumulative sums of the resulting sequence $\{2, 5, 9, 17\}$ are obtained as 2, 2 + 3, 2 + 3 + 4, and 2 + 3 + 4 + 8. Instead of the operator +, any binary operation can be specified as an argument of the second version. The return value indicates the end of the result sequence.

```
i = adjacent_difference(first, last, result);
i = adjacent_difference(first, last, result, binary_op);
```

These algorithms are the inverses of the previous ones. For example, with a given sequence {2, 5, 9, 17}, the first version computes the following result: {2, 3, 4, 8}, the elements of which are obtained as 2, 5 – 2, 9 – 5, and 17 – 9. The second version enables us to specify any binary operation to be used instead of subtraction.

The following program illustrates the above algorithms:

```
// numeric.cpp: Numerical algorithms.
#include <iostream>
#include <numeric>
#include <algorithm>
#include <functional>
using namespace std;

double power(int x, int n)
{   double y = 1;
    for (int k=0; k<n; ++k) y *= x;
    return y;   // x raised to the power n
}

int main()
{   const int n = 3;
    int a[n] = {4, 2, 3}, sum = 0;
    sum = accumulate(a, a + n, sum);
    cout << "Sum of all elements: " << sum << endl;
    // 4 + 2 + 3 = 9

    int prod = 1;
    prod = accumulate(a, a + n, prod, multiplies<int>());
    cout << "Product of all elements: " << prod << endl;
    // 4 * 2 * 3 = 24

    int b[n] = {3, 4, 2}, inprod = 0;
    inprod = inner_product(a, a + n, b, inprod);
    cout << inprod << endl;
    // 0 +  4 * 3  +  2 * 4  +  3 * 2  =  26

    int product=1;
    product = inner_product(a, a + n, b, product,
        multiplies<double>(), power);
    cout << product << endl;
    // 1 * power(4, 3) * power(2, 4) * power(3, 2) =
    // 1 * 64 * 16 * 9 = 9216

    int c[n], *iEnd;   // a = {4, 2, 3}
    iEnd = partial_sum(a, a + n, c);
    copy(c, iEnd, ostream_iterator<int>(cout, " "));
    cout << endl; // Output: 4 6 9
```

```
    int d[n];
    iEnd = adjacent_difference(c, c + n, d);
    copy(d, iEnd, ostream_iterator<int>(cout, " "));
    cout << endl; // Output: 4 2 3
    return 0;
}
```

9.15 Bit Sequences: *bitset*

To store a sequence of n bits, where n can be very large but is known at compile time, we use the type *bitset<n>*. An object of this type is similar to an array of n bits in that it allows the subscripting operator. For example, after

```
#include <bitset>
using namespace std;
...
const int n = 1000;   // const is essential here
bitset<n> b;
```

we can write

```
b[i] = 1;
b[j] = 0;
while (k < n && b[k] == 1) ++k;
```

for any nonnegative i, j and k less than 1000. It goes without saying that we can replace 1 with *true* and 0 with *false* in these statements. Besides, this class *bitset<n>* has the member functions *set*, *reset* and *test*, so we can replace the above statements with the following ones, which may be more efficient:

```
b.set(i);
b.reset(j);
while (k < n && b.test(k)) ++k;
```

This class *bitset<n>* will be useful in Exercise 9.7.

Exercises

9.1*   Write a program which reads a positive integer x as well as the base (or *radix*) b ($2 \leq b \leq 9$) of a number system to be used for output. For example, if $x = 19$ and $b = 8$, the output is

   23

because $19 = 2 \times 8 + 3$

Hint: since it is easy to compute the digits from right to left, using integer division with b as a divisor, use a stack container to store these digits, so the one computed last will be available first for output.

9.2*   We are given 25 gears with the following numbers of teeth:

30	35	37	40	45
47	50	52	55	57
60	65	68	70	75
78	80	82	85	86
87	90	95	97	99.

In order to transmit power from one shaft to another, we need to use pairs of gears, as illustrated in Figure 9.7. The left and the right gears have a and b teeth, respectively. In view of the allowed center distances d, the sum of the numbers of teeth must satisfy

$$130 \leq a + b \leq 140$$

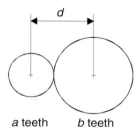

Figure 9.7. Gears

Furthermore, we are only interested in pairs (a, b) that give a gear ratio $q = a/b$ satisfying $0.5 \leq q < 1$. Write a program that produces a table of all allowed pairs (a, b), together with their gear ratios q, where all values of q are to appear in ascending order. Use the *sort* algorithm for this purpose.

a	b	q
.	.	.
.	.	.
.	.	.
.	.	.

9.3   Use a deque to add and remove numbers at random in the following way. Generate a random number, using the function *rand*(), which is declared in the header *<cstdlib>* and generates nonnegative integers at random. For each generated integer x, determine its last decimal digit, d. If $d < 3$, insert x at the front. Otherwise, if $d < 6$, add x at the back. Otherwise, if the deque is empty, do nothing at all. Otherwise, if $d < 8$, remove the element at the front. Otherwise, remove the element at the back. Show the contents of the deque each time it is modified. Let the user specify how many modifications are required.

9.4 Write a program that reads text from the keyboard, and that, for each word that is read, displays the numbers of the lines on which that word occurs. Use a map, each element of which is a pair (k, v), where the key k is a word and the value v is a set containing the line numbers of that word. You can use the types *settype* and *maptype* defined as follows:

```
typedef set<int> settype;
typedef map<string, settype> maptype;
```

9.5 Read a sequence a of integers, followed by a nonnumeric character. Skip this character and then read another sequence, b, of equal length. Build yet another sequence, c, again of the same length, such that each element $c[i]$ is equal to the larger of $a[i]$ and $b[i]$.

9.6 Write a program that reads two lines of text. Produce

a. A line of output containing all characters that occur in the input text.
b. A line of output containing all characters that occur on both the first and the second input line.

On each output line, a character must not occur more than once, and the characters must occur in alphabetic order. For example, if we have the input lines

```
program
computer
```

the output should be as follows:

```
acegmoprtu
mor
```

9.7* Write a program that finds all prime numbers less than 100 000, using the *sieve of Eratosthenes*, which works as follows. The smallest prime number is 2; furthermore, a positive integer n is a prime number if it is not a multiple of any smaller prime number. You can use a *bitset* (see Section 9.15), the bits of which we denote as

$$b_0, b_1, b_2, ..., b_{99999}$$

We want each bit b_i to be 0 if i is a prime number, and 1 if it is not. Initially we set $b_0 = b_1 = 1$ and $b_i = 0$ for all i greater than 1. As 2 is a prime number, b_2 remains 0. Obviously, no multiple of 2 is a prime number. We therefore assign the value 1 to b_4, b_6, b_8, and so on. Similarly, b_3 remains 0, but we assign 1 to b_6, b_9, b_{12}, and so on. Examining b_4, we find that it has already obtained the value 1, which means that 4 is a multiple of a smaller prime number; we then know that all multiples of 4 also have been set to 1; so the fact that b_4 is 1 means that we can immediately proceed to the next element, b_5. As this is 0, we do not alter it, but assign 1 in b_{10}, b_{15}, b_{20}, and so on. We continue this process until all elements b_i have their correct values. Note that you can stop as soon as you have reached an element b_j such that $j^2 > 100\,000$. Write all prime numbers found in this way to the file *prime.dat*, and count how many there are. (The correct answer is 9592.) Also, display the greatest prime number that is less than 100 000. As we will see in Chapter 10, we can write to a file, such as *prime.dat*, using normal output operations, simply replacing *cout* with *out*, after we have opened this stream *out* for the file *prime.dat* as follows:

```
ofstream out("prime.dat");
```

9.8* Write a program to solve the Josephus problem. The program reads two positive integers, *n* and *k*. Suppose that *n* persons form a circle. In clockwise order, we assign the numbers 1, 2, ..., *n* to them. Starting at person 1 and counting clockwise, we remove the *k*th person from the circle. In the reduced circle, we continue with the person following the one just removed and, resuming counting from 1 to *k*, again eliminate the *k*th person. This process is repeated until only one person remains: we want to know the number of this person.

9.9   Solve Exercise 6.5, but using a vector rather than a pointer in the class *verylongint*. (A more realistic class for large integers, also based on STL, can be found in *STL for C++ Programmers*, listed in the Bibliography.)

10

Stream I/O

10.1 Streams

This chapter is based on declarations in the header *<iostream>* and some others. As we know, this line causes the shift operators >> and << (discussed in Section 3.3), to be overloaded for input and output (I/O) operations. When we use these operators for I/O operations, we call their first operands *streams*. Streams indicate where input data is to be found and where output data is to be written. There are four standard streams, which are immediately available:

cin   The standard input stream.
cout   The standard output stream.
cerr   The standard error output stream, to be used for error messages.
clog   A buffered version of *cerr*, more suitable for large amounts of error messages.

The difference between *cerr* and *clog* is that output buffers are flushed each time *cerr* is used, so that the output is sooner available on the external device (which, by default, is the video screen). On the other hand, with large amounts of messages, the buffered version *clog* is more efficient.

The type of *cin* is a class, called *istream*. Similarly, the streams *cout*, *cerr*, and *clog* have type *ostream*. Both *istream* and *ostream* are declared in the header file *<iostream>* as classes derived from another class, *ios_base*, also declared in this header file. As we know, this means that all members of *ios_base* are also members of *istream* and *ostream*.

As we have done when discussing strings in Chapter 5, we have simplified the above discussion a little, as we will do in the sections that follow. In Section 7.4 we have seen that the type string is actually defined as

```
typedef basic_string<char> string;
```

In the same way, the stream types discussed in this chapter are actually obtained by supplying class templates with the template argument *char*. The typedef statements that accomplish this all have the same pattern as the above one. For example, the types *ostream* and *istream* are defined as follows:

```
typedef basic_ostream<char> ostream;
typedef basic_istream<char> istream;
```

10.2 Output

We will discuss output (also known as *insertion*) by using the well-known stream *cout* as an example. Since all facilities for *cout* are also available for other output streams, including those created by ourselves, everything dealt with here is also relevant to file output, to be discussed in Section 10.4.

The standard left-shift operator, <<, is overloaded, so that it denotes an output operation instead of left-shift if its left operand has type *ostream*. In this case, its precise meaning also depends on its right operand. As discussed in Section 3.5, the << operator is left-associative. For example, if both the value of variable *ch* and an equal sign are to be displayed (or 'printed', as we sometimes say), we can write

```
cout << ch << '=';
```

which means

```
(cout << ch) << '=';
```

In Section 6.6, we saw that

```
s = u + v;
```

where *s*, *u*, and *v* are objects of a class in which *operator+* is a member function, is simply a convenient notation for

```
s = u.operator+(v);
```

Analogously, the expression

```
cout << i;
```

can be written as

```
cout.operator<<(i);
```

Although the latter is rather cumbersome to write, it shows very clearly that *operator<<* is used here as a member function of class *ostream* (which is the type of *cout*). The return value of this function is a reference to the object (*cout*) written in front of the dot. It follows that the type of *cout << i* is the same as that of *cout*, namely *ostream*. This explains why a expression such as *cout << i* can be followed by <<.

We have seen in Section 6.6 that an operator function need not necessarily be a class member function. For example, the function *operator<<* that accepts a *string* object is a normal function, not a member function. In other words, with *s* of type *string*, the meaning of

```
cout << s;
```

is *not*

```
cout.operator<<(s);
```

but rather

```
operator<<(cout, s);
```

Remember, *string* is a class, defined in the header *<string>*, so it is logical that this particular *operator<<* function is declared in this header, not in *<iostream>*, which explains this curious distinction between the *operator<<* functions for the types *int* and *string*. Fortunately, we need hardly be aware of this distinction when we use the operator << in practice.

Precedence of the << operator

To avoid incomprehensible error messages or incorrect results, we must bear in mind that << is an operator with a given precedence. Since the arithmetic operators have higher precedence than <<, we can write, for example,

```
cout << i + j << ' ' << i - j;
```

However, as we have seen in Section 3.6, there are many operators whose precedence is lower than that of <<. We must therefore not forget to use parentheses in statements such as

```
cout << (a < b);
cout << (code & mask);
cout << (a < b ? a : b);
```

Built-in inserter types

The type of *expression* in

```
cout << expression
```

is referred to as an *inserter type*, because it determines which of all the << operator functions is actually to be used to insert the value of *expression* in the output stream. For example, if this type is *char*, the << operator that is actually used is the *char* inserter; if this type is *int*, another << operator is used, namely the *int* inserter, and so on. In general, if the above expression has type *T*, the << operator used here is the *T* inserter, and *T* is the inserter type. The following inserter types are supported by the header *<iostream>*:

> *bool*
> *char* (plain, signed and unsigned)
> *short* (signed and unsigned)
> *int* (signed and unsigned)
> *long* (signed and unsigned)
> *const char** (as well as the signed and unsigned versions)
> *float*
> *double*
> *long double*
> *void** (displays an address in hexadecimal form)

As we know, the output operator << also applies to strings, so we might like to add

> *string*

to the above list of types. However, as we discussed a moment ago, there is a distinction in the sense that this operator is declared in the header *<string>*, not in *<iostream>*.

For those who are familiar with the C language, it may be helpful to know that, after the declarations

```
int i;
long l;
double d;
```

the stream-I/O statements

```
cout << i;
cout << l;
cout << d;
```

give the same results as the following C-style I/O statements (which, incidentally, are also available in C++):

```
printf("%d", i);
printf("%ld", l);
printf("%g", d);
```

For integers, as many positions are used as are necessary, and floating-point output may appear in fixed as well as in floating notation. For example the output of

```
int k = 12;
double d1 = 34, d2 = 0.0001, d3 = 0.000000002;
cout << k << " " << d1 << " " << d2 << " " << d3 << endl;
```

is as follows:

```
12 34 0.0001 2e-009
```

As we will see below, we can specify how to format the output by using manipulators, which is especially important for the output of tables.

Besides the << operator, there are also some more primitive output facilities in the form of the *ostream* member functions *put* and *write*. If we want to display only one character, say, stored in the variable *ch*, we can write

```
cout.put(ch);
```

instead of

```
cout << ch;
```

With a given address *a* (which may be the name of an array), we can use

```
cout.write(a, n);
```

to write *n* consecutive bytes, starting at address *a*. With this *write* function, null bytes do not act as string terminators. This function will actually be more useful for output to files on disk than for screen output. Rather than in connection with *cout*, it will be used with similar stream objects for files, as we will see in Section 10.4.

Manipulators for output

When we use <<, normally as many positions are used as are needed to represent the value of the right-hand operand. For example, with $i = 7$, the output produced by

```
cout << i;
```

takes only one position, while it would take four positions with $i = 8243$. When printing a table, we normally want columns with right-aligned numbers. This can be done by using a so-called manipulator, *setw*. For example, we can write

```
i = 10;
cout << setw(3) << i << setw(7) << i * i * i;
```

to print i in three and i^3 in seven positions. In contrast to manipulators without arguments, such as *endl*, those with arguments (such as *setw*) require the header *<iomanip>*. In other words, the above fragment requires the following program lines at the top of the program:

```
#include <iostream>
#include <iomanip>
```

As usual, we also write either the using directive

```
using namespace std;
```

or (in the case of the above fragment) the following using declarations:

```
using std::setw;
using std::cout;
```

In this example the output will be

```
b10bbb1000
```

where each b denotes a space character. If the width given by *setw* is too small to accommodate the output data, as many positions are used as are required. In other words, the minimum number of positions are used with the default width 0. For example, the output of

```
cout << setw(3) << 12345;
```

will be

```
12345
```

and it would not make any difference if, instead of 3, we wrote 0, 1, 2, 4, or 5 as an argument of *setw*, or if we simply omitted *setw*(3) <<.

The manipulator *setw* applies only to one output item, after which the default width of 0 is restored. For example, the second occurrence of *setw*(4) in

```
cout << setw(4) << 12 << setw(4) << 34;
```

is required to produce the output

```
12    34
```

since it would otherwise apply only to 12, so that

```
cout << setw(4) << 12 << 34;
```

would produce

```
1234
```

Besides *setw*, there are some more manipulators. Here is a list of manipulators that we can use for output:

setw(n)	Set field width to *n*
setfill(ch)	Set fill character to *ch*
endl	Insert newline (can be used instead of '\n') and flush
ends	Insert null character (to terminate a string) and flush
flush	Flush output stream (output of data from buffer)
setbase(n)	Set conversion base to *n* (8, 10, 16)
setiosflags(f)	Set format bits specified by the *ios_base::fmtflags* argument *f*
resetiosflags(f)	Reset format bits specified by the *ios_base::fmtflags* argument *f*

The following manipulators remain in force until further notice:

setprecision(n)	Set floating-point precision to *n* digits
dec	Use decimal conversion (default)
hex	Use hexadecimal conversion
oct	Use octal conversion
boolalpha	Output the words *true* and *false* (instead of the digits 1 and 0)
noboolalpha	Output the digits 1 and 0 instead of the words *true* and *false* (default)
showbase	Insert a leading 0 for octal and 0*x* for hexadecimal data
noshowbase	Omit a leading 0 for octal and 0*x* for hexadecimal data (default)
fixed	Fixed-point floating point output (very usual in tables)
scientific	Scientific format. For example, 1.234500*e*+008.
showpoint	Output decimal point and trailing zeros. For example, 25.0 is formatted as 25.0000
noshowpoint	Omit trailing zeros and a decimal point preceding them. For example, 25.0 is formatted as 25 (only two digits) (default).
showpos	Output explicit + at the beginning of positive (decimal) numbers
noshowpos	Omit + at the beginning of positive numbers (default)
uppercase	Use *X* and *E* rather than *x* and *e* in the output of numbers
nouppercase	Use *x* and *e* rather than *X* and *E* in the output of numbers (default)
right	Align right, with blank spaces on the left (default)
left	Align left, with blank spaces on the right
internal	If numbers start with an explicit + (due to *showpos*) and blank spaces are to be inserted, do this after the +

Only for manipulators that have parameters do we have to use the header file *<iomanip>*.

The manipulator *setiosflags* enables us to specify all kinds of formatting requirements by setting certain bits, called format state flags, in its argument *f*. Similarly, *resetiosflags* reset such bits (which means that we make them equal to zero). In most cases it is simpler to use some other manipulators instead. For example, most programmers will prefer

```
cout << fixed << showpoint << 20.0 << endl; // 20.000000
```

to

```
ios_base::fmtflags f =
    (ios_base::fixed | ios_base::showpoint);
cout << setiosflags(f) << 20.0 << endl;
```

or

```
cout << setiosflags(ios_base::fixed | ios_base::showpoint)
        << 20.0 << endl;
```

Recall that we have used the manipulators *fixed*, *setw*, and *setprecision* in program *table.cpp* of Section 2.5

The *setf* function

Instead of using the *setiosflags* manipulator, we can use the *setf* member function of class *ostream* to specify *ios_base::fixed*. We will briefly discuss *setf* since manipulators such as *hex* are based on them, as we will see shortly in a program that defines such a manipulator (named *hexadecimal* instead of *hex*) of our own. Instead of

```
cout << fixed;
```

or

```
cout << setiosflags(ios_base::fixed);
```

we can write

```
cout.setf(ios_base::fixed, ios_base::floatfield);
```

The first argument of *setf* depends on the second, as shown below. Note that all these names must be preceded by *ios_base::*.

Possible first arguments of *setf*	Second argument
fixed, scientific	floatfield
dec, doc, hex	basefield
left, right, internal	adjustfield

We may regard working with the function *setf* as a lower-level activity than using the standard manipulators.

Another example of using manipulators

Manipulators are easy to use and in most cases we prefer them to the *setf* function. We should bear in mind that the *setw* manipulator affects only the immediately following output operations. By contrast, the setting specified by the manipulator *setprecision* remains in effect until further notice. Let us use the following table as an example:

```
Left                Right           Hexa-
justified          justified         decimal
5       125        5      125      0X5      0X7D
6       216        6      216      0X6      0XD8
7       343        7      343      0X7     0X157
8       512        8      512      0X8     0X200
9       729        9      729      0X9     0X2D9
10     1000       10     1000      0XA     0X3E8
```

This table was produced by the following program:

```cpp
// manip.cpp: A demonstration of some manipulators.
#include <iostream>
#include <iomanip>
using namespace std;

int main()
{   cout << showbase << uppercase
         << "Left               Right          Hexa-\n"
         << "justified       justified        decimal\n";
    for (int i=5; i<=10; i++)
    {   cout << dec << left
             << setw(5) << i << setw(8) << i * i * i

             << right
             << setw(2) << i << setw(8) << i * i * i

             << hex << setw(8) << i
             << setw(8) <<   i * i * i << endl;
    }
    return 0;
}
```

Note that we have to use *setw*(8) three times to make each of the last three columns of the table appear in eight positions. By contrast, we need not repeat the *hex* manipulator for the last column of our table because we used it for the second last column so it is still in effect.

Because of the use of the manipulators *showbase* and *uppercase*, the hexadecimal numbers in this table begin with 0*X*. If we had omitted *showbase*, we would have obtained, for example, 3*E*8 instead of 0*X*3*E*8. If we had omitted *uppercase*, we would have obtained 0*x*3*e*8 if showbase was still present and 3*e*8 if this manipulator was also omitted.

Alignment of strings in tables

We have demonstrated the alignment of strings in tables in program *align.cpp*, in Section 5.10. In that program, left alignment of a column of strings is realized by the manipulator *left* while the manipulator *right* is used for numbers.

Boolean values

Values of type *bool* are displayed as 1 (for *true*) and 0 (for *false*), unless we use the manipulator *boolalpha*. This setting then remains in force until we use the manipulator *noboolalpha*. For example, the program produces output as shown in comments:

```
// booleans.cpp: The manipulators boolalpha and noboolalpha.
#include <iostream>
using namespace std;

int main()
{   cout << true << " " << false << endl      // 1 0
         << boolalpha << true << endl;         // true
    cout << false << endl;                     // false
    cout << noboolalpha << true << endl;       // 1
    return 0;
}
```

Writing our own manipulators

We can define manipulators for output ourselves. This is very simple for manipulators that have no parameters: all we have to do is to write a function that takes an *ostream* reference parameter and returns a similar result. This parameter, say *s*, is then used in the function for the desired output operation, which can have the form

```
s.setf(...);
```

after which *s* provides the reference to an *ostream* that our manipulator function is to return. Let us demonstrate this by defining the manipulator *hexadecimal*, which does the same as the standard manipulator *hex*. The following program illustrates that this manipulator is based on the function *setf*:

```
// mymanip.cpp: A manipulator defined by ourselves.
#include <iostream>
using namespace std;

ostream &hexadecimal(ostream &s)
{   s.setf(ios_base::hex, ios_base::basefield);
    return s;
}

int main()
{   cout << hexadecimal << 17 << endl; // Output: 11
    return 0;
}
```

Although this is a very small program, it will at first sight be difficult to understand. As we have discussed in Section 5.15, the name of a function, not followed by a pair of parentheses and optionally preceded by the address-of operator &, represents the address of that function, otherwise known as a pointer to it. This is the case here with the way *hexadecimal* is used in the *main* function. The above output statement is equivalent to the following one, in which the optional & has been inserted:

```
cout << &hexadecimal << 17 << endl; // Output: 11
```

There is an *ostream* member function *operator<<* that takes a pointer to a function as an argument, and this function *operator<<*, which is used here, takes our own function hexadecimal, or rather, its address, as an argument.

So much for defining manipulators that do not take arguments. It is also possible to define manipulators that do, and again, no new language elements are required to accomplish this. The C++ class concept provides us with all the tools we need to define manipulators both with and without parameters. Since this subject is rather technical and possibly not essential for most C++ programmers, we will not discuss this subject here, but rather refer to Appendix A.

Inserters for user-defined types

So far, in this chapter, we have only used built-in inserter types, such as *char*, *int*, *float*, and so on. Everything we did with the << operator could also be done with the old *printf* function, with which every C programmer is familiar and which will be briefly discussed in Section 11.8. An important advantage of << over *printf* is the possibility of applying << to types of our own by means of operator overloading, as we did in the program *operator.cpp* of Section 6.6, writing

```
cout << "The sum of (3, 1) and (1, 2) is "
        << s       // This is our own operator <<
        << endl;
```

where *s* is variable of our own type *vec*. This was possible because of the following function:

```
ostream &operator<<(ostream &os, const vec &v)
{  v.printvec(os);
   return os;
}
```

This function is based on the public member function *printvec*, which is defined inside class *vec* as follows:

```
void printvec(ostream &os)const
{  os << "(" << x << ", " << y << ")";
}
```

10.3 Input

The right-shift operator >>, overloaded in the header *<iostream>*, has a first operand of type *istream* (also defined in this header file). This operator is used for input, or, more technically, *extraction*. For example, if *x* has type *float*, the statement

```
cin >> x;
```

reads a number from the standard input stream, which is usually the keyboard, and assigns it to the second operand *x*. This can be done because *cin* (which is the first operand) is declared in *<iostream>* as being of type *istream* and because there is a *float* extractor >>. The type of the expression that follows >> is referred to as the *extractor type*. The expression *cin >> x* (without a terminating semicolon) yields a reference to the *istream* object *cin*, so that it can in turn be used as the first operand of a >> operator, as is done in

```
(cin >> x) >> y
```

and so on. Since the operator >> is left associative, the parentheses in this expression are superfluous and are therefore usually omitted.

When we are using >> for built-in types, any leading white-space characters are skipped by default. This is convenient in the following case:

```
float x;
char ch;
cout << "Enter a number: "; cin >> x;
cout << "Continue? (y/n): "; cin >> ch;
if (ch == 'y') ...
```

After entering a number, the user will press the enter key, which is the same as entering a newline character. Then the next character to be read would be this newline character, but because any leading white-space characters are skipped, the value that is stored in the variable *ch* will not be this newline character but one of the characters *y* or *n* (assuming that the user behaves sensibly).

Unlike the above situation, we sometimes want to read exactly one character, whether it is white-space or not. We can do this by using the manipulator *noskipws*, writing, for example,

```
cin >> noskipws >> ch;
```

This manipulator *noskipws* is based on the (somewhat lower level) *istream* member function *get*, so we can also write

```
cin.get(ch);
```

or

```
ch = cin.get();
```

In many applications we want to read one character in a loop until some terminating character is read. As we get one character too many in this way, there is a need for putting it back into the input stream. This can be done by writing, for example,

```
cin.putback(ch);
```

Strangely enough, the argument *ch* of this *putback* function call may be different from the character that was read most recently. To understand this, we must know that there is an input buffer, in which putback writes the given character so it will be read in the next input operation. In most cases the only thing we want is to put back the most recently read character in the input buffer. In such cases, we may as well write the following instead of the above statement:

```
cin.unget();
```

Yet another way to look ahead, is by using the member function *peek*. The following program demonstrates this function. The user will enter zero or more letters followed by an integer. Using a for-loop in which we read letters, we terminate this loop only when we have 'seen' the first digit of the integer, but this should not yet really have been read so it can still be read as part of the integer that we read after the letters:

```cpp
// peekdemo.cpp: Looking ahead.
#include <iostream>
#include <cctype>
#include <string>
using namespace std;

int main()
{   cout << "Enter some letters, "
         "immediately followed by an integer: ";
    string s;
    for (;;)
    {   int ch = cin.peek();
        if (isdigit(ch)) break;
        ch = cin.get();
        s += ch;
    }
    int x;
    cin >> x;
    cout << "Letters: " << s << endl;
    cout << "Integer: " << x << endl;
    return 0;
}
```

If the user enters

```
AAA123
```

then the output of this program is

```
Letters: AAA
Integer: 123
```

It may look strange that we have used type *int* instead of *char* for *ch* but the *peek* function really returns an *int* value, of which normally only the eight least significant bits are used (for a character) and all other bits are zero. This is a way of testing for 'end of file', as we will see in Section 10.4. For the same reason, the function *get* without parameters (used in the above for-loop) returns such an integer, which normally contains a character in its final eight bits. Implicit conversion from *int* to *char* takes place in the operation *s += ch*.

Using the above function *get* instead of *peek*, we could have written the above for-loop as follows, with the program behaving in the same way:

```
for (;;)
{   char ch;
    cin.get(ch);
    if (isdigit(ch)) {cin.unget(); break;}
    s += ch;
}
```

Finally, we could have replaced

```
cin.unget();
```

with

```
cin.putback(ch);
```

in this fragment. If you like strange effects, you might try to write the following instead of the last statement:

```
cin.putback('9');
```

In this case, the integer 123 entered by the user would lead to the integer 923 in the output.

Reading C-style strings

The class *istream* also has a *get* member function to read C-style strings. For example, if we have a char array *str* with at least 40 elements, we can write

```
cin.get(str, 40);
```

This call reads at most 39 characters, which are placed into *str*, followed by a null character. We can also use a third argument, of type *char*, which has '\n' as its default value. It indicates that reading characters is to terminate as soon as this character (given as the third argument or '\n' otherwise) has been read, that is, if this happens before 39 characters have been read. The terminating character, if found, is still available in the input stream, so it will be encountered when the next item is read.

The latter aspect is very inconvenient if we want to read several lines of text. For example, the fragment

```
cin.get(str1, 40);   // OK
cin.get(str2, 40);   // ???
```

is not practical. In the first statement, the terminating newline character is detected but not read. The second then immediately encounters it, so reading terminates as soon as it begins, and the empty string (consisting of '\0') is placed in *str2*. One way to solve this problem is by inserting

```
cin >> ws;    // Skip white-space characters
```

between the above two calls. As we will see shortly, *ws* is a standard manipulator for input. It will be clear that this solution is not particularly elegant.

Fortunately, there is also the *istream* member function *getline* to read C-style strings. The following fragment will be more useful than the similar one above:

```
cin.getline(str1, 40);   // OK
cin.getline(str2, 40);   // OK
```

As with *get*, a third argument can be supplied in case a terminating character other than '\n' is desired. Function *getline* not only detects but also reads the terminating character, so in a subsequent call to this input function it will no longer be in the way. This terminating character (usually '\n') is not stored in our variables (*str1* and *str2* in this example).

It is not necessary to use a terminating character. If we want to read exactly 40 bytes, irrespective of their values, and to store them into *str*, without appending a null character, we can use the *read* member function, to be discussed in Section 10.4:

```
cin.read(str, 40);
```

Reading standard strings

We must not confuse the *istream* member function *getline*, used for C-style strings as discussed above, with the function *getline* for standard strings, which we used already in Section 1.6. The latter is not a member function of a class but a normal function. Notice the difference:

```
char str1[40];
cin.getline(str1, 40);   // Read C-style string
string s;
getline(cin, s);         // Read standard string
```

This last *getline* function is available only if we use the header *<string>*. In other words, it is more closely related to the class *string* than to the class *istream*, so it is not a member function of the latter class and we have to supply an *istream* object, such as *cin*, as an argument. It goes without saying that reading a standard string is easier and more elegant than reading a C-style string because we need not specify some maximum length imposed by an array length. Again, the terminating character, which is usually '\n', is read in but not stored in the string variable *s*.

Built-in extractor types

As we know, whether or not expressions such as

```
cin >> x
```

are allowed depends on the type of *x*, which is referred to as an *extractor type*. The following types are valid extractor types based on the header *<iostream>*:

> *char* (plain, signed, and unsigned)
> *short* (signed and unsigned)
> *int* (signed and unsigned)
> *long* (signed and unsigned)
> *char** (to read C-style strings)
> *float*
> *double*
> *long double*

Besides these, many other types can appear as extractor types by overloading the operator >> for them. This applies to types of our own, but also for standard library types, such as

> *string* (see remark below)

The operator >> for the input of type *string* is defined in the header *<string>*, which implies that it is not a member function of the class *istream*. This is similar to what we discussed for the operator << for the output of standard strings in Section 10.2.

In general, the format of numeric input data must be the same as that used in C++ programs, except for suffixes, such as *L* in 123*L*, which are not allowed.

When reading C-style strings (using the operator >>), any leading white-space characters are skipped; the next non-white-space characters are read and stored until another white-space character is found. A final null character is then appended. The character that follows the final character of the input item (a number, a character, or a string) is still in the input buffer, so that it will be encountered in the next input operation. Except for the final null character, reading standard strings is similar. Actually, reading a string by using >> could better be referred to as 'reading a word'. For example, consider the following program:

```
// rword.cpp: Reading a word.
#include <iostream>
#include <string>
using namespace std;

int main()
{   string s;
    cout << "Enter some text: ";
    cin >> s;
    cout << "The following has been read: " << s << endl;
    return 0;
}
```

Here is a demonstration, which clearly shows that this program reads only a single word:

```
Enter some text:     New York
The following has been read: New
```

Note that some spaces were entered before the word *New*, but these do not appear in the output because they were skipped and therefore not stored in *s*. We could try to suppress this skipping of leading white-space characters by using the manipulator *noskipws*, which we discussed in the context of reading a single character. However, this attempt will fail. Suppose we use this manipulator in the input statement of the above program, writing

```
cin >> noskipws >> s;
```

After this modification of the program, the above demonstration, with spaces preceding the word *New*, would produce no output at all:

```
Enter some text:     New York
The following has been read:
```

This is because white-space characters are not skipped so that the first space acts as the end of the input.

In contrast, the first word of the input is read if it is not preceded by spaces, as the following demonstration shows:

```
Enter some text: New York
The following has been read: New
```

Both the original program and the modified one behave in the same way with this input.

Manipulators for input

There are several manipulators for input, as shown below. The header *<iomanip>* must be included for those manipulators which have a parameter. For each of the manipulators *dec*, *hex*, *oct*, *boolalpha*, *noboolalpha*, *skipws*, and *noskipws*, its remains in force until further notice:

setw(*n*)	Set field width to *n*
ws	Skip any white-space characters (immediately)
skipws	Skip leading white-space characters (default) in next input operation
noskipws	Do not skip leading white-space characters
dec	Use decimal conversion (default)
hex	Use hexadecimal conversion
oct	Use octal conversion
boolalpha	Accept *true* and *false* (not 1 and 0)
noboolalpha	Accept 1 and 0 (not *true* and *false*) (default)
setiosflags(*f*)	Set format bits specified by the *ios_base::fmtflags* argument *f*
resetiosflags(*f*)	Reset format bits specified by the *ios_base::fmtflags* argument *f*

With input, we can use the *setw* manipulator as follows to read C-style strings without any risk of exceeding array bounds:

```
char buf[40];
cin >> setw(40) >> buf;
```

In this way, reading terminates when 39 characters, followed by '\0', have been placed in *buf*, unless a white-space character is encountered sooner. (Recall that, first, any leading white-space characters are skipped and, second, any white-space character terminates the process of reading normal characters.)

The *ws* manipulator 'eats' white-space characters. Recall that we have already discussed it in our above discussion about reading C-style strings.

There is a subtle distinction between *skipws* and *ws*. While *ws* immediately skips any white-space characters in the input, *skipws* only sets a flag so that any white-space characters in the input will be skipped in any input operations that follow. We have discussed the manipulators *skipws* and *noskipws* at the beginning of this section. In many cases, the default *skipws* is what we want. If, occasionally, we use *noskipws* because we want to read the next character even if this is a white-space character, it might be necessary to restore the old situation by using *skipws*. This is the case if we subsequently want to read numbers, for otherwise any white-space characters still present in the input buffer (because the user pressed the Enter key after previous input) would cause the attempt to read a number to fail.

The *dec*, *hex* and *oct* manipulators enable us to use not only decimal but also hexadecimal and octal numbers as input.

If we write *cin* >> *b*, where *b* has type *bool*, the user has to enter 1 or 0 as representations of *true* and *false*, unless we have indicated by means of the manipulator *boolalpha* that the user will enter one of the words *true* and *false*.

Possible argument values of *setiosflags* and *resetiosflags* are the format state flags discussed in Section 10.2. For example, we can write

```
cin >> resetiosflags(ios_base::skipws);
```

if we want to reset the flag for skipping white-space characters (which is set by default).

Extractors for user-defined types

As we have seen in Section 6.7, when discussing the program *modulo.cpp*, we can overload the operator >> for types defined by ourselves, which is similar to overloading the operator <<. If we wanted to use the operator >> for the input of *vec* objects, discussed in Section 6.6, we could write

```
istream &operator>>(istream &s, vec &u)
{   float x, y;
    s >> x >> y;
    u = vector(x, y);
    return s;
}
```

With this operator function, we can read a number pair by using >> only once, as in

```
vector v;
cin >> v;
```

10.4 File I/O

For input from and output to files on disk, we can use *ifstream* and *ofstream*, which are classes derived from *istream* and *ostream*, respectively, and declared in the header file *<fstream>*. Figure 10.1 shows how the I/O classes discussed in this chapter are related. The base class *ios_base* was mentioned in Section 10.1.

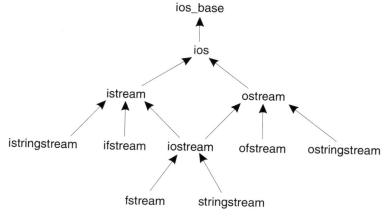

Figure 10.1. Classes for stream I/O

In accordance with the rather informal way we are discussing streams, this diagram is somewhat simplified. Actually, all stream classes in this diagram, except *ios_base*, are templates parameterized on the character type. For example,

```
istream
```

is an abbreviated form of

```
basic_istream<char>
```

and I would have been more accurate if I had written, for example, *basic_istream< >*
instead of just *istream* in Figure 10.1, but this diagram is clearly more readable in its
present form.

The class *ifstream* inherits the extraction operations from *istream*, while *ofstream*
inherits the insertion operations from *ostream*. The following program shows that, in calls
to their constructors, we can associate *ifstream* and *ofstream* objects with real files. It
copies file *aa* to file *bb* and counts how many characters are copied:

```
// copyaabb.cpp:
//     This program copies characters from file aa to file bb.
#include <iostream>
#include <fstream>
using namespace std;

int main()
{   char ch;
    int n=0;
    ifstream ff("aa");
    if (!ff)
    {   cout << "Cannot open aa for input\n";
        return 1;
    }
    ofstream gg("bb");
    if (!gg)
    {   cout << "Cannot open bb for output\n";
        return 1;
    }
    while (ff.get(ch))
    {   gg.put(ch);
        n++;
    }
    cout << n << " characters copied.\n";
    return 0;
}
```

The stream *ff* is opened and associated with the file *aa* by defining *ff* as an object of class
ifstream and by supplying the string *"aa"* as an argument for the *ifstream* constructor. In
the same way, the stream *gg* is opened for the file *bb*. If the file *aa* contains the contents

```
XYZ
PQR
```

with two newline characters, then after copying these contents to file bb the following line is displayed:

```
8 characters copied.
```

If you use MS-DOS, a newline character is represented by two characters (carriage return and line feed), so the files *aa* and *bb* actually consist of 10 bytes, which you can verify with the *dir* command. This way of dealing with newline characters applies to streams opened in the (default) text mode. In contrast, we can open streams in binary mode, as we will be discussing shortly.

Using the operator ! (with *not* as its usual meaning) for a stream, as in, for example,

```
if (!ff)
```

causes the member function *operator*! to be called, which returns the value of another member function, *fail*. In other words, instead of the condition just shown we could have written

```
if (ff.operator!())
```

which is turn equivalent to

```
if (ff.fail())
```

So much for the operator !. You may wonder if logical tests on streams are only possible by using this operator. This is not the case. For example, instead of

```
if (!ff)
{   cout << "Cannot open aa for input\n";
    return 1;
}
```

we might have written the following (admittedly very clumsy) if-statement with the same effect:

```
if (ff) ; // OK
else
{   cout << "Cannot open aa for input\n";
    return 1;
}
```

In this situation, the conversion member function declared as

```
operator void*() const;
```

is called, so that *ff* is converted to a void-pointer (see Section 5.3) which is zero if an I/O operation has failed. More precisely, the fragment

```
if (ff)
```

actually means

```
if (static_cast<void *>(ff))
```

which is equivalent to

```
if (!ff.fail())
```

Recall that we have discussed conversion member functions in Section 6.7, using

```
operator int(){return t;}
```

as an example in the class *modulo*.

Testing for end-of-file when using *get* functions

What we have just been discussing is also relevant to the following fragment:

```
while (ff.get(ch))
{   gg.put(ch);
    n++;
}
```

The function *get* that is used here returns the stream *ff*. Because the expression

```
ff.get(ch)
```

occurs in a logical context, it is converted to a pointer, which is nonzero if the input operation was successful and zero if it failed. We could have tested for end of file in several other ways. First, we can replace the first line of the above while-statement with the following one, if we like:

```
while (ff.get(ch), !ff.fail())
```

Instead, we can use this line, with the same effect:

```
while (ff.get(ch), ff)
```

We will see in the next section that there is a stream member function *eof*, which returns true after an input attempt has failed. Using this function, we can write

```
while (ff.get(ch), !ff.eof())
```

or even

```
while (!ff.get(ch).eof())
```

which is possible because *ff.get*(*ch*) returns the stream *ff*, as we have seen,

There is also a function *get* without parameters. This also reads a character and returns this as its function value. However, this function value is of type *int*, for the sole purpose of enabling us to test for end of file. Using this function, we can write

```
int ch;  // instead of char ch;
while ((ch = ff.get()) != EOF)
```

This value *EOF* is usually equal to –1, represented by, for example, 32 one-bits. This is different from any byte value, since these consist of only 8 bits.

Opening and closing a stream

As we know, the definition of a class variable, such as *ff*, in

```
ifstream ff("aa");
```

invokes a constructor for the class *ifstream*. We may omit a file name (*aa*) here, so that we can associate the stream *ff* with a file later by using the member function *open*. There is also a member function *close*, so we can close a stream and re-open it later:

```
ifstream ff;        // No file opened yet.
...
ff.open("aa");      // Open file aa.
...
ff.close();         // Close file aa.
...
ff.open("aaa");     // Open file aaa.
```

The *open* member function of *ifstream* accepts an optional second argument, as does the *ifstream* constructor. The following list shows values that we can combine using the bitwise or-operator (|) and then supply as this second argument:

ios_base::app	Append: new date is added at the end of the file
ios_base::ate	Open and seek to end of file (pronounced 'at end')
ios_base::binary	I/O to be done in binary mode, not in text mode
ios_base::in	Open for reading (default for *ifstream*)
ios_base::out	Open for writing (default for *ofstream*)
ios_base::trunc	Truncate file to length zero (default for *ofstream*)

For example, suppose we want to write bytes that do not necessarily represent characters and to add these bytes to the end of the existing file *data.bin*. We can then open the stream *ff* for this file as follows:

```
ofstream ff("data.bin", ios_base::app | ios_base::binary);
```

Alternatively, we can use the *open* function, writing

```
ofstream ff;
ff.open("data.bin", ios_base::app | ios_base::binary);
```

Opening a file in the binary mode, as just demonstrated, is recommended for files to which we write and from which we read arbitrary data. In particular, the program *copyaabb.cpp* is a good candidate for using the binary mode. We can easily make this program more generally applicable by replacing the declarations of *ff* and *gg* with the following ones.

```
ifstream ff("aa", ios_base::binary);
ofstream gg("bb", ios_base::binary);
```

After this modification, copying by means of this program is not restricted to text files, but we can also use it for, say, executable files or zip files. Trying to do this by using the original program (which uses text mode) may fail for files that contain certain byte values, such as $0x1A$ (or Ctrl+Z) which, depending on the operating system, causes the copying process to terminate. There are no such problems with reading and writing files in binary mode. There is another difference between the original program *copyaabb.cpp* and the one modified for binary mode. If we use it for the same input file

```
XYZ
PQR
```

the final value of the count variable n would be 10, the same value as shown by the *dir* command, instead of 8 (with MS-DOS, that is). This is because the 'newline character' at the end of each line actually consists of two bytes, $0x0D$ (carriage return) and $0x0A$ (line feed). In text mode this pair of bytes is read in a single call to *get* and internally represented as $0x0A$ (denoted in program text as '\n'). On output, the inverse operation takes place, that is, the function *put* writes the character '\n' as the pair of bytes just mentioned. In contrast, in binary mode each call to *get* or *put*, if successful, reads or writes exactly one byte.

Writing and reading class objects

Suppose we have a class, say, *article*, the objects of which we want to write to a file so that we can read them later. For example, using a stream *ff* which is opened for some file on disk, we want to be able to write (or *save*) an object x of type *article* to the stream *ff* as follows:

```
x.writeObject(ff);
```

Similarly, we want to read (or *load*) x from stream *ff* by means of

```
x.readObject(ff);
```

For simple classes, containing no pointers, strings, STL containers, and so on, it is tempting to make such member functions *writeObject* and *readObject* very simple by using the statements

```
ff.write((char*)this, sizeof(*this));
```

and

```
ff.read((char*)this, sizeof(*this));
```

respectively. It will then be necessary to open the stream *ff* in the binary mode. However, we should realize that this way of writing and reading is not portable: 'records' written on one machine may possibly be unreadable on another because of differences in the sizes of data types and in the way data members are stored in a class object. Besides, classes often contain strings and we have seen at the end of Section 6.8 that the operator *sizeof* is no good if we want to know how many bytes a string takes. The above calls to *write* and *read* are based on the assumption that all data in question is stored in a consecutive block of memory, which is not correct if *article* contains strings (or other advanced containers, such as vectors or lists). The following program therefore takes a different approach. It uses text mode rather than binary mode to increase portability:

```cpp
// saveload.cpp: Writing and reading class objects
#include <iostream>
#include <fstream>
#include <string>
using namespace std;

class article {
public:
    article(const string &ss = "", float xx = 0)
        : s(ss), x(xx){}
    void writeObject(ofstream &ff)const
    {   ff << s << endl;
        ff << x << endl;
    }
    bool readObject(ifstream &ff)
    {   getline(ff, s);
        ff >> x;
        char ch;
        ff.get(ch);
        return ff.good() && ch == '\n';
    }
    void show()const{cout << s << " " << x << endl;}
private:
    string s;
    float x;
};
```

```
int main()
{  ofstream ff("test.txt");
   article a("pencil", 1.23F), b("pen", 4.56F);
   a.writeObject(ff);
   b.writeObject(ff);
   ff.close();

   ifstream gg("test.txt");
   article a1, b1;
   if (!a1.readObject(gg) || !b1.readObject(gg))
      cout << "Could not read two articles.\n";
   else
   {  a1.show();    // pencil 1.23
      b1.show();    // pen 4.56
   }
   return 0;
}
```

In the *main* function of this program, the function *writeObject* writes the objects *a* and *b* to the file *test.txt*. Later the function *readObject* reads the same values to place them in the objects *a*1 and *b*1, which are then displayed. In the function *readObject*, *getline* reads the terminating character '\n' but does not store it in the string variable, so that the output statement

```
ff << s << endl;
```

corresponds with the input statement

```
getline(ff, s);
```

with regard to this character, despite the difference in appearance of these statements.

If we ourselves had to program all classes that we use, it would be a good idea to supply each with *writeObject* and *readObject* functions, in such a way that, for a given class *A* containing members of other classes *B*1, *B*2, ... (like class *article* containing a member of class *string*), the *writeObject* and *readObject* functions of class *A* could be expressed in those of *B*1, *B*2, ... (This principle is referred to as *serialization* and it is an important subject both of the Microsoft Foundation Classes and of Java.)

10.5 Random Access

The binary mode, introduced in the previous section, is especially useful in connection with random access to files. This is because we want to count bytes rather than characters, and, as we have seen, not every character corresponds to one byte. The *fstream* member functions to be used for random access are *seekg* for input and *seekp* for output. As the final letters of these function names indicate, we distinguish between a 'get position' for input and a 'put position' for output.

Suppose we open stream *f* as follows:

```
f.open("info", ios_base::in | ios_base::out |
                ios_base::binary | ios_base::trunc);
```

Since this file is opened for both input and output, there is a 'get position' and a 'put position.' With sequential access, as used so far, these positions are initially at the beginning of the file and gradually move towards its end as we use input and output operations, respectively. With random access, however, we can choose any position in the file as its current get position or put position. For example, the statement

```
f.seekg(i);
```

sets the current get position of stream *f* to *i*. This argument *i* has type *pos_type* (usually defined as *long* or *unsigned long*) and is in fact a byte number, counting from 0 for the first byte of the file. There is a similar stream member function *seekp* for output. Alternatively, we can use another argument, which specifies the position relative to which we must count, using an *off_type* argument *offset* (where *off_type* is usually defined as *long*):

```
f.seekg(offset, ios_base::beg);
f.seekg(offset, ios_base::cur);
f.seekg(offset, ios_base::end);
```

For the first, the second, and the third of these statements, an offset 0 refers to the beginning, the current position, and the end, respectively. With *ios_base::end*, real file positions are obtained by using negative offset values. Again, *seekg* is to be used for input. The function *seekp*, for output, can also have two arguments, with the same meaning.

There are also two member functions, *tellg* and *tellp*, to determine the current get and put positions. For example, we can write

```
pos_type posget = f.tellg(), posput = f.tellp();
```

Program *update.cpp* demonstrates the use of random access. It asks the user to enter a nonnegative (possibly long) integer *n*, which will be the number of *long int* values to be written in the file *info*. First, the *n* values 0, 10, 20, ..., 10(*n* – 1) are sequentially written to the file. If this file already exists, it is 'truncated,' that is, its old contents are destroyed. Then the user is requested to enter another nonnegative (long) integer *i*, less than *n*. The *i*th stored value (counting from 0) is then displayed, and we are requested to enter an increment value by which the displayed value will be increased. Before and after this updating action, the file contents are displayed, so that you can see what happens. Let us begin with a demonstration:

```
Demonstration of updating a binary file.
How many long ints are to be written? 4
0
10
20
30
Enter a nonnegative integer less than 4: 2
20
Enter increment: 7
0
10
27
30
```

In this case the integer positions are numbered 0, 1, 2, 3, so entering 2 implies that the third integer, 20, is to be updated. With increment 7, its new value is 27. Program *update.cpp* contains some new elements, to be discussed shortly:

```cpp
// update.cpp: Updating a file by using random access.
#include <iostream>
#include <fstream>
#include <cstdlib>
#include <string>
using namespace std;

void display(fstream &f)
{   long x;
    f.seekg(0);
    for (;;)
    {   f.read((char *)(&x), sizeof(x));
        if (f.eof()) break;
        cout << x << endl;
    }
    f.clear();
}

void check(fstream &f, const string &s)
{   if (! f.good())
    {   cout << "I/O error: " << s << endl;
        exit(1);   // See Section 11.9
    }
}

int main()
{   long n, x, incr, i;
    cout << "Demonstration of updating a binary file.\n";
    cout << "How many long ints are to be written? ";
    cin >> n;
```

```
    fstream f("info.bin", ios_base::in | ios_base::out |
                ios_base::binary | ios_base::trunc);
    check(f, "cannot open file info.bin");

    for (i=0; i<n; i++)
    {   x = 10 * i;
        f.write((char *)(&x), sizeof(x));
        check(f, "write fails");
    }
    display(f);

    do
    {   cout <<
        "Enter a nonnegative integer less than " << n << ": ";
        cin >> i;
    }   while (i < 0 || i >= n);
    f.seekg(i * sizeof(x), ios_base::beg);
    f.read((char *)(&x), sizeof(x));
    check(f, "read fails");
    cout << x << endl;
    cout << "Enter increment: "; cin >> incr;
    x += incr;
    f.seekp(i * sizeof(x), ios_base::beg);
    f.write((char *)(&x), sizeof(x));
    check(f, "write fails");
    display(f);
    return 0;
}
```

The stream member functions *read* and *write* are used for *unformatted* (or *binary*) input and output. We use them if we want the internal and the external representation of data to be identical. These functions take two arguments: the begin address, which must be of type pointer-to-char, and the number of bytes to be read or written. Besides the actual input and output operations, some checks are performed, which we will discuss in the next section.

Program *update.cpp* contains four statements of the following form and in this order:

```
f.seekg(...);   // Specify position in file
f.read(...);    // Read some data and store it in a variable
...             // Modify that variable
f.seekp(...);   // Specify the same position as above
f.write(...);   // Write the modified variable
```

This pattern is typical for programs that perform update operations based on random access. In programs that are more realistic than *update.cpp*, these four statements usually occur in a loop, the variable in question is usually of some structure type, and the corresponding data items are often referred to as *records*.

10.6 Error States

In class *ios_base* there is a (protected) state member, the bits of which are called *status bits*. It can be consulted after I/O operations to check if these operations have been successful. For this purpose, the following constants can be useful:

ios_base::eofbit	End of file was reached in an input operation
ios_base::failbit	An input or output operation failed
ios_base::badbit	A very serious error occurred
ios_base::goodbit	None of the three bits above are set

One way to use these symbolic values is by calling the member function *rdstate* to obtain the state, and to check if, say, the bit known as *failbit* in it is equal to 1, as the following fragment shows:

```
f.write(str, n);
if (f.rdstate() & ios_base::failbit)
{ ... // I/O operation failed
}
```

Instead, we can test the status bits by special member functions. These return an int value as specified below:

eof( )	Returns nonzero if *eofbit* is set. Otherwise, it returns zero.
fail( )	Returns nonzero if *failbit*, *badbit*, or *hardfail* is set. Otherwise, it returns zero.
bad( )	Returns nonzero if *badbit* or *hardfail* is set. Otherwise, it returns zero.
good( )	Returns nonzero if no error bits are set. Otherwise, it returns zero.

For example, instead of the line

```
if (f.rdstate() & ios_base::failbit)
```

which we used in the above fragment, it is much easier to write the following, with the same effect:

```
if (f.fail())
```

We can clear (or set) the error bits ourselves by calling the stream member function *clear*, declared as

```
void clear(iostate state = goodbit);
```

Its argument, if present, will be assigned to the state member. Normally, we use this function to clear the error bits after we have found some of them to be set. Our program *update.cpp* calls the member functions *eof* and *clear* in the function *display*. The member function *good* is called in our function *check*.

User-defined I/O operators and error states

Several times we have used tests of the following types to check if I/O, and in particular input operations, were successful:

```
if (cin >> x) ...
if (!cin.fail()) ...
if (cin.good()) ...
if (cin) ...
```

in which *cin* may be replaced with other streams. This works very well as long as we use a standard input operator >>. However, we may want to define an *operator>>* function of our own which reads some characters and/or numbers and perform a test on the correctness of the input data. Then the question arises what to do if this test fails in view of the above fragments. For example, suppose we have a class *price*, and want to supply this with an input operator which reads a dollar sign followed by a number of type *double*, followed by a newline character '\n'. The latter implies that a price cannot be followed by any other data on the same input line. It should then be possible to use this operator as follows to read a price and test whether it satisfies these requirements:

```
price pr;
if (cin >> pr)
   cout << "Price entered: " << pr.getPrice() << endl;
else
{  cout << "Input incorrect\n";
   cin.clear();
}
```

Note the use of *cin.clear*( ) to make subsequent input operations possible. It should also be possible to use the statement

```
cin >> pr;
```

and then test for validity of the input data in one of the following ways:

```
if (!cin.fail()) ...
if (cin.good()) ...
if (cin) ...
```

The solution to this problem is based on the stream member function *setstate*, as the following demonstration program shows:

```
// failtest.cpp: Making a user-defined input
//               operator >> suitable for the
//               usual test on success or failure.
#include <iostream>
using std::cout;
using std::cin;
using std::endl;
using std::istream;
```

```
using std::ostream;
using std::ios_base;

class price {
public:
   friend istream &operator>>(istream &is, price &pr);
      // requires dollar sign followed by a real number
   double getPrice()const{return x;}
private:
   double x;
};

istream &operator>>(istream &is, price &pr)
{  char ch;
   is >> ch >> pr.x;
   bool wrong = (is.fail() || ch != '$');
   is.clear();
   is.get(ch);
   wrong |= (ch != '\n');
   while (ch != '\n') is.get(ch);
   if (wrong) is.setstate(ios_base::failbit);
   return is;
}

int main()
{  cout <<
       "Enter a price (dollar sign, followed by number)\n";
   price pr;
   if (cin >> pr)
      cout << "Price entered: " << pr.getPrice() << endl;
   else
   {  cout << "Input incorrect\n";
      cin.clear();
   }
   cout << "Enter an integer: ";
   int i;
   cin >> i;
   cout << "Integer entered: " << i << endl;
   return 0;
}
```

If we omitted the call *cin.clear( )* in the *main* function of this program, then, once an invalid price is entered, it would not be possible to read the integer *i* near the end of this program. There is also a call to this function *clear* in the function *operator>>*. This is necessary because we want to read an entire input line, so we have to clear the 'fail bit' if this is set by the attempt to read a character and an integer, for example, because the user enters $A. The variable *wrong* (in the function *operator>>*) is given the value *true* in the following cases (and *false* otherwise):

- if the fail bit is set after the attempt to read a character and an integer
- if the first character read is not a dollar sign
- if the number is not immediately followed by a newline character

The essential point is the following statement, which applies if the variable *wrong* is equal to *true*:

```
is.setstate(ios_base::failbit);
```

Note that this statement must not be executed before we enter the while-loop that skips the remaining characters (including '\n') for otherwise nothing would be read in that loop.

10.7 In-memory Format Conversion Revisited

In Section 5.14 we discussed in-memory format conversion, which will be much clearer now that we are familiar with classes and streams. Let us consider another example program in which this kind of conversion is applied:

```
// inmemfc.cpp: In-memory format conversion.
#include <iostream>
#include <sstream>
#include <iomanip>
#include <string>
using namespace std;

int main()
{   float x = 2.5;
    // From binary to text (output to a string):
    ostringstream oo;
    oo << "Test:\n"                    // 6 characters
       << setfill('*') << setw(8)
       << setprecision(3) << x * x     // 8 characters
       << endl;                        // 1 character ('\n')
    string s = oo.str();
    cout << s << "Length: " << s.length() << endl;
                        // 6 + 8 + 1 = 15 characters

    // From text to binary (input from a string):
    string t = "0.01234567 89";
    double y;
    int i;
    istringstream ii(t);
    ii >> y >> i;
    cout << "y + i = " << fixed
         << setprecision(10) << y + i << endl;
    return 0;
}
```

After writing

```
ostringstream oo;
```

we can use the object *oo* in the same way as *cout*, but the result is written in a string that belongs to *oo* and that later is available as the expression *oo.str*( ). The first three of the following output lines, produced by the program, show that we obtain a string of length 15, including two newline characters:

```
Test:
****6.25
Length: 15
y + i = 89.0123456700
```

So much for output to a string by using the class *ostringstream*. Similarly, there is a class *istringstream* for input from a string, as the second part of the program demonstrates. Using an available string *t*, we create a corresponding *istringstream* object *ii* by writing

```
istringstream ii(t);
```

After this, we can read from the stream *ii* in the same way as from a real input stream, such as *cin*. This is demonstrated here by reading the real number 0.01234567 and the integer 89 into the *double* variable *y* and the *int* variable *i*, respectively. We then display the value *y* + *i* to show that the input operation was successful.

Exercises

Unless stated otherwise, the names of the files involved in the following exercises are to be read from the keyboard after an appropriate request from your program.

10.1   Display the longest line of a given text file.

10.2   A given text file contains only words, separated by white-space characters. Count how many distinct words there are in the file. Store every word only once by using a set (see Chapter 8).

10.3   The text of a given file has been typed by someone with little typing experience, which explains that not every comma character in the file is followed by a space character. Copy the file to a corrected version in which each comma is followed by a space. (If there is already a space after a comma, you must not insert another one.)

10.4   Two text files are given, each of which contains a sequence of integers in increasing order. Merge these files to obtain an output file in which all numbers read from the original files occur in increasing order.

10.5   As 10.4, but with words in alphabetic order instead of integers in increasing order.

10.6   Read a file name from the keyboard and try to open a file with that name to see if such a file exists. If not, create this file and write n zeros to it, where n is also read from the keyboard. If the file already exists, repeatedly read an integer k (less than n) from the keyboard to update the integer in position k in the file, according to directions given by the user. After reading the integer in the kth position, display it, and give the user the opportunity to replace it with another integer. The positions are numbered from 0. Use binary I/O and random access.

10.7   A text file contains records, each consisting of a name of at most 25 characters and an integer. Read this text file to build a binary file with the same records in alphabetic order of the names. After this, display the contents of the binary file.

10.8* A file contains the integer n, followed by two sequences: first, n integers a_i and, second, n integers b_i. Compute $\Sigma \max(a_i, b_i)$, that is, the sum of the n larger values of each pair (a_i, b_i). The name of the input file is to be entered on the keyboard.

10.9* A given input file contains the values x_1, y_1, x_2, y_2, ..., x_n, y_n, in that order. Each pair (x_i, y_i) represents a point in the xy-plane. Compute the coefficients a and b of the equation

$$y = a + bx$$

which represents a regression line, that is, a straight line. This line fits best through the set of n given points in the sense of the method of *least squares*, according to which we have to solve the following system of linear equations for a and b:

$$an \;\;+\;\; b\,\Sigma\, x_i \;\;=\;\; \Sigma\, y_i$$
$$a\,\Sigma\, x_i \;+\; b\,\Sigma\, x_i^2 \;=\; \Sigma\, 2x_i y_i$$

10.10 A file contains the positive integers k and n, followed by $k \times n$ real numbers in a table with k rows and n columns. Compute the arithmetic means of each of the n columns. The name of the input file is to be supplied as a program argument.

10.11* Count how many decimal integers occur in a given text file, and compute their sum. The integers may be separated by any sequences of nonnumeric characters. The name of the input file is to be supplied as a program argument. For example, the file consisting of the two lines shown below contains five integers, the sum of which is 1034.

```
123.111?abc200
500 100def
```

10.12* Write a program which reads the name of a text file from the keyboard to produce a concordance for all words in this file. All these words are to be printed (only once) in alphabetic order, followed by the numbers of the lines on which they occur. Upper-case and lower-case letters are to be regarded as identical. For example, with the input file

```
To be or
not to be,
that is the question.
```

the following concordance is produced:

```
be              1   2
is              3
not             2
or              1
question        3
that            3
the             3
to              1   2
```

10.13* Write a program that looks for all occurrences of a given word in a given text file. Both the word (consisting of letters only) and the file name are supplied as program arguments. Print each line of the file in which the given word occurs.

10.14 In a factory, there is a machine that examines a great many samples of, say, a liquid product. For each sample, the machine checks whether or not each of the elements E0, E1, ..., E7 is present in the sample, and the eight answers are coded (as 1 for present and 0 for absent) in the bits b_0, b_1, ..., b_7 of a byte. The machine just mentioned writes all these bytes in the file *element.dat*. Write a program that reads this file, and, for each of the eight elements, counts how many times it has been present in the tested samples. In other words, your program has to produce a frequency distribution for the eight individual bits of all bytes stored in the file *element.dat*.

10.15* Write a program that can read any text file to display both its longest and its second longest line. If several lines are candidates for being the longest, only the first is to be taken. The same applies to the second longest line.

10.16 Write a program to count how many times a given word, read from the keyboard, occurs in a given text file. You should look for whole words only. For example, the word *under* occurs only once in the following text (with *un* on the second and *der* on the third line):

```
The importance of understanding the
wise lessons presented in the book un-
der consideration is easily under-
estimated.
```

10.17*Write a program that examines if two given text files contain exactly the same words, regardless of their order and frequency. Two files, say, *A* and *B*, contain the same words if each word that occurs in *A* also occurs in *B* and each word of *B* also occurs in *A*.

10.18 Write a program which takes the names of an input and an output file as program arguments. We want to apply a process technically known as *justification* to this file. This implies that, except for the final line of the file, the final words of all lines are right aligned, so that the right margin of the page is made even. The modified version is to be written to the output file. Each character has the same width. The program is to read a desired line length from the keyboard. In the input file, any sequence of white-space characters acts as a word separator. Each line of the output file is to contain as many words as the given line length permits, and the words are to be separated by at least one space character, but zero or more additional space characters are to be distributed as evenly as possible between the words to make the line have exactly its required length.

10.19*Write a program that can read any text file to check it with regard to matching parentheses and braces. These are allowed to occur only in pairs and arranged in the usual way. For example, the following is correct:

```
({(( ... )( ... ))}( ))
```

Note that all parentheses ( ) between the two braces { } are paired in the proper way. Incorrect examples are:

```
{(})
{)(}
```

10.20 Write a program that reads a file containing a (possibly incorrect) C++ program. The program checks the correctness of strings and (both C- and C++-style) comments. Recall that C-style comments cannot be nested, so that

```
/* abc // def " /* ghi */
```

is a single C-style comment. Similarly,

```
// /*    aaa
```

is a valid C++-style comment, and

```
" jkl // mno /* pqr "
```

is a valid string literal. The double quote is to be ignored if it occurs in a string, preceded by a backslash (as in "\""), or in a character constant ('"'). The double-quote pairs of a string must be on the same line, unless lines are continued by means of the backslash (\).

11

Some Older Library Functions

This chapter is about some useful library functions, which are available to both C and C++ programmers. Since this chapter may be useful as a reference, the headers that we need for these functions are presented in alphabetical order. To use a function, we want to know its number of arguments, their types, and the type of its return value. This information will be given in the form of function declarations.

We can include headers in two ways. The older way is by using the file-name extension *.h*, after which the names in question are not in the namespaces *std*. For example, we can write

```
#include <assert.h>
```

Instead, we can adopt the C++ style by omitting *.h*, adding a *c* at the beginning of the header name, and use the namespace *std*. Therefore, instead of the above line we can write

```
#include <cassert>
using namespace std;
```

11.1 Diagnostics: *<cassert>*

```
void assert(int expression);
```

If *expression* is zero (or *false*), an error message, such as

```
Assertion failed: expression, file filename, line nnn
```

appears, after which the program terminates execution. For example, if we compute some variable *x* and, during debugging, we want to check if this value is less than 1000, we can write

```
assert(x < 1000);
```

Instead of deleting this and similar statements when, after debugging, we no longer need them, we can insert the line

```
#define NDEBUG 1
```

at the top of the program, that is, before the line *#include <cassert>*. Because of this definition of *NDEBUG*, the compiler will ignore all calls to *assert*. For example, in the following program, the call to *assert* will have no effect because of the definition of *NDEBUG*:

```
// assert.cpp: Assertion ineffective because of NDEBUG.
#define NDEBUG 1
#include <iostream>
#include <cassert>
using namespace std;

int main()
{   int x = 2000;
    assert(x < 1000);
    cout << "Ready.\n";
    return 0;
}
```

If we remove the definition of *NDEBUG*, the program will terminate abnormally.

11.2 Character Classification: *<cctype>*

In the following list, the declaration of each function is followed by a description of its return value:

`int isalnum(int ch);`	$\neq 0$ (*true*) if *ch* is a letter or a digit (and 0 otherwise)
`int isalpha(int ch);`	$\neq 0$ if *ch* is a letter
`int iscntrl(int ch);`	$\neq 0$ if *ch* is a control character
`int isdigit(int ch);`	$\neq 0$ if *ch* is a decimal digit
`int isgraph(int ch);`	$\neq 0$ if *ch* is a printable character, other than white-space
`int islower(int ch);`	$\neq 0$ if *ch* is a lower-case letter
`int isprint(int ch);`	$\neq 0$ if *ch* is a printable character, including a space character
`int ispunct(int ch);`	$\neq 0$ if *ch* is a printable character other than a letter, a digit, or a white-space character
`int isspace(int ch);`	$\neq 0$ if *ch* is a space, a form feed, a newline, a carriage return, a tab, or a vertical tab
`int isupper(int ch);`	$\neq 0$ if *ch* is an upper-case letter
`int isxdigit(int ch);`	$\neq 0$ if *ch* is a hexadecimal digit

There are also two functions to convert the case of letters:

`int tolower(int ch);`   The lower-case letter whose upper-case counterpart is *ch*. If *ch* is not an upper-case letter, the return value is *ch*.

`int toupper(int ch);`   The upper-case letter whose lower-case counterpart is *ch*. If *ch* is not an upper-case letter, the return value is *ch*.

For example, suppose that, if a character *ch* denotes a lower-case letter, we want to convert it to the corresponding upper-case letter. If *ch* does not denote a lower-case letter, it is not to be altered. We then write

```
ch = toupper(ch);
```

11.3 Error Numbers: *<cerrno>*

If we write

```
#include <cerrno>
```

in our program, then after an error occurs we can consult the value of the system variable *errno* to obtain more information about that error. Two symbolic constants are defined in this header *<cerrno>*:

EDOM   is assigned to *errno* in the case of a domain error, as occurs, for example, if we try to compute *sqrt*(−1) (with *sqrt* declared in *<cmath>*).

ERANGE   is assigned to *errno* in the case of a range error, as occurs, for example, if we try to compute *exp*(1*e*8).

The following program illegally attempts to compute the square root of a negative number. It also uses the related function *strerror* (see Section 11.10):

```
// errno.cpp: Demonstration of errno.
#include <iostream>
#include <cerrno>
#include <cmath>
#include <string>
using namespace std;

int main()
{   double x = -1;
    double y = sqrt(x);  // Error since x is negative
```

```
    if (errno == EDOM)
    {   cout << "EDOM\n"; // Output: EDOM
        cout << strerror(errno) << endl;
    }
    return 0;
}
```

With Visual C++ 6.0 this program produces the following output:

```
EDOM
Domain error
```

11.4 Floating-point Precision: *<cfloat>*

The results of our computations may depend on our hardware. The header file *<cfloat>* supplies us with detailed information about the floating-point arithmetic that is used. In this section the names that we use for this purpose are listed, together with their meaning and (between parentheses) the minimum or maximum values considered acceptable by ANSI. To explain some new notions, we will first briefly discuss some fundamentals of the floating-point representation of numbers. Note that our discussion is only about principles. The floating-point format actually used on your machine may be slightly different from what is discussed below.

A real number x can be approximated

$$x \approx m \times 2^n$$

where n is integer and m satisfies the following condition to *normalize* the representation:

$$0.5 \le |m| < 1 \quad \text{or} \quad m = 0 \quad \text{(in the latter case, we also have } n = 0)$$

We call m the *mantissa* and n the *exponent* of the floating-point representation (m, n). Instead of 2, a different base, say, b, may be raised to the power n (in which case the number 0.5 in the above normalization condition is replaced with $1/b$). This base is also known as the *radix* of the floating-point representation. The normalization condition makes the representation of x by the pair (m, n) unique (except for round-off errors). For example, with $x = 9/4$, we have

$$m = 9/16, \quad n = 2$$

Instead of x, both its (approximated) mantissa m and its exponent n are stored. Although x may have very large and very small absolute values, the numbers m and n that represent x can very well be stored in fixed numbers of bits. These numbers of bits determine both the precision and the maximum magnitude of x.

The above background information may be helpful in understanding the meaning of the following symbolic constants, defined in *<cfloat>*:

`FLT_RADIX`	Radix of the floating-point representation; for example, 2 or 16.
`FLT_ROUNDS`	Floating-point rounding mode for addition.

Special information about type *float*:

`FLT_DIG`	Precision: number of decimal digits (at least 6).
`FLT_EPSILON`	Smallest number x such that $1.0 + x \neq 1.0$ (x is at most 10^{-5}).
`FLT_MANT_DIG`	Number of digits of the mantissa when this is written in the number system with radix *FLT_RADIX*.
`FLT_MAX`	Maximum float value (at least 10^{37}).
`FLT_MAX_EXP`	Greatest n such that $FLT\_RADIX^n - 1$ can be represented.
`FLT_MIN`	Smallest positive normalized value of type *float* (at most 10^{37}).
`FLT_MIN_EXP`	Smallest n for which 10^n can be normalized.

Special information about type *double*:

`DBL_DIG`	Precision: number of decimal digits (at least 6).
`DBL_EPSILON`	Smallest number x such that $1.0 + x \neq 1.0$ (x is at most 10^{-5}).
`DBL_MANT_DIG`	Number of digits of the mantissa when this is written in the number system with radix *FLT_RADIX*.
`DBL_MAX`	Maximum float value (at least 10^{37}).
`DBL_MAX_EXP`	Greatest n such that $FLT\_RADIX^n - 1$ can be represented.
`DBL_MIN`	Smallest positive normalized value of type *float* (at most 10^{37}).
`DBL_MIN_EXP`	Smallest n for which 10^n can be normalized.

11.5 Maximum Integer, etc.: *<climits>*

All elementary types for which no floating-point representation is used are sometimes called integral types. The header *<climits>* supplies us with very useful information about these types:

CHAR_BIT	Number of bits in a char (at least 8).
CHAR_MAX	Maximum *char* value.
CHAR_MIN	Minimum *char* value.
INT_MAX	Maximum *int* value (+32767 or greater).
INT_MIN	Minimum *int* value (32767 or less).
LONG_MAX	Maximum *long* value (+2147483647 or greater).
LONG_MIN	Minimum *long* value (2147483647 or less).
SCHAR_MAX	Maximum *signed char* value (+127 or greater).
SCHAR_MIN	Minimum *signed char* value (127 or less).
SHRT_MAX	Maximum *short* value (+32767 or greater).
SHRT_MIN	Minimum *short* value (32767 or less).
UCHAR_MAX	Maximum *unsigned char* value (255 or greater).
UINT_MAX	Maximum *unsigned int* value (65535 or greater).
ULONG_MAX	Maximum *unsigned long* value (4294967295 or greater).
USHRT_MAX	Maximum *unsigned short* value (65535 or greater).

11.6 Mathematical Functions: *<cmath>*

In Section 4.7, we discussed a number of mathematical standard library functions. Here are their declarations once again:

```
double cos(double x);
double sin(double x);
double tan(double x);
double exp(double x);
double log(double x);
double log10(double x);
double pow(double x, double y);
double sqrt(double x);
double floor(double x);
double ceil(double x);
double fabs(double x);
double acos(double x);
double asin(double x);
double atan(double x);
double atan2(double y, double x);
double cosh(double x);
double sinh(double x);
double tanh(double x);
```

The header *<cmath>* also declares four functions that are associated with floating-point representation, discussed in Section 11.4:

`double ldexp(double x, int n);`	Returns $x \times 2^n$.
`double frexp(double x, int *exponent);`	See below.
`double modf(double x, double *ip);`	See below.
`double fmod(double x, double y);`	See below.

As you can see, *ldexp* computes a floating-point number from its mantissa and its exponent. The opposite of this is done by *frexp*. For example, after the execution of

```
int n;
double x, mantissa;
x = ...;
mantissa = frexp(x, &n);
```

we have

$$x = mantissa \times 2^n$$

where

$$0.5 \le |\,mantissa\,| < 1 \quad \text{if } x \ne 0$$
$$mantissa = n = 0 \qquad \text{if } x = 0$$

We can use *modf* to split a real number x into its integral part n and its fraction f. For example, consider the call to *modf* in

```
int n;
double x, f;
x = ...;
f = modf(x, &n);
```

After this call, the sum of $n + f$ is equal to x, the signs of n and f are the same as that of x, and $f < 1$. For example, 123.456 is split into 123 and 0.456 in this way.

The function *modf* should not be confused with *fmod*, which computes the remainder when one floating-point number is divided by another. After

```
double a, b, r;
a = ...; b = ...;      // b unequal to 0
r = fmod(a, b);
```

the value of r is such that $a - r$ is a whole multiple of b, the sign of r is the same as that of a, and

$$0 \le |r| < |b|$$

For example, *fmod*(2.8, 1.1) is equal to 0.6 (= $2.8 - 2 \times 1.1$).

Besides the function declarations mentioned above, we also find the definition of the following symbolic constant in *<cmath>*:

HUGE_VAL   A very large positive value of type double.

11.7 Variable-length Argument Lists: *<cstdarg>*

We are already familiar with two methods (namely default arguments and function overloading, discussed in Sections 4.5 and 4.8, respectively) to define functions that can be called with different numbers of arguments, so that we can write, for example, *f*(*a*) and *f*(*a*, *b*). These two methods are available only in C++. There is a third way, which is also available in plain C. It is more general than the others, in that the function declaration does not limit the number of arguments. On the other hand, it does not provide for argument checking and conversion, as the others do.

We will consider the beginning of a function, *fun*, the first three parameters, *c*, *x*, and *k* of which have the types *char*, *float*, and *int*, respectively. In total, the number of arguments is $3 + n$ ($n \geq 0$). The first three arguments supply *fun* with information to determine how many arguments follow and what the type of each of these is. Then we write the first line of function *fun* as follows:

```
int fun(char c, float x, int k, ...)
```

Note that this should be taken literally, including the three dots. If we want a separate declaration of *fun*, this takes the same form as this line followed by a semicolon.

We then introduce a variable, traditionally called *argp*, of type *va_list* (defined in the header *<cstdarg>*), writing the following line at the beginning of *fun*:

```
va_list argp;
```

This variable *argp* will act as a pointer to the next argument to be used. This process is initialized by executing the following macro call:

```
va_start(argp, k);
```

This expresses that *argp* is to point to the argument that follows the one that corresponds to parameter *k*. In order to obtain the value of the argument pointed to by *argp*, we must not use the normal notation **argp*, but, instead, we write:

```
va_arg(argp, type)
```

where *type* is the type of the argument pointed to by *argp* (which means that *type* is also the type of this whole macro call). For example, we can call *va_arg* as follows:

```
y = va_arg(argp, double);
```

As an important side effect, *va_arg* alters *argp*, so that it points to the next argument, and so on. Therefore *va_arg* will in practice be called in a loop. After the termination of this loop, the following macro call is to be executed:

```
va_end(argp);
```

A complete program that uses variable-length argument lists is given below. The number of arguments used in calls to the function *sum* is unlimited. It is essential that these arguments, except for the first, have type *double*. For example, we must not replace 10.0 (of type *double*) with 10 (of type *int*) or 10.0F (of type *float*) in the *main* function below. The first argument has type *int*. It specifies how many arguments of type *double* follow, so that function *sum* can compute their sum:

```
// vararg.cpp: Variable-length argument lists.
#include <cstdarg>
#include <iostream>
using namespace std;

int main()
{   double sum(int n, ...); // Literal program text!
    cout << sum(1, 9.87) << endl;
    cout << sum(5, 10.0, 20.0, 30.0, 40.0, 50.0) << endl;
    return 0;
}

double sum(int n, ...)      // Literal program text!
// n is the number of arguments that follow.
{   va_list argp;
    double s = 0;
    va_start(argp, n);
    while (n--) s += va_arg(argp, double);
    va_end(argp);
    return s;
}
```

Note that the curious parameter list, containing three dots, occurs both in the declaration and in the definition of the function *sum*. The first call to *sum* in the *main* function computes a sum of only one term, 9.87, while the second computes

$$10 + 20 + 30 + 40 + 50 = 150$$

which explains the following output of this program:

```
9.87
150
```

11.8 Input and Output: *<cstdio>*

Besides the typical C++ stream I/O, discussed in Chapter 10, the traditional C 'standard I/O,' with header *<stdio.h>* or *<cstdio>* is also available for C++ programmers. Since the use of these I/O facilities is widespread, we will pay some attention to them in this section, or rather, to the well-known functions *printf* and *scanf*. After this, we will briefly discuss their counterpart for files, *fprintf* and *fscanf*, and those for in-memory format conversion, *sprintf* and *sscanf*.

The function *printf*

Traditionally, *printf* is used for formatted output to the stream *stdout*, that is, to the screen. We often speak about *printing* rather than 'writing to *stdout*'. A call to *printf* has the form

```
printf(formatstring, arg1, arg2, ...)
```

in which the first argument (which we will refer to as *format string*) is a C-style string, which can be followed by any number of arguments. (Recall that we have discussed variable-length argument lists, as used here, in the previous section.) Although *printf* is often used as a 'void function,' it returns a value, which is normally equal to the number of characters that are written. In case of an error, the return value is negative.

In accordance to Section 5.4, the format string is passed to *printf* in the form of an address. For example, in

```
printf("Temperature: %4.1f degrees centigrade.", temp);
```

the address of the first character (*T*) of the format string is passed to *printf*, and this function itself can determine the length of the string because of the null character, internally stored at its end. The fact that an address is passed as an argument explains that the first argument of *printf* can have other forms that also result in addresses. Examples are the name of an array in which a format string is stored, and a conditional expression, as in:

```
char fstr[80] = "If x = %f and y = %f, then z is ";
float x, y, z;
...
printf(fstr, x, y);
printf(z < 0 ? "negative." : z > 0 ? "positive." : "zero.");
```

The format string can contain two kinds of objects:

- Characters to be printed literally
- Conversion specifications

There must be a conversion specification for each of the arguments *arg*1, *arg*2, and so on. Each conversion specification begins with % and ends with a conversion character. There may be something, such as a 'precision,' between these two characters. Let us start with the conversion characters themselves:

d   The (*int*) argument is converted to decimal representation. (Instead of *d*, we may use *i* with the same meaning.)

o   The (int) argument is converted to octal representation, without a leading zero.

x   The (*int*) argument is converted to hexadecimal representation, without a prefix 0*x*. In addition to the digits 0, ..., 9, the lower case letters *a*, ..., *f* are used. We can also write *X* instead of *x*, with the effect that capital letters *A*, ..., *F* are used instead of lower case letters.

u   The (*int* or *unsigned*) argument is converted to unsigned decimal representation. This implies that the leftmost bit of the argument is used as a value bit, not as a sign bit.

c   The (*char* or *int*) argument is (or is interpreted as) a single character.

s   The argument is a string, or, technically, the address of the first element of a character array. The characters starting at this address are printed until a null character is reached or until as many characters have been printed as indicated by the precision (between % and *s*).

f   The (*float* or *double*) argument is converted to decimal representation of the form [–]*mmm.dddddd*, in which the default precision (that is, the number of digits *d* in the form just mentioned) is 6. The result is neatly rounded. If we use 0 as a precision, the decimal point is suppressed.

e   The (*float* or *double*) argument is converted to decimal representation of the form [–]*m.dddddd*e±*xx*, in which the number of digits *d* is given by the precision (between % and *e*). The default precision is 6. If we write 0 as a precision, the decimal point is suppressed. If we write *E* instead of *e*, then *E* instead of *e* appears in the output.

g   The (*float* or *double*) argument is converted by means of %*f* or %*e* (or %*E* if we write *G* instead of *g*). In most cases, %*f* will be used; %*e* (or %*E*) is used if the exponent is either less than 4 or greater than the given precision. Neither a point at the end nor any trailing zeros are printed.

p   The argument must have a pointer type, that is, it must be an address. This address is printed in a system-dependent way.

n   The argument must be the address of an integer variable. The number of characters printed so far by the current call to *printf* is placed into that variable. (Nothing is printed.)

%   This is not really a conversion character, and there is no corresponding argument. We simply write %% if we want to include the character % in the output.

Between % and the conversion character, we can insert:

1.   Flags (in any order):

–   The converted argument is left aligned in the positions that are available. (Normally, we do not want this for numerical output, but we do for strings.)

+   The number being printed is preceded by a plus sign if it is positive and by a minus sign it is negative. (Without this flag, a negative number is preceded by a minus sign but a positive one not by a plus sign.)

space If a plus or minus sign is omitted, a space character is printed instead.

0   Numbers are padded with zeros (not with space characters) on the left.

An alternative form is used. This form depends on the conversion character as follows. If used in combination with *o* (denoting *octal*), the first digit is 0. With *x* or *X* (denoting *hexadecimal*), there is a prefix 0x or 0X if the value is unequal to zero. With *e*, *E*, *f*, *g*, and *G*, a decimal point always appears in the output; with *g* and *G* trailing zeros are printed.

2.   A number (written as a sequence of decimal digits), indicating the field width. The converted argument is printed in a field of that width or more if more positions are needed. Any room not needed is padded on the left, or, in the case of the – flag, on the right. The padding character is a space, or, in the case of the flag 0, it is 0. See also the remark below.

3.   A period, which separates the field width (see 2) from the precision (see 4).

4.   A number (written as a sequence of decimal digits), indicating the precision. In the case of a string, this is the maximum number of characters to be printed. With f, e, E, it is the number of digits printed after the decimal point; with g and G, it is the number of significant digits. In the case of an integer, it is the minimum number of digits to be printed, with leading zeros if needed. See also the remark below.

5.   A length modifier h, l, or L. We use h if the argument is *short* or *unsigned short*, l if it is *long* or *unsigned long*, and L if it is *long double*.

Remark:

We can write an asterisk (*) for the field width (see 2) and/or for the precision (see 4). If we do, the argument in question must be preceded by one or two special arguments (depending on whether one or two asterisks are being used). These additional arguments must be of type *int*, and their numerical values are taken as the field width and the precision, respectively. In the following program, the value of x is printed with both the field width and the precision given by special arguments, while k has only one special argument, used for its width:

```
// asterisk.cpp: Asterisks in conversion specifications for
//                printf.

#include <stdio.h>

int main()
{  int width = 5, precision = 2,
       k = 1234;
   double x = 9.87654321;
   printf("x =%*.*f   k =%*d\n",
          width, precision, x, width, k);
   return 0;
}
```

The output of this program is:

```
x = 9.88   k = 1234
```

The function *scanf*

We use *scanf* for input from *stdin*, which usually corresponds to the keyboard. A call to this function has the following form:

```
scanf(format string, arg1, arg2, ...)
```

Actually, *scanf* expects an address as its first argument, in the same way as *printf* does. The arguments that follow, *arg*1, *arg*2, ... also denote addresses: they specify where the data items that are read are to be placed.

The return value of *scanf* is equal to the number of data items that have been read and assigned to variables, or to *EOF* if nothing could be read because we were reading from a file the end of which was encountered. As we have seen in Section 10.4, this *EOF* value is usually equal to –1.

The format string contains conversion specifications, each of which starts with % and ends with a conversion character. The following conversion characters can be used with *scanf*:

d   The input is a decimal integer and the corresponding argument has type *int**. (The latter notation means *pointer-to-int*, which is the type of, for example, &*i*, where *i* has type *int*). We must use *%ld* for a *long** and *%hd* for a *short** argument, as we will discuss shortly.)

i   The input is an integer in decimal, octal, or hexadecimal representation. For example, 19 is decimal, 023 octal, and 0*x*13 hexadecimal. The argument has type *int**.

o   The input is an octal integer, with or without leading 0. The argument is *int**.

u   The input is an unsigned integer. It cannot be negative, but, on the other hand, its value can be about twice as large as that of type *int*. The argument has type *unsigned int**.

x   The input is a hexadecimal integer, with or without a prefix 0*x* or 0*X*. The argument has type *int**.

c   The input consists of a character sequence, the length of which is given by the precision (between % and *c*); if no precision is given, only one character is read. In contrast to the other conversion specifications, the character being read can be a white-space character (unless *%c* is preceded by a space character). No null character is added at the end. The argument has type *char**.

s   As with numeric input data, any leading white-space characters are skipped. Then all characters are read, either until as many have been read as indicated by the precision or until a white-space character follows. A null character is added at the end. The argument has type *char** and must be the start address of an area large enough to store all characters read, including the null character.

f   The input consists of a number, represented as a floating-point or an integer constant, and possibly preceded by a sign. The argument has type *float**. Instead of *f*, we may write *e* or *g*. (We must write *%lf* in the case of a *double** argument, as we will discuss below.)

p   The input is an address, as printed by *printf("%p", ...)*. The argument is the address of a pointer (to any type).

n   The number of characters read so far in the current call to *scanf* is stored in the variable the address of which is given by the argument. The argument has type *int**. Nothing is read.

[...]   Characters are read only as far as they belong to the set of characters occurring between these brackets. The first character not belonging to this set terminates reading and is considered not to be read. A null character is added at the end. The argument has type *char**. (The set of characters between the brackets must not be empty; this convention makes it possible to recognize the first] in []...] as a character that belongs to the set.)

[^...] As [...], except that characters are read that do *not* belong to the set of characters specified between the brackets.

The following example illustrates how *%n* and *%[...]* work. First, all characters different from the five characters . , ; ? ! are read and stored in array *str*. Then one more character is read (which can only be one of the five characters just mentioned) and stored in the variable *ch*. The total number of characters that are read is stored in the variable *k*:

```
// scanfadv.cpp: Some advanced conversion specifications
//                    for scanf.
#include <stdio.h>

int main()
{   int k;
    char str[80], ch;
    printf("Enter a line of text, ending with a "
           "punctuation character:\n");
    scanf("%[^.,;?!]%c%n", str, &ch, &k);
    printf("str=%s  ch=%c  k=%d\n", str, ch, k);
    return 0;
}
```

Here is a demonstration of this program:

```
Enter a line of text, ending with a punctuation character:
Good morning!
str=Good morning  ch=!  k=13
```

Between % and the conversion character there can be

-       An asterisk (*). A data item is then skipped in the input stream, that is, it is read but not assigned to a variable. There must be no argument corresponding to the conversion specification in question.

-       A number (written as a sequence of decimal digits) indicating the maximum field width. This is particularly useful when we are reading strings, because it enables us to prevent array overflow in case more characters are read than the data area in which they are stored permits. For example, in

```
char str[10];
scanf("%9s", str);
```

not more than nine characters will be read. With the null character at the end, at most ten array elements of str will be used, as is permitted here.

One of the letters *l* (to be used for the types *double** and *long**), *L* (for type *long double**), and *h* (for type *short**). For example, the letter *l* must precede the conversion characters *f*, *e*, and *g*, if the argument has type pointer-to-double, as is the case in

```
double xx;
scanf("%lf", &xx);
```

Writing "*%f*" here would be a very serious error: the compiler would not detect this, but things would go wrong during program execution. With an argument of type *long double**, we would need *%Lf*. Similarly, the letter *l* must precede the conversion characters *d*, *i*, *n*, *o*, *u*, and *x*, if the argument is *long**, and the letter *h* must precede them if it is *short**.

With *printf*, it is quite usual to include text other than conversion specifications in format strings. This is done far less often with *scanf*, because such text is not printed but expected in the input! For example, in

```
scanf("%d/%d/%d", &day, &month, &year);
```

the slashes in the format string force the user to separate the numerical values for day, month, and year by slashes, as in

```
31/12/1989
```

Since *%d* permits the data items to be preceded by white-space characters, the input can also have other forms, such as

```
31/     12/
1989
```

However, in the input data, white-space characters must not precede the slashes. If we want them to be permitted, we must write at least one space character immediately before the slashes in the format string. (We may as well write space characters following the slashes to make the format string more readable, although this has no effect.) The following call to *scanf* is therefore more practical:

```
scanf("%d / %d / %d", &day, &month, &year);
```

For example, it accepts the following input:

```
31    /    12/1990
```

Note that the presence of spaces in the format string does not oblige us to enter corresponding space characters in the input, as the final part, 12/1990, in this example illustrates.

Space characters in the format string are particularly important in combination with %c. If the input data

```
123    A
```

is read by

```
scanf("%d %c", &n, &ch);
```

then the character A is stored in the variable *ch*. However, if it is read by

```
scanf("%d%c", &n, &ch);
```

(in which there is no blank space between %d and %c), then, after reading 123, the first character that follows is read and stored in ch. In our example, this is a space character.

When we are using *scanf* to read data from the keyboard, program execution resumes only after we have pressed the Enter key, or, in other words, after we have entered a newline character. Although obviously the computer has seen this newline character, it is considered not to have been read yet. In most cases this will not cause any trouble in any call to *scanf* that follows because the latter will skip over leading white-space characters. However, %c skips over white-space characters only if, in the format string, this conversion specification is preceded by a white-space character. Therefore the space character in the format string on the fourth line of the following program fragment is by no means superfluous:

```
printf("Enter an integer: ");
scanf("%d", &n);
printf("Enter a character: ");
scanf(" %c", &ch);
```

Note that you cannot skip over the newline character following the integer by replacing the second of these program lines with

```
scanf("%d\n", &n); // Error
```

If you try this, you will notice that \n (or, in general, a white-space character) at the end of the format string has a very undesirable effect. It is interpreted as a command to skip over any white-space characters in the input, until a different character is entered. This means that after entering an integer and pressing the Enter key, the machine will wait until a different character is entered and the Enter key is pressed again. (Recall that the latter is usual: only when the Enter key is pressed is the input, as far as needed by the program, actually processed.) Although all this is already very unpleasant, things may even be worse if there are subsequent calls to *scanf*, for then all these additional characters entered are still available in the input stream and will therefore turn up when we do not want or expect them.

Files

Many I/O functions declared in *stdio.h* make use of type *FILE*, also defined in this header. We have access to files (on disk) by using file pointers of type pointer-to-*FILE*, or type *FILE**, for short. There are three standard file pointers, also called streams, namely *stdin*, *stdout*, and *stderr*. They are normally used for input from the keyboard, output to the video display, and the display of error messages, respectively.

Since we focus in this book on the typical C++ stream I/O facilities, our discussion of C-style file I/O will not be complete. Now that we have paid so much attention to *printf* and *scanf*, we select two similar functions, *fprintf* and *sscanf*, to discuss this type of file I/O. These two functions accept the same format strings as *printf* and *scanf*.

Before we can write to or read from files, we have to open them by using the function *fopen*. When we do not want to use a file anymore, we can close it by using *fclose*. The following program demonstrates these four functions (*fopen*, *fclose*, *fprintf*, and *fscanf*). It assumes that there is a text file *num.txt*, which can contain any number of integers, separated by white-space characters. The sum of these is computed and both displayed on the screen and written to another file, *outsum.txt*:

```
// numio.cpp: This program reads integers from the file
//            num.txt and computes their sum. It terminates
//            as soon as an invalid character is encountered
//            or the end of the file is reached. The sum is
//            displayed and also written to the file
//            outsum.txt.
#include <stdio.h>
#include <stdlib.h>

int main()
{   int sum = 0, x;
    FILE *fp = fopen("num.txt", "r");
    if (fp == NULL)
    {   printf("File num.txt not available.\n");
        exit(1);
    }
```

```
    while (fscanf(fp, "%d", &x) == 1)
       sum += x;
    if (!feof(fp))
    {  printf("Invalid character read.\n");
    }
    fclose(fp);
    printf("The sum (also written to outsum.txt) is: %d\n",
       sum);
    FILE *fpsum = fopen("outsum.txt", "w");
    fprintf(fpsum, "%d\n", sum);
    fclose(fpsum);
    return 0;
}
```

The association of the file *num.txt* with the file pointer *fp* follows from the following statement:

```
    FILE *fp = fopen("num.txt", "r");
```

The second argument, "*r*", indicates that we will read from this file, so we open it for input. Similarly, we use "*w*" for output files, as this program shows for the file *outsum.txt*. The file pointer returned by *fopen* is used as the first argument in calls to *fprintf* and *fscanf*, so that the format string is the second argument in these function calls. Like *scanf*, the function *fscanf* returns the number of successfully read data items, which should be 1 in this program, since in each call to *fscanf* we read only one integer, except for the final one, which fails and returns the value *EOF* instead of 1. This explains the correct termination of the while-loop. After end of file is encountered the function *feof* will return a nonzero value (which we interpret as *true*). If the file contains an invalid character, such as a letter, a call to *fscanf* will fail while returning neither 1 nor *EOF*, but the value 0. We could have used this return value for this purpose, instead of using the function *feof*. In the case of the failure of *fscanf* due to an invalid input character, *feof* returns 0, so that *!feof(fp)* is 1 (or *true*).

Closing the files by calls to *fclose* is not really necessary in this program, since all files will be automatically closed on normal program termination, including the case that the function *exit* (see Section 11.9) is executed.

In-memory format conversion

The header *<stdio.h>* also enables us to use the functions *sprintf* and *sscanf* for in-memory format conversion. They form the C-style counterpart of the facilities based on the header *<sstream>* and discussed in Section 10.7. The following program demonstrate these two functions. We use the *sprintf* here to convert the result of the computation $x * x$, where $x = 2.5$, to a sequence of characters and to store this as the null-terminated string "6.25" in the character array *s*. So much for the conversion of the internal binary to text format of a number. Then the opposite conversion is demonstrated, by starting with a (C-style) character string *t*, containing the decimal representation of two numbers, and converting these to their internal binary format:

```
// sprintf.cpp: In-memory format conversion using
//              sprintf and sscanf.
#include <stdio.h>

int main()
{   float x = 2.5;

    // From binary to text (output to a C-style string):
    char s[100];
    sprintf(s, "The square of 2.5 is %f\n", x * x);
    // Show the result:
    printf(s);

    // From text to binary (input from a C-style string):
    char *t = "0.01234567 89";
    double y;
    int i;
    sscanf(t, "%lf %d", &y, &i);
    printf("y = %f   i = %d\n", y, i);
    return 0;
}
```

11.9 Miscellaneous: *<cstdlib>*

The header *<cstdlib>* declares a set of functions for various purposes. A selection out of this set is listed and briefly discussed below:

double atof(const char *s);

If the string *s* contains a valid character representation of a number, then this number, converted to type *double*, is returned. If not, *errno* is given a nonzero value; see Section 11.3.

int atoi(const char *s);

As *atof*, except that *s* is converted to type *int*.

long atol(const char *s);

As *atof*, except that *s* is converted to type *long*.

void exit(int status);

Causes normal program termination; any open files are closed, as if the program terminates normally without calling *exit*. The use of the argument *status* is system dependent; its normal values are 0 for success and 1 for failure. Instead of 0 and 1, the symbolic constants *EXIT_SUCCESS* and *EXIT_FAILURE*, defined in *cstdlib*, may be used.

```
int atexit(void (*fcn)(void));
```

Registers the function *fcn*, so that the latter will be called when the program (normally) terminates. The return value is nonzero if the registration cannot be made. If you register more than one function in this way, the most recently registered one is executed first, and so on, as the following example shows:

```cpp
// atexit.cpp: A demonstration of atexit.
#include <iostream>
#include <cstdlib>
using namespace std;

void ready(void)
{   cout << "Ready.\n";
}
void almost_ready(void)
{   cout << "Almost ready.\n";
}

int main()
{   atexit(ready);
    atexit(almost_ready);
    cout << "Not ready.\n";
    return 0;
}
```

The output of this program is as follows:

```
Not ready.
Almost ready.
Ready.
```

```
int system(const char *s);
```

The string *s* is passed to the command processor of the operating system, so that it will be interpreted and executed as a command. The value returned by system is system dependent.

```
int abs(int n);
```

Returns the absolute value of its argument *n*. Remember, *abs* can be used only for *int* arguments. See also *labs* and *fabs*.

```
long labs(long n);
```

Returns the absolute value of its *long* argument *n*.

```
int rand(void);
```

Returns a nonnegative pseudo-random integer, not greater than *RAND_MAX*. This symbolic constant is defined in *<cstdlib>* and is not less than 32767. See also *srand*.

```
void srand(unsigned int seed);
```

Specifies that *seed* is to be used as the initial value in the process of generating pseudo-random numbers by means of successive calls to *rand*. If we do not call *srand*, that initial value is 1. We can use *srand* if the same pseudo-random number sequence is to be generated more than once. For each sequence, we call *srand* with the same argument, prior to entering the loop in which calls to *rand* generate the elements of that sequence. On the other hand, we may want to write a program that generates a sequence of pseudo-random numbers that is different each time the program is executed. Then each time the *seed* value must be different. This can be achieved by using the function *time* (to be discussed in Section 11.11), because this function supplies us with a different value each time the program is executed.

```
void *malloc(size_t nbytes);
```

Low-level request for a block of memory, with block size *nbytes*. Returns the start address of the allocated memory, or *NULL* (= 0) in the case of failure.

```
void *calloc(size_t nobj, size_t objectsize);
```

Similar to *malloc*, but to be used for an array of *nobj* elements, each taking *objectsize* bytes. The allocated memory is set to zero.

```
void *realloc(void *p, size_t nbytes);
```

As *malloc*, but to be used to increase or decrease the size of a block of memory allocated previously by using *malloc*, *calloc*, or *realloc*, and pointed to by *p*.

```
void free(void *p);
```

Releases memory pointed to by *p* and allocated by one of the above three functions.

11.10 C-style String Functions: *<cstring>*

The word *string* is used as short-hand for *C-style string* throughout this section. We have discussed the first three of the following functions in Section 5.6:

```
size_t strlen(const char *s);
```

Returns the logical length of the string *s*. For example, *strlen*("*ABC*") = 3. Note that "*ABC*" takes four bytes because of the terminating null character.

```
int strcmp(const char *s1, const char *s2);
```

Returns a negative value if, in the sense of alphabetic-lexicographic ordering, $s1 < s2$, a positive value if $s1 > s2$, and zero if $s1 = s2$.

```
char *strcpy(char *dest, const char *src);
```
Copies the source *src* to the destination *dest* (up to and including the terminating null character) and returns *dest*.

```
int strncmp(const char *s1, const char *s2, size_t maxlen);
```
As *strcmp*, but at most *maxlen* characters are compared.

```
char *strncpy(char *dest, const char *src, size_t maxlen);
```
As *strcpy*, but at most *maxlen* characters are copied.

```
char *strcat(char *dest, const char *src);
```
Performs concatenation: the characters of *src* are copied and placed after those of *dest*. Returns *dest*.

```
char *strncat(char *dest, const char *src, size_t maxlen);
```
As *strncat*, but at most *maxlen* characters are copied.

```
char *strchr(const char *s, int ch);
```
Returns the address of the first occurrence of character *ch* in string *s*, or *NULL* if *ch* does not occur in *s*.

```
char *strrchr(const char *s, int ch);
```
Returns the address of the last occurrence of character *ch* in string *s*, or *NULL* if *ch* does not occur in *s*.

```
size_t strspn(const char *s1, const char *s2);
```
Returns the length of the longest possible prefix of *s*1 consisting of characters that also occur in *s*2.

```
size_t strcspn(const char *s1, const char *s2);
```
Returns the length of the longest possible prefix of *s*1 consisting of characters that do not occur in *s*2.

```
char *strpbrk(const char *s1, const char *s2);
```
Searches *s*1 (starting at *s*1[0]) for a character that also occurs in s2. If such a character is found, its address is returned; if not, the return value is *NULL*.

```
char *strstr(const char *s1, const char *s2);
```
Searches *s*1(starting at *s*1[0]) for a substring identical with *s*2. If this substring is found, its start address is returned; if not, the return value is *NULL*.

```
char *strerror(int errnum);
```
Returns (the address of) a string that contains an error message belonging to the current value of *errnum*. See Section 11.3 for a demonstration of this function.

```
char *strtok(char *s1, const char *s2);
```

Consider the call *strtok(s1, s2)*. Then a *token* is defined as a substring of *s1* consisting of characters that do not occur in *s2*. An additional requirement is that a token cannot be a substring of a longer token. An example will make this clear. Consider the call *strtok("!ABC.;DEF", ";?.!/")*. Here we have precisely two tokens, namely *ABC* and *DEF*. The value returned by *strtok(s1, s2)* is the address of the first token in *s1*. After this initial call, we can write a loop in which the call *strtok(NULL, s2)* occurs. Each time, *strtok* returns the next token in the string *s1* supplied in the initial call. If no more tokens are to be found, *strtok* returns *NULL*. Each time a token is found in *s1*, the first character that follows this token is overwritten by the null character.

The following functions manipulate byte sequences that are not necessarily strings. Remember that a (C-style) string ends with a null character, on which most functions rely. The following do not. They can therefore also deal with byte sequences that may contain null characters in any positions.

```
void *memcpy(void *dest, const void *src, size_t n);
```

Copies *n* bytes from *src* to *dest* and returns *dest*. The result is undefined if *src* and *dest* overlap.

```
void *memmove(void *dest, const void *src, size_t n);
```

The same as *memcpy*, except that *src* and *dest* may overlap.

```
int memcmp(const void *s1, const void *s2, size_t n);
```

The same as *strncmp* (discussed above), except that comparing characters does not terminate if a null character is encountered.

```
void *memchr(const void *s, int ch, size_t n);
```

Returns the address of the first occurrence of character *ch* in *s*[0], ..., *s*[*n*−1], or *NULL* if *ch* does not occur in this sequence.

```
void *memset(void *s, int ch, size_t n);
```

Assigns *ch* to all elements *s*[0], ..., *s*[*n*−1], and returns *s*.

11.11 Time and Date: *<ctime>*

The types *time_t* and *clock_t* are defined in the header *<ctime>* to represent the time as a number. These types may be defined, for example, as *long*. Bearing this in mind will be helpful in understanding the following function declarations:

```
time_t time(time_t *pt);
```

Returns the current calendar time, expressed in seconds. The return value may be the time elapsed since January 1st 1970, 0.00 h GMT. If the time is not available, −1 is returned. If *pt* is not *NULL*, the return value is also assigned to **pt*.

```
double difftime(time_t t2, time_t t1);
```
Returns the difference $t2 - t1$, expressed in seconds.

```
clock_t clock(void);
```
Returns the processor time used since the beginning of program execution. This time is expressed in *ticks*. The number of ticks per second is given by the symbolic constant *CLOCKS_PER_SEC*, defined in *<ctime>*. It follows that a single tick is equal to $1.0/CLOCKS\_PER\_SEC$ seconds. If the time is not available, the return value is -1.

To make the time available in other forms, type *tm* is defined in *<ctime>* as follows:

```
struct tm
{   int tm_sec;    // Seconds (< 60) after the minute
    int tm_min;    // Minutes (< 60) after the hour
    int tm_hour;   // Hours (< 24) since midnight
    int tm_mday;   // Day of the month (<= 31)
    int tm_mon;    // Month: 0 = Jan., ..., 11 = Dec.
    int tm_year;   // Years since 1900
    int tm_wday;
       // Day of the week: 0 = Sunday, ..., 6 = Saturday
    int tm_yday;
       // Day of the year: 0 = Jan. 1st, 31 = Feb. 1st
    int tm_isdst; // Daylight Saving Time:
       //   Positive: Daylight Saving Time in effect
       //   0:        Daylight Saving Time not in effect
       //   Negative: The information is not available
};
```

The following functions are based on this type. The functions *localtime*, *gmtime*, *asctime* and *ctime* return the addresses of static objects, which may be overwritten by subsequent call to these functions.

```
tm *localtime(const time_t *pt);
```
Converts the time **pt*, as returned by *time*, into local time.

```
tm *gmtime(const time_t *pt);
```
Converts the time **pt*, as returned by *time*, into Universal Coordinated Time (UTC), which was formerly known as Greenwich Mean Time (GMT). It returns *NULL* if the UTC is not available.

```
char *asctime(const tm *pt);
```
Converts the time available in the structure **pt* into a string of the following form:

```
Fri Jul 14 09:06:43 1990\n\0
```

```
char *ctime(const time_t *pt);
```
Returns a string similar to the one returned by *asctime*, but based on the time available in **pt* (as returned by *time*). Therefore *ctime(pt)* is equivalent to *asctime(localtime(pt))*.

```
time_t mktime(tm *pt);
```

Converts the local time given in *pt* into calendar time in the same representation as that used by *time*.

```
size_t strftime(char *s, size_t smax, const char *fmt,
                const tm *pt);
```

Formats the date and time information given in *pt* according to the format string *fmt*, which can contain special conversion specifications listed below. Like *sprintf*, discussed in Section 11.8, *strftime* places the resulting string into a memory area the address of which is given by its first argument, *s*. No more than *smax* characters are transmitted to *s*. If *smax* is too small to place all characters that are generated into *s*, the return value is 0; otherwise it is the number of characters placed into *s*, excluding the null character, which is written at the end. Ordinary characters in *fmt*, not belonging to conversion specifications, are copied into *s*. The following conversion specifications can be used:

%a	Abbreviated weekday name.
%A	Full weekday name.
%b	Abbreviated month name.
%B	Full month name.
%c	Date and time.
%d	Two-digit day of the month (01–31).
%H	Two-digit hour (24-hour clock) (00–23).
%I	Two-digit hour (12-hour clock) (00–12).
%j	Three-digit day of the year (001–366).
%m	Two-digit month (01–12).
%M	Two-digit minute (00–59).
%p	AM or PM.
%S	Two-digit second (00–59).
%U	Two-digit week number with Sunday as the first day (00–53).
%w	Weekday, where 0 is Sunday (0–6).
%W	Two-digit week number with Monday as the first day (00–53).
%x	Date.
%X	Time.
%y	Two-digit year without century (00–99).
%Y	Year with century.
%Z	Time zone name, or no characters if no time zone.
%%	Character %.

As you can see, these conversion specifications are quite different from those used for *sprintf*. Note also that, unlike *sprintf*, *strftime* has a fixed number of arguments. All conversion specifications refer to the same structure object, the address of which is given as the last argument. The order of the conversion specifications in the format string may be different from the order of the members in that structure.

Since most of the functions discussed in this section have addresses as arguments, we will often have to use the operator &. Some of these functions are used in the following demonstration program:

```cpp
// timedemo.cpp: Demonstration of time and date functions.
#include <ctime>
#include <iostream>
using namespace std;

int main()
{  time_t t = time(NULL);
   tm s = *localtime(&t);
   cout << "Time in structure s (of type tm):\n";
   cout << " sec="   << s.tm_sec
        << " min="   << s.tm_min
        << " hour="  << s.tm_hour
        << " mday="  << s.tm_mday
        << " mon="   << s.tm_mon
        << " year="  << s.tm_year << endl;
   cout << " wday="  << s.tm_wday
        << " yday="  << s.tm_yday
        << " isdst=" << s.tm_isdst << endl;
   cout << "Time obtained by asctime          : "
        << asctime(&s);
   cout << "The same result obtained by ctime: "
        << ctime(&t);
   cout << "The following lines contain data "
           "obtained by using strftime:\n";
   char str[80];
   strftime(str, 80,
      " Time: %M minutes after %I o'clock %p\n"
      " Day:  %A, %B %d, 20%y", &s);
   cout << str << endl;
   return 0;
}
```

At the moment this program was executed, the result was as shown below. Note the strange output *year* = 100, which denotes the number of years since 1900:

```
Time in structure s (of type tm):
 sec=41 min=34 hour=14 mday=27 mon=10 year=100
 wday=1 yday=331 isdst=0
Time obtained by asctime          : Mon Nov 27 14:34:41 2000
The same result obtained by ctime: Mon Nov 27 14:34:41 2000
The following lines contain data obtained by using strftime:
 Time: 34 minutes after 02 o'clock PM
 Day:  Monday, November 27, 2000
```

Exercises

11.1   Write a program to demonstrate the functions *isalpha*, *isxdigit*, and *toupper*, discussed in Section 11.2.

11.2*   Write a program equivalent to *table.cpp* of Section 2.5, but based on C-style output as discussed in Section 11.8.

11.3   Use the function *rand* (see Section 11.9) to generate 50 sequences of three letters, taken at random out of the alphabet. Note how few of these sequences are existing 3-letter words.

11.4   Why does the following program terminate abnormally, despite the definition of *NDEBUG*?

```
#include <assert.h>
#define NDEBUG 1

int main()
{  assert(false);
   return 0;
}
```

More about Manipulators

Manipulators without Parameters

We have seen in Section 10.2 how we can define manipulators without parameters. Program *mymanip.cpp* of that section is also shown below:

```cpp
// mymanip.cpp: A manipulator defined by ourselves.
#include <iostream>
using namespace std;

ostream &hexadecimal(ostream &s)
{   s.setf(ios_base::hex, ios_base::basefield);
    return s;
}

int main()
{   cout << hexadecimal << 17 << endl; // Output: 11
    return 0;
}
```

We will now discuss in more detail how this way of defining a manipulator fits into the C++ language. Remember that the expression

```cpp
cout << hexadecimal
```

is actually a convenient notation for the following call to the *ostream* member function *operator<<*, in which *hexadecimal* is the argument:

```cpp
cout.operator<<(hexadecimal)
```

Since the name of a function, not followed by an open parenthesis, gives the address of that function, this call makes sense only if there is a function *ostream::operator<<* that takes a pointer to a function as its parameter. More precisely, this parameter type must be 'pointer to function taking an *ostream&* argument and returning an *ostream&*,' for that is the type of this argument *hexadecimal*. There is indeed such a function *operator<<*, defined in the header *<iostream>* like this:

```
ostream& operator<<(ostream& (*f)(ostream&))
{   return (*f)(*this);
}
```

Our expression *cout << hexadecimal* is apparently a call to this function, with argument *hexadecimal* corresponding to parameter *f* and *cout* corresponding to **this*. The return-statement of this function implies that the value of *cout << hexadecimal* is equal to *hexadecimal(cout)*. We see that our own manipulator function *hexadecimal* is called in this return statement, and that manipulators (without parameters) do not require any additional C++ language extensions at all.

Another possible solution

Even if there were no definition of *operator<<* (taking a function as its argument) such as the one shown above, it would be possible to implement the manipulator *hexadecimal*. To demonstrate this, we must realize that in

```
cout << hexadecimal
```

the identifier *hexadecimal* must be some object, of a specific type. As we have seen, this was a pointer type in our previous solution. Since function calls always contain parentheses, this occurrence of *hexadecimal* cannot represent a function call. It can be a variable, but not one of a standard type such as *int* because there are already *<<* operators for such types. We will therefore define a new class, and *hexadecimal* will be an object of this class. We need this class only to overload the *<<* operator, so there is no need to store any data in objects of such types. This may explain the curious fact that the following program is based on a class (*ManipType*) which does not have any members at all. Another peculiar aspect of the following program is that the parameter *m* in the *operator<<* function is not used at all in this function:

```
// mymanip1.cpp: A manipulator defined by using a special
//                      class.
#include <iostream>
using namespace std;

class ManipType {} hexadecimal;

ostream& operator<<(ostream& s, ManipType m)
{   s.setf(ios_base::hex, ios_base::basefield);
    return s;
}
```

```
int main()
{   cout << hexadecimal << 17 << endl; // Output: 11
    return 0;
}
```

Although this program produces the same output as the original version, *mymanip.cpp*, it is essentially different: the actual work is now done in an overloaded *operator<<* function, and *hexadecimal* is now a class object. The requirement that this rather funny class *ManipType* should be supplied in this program makes our first solution, demonstrated in program *mymanip.cpp*, preferable.

Defining Manipulators with Parameters

Besides manipulators without parameters, such as the standard manipulator *hex* and our own manipulator *hexadecimal*, we have also seen some that take an *int* argument. An example of those is *setprecision*. We will now see how such manipulators fit into the language, so we will be able to write manipulators with parameters ourselves. As an example, we will define the manipulator *horline*( ). It displays a horizontal line consisting of minus signs, and it takes an *int* argument indicating how many minus signs are to be displayed. For example, by writing

```
cout << horline(5) << "Ready.\n";
```

we will obtain the following output line:

```
-----Ready.
```

As usual, this new manipulator should be general in the sense that it can be used not only for *cout* but for any *ostream* object.

Since *horline*(5) has the syntactical form of a function with an int argument, we might try to define such a function, and make this function display the minus signs. However, it is not immediately clear what value type this function should return. Besides, no information about any output stream would be available in such a function: if we used *cout << ' '* in this function, its use would be restricted to *cout*. We therefore see that the actual output actions are to be done by an overloaded << operator. This suggests using a new type, different from all existing types so a new and unique function *operator<<* can be defined. We therefore define the class *horline* in such a way that *horline*(5) is a constructor call. We can then store the value 5 in the object generated by this call. Here is a complete program that demonstrates all this:

```
// parmanip.cpp: Defining a manipulator with a parameter.
//               Both class 'horline' and operator<< are
//               specific for this manipulator.
#include <iostream>
using namespace std;

class horline {
public:
    int n;
    horline(int nn):n(nn){}   // Use nn to initialize n.
};
```

```
ostream& operator<<(ostream& s, horline& h)
{  for (int i=0; i<h.n; i++) s << '-';
   return s;
}

int main()
{  cout << horline(5) << "Ready.\n";
   return 0;
}
```

To understand this program, it will be helpful to remember that the expression

```
cout << horline(5)
```

is here equivalent to the following one

```
operator<<(cout, horline(5))
```

B

Table of ASCII Values

HEX	DEC	CHAR	HEX	DEC	CHAR	HEX	DEC	CHAR	HEX	DEC	CHAR
00	0	^@ NUL	20	32	space	40	64	@	60	96	`
01	1	^A SOH	21	33	!	41	65	A	61	97	a
02	2	^B STX	22	34	"	42	66	B	62	98	b
03	3	^C ETX	23	35	#	43	67	C	63	99	c
04	4	^D EOT	24	36	$	44	68	D	64	100	d
05	5	^E ENQ	25	37	%	45	69	E	65	101	e
06	6	^F ACK	26	38	&	46	70	F	66	102	f
07	7	^G BEL	27	39	'	47	71	G	67	103	g
08	8	^H BS	28	40	(	48	72	H	68	104	h
09	9	^I HT	29	41	)	49	73	I	69	105	i
0A	10	^J LF	2A	42	*	4A	74	J	6A	106	j
0B	11	^K VT	2B	43	+	4B	75	K	6B	107	k
0C	12	^L FF	2C	44	,	4C	76	L	6C	108	l
0D	13	^M CR	2D	45	-	4D	77	M	6D	109	m
0E	14	^N SO	2E	46	.	4E	78	N	6E	110	n
0F	15	^O SI	2F	47	/	4F	79	O	6F	111	o
10	16	^P DLE	30	48	0	50	80	P	70	112	p
11	17	^Q DC1	31	49	1	51	81	Q	71	113	q
12	18	^R DC2	32	50	2	52	82	R	72	114	r
13	19	^S DC3	33	51	3	53	83	S	73	115	s
14	20	^T DC4	34	52	4	54	84	T	74	116	t
15	21	^U NAK	35	53	5	55	85	U	75	117	u
16	22	^V SYN	36	54	6	56	86	V	76	118	v
17	23	^W ETB	37	55	7	57	87	W	77	119	w
18	24	^X CAN	38	56	8	58	88	X	78	120	x
19	25	^Y EM	39	57	9	59	89	Y	79	121	y
1A	26	^Z SUB	3A	58	:	5A	90	Z	7A	122	z
1B	27	^[ESC	3B	59	;	5B	91	[	7B	123	{
1C	28	^\ FS	3C	60	<	5C	92	\	7C	124	|
1D	29	^] GS	3D	61	=	5D	93	]	7D	125	}
1E	30	^^ RS	3E	62	>	5E	94	^	7E	126	~
1F	31	^_ US	3F	63	?	5F	95	_	7F	127	DEL

Answers to Exercises

This Appendix contains the author's solutions to those exercises which, in the previous chapters, show an asterisk after their exercise number. For all exercises of this book, included those not covered by this Appendix, you can obtain machine-readable solutions from the website mentioned in the Preface.

Exercise 1.1

```
// p01_01.cpp: Name and address.
#include <iostream>
using namespace std;

int main()
{   cout << "John Brown\n"
         << "1234 Church Street\n"
         << "London\n";
    return 0;
}
```

Exercise 1.2

```
// p01_02.cpp: Computing your age.
#include <iostream>
using namespace std;

int main()
{   int curYear, yearOfBirth;
    cout << "Current year:   ";
    cin >> curYear;
    cout << "Year of birth: ";
    cin >> yearOfBirth;
```

```
        cout << "Your computed age at the end of this\n"
             << "year is " << curYear - yearOfBirth << endl;
        return 0;
}
```

Exercise 1.3

a. 15
b. −16
c. $2^k - 1$
d. -2^k

Exercise 1.4

a. 00000000 00000000 00000000 000010011
b. 11111111 11111111 11111111 111111000

Exercise 1.5

```
// p01_05.cpp: Output of double quotes and slashes.
#include <iostream>
using namespace std;

int main()
{   cout << "One double quote: \"\n"
             "Two double quotes: \"\"\n"
             "Backslash: \\\n";
    return 0;
}
```

Exercise 1.6

```
include <iostream>   // should be: #include <iostream>

int main();          // should be: int main()
{  int i, j          // should be: {  int i, j;
    i = 'A';          // is correct
    j = "B";          // should be: j = 'B';
    i = 'C' + 1;      // is correct
    cout >> "End of    // should be: std::cout << "End of "
       program/n";    // should be: "program\n";
    return 0          // should be: return 0;
}
```

Exercise 1.7

```
// p01_07.cpp: Exercise 1.7. Hexadecimal constant
#include <iostream>
using namespace std;

int main()
{   cout << 0x55555555 << endl;
    return 0;
}
```

Exercise 1.8

```
Single quote: '
Double quote: "
Backslash: \
The End.
```

Exercise 2.1

```cpp
// p02_01.cpp: The largest of some positive integers.
#include <iostream>
using namespace std;

int main()
{  int x, maximum = 0;
   cout << "Enter some positive integers, followed\n"
           "by a negative integer:\n";
   for (;;)
   {  cin >> x;
      if (x < 0)
         break;
      if (x > maximum)
         maximum = x;
   }
   cout << "Largest: " << maximum << endl;
   return 0;
}
```

Exercise 2.2

```cpp
// p02_02.cpp: The average of some positive numbers.
#include <iostream>
using namespace std;

int main()
{  double x, sum = 0;
   int n = 0;
   cout << "Enter some positive numbers, followed by a\n"
           "negative number:\n";
   for (;;)
   {  cin >> x;
      if (x < 0) break;
      sum += x;
      ++n;
   }
   if (n == 0)
      cout << "No numbers read.\n";
   else
      cout << "Average: " << sum/n << endl;
   return 0;
}
```

Exercise 2.3

```cpp
// p02_03: Sum of final two decimal digits.
#include <iostream>
using namespace std;

int main()
{  int x;
   cout << "Enter an integer: ";
   cin >> x;
   if (x < 0) x = -x;
   cout << "The sum of the final two digits is "
        << x % 10 + x % 100 / 10 << endl;
   return 0;
}
```

Exercise 2.4

```cpp
// p02_04.cpp: Given an sequence of 20 integers, how
//             often is an element of this sequence
//             immediately followed by a smaller one?
#include <iostream>
using namespace std;

int main()
{  int xOld, xNew, i, nLargePrecedesSmall = 0;
   cout << "Enter 20 integers: \n";
   cin >> xOld;
   for (i=2; i<=20; ++i)
   {  cin >> xNew;
      if (xOld > xNew)
         nLargePrecedesSmall++;
      xOld = xNew;
   }
   cout << "A larger integer is immediately followed by "
        << "a smaller one " << nLargePrecedesSmall
        << " times.\n";
   return 0;
}
```

Exercise 2.5

```cpp
// p02_05.cpp: The second smallest of an input sequence
//             of 10 integers.
//             Note that the second smallest of
//             1 1 1 1 2 3 4 5 6
//             is 2, not 1.
#include <iostream>
using namespace std;

int main()
{  int x, minimum, secondSmallest;
   cout << "Enter 10 integers:\n";
```

```
      cin >> x;
      minimum = secondSmallest = x;
      for (int i=1; i<10; ++i)
      {  cin >> x;
         if (minimum == secondSmallest)
         {  if (x < minimum) minimum = x;
            else secondSmallest = x;
         }
         else
         if (x < minimum)
         {  secondSmallest = minimum;
            minimum = x;
         }
         else
         if (x > minimum && x < secondSmallest)
            secondSmallest = x;
      }
      if (minimum == secondSmallest)
         cout << "Ten equal integers read.\n";
      else
         cout << "The second smallest is "
              << secondSmallest << endl;
      return 0;
}
```

Exercise 2.6

```
// p02_06.cpp: Three sides of a triangle?
#include <iostream>
using namespace std;

int main()
{  double a, b, c, h;
   const double eps = 1e-8;
   cout << "Enter three numbers a, b and c: ";
   cin >> a >> b >> c;
   if (a > c){h = a; a = c; c = h;} // Now c >= a
   if (b > c){h = b; b = c; c = h;} // Now c >= b
   if (a + b < c + eps)
      cout << "No triangle possible with these data.\n";
   else
   {  double v = a * a + b * b - c * c;
      if (v < -eps)
         cout << "The triangle has an obtuse angle.\n";
      else
      if (v > +eps)
         cout << "The triangle has three acute angles\n";
      else cout << "This is a right angled triangle.\n";
   }
   return 0;
}
```

Exercise 2.7

```
// p02_07.cpp: Compute all sequences of two or more successive
//             integers whose sum is equal to a given number.
//             The solution below is not the simplest one, but
//             it is very efficient in that it does not contain
//             any nested loops.
#include <iostream>
using namespace std;

int main()
{   int s, n, k, ndiv2, t1, tn;
    cout << "Enter the desired sum: ";
    cin >> s;
    for (n=2; n<s; ++n) // n will be the number of terms
    {   k = s/n;
        ndiv2 = n/2;
        tn = k + ndiv2;
        t1 = tn - n + 1;
        if (t1 < 1) break;
        if (n % 2 == 1 && s % n == 0
        || n % 2 == 0 && s % 2 == 1 && 2 * s % n == 0)
            cout << s << " = " << t1 << " + ... + "
                 << tn << " (" << n << " terms)\n";

    }
    return 0;
}
```

Exercise 2.8

```
// p02_08.cpp: A generalized chessboard.
#include <iostream>
using namespace std;

int main()
{   int n, k;
    const char white = ' ', black = '*';
    cout << "Chessboard of n x n squares; each black square\n"
         << "consists of k x k asterisks.\n"
         << "Enter n and k: ";
    cin >> n >> k;
    int nk = n * k;
    for (int I=0; I<nk; ++I)      // Line number I (0,...,nk-1)
    {   int i = I/k;              // Row number i (0,..., n-1)
        for (int J=0; J<nk; ++J) // Position J (0,...,nk-1)
        {   int j = J/k;          // Column number (0,...,n-1)
            // If n is even, the upper-left square (i = j = 0) is
            // white, while it is black if n is odd:
            if ((i + j) % 2 == n % 2) cout << white;
            else cout << black;
```

```
                  // The above can be programmed more elegantly by
                  // using ?:, as we will see in Section 3.1.
            }
         cout << endl;
      }
   return 0;
}
```

Exercise 2.9

```
// p02_09.cpp: Smallest and largest integer and their
//                positions in a given sequence of length 20.
#include <iostream>
using namespace std;

int main()
{   int minim, maxim, iMin, iMax, x, i;
    cout << "Enter 20 integers:\n";
    cin >> minim;
    maxim = minim; iMin = iMax = 1;
    for (i=2; i<=20; ++i)
    {   cin >> x;
        if (x < minim){minim = x; iMin = i;}
        if (x >= maxim){maxim = x; iMax = i;}
    }
    cout << "Smallest: " << minim
         << " (first occurrence at position: " << iMin
         << ").\n";
    cout << "Largest:  " << maxim
         << " (last occurrence at position:  " << iMax
         << ").\n";
    return 0;
}
```

Exercise 2.10

```
// p02_10.cpp: With a given n x n matrix, compute the
//                maximum distance of a nonzero element to the
//                main diagonal. (This distance is zero if only
//                this diagonal contains nonzero elements.)
#include <iostream>
#include <cstdlib>
using namespace std;

int main()
{   int n, max = 0, i, j, d;
    float x;
    cout << "Enter n: ";
    cin >> n;
    cout << "Enter all n x n matrix elements:\n";
```

```
for (i=1; i<=n; ++i)
for (j=1; j<=n; ++j)
{  cin >> x;
   if (x != 0)
   {  d = abs(i - j);
      if (d > max) max = d;
   }
}
cout << "The desired distance is equal to " << max
     << endl;
cout << "(This is the maximum value of |i - j|\n"
     "for which aij is nonzero.)\n";
return 0;
}
```

Exercise 3.2

```
// p03_02.cpp: How many numbers, read from the keyboard,
//              are multiples of 2, 3, and 5?
#include <iostream>
using namespace std;

int main()
{  int x, n2 = 0, n3 = 0, n5 = 0;
   cout << "Enter some integers, followed by a "
           "nonnumeric character:\n";
   while (cin >> x)
   {  if (x % 2 == 0) n2++;
      if (x % 3 == 0) n3++;
      if (x % 5 == 0) n5++;
   }
   cout << n2 << " multiples of 2\n";
   cout << n3 << " multiples of 3\n";
   cout << n5 << " multiples of 5\n";
   return 0;
}
```

Exercise 3.3

```
// p03_03.cpp: Sum of 1st, 3rd, 6th, 10th, 15th,... elements
//              of a number sequence entered by the user.
#include <iostream>
using namespace std;

int main()
{  float x, s = 0;
   int i = 0, iAdd = 1, diff = 1;
   cout <<
      "Add numbers followed by a nonnumeric character: \n";
```

```
    while (cin >> x)
    {  if (++i == iAdd)
       {  s += x;
          iAdd += ++diff;
       }
    }
    cout <<
       "Sum (of 1st, 3rd, 6th, 10th, 15th,... number) is "
          << s << endl;
    return 0;
}
```

Exercise 3.12

```
// p03_12.cpp: Read ten integers and compute the position
//    of the one that is equal to the final one. If there
//    are several, take the first that you encounter.
#include <iostream>
using namespace std;

int main()
{  int a[10], i;
   cout << "Enter 10 integers (a[0], ..., a[9]):\n";
   for (i=0; i<10; ++i)
      cin >> a[i];
   i = 0;
   while (a[i] != a[9]) ++i;
   cout << "a[" << i << "] = a[9]\n";
   return 0;
}
```

Exercise 3.14

```
// p03_14.cpp: Frequency diagram.
#include <iostream>
#include <iomanip>
using namespace std;

int main()
{  int a[25], i, j, max = 0;
   cout <<
      "Enter 25 positive integers, not greater than 40:\n";
   for (j=0; j<25; ++j)
   {  if (!(cin >> a[j]) || a[j] <= 0 || a[j] > 40)
      {  cout << "Incorrect input.\n";
         return 1;
      }
      if (a[j] > max) max = a[j];
   }
   cout << endl;
```

```
   for (i=max; i>0; --i)
   {  for (j=0; j<25; ++j)
         cout << (a[j] >= i ? "  I" : "   ");
      cout << endl;
   }
   for (j=0; j<25; ++j)
      cout << setw(3) << j;
   cout << endl;
   return 0;
}
```

Exercise 3.15

```
// p03_15.cpp: Count how often each of the integers
//             0, 1, ..., 15 occurs in an input sequence.
#include <iostream>
#include <iomanip>
using namespace std;

int main()
{  int i, a[16] = {0};
   cout << "Enter integers, followed by a nonnumeric "
           "character:\n";
   while (cin >> i) if (i >= 0 && i < 16) a[i]++;
   cout << "\nThe integers 0, 1, ..., 15 have been entered "
      "with the following frequencies:\n\n";
   cout << "Number   Frequency\n";
   for (i=0; i<16; ++i)
      if (a[i] > 0)
         cout << setw(4) << i << setw(9) << a[i] << endl;
   return 0;
}
```

Exercise 3.16

```
// p03_16.cpp: A symmetric table.
#include <iostream>
#include <iomanip>
using namespace std;

int main()
{  int i, j, n;
   cout << "Enter a (reasonably small) positive integer n: ";
   cin >> n;
   cout << endl;
   for (i=1; i<=n; ++i)
   {  for (j=1; j<=n; ++j)
         cout << setw(3) << (i < j ? i : j);
      cout << endl;
   }
   return 0;
}
```

Exercise 3.17

```
// p03_17.cpp: Average, variance, and range of a sequence of
//             real numbers.
#include <iostream>
using namespace std;

int main()
{   double x, s = 0, s2 = 0, minim, maxim;
    int n = 0;
    cout << "Enter two or more numbers, followed by a "
            "nonnumeric character:\n";
    while (cin >> x)
    {   ++n;
        if (n == 1) minim = maxim = x; else
        {   if (x < minim) minim = x;
            if (x > maxim) maxim = x;
        }
        s += x;
        s2 += x * x;
    }
    if (n < 2) cout << "At least two numbers, please.\n"; else
    {   cout << "Average:  " << s/n << endl;
        cout << "Variance: " << (s2 - s * s / n)/(n - 1)
             << endl;
        cout << "Range:    " << maxim - minim << endl;
    }
    return 0;
}
```

Exercise 4.3

```
// p04_03.cpp: Display all positive integers x less than 100,
//             such that a given digit d occurs both in x and
//             in x * x.
#include <iostream>
#include <iomanip>
using namespace std;

bool occursIn(int d, int x)   // Does digit d occur in integer x?
{   while (x != 0)
    {   if (d == x % 10)
            return true;
        x /= 10;
    }
    return false;
}

int main()
{   int d, x;
    cout << "Enter a decimal digit (0 - 9): ";
    cin >> d;
```

```
    for (x=1; x<100; ++x)
    {  if (occursIn(d, x) && occursIn(d, x * x))
          cout << setw(2) << x << setw(6) << x * x << endl;
    }
    return 0;
}
```

Exercise 4.5

```
// p04_05.cpp: Writing a number as a product of prime factors.
#include <iostream>
using namespace std;

void tryFactor(unsigned long *p, unsigned i)
{  static int factorPrinted = 0;
   while (*p % i == 0)
   {  if (factorPrinted) cout << " x "; else
      {  cout << " = ";
         factorPrinted = 1;
      }
      cout << i;
      *p /= i;
   }
}

int main()
{  unsigned long a, a0, i;
   do
   {  cout << "Enter a positive integer: ";
      cin >> a;
   }  while (a < 1);
   a0 = a;
   cout << endl << a;
   tryFactor(&a, 2);
   for (i=3; i*i <= a0; i+=2)
      tryFactor(&a, i);
   if (a > 1) tryFactor(&a, a);
   cout << endl;
   return 0;
}
```

Exercise 4.8

```
// p04_08.cpp: Solution to the Towers of Hanoi problem.
#include <iostream>
using namespace std;

/* A tower of n disks is moved from peg src to
   peg dest; peg aux may be used temporarily.
*/
```

```
void Hanoi(char src, char aux, char dest, int n)
{  if (n > 0)
   {  Hanoi(src, dest, aux, n-1);
      cout << "Disk " << n << " from peg " <<
              src << " to peg " << dest << '.' << endl;
      Hanoi(aux, src, dest, n-1);
   }
}

int main()
{  int n;
   cout << endl;
   cout << "Enter n, the number of disks: ";
   cin >> n;
   Hanoi('A', 'B', 'C', n);
   cout << endl;
   return 0;
}
```

Exercise 4.11

```
// p04_11.cpp: Real quadratic equation ax2 + bx + c = 0.
#include <iostream>
#include <cmath>
using namespace std;

int main()
{  double a, b, c, D, sq;
   const double eps = 1e-8;
   cout << "Enter a, b, and c: ";
   cin >> a >> b >> c;
   if (a == 0)
   {  if (b == 0)
      {  if (c == 0)
            cout << "Any x is a root of this equation.\n";
         else cout << "No solution.\n";
      }
      else // a == 0, b != 0:
         cout << "x = " << -c/b << endl;
   }
   else   // a != 0
   {  D = b * b - 4 * a * c;
      if (D < -eps) cout << "No solution.\n"; else
      if (D > +eps)
      {  sq = sqrt(D);
         cout << "Two roots: " << (-b+sq)/(2*a)
              << " and " << (-b-sq)/(2*a) << endl;
      }
      else cout << "Two equal roots: " << -b/(2*a) << endl;
   }
   return 0;
}
```

Exercise 4.12

```
// p04_12.cpp: Compute the maximum of
//             |a2-a1|, |a3-a2|, ..., |a20-a19|,
//             where the sequence a1, a2, ..., a20
//             is read from the keyboard.
#include <iostream>
#include <cstdlib>
using namespace std;

int main()
{   int maxdif = 0, x, xOld, dif;
    cout << "Enter 20 integers:\n";
    cin >> x;
    for (int i=2; i<=20; ++i)
    {   xOld = x;
        cin >> x;
        dif = abs(x - xOld);
        if (dif > maxdif) maxdif = dif;
    }
    cout << "The maximum absolute difference between any\n"
         << "two elements in the sequence is equal to "
         << maxdif << endl;
    return 0;
}
```

Exercise 4.13

```
// p04_13.cpp: The equation sin x - 0.5x = 0 solved
//             numerically by using Newton-Raphson.
#include <iostream>
#include <iomanip>
#include <cmath>
using namespace std;

double f(double x){return sin(x) - 0.5 * x;}
double f1(double x){return cos(x) - 0.5;}

int main()
{   double x = 3, x0 = 0, y;
    int i;
    cout << "Intermediate results:\n"
         << setiosflags(ios::showpoint | ios::showpos);
    for (i=1; i<100; ++i)
    {   y = f(x);
        cout << "x = "
             << fixed << setprecision(16) << x
             << "        y = "
             << scientific << setprecision(4) << y
             << endl;
```

```
        if (fabs(y) < 1e-12 && fabs(x - x0) < 1e-12) break;
        x0 = x;
        x = x - y/f1(x);
    }
    cout << "\nThe solution to sin x - 0.5x = 0\n"
            "(to twelve decimals) is "
         << fixed << setprecision(12) << x << ".\n";
    cout << "Number of iteration steps: "
         << showpos << i << endl;
    if (i == 100)
        cout <<
           "Result unreliable (no convergence in 100 steps).\n";
    return 0;
}
```

Exercise 4.14

```
/* p04_04.cpp: Ladder against wall.
   The ladder is the hypotenuse BC of triangle ABC.
   AB is on the floor and AC on the wall.
   BC is equal to the given ladder length L and
   touches the square ADEF (with sides equal to 1)
   at E, where D is on AB and F on AC.
   We make use of the variables a = BE and b = EC,
   and we will solve this problem both analytically
   and iteratively. (Obviously, only one solution
   is actually required.)
   The functions 'analytical' and 'iterative' below
   take the ladder length L as an argument and
   return the desired distance x = DB.
*/
#include <iostream>
#include <cmath>
#include <cstdlib>
using namespace std;

void error()
{   cout << "Enter a reasonable value of L "
            "(between 2.83 and 1000000)\n";
    exit(1);
}

double analytical(double L)
{   /* With alpha = angle DBE = angle FEC we have
       cos alpha = 1/b and sin alpha = 1/a. It follows that
       1/(b*b) + 1/(a*a) = 1. Furthemore, a + b = L.
       Therefore a*a + b*b = a*a*b*b and
       a*a + 2ab + b*b = L*L.
       Combining these equations, we find a*a*b*b + 2ab = L*L.
       We set p = ab, obtaining p*p + 2p - L*L = 0.
```

```
        Solving this for p, we find p = sqrt(L*L + 1) - 1.
        From ab = p and a + b = L it follows that
        b*b - Lb + p = 0, so b = (L + sqrt(L*L - 4p))/2.
        Since x : a = 1 : b we have
        x = a/b = ab/(b*b) = p/(b*b).
   */
   double p, b, L2 = L * L, Discr;
   p = sqrt(L2 + 1) - 1;
   Discr = L2 - 4 * p;
   if (Discr < 0) error();
   b = (L + sqrt(L2 - 4 * p))/2;
   return p/(b * b); // = x
}

double iterative(double L, int &i)
{   const double eps = 1e-12;
    double xLow = eps, xHigh = 1, x, a, b, delta, h;
    // x will be between xLow and xHigh.
    for (i=0; i<1000; ++i)
    {   x = (xLow + xHigh)/2;
        a = sqrt(x * x + 1); // Pythagoras (triangle DBE)
        b = a/x;             // Because x : a = 1 : b
        h = a + b;           // Hypotenuse
        delta = h - L;       // Should be zero
        if (delta > eps) xLow = x;       // x was too small
        else if (delta < -eps) xHigh = x; // x was too large
        else break;          // fabs(delta) <= eps
    }
    if (i == 1000) error();
    return x;
}

int main()
{   double L;
    int n;
    cout << "Ladder length L: ";
    cin >> L;
    cout << "Computed analytically: x = " << analytical(L)
         << endl;
    cout << "Computed iteratively:  x = " << iterative(L, n)
         << endl;
    cout << "(computed in " << n << " iteration steps)\n";
    return 0;
}
```

Exercise 4.15

```
// p04_15.cpp: Compute e, using a series.
#include <iostream>
#include <cmath>
using namespace std;
```

```
#define NR_OF_TERMS_REQUIRED 1

#if NR_OF_TERMS_REQUIRED
int iGlobal;  // Only for debug version
#endif

double exp1(double x)
{  const double eps = 1e-10;
   double s, t;
   bool neg = (x < 0);
   if (neg) x = -x;
   s = 1 + x;
   t = x;
   int i = 2;
   // Already 2 terms computed; t = most recently used term
   // In the following loop we start with the third
   // term, t = x * x / (2!)
   do s += (t *= x/i++); while (t > eps);
   // i = number of used terms of the series
#if NR_OF_TERMS_REQUIRED
   iGlobal = i;  // Only for debug version
#endif
   return neg ? 1/s : s;  // exp(-x) = 1/exp(x)
}

int main()
{  double x;
   cout << "Enter x: ";
   cin >> x;
   cout << "Standard library function: exp(x) = "
        << exp(x) << endl;
   cout << "Our own function exp1(x) =          "
        << exp1(x) << endl;
#if NR_OF_TERMS_REQUIRED
   cout << iGlobal << " terms of series computed" << endl;
#endif
   return 0;
}
```

Exercise 4.16

```
// p04_16.cpp: Continued fraction.
#include <iostream>
#include <cstdlib>
using namespace std;

long gcd(long a, long b)  // Greatest Common Divisor
{  return b ? gcd(b, a % b) : a;  // See Exercise 4.7
}
```

```cpp
int main()
{   long a0, b0, a, b, d, q, r;
    cout << "Enter the positive integers a and b (a < b)\n"
            "of fraction a/b:\n";
    cin >> a0 >> b0;
    if (a0 <= 0 || b0 <= 0)
    {   cout << "a and b must be positive.\n";
        exit(1);
    }
    if (a0 >= b0)
    {   cout << "a must be less than b.\n";
        exit(1);
    }
    if ((d = gcd(a0, b0)) == 1)
    {   a = a0;
        b = b0;
    }
    else
    {   a = a0/d; b = b0/d;
        cout << "Instead of " << a0 << "/" << b0 << ", we take "
                << a << "/" << b << endl;
    }
    cout << "The following sequence represents the "
            "desired continuous fraction:\n";
    while (a)
    {   q = b / a;
        r = b % a;
        cout << q << " ";
        b = a;
        a = r;
    }
    cout << endl;
    return 0;
}
```

Exercise 4.17

```cpp
// p04_17.cpp: For the given sequence a1, a2, ..., an,
//             we look for pairs (i, j) (i < j) so that
//             gcd(ai, aj) = 1.

#include <iostream>
#include <iomanip>
#include <cstdlib>
using namespace std;

int gcd(int a, int b)     // see also Exercise 4.7
{   return b ? gcd(b, a % b) : a;
}
```

```cpp
int main()
{   int n, i, j;
    int *a;
    cout << "Enter n, followed by a sequence of n integers: ";
    cin >> n;
    a = new int[n+1];
    for (i=1; i<=n; ++i) cin >> a[i];
    cout << "Pairs (i, j) (where i and j range from 1 to n),\n"
            "followed by ai and aj so that gcd(ai, aj) = 1, :\n";
    for (i=1; i<=n; ++i)
    for (j=i+1; j<=n; ++j)
        if (gcd(a[i], a[j]) == 1)
            cout << setw(3) << i << " " << setw(3) << j
                 << "      " << "==>" << setw(5) << a[i] << "  "
                 << setw(5) << a[j] << endl;
    delete[]a;
    return 0;
}
```

Exercise 4.18

```cpp
// p04_18.cpp: Fibonacci sequence.
#include <iostream>
#include <cmath>
using namespace std;

int main()
{   long previousF = 0, F = 1, h;
    const long double pi = 3.14159265358979323846;
    unsigned n, i;
    cout << "Enter the (nonnegative) integer n: ";
    cin >> n;
    if (n == 0) {cout << "F(0) = 0\n"; return 0;}
    if (n == 1) {cout << "F(1) = 1\n"; return 0;}
    for (i=1; i<n; ++i)
    {   h = previousF;
        previousF = F;
        F = F + h;
        if (F < 0)
        {   cout <<
            "n too large: F(n) does not fit into 'long int'!\n";
            return 1;
        }
    }
    cout << "F(" << n << ") = " << F << endl;
    cout << "F(" << n << ")/F(" << n - 1 << ") = "
         << static_cast<double>(F)/previousF << endl;
    cout << "For large n, this value is an approximation of\n"
         << "the mathematical constant tau, which we can\n"
         << "also compute in the following two ways:\n";
```

```
   cout << "tau = 2 * cos(pi/5) = " << 2 * cos(pi/5) << endl;
   cout << "tau = 0.5 * (1 + sqrt(5)) = "
        << 0.5 * (1 + sqrt(5)) << endl;
   return 0;
}
```

Exercise 5.1

```
// p05_01.cpp: Output line is reverse of input line.

#include <iostream>
#include <string>
using namespace std;

int main()
{  string s;
   cout << "Enter a line of text:\n";
   getline(cin, s);
   cout << "Reversed:\n";
   for (int i=s.length() - 1; i>=0; --i)
      cout << s[i];
   cout << endl;
   return 0;
}
```

Exercise 5.2

```
// p05_02.cpp: The same as Exercise 5.1 but without
//              type 'string'.

#include <iostream>
#include <string.h>
using namespace std;

int main()
{  const int N = 200;
   char s[N];
   cout << "Enter a line of text:\n";
   int i = N - 1;
   s[i] = '\0';
   char ch;
   while (cin.get(ch), ch != '\n' && i > 0)
      s[--i] = ch;
   if (ch != '\n') // Happens only if length >= N
      cout << "Input string truncated.\n";
   cout << "Reverse:\n";
   cout << s + i << endl;  // or: &s[i]
   return 0;
}
```

Exercise 5.4

```cpp
// p05_04.cpp: For each element in a sequence of length 20,
//             count how many smaller elements follow.
#include <iostream>
using namespace std;

int main()
{  const int N = 20;
   int a[N], n, x, i, j;
   cout << "Enter " << N << " integers:\n";
   for (i=0; i<N; ++i)
      cin >> a[i];
   for (i=0; i<N; ++i)
   {  n = 0; x = a[i];
      for (j=i+1; j<N; ++j)
         if (a[j] < x) n++;
      cout << "After " << x << " in position " << i + 1
           << ", " << n << " smaller elements follow.\n";
   }
   return 0;
}
```

Exercise 5.8

```cpp
// p05_08.cpp: Pascal's triangle.
#include <iostream>
#include <iomanip>
using namespace std;

int main()
{  const int MAX = 12;
   int a[MAX+1], i, j, n;
   cout << "Enter n (at most " << MAX << "): ";
   cin >> n;
   if (n > MAX)
   {  cout << "Too large.\n";
      return 1;
   }
   for (i=0; i<=n; ++i)
   {  a[i] = 1;
      for (j=i-1; j>=1; --j)
         a[j] = a[j-1] + a[j];
      for (j=(n-i)*3; j>0; --j)
         cout << ' ';
      for (j=0; j<=i; ++j)
         cout << setw(6) << a[j];
      cout << endl;
   }
   return 0;
}
```

Exercise 6.3

```cpp
// p06_03.cpp: Difference between two dates of
//              the same (non-leap) year.
#include <iostream>
#include <cstdlib>
using namespace std;

class Dates {
public:
    Dates()
    {  int c[13]; // Calendar
       c[1] = 31; c[2] = 28; c[3] = 31; c[4] = 30;
       c[5] = 31; c[6] = 30; c[7] = 31; c[8] = 31;
       c[9] = 30; c[10]= 31; c[11]= 30; c[12]= 31;
       preceding[0] = 0;
       for (int i=1; i<12; ++i)
          preceding[i+1] = preceding[i] + c[i];
    }
    void read2()
    {  cout << "Enter two dates, each coded as a 4-digit "
               "integer (mmdd):\n";
       absDayNr1 = dayNr();
       absDayNr2 = dayNr();
    }
    int difference(){return absDayNr2 - absDayNr1;}
private:
    int absDayNr1, absDayNr2, preceding[13];

    int dayNr()
    {  int mmdd, mm, dd;
       cin >> dec >> mmdd;
           // 'dec' required; otherwise 0101 would be octal
       dd = mmdd % 100;
       mm = mmdd / 100;
       if (dd < 1 || dd > 31 || mm < 1 || mm > 12)
       {  cout << "Invalid input.\n";
          exit(1);
       }
       return preceding[mm] + dd;
    }
};

int main()
{  Dates dd;
   dd.read2();
   cout << "The second date falls " << dd.difference()
        << " after the first.\n";
   return 0;
}
```

Exercise 6.4

```cpp
// p06_04.cpp: All sequences of length n, with each element
//              ranging from a given lower bound to a given
//              upper bound.
#include <iostream>
#include <iomanip>
using namespace std;

class VarNestedLoops {
public:
   VarNestedLoops(int n)
   {  r = new int[n]; l = new int[n]; u = new int[n];
      this->n = n;
   }
   ~VarNestedLoops(){delete[]r; delete[]l; delete[]u;}
   void readBounds()
   {  cout <<
      "Enter n input lines, each with two integers, the\n"
      "lower and upper bounds li and ui, where li <= ui:\n";
      for (int i=0; i<n; ++i)
         cin >> l[i] >> u[i];
   }
   void generate(int k = 0)
   {  if (k == n)
         display_r();
      else
         for (r[k] = l[k]; r[k] <= u[k]; ++r[k])
            generate(k+1);
   }
private:
   int n, *r, *l, *u;

   void display_r()
   {  for (int i=0; i<n; ++i)
         cout << setw(6) << r[i];
      cout << endl;
   }
};

int main()
{  cout << "Enter a (small) positive integer n: ";
   int n;
   cin >> n;
   VarNestedLoops v(n);
   v.readBounds();
   cout << "Result:\n";
   v.generate();
   return 0;
}
```

Exercise 6.6

```cpp
// p06_06.cpp: Write a program that reads an integer n and
//             displays all possible sequences of n bits in
//             which no successive zeros occur.
#include <iostream>
using namespace std;

class BitSequences {
public:
   BitSequences(int n)
   {  this->n = n;
      r = new int[n];
   }
   ~BitSequences(){delete[]r;}

   void generate(int k = 0)
   {  // This function will print the fixed
      // values r[0], r[1], ..., r[k-1],
      // followed by all possible values of
      // r[k], r[k+1], ..., r[n-1].
      // To achieve this, both for r[k] = 0 (if allowed)
      // and for r[k] = 1,
      // we recursively call generate(k + 1):
      if (k == n) printn(); else
      {  if (k == 0 || r[k-1] != 0)
         {  r[k] = 0;
            generate(k+1);
         }
         r[k] = 1;
         generate(k+1);
      }
   }

private:
   int n, *r;

   void printn()
   {  for (int i=0; i<n; ++i) cout << r[i];
      cout << endl;
   }
};

int main()
{  cout << "Enter the sequence length n: ";
   int n;
   cin >> n;
   BitSequences b(n);
   b.generate();
   return 0;
}
```

Exercise 7.1

```
// p07_01.cpp: Function template to display three values
//              in ascending order.
#include <iostream>
#include <string>
using namespace std;

template <class T>
void displaysorted3(T p, T q, T r)
{   T t;
    if (q < p){t = p; p = q; q = t;}
    if (r < q){t = q; q = r; r = t;}
    // Now r is the largest
    if (p < q)
       cout << p << " " << q;
    else
       cout << q << " " << p;
    cout << " " << r << endl;
}

int main()
{   double x = 3.4, y = 7.5, z = 1.2;
    string s("John"), t("Peter"), u("Nicholas");
    displaysorted3(x, y, z);
    displaysorted3(s, t, u);
    return 0;
}
```

Exercise 8.1

```
// p08_01.cpp: Input of integers with exception handling.
#include <iostream>
using namespace std;

class NumInputFailure { };

void readInt(int &x)
{   cin >> x;
    if (cin.fail())
       throw NumInputFailure();
}

int main()
{   int k, n;
    cout << "Enter two integers:\n";
    try
    {   readInt(k);
        cout << "Read: k = " << k << endl;
        readInt(n);
        cout << "Read: n = " << n << endl;
    }
```

```
    catch (NumInputFailure)
    {  cout << "Could not read a number.\n";
       exit(1);
    }
    return 0;
}
```

Exercise 9.1

```
// p09_01: Read an integer and display its digits in
//         the number system with base b, where b (at
//         least 2 and at most 10) is also read from
//         the keyboard.
//         Use a stack to store these digits.
#include <iostream>
#include <stack>
using namespace std;

int main()
{  cout << "Enter an integer: ";
   long x;
   cin >> x;
   cout <<
       "Enter the base of the desired number system (2-10): ";
   int b;
   cin >> b;
   if (b < 2 || b > 10){cout << "Invalid.\n"; return 1;}

   stack<int> s;
   if (x == 0){cout << "0\n"; return 0;}
   if (x < 0){cout << "-"; x = -x;}
   while (x)
   {  s.push(x % b);
      x /= b;
   }
   while (!s.empty())
   {  cout << s.top();
      s.pop();
   }
   cout << endl;
   return 0;
}
```

Exercise 9.2

```
// p09_02.cpp: Pairs of gears.
//    The q-values will appear in ascending order.
#include <iostream>
#include <iomanip>
#include <utility>
#include <algorithm>
```

```
using namespace std;
using namespace std::rel_ops;

struct line {
   bool operator<(const line &y)const
   {  return q < y.q;
   }
   bool operator==(const line &y)const
   {  return q == y.q;
   }
   int a, b;
   float q;
};

int main()
{  int a, b, s, k = 0;
   float q;
   int z[]={30, 35, 37, 40, 45,
            47, 50, 52, 55, 57,
            60, 65, 68, 70, 75,
            78, 80, 82, 85, 86,
            87, 90, 95, 97, 99};
   const int n = sizeof(z)/sizeof(z[0]);
   line pairs[n * n / 2 + 1];

   // In total, there are n * n ordered pairs (a, b).
   // Among these, there are as many with q < 1 as there
   // are with q > 1. Only those with q < 1 are acceptable,
   // which means that the number of output lines will
   // not exceed n * n / 2 + 1. This explains the size of
   // the above array pairs, in which we store triples
   // (a, b, q) before we sort them:

   for (int i=0; i<n; ++i)
   for (int j=i+1; j<n; ++j)
   {  a = z[i];
      b = z[j];
      s = a + b;
      if (s >= 130 && s <= 140)
      {  q = float(a)/b;
         if (q >= 0.5) // q < 1 is true because z[i] < z[j]
         {  pairs[k].a = a;
            pairs[k].b = b;
            pairs[k++].q = q;
         }
      }
   }
   sort(pairs, pairs + n);
   cout << "The following " << k <<
           " pairs satify the requirements:\n";
   cout << "    a     b          q\n";
```

```
    for (int h=0; h<k; ++h)
    {  cout << setw(4) << pairs[h].a
              << setw(4) << pairs[h].b
              << fixed << setw(12) << setprecision(5)
              << pairs[h].q << endl;
    }
    return 0;
}
```

Exercise 9.7

```
// p09_07.cpp. Sieve of Eratosthenes
// (computing all prime numbers under 100000).

#include <iostream>
#include <fstream>
#include <bitset>
using namespace std;

int main()
{  int i;
   long k, maximum, howmany = 0;

   const int n = 100000, sqrtn = 317;
   // 316 * 316 = 99856 and 317 * 317 = 100489.
   // If you change n, you should make sqrtn equal to the
   // square root of n, rounded up to an integer.

   bitset<n> b;
   // b[i] = 1 means: the integer i has a nontrivial divisor
   // (i = 2, 3, 4, ...)
   for (i=2; i<sqrtn; ++i)
     if (!b.test(i)) // i.e. b[i] == 0, i is prime,
       for (k=long(i)*i; k<n; k+=i) b.set(k);
   ofstream out("prime.dat");
   for (k=2; k<n; ++k)
   {  if (!b.test(k))
      {  out << k << endl;
         maximum = k;
         howmany++;
      }
   }
   cout << "There are " << howmany
        << " prime numbers less than "
        << n
        << ".\n";
   cout << "The largest of these is "
        << maximum
        << " (see also the file prime.dat).\n";
   return 0;
}
```

Exercise 9.8

```
// p09_08.cpp: Josephus problem, solved with list container.
#include <iostream>
#include <list>
using namespace std;

typedef list<int>::iterator iter;

iter step(list<int> &L, iter i)
{   iter i1 = ++i;
    return (i1 == L.end() ? L.begin() : i1);
}

int main()
{   int n, k, j;
    cout << "Initially, n persons are placed in a circle.\n"
            "All persons in the circle are visited in turn\n"
            "and each time the kth person is removed.\n"
            "Enter n and k: ";
    cin >> n >> k;
    list<int> L;
    for (j=1; j<=n; ++j) L.push_back(j);
    iter i1 = L.end(), i;
    --i1;
    for (j=0; j<n; ++j)
    {   for (int h=1; h<=k; ++h)
        {   i = i1;
            i1 = step(L, i);
        }
        cout << "This person is now removed: " << *i1 << endl;
        L.erase(i1);
        i1 = i;
    }
    return 0;
}
```

Exercise 10.8

```
// p10_08.cpp: Read the numbers
//             n, a1, a2, ..., an, b1, b2, ..., bn,
//             in that order, from an input file, and
//             compute the sum of all values max(ai, bi)
//             (i = 1, 2, ..., n).

#include <iostream>
#include <fstream>
#include <string>
#include <cstdlib>
using namespace std;
```

```
void error(const char *s)
{   cout << s << endl;
    exit(1);
}

int main()
{   cout << "Input file name: ";
    string fname;
    cin >> fname;
    ifstream in(fname.c_str());
    if (in.fail()) error("Cannot open input file.\n");
    int i, n;
    double *a, sum = 0, x;
    in >> n;
    a = new double[n];
    for (i=0; i<n; ++i)
    {   in >> a[i];
        if (in.fail()) error("Too few numbers in input file");
    }
    for (i=0; i<n; ++i)
    {   in >> x;
        if (in.fail()) error("Too few numbers in input file");
        sum += (a[i] > x ? a[i] : x);
    }
    cout <<
        "The sum of all max(ai, bi) values is " << sum << endl;
    delete[] a;
    return 0;
}
```

Exercise 10.9

```
// p10_09.cpp: Compute the coefficients a and b of the
//             regression line y = a + bx.
#include <iostream>
#include <fstream>
#include <string>
using namespace std;

int main()
{   int n = 0;
    double x, y, sx = 0, sx2 = 0, sy = 0, sxy = 0, D;
    cout << "Enter the name of an input file, which\n"
         << "contains pairs of numbers x, y, to be used\n"
         << "for linear regression: ";
    string fname;
    cin >> fname;
    ifstream in(fname.c_str());
    if (in.fail())
    {   cout << "Cannot open input file.\n";
        return 1;
    }
```

```
   while (in >> x >> y)
   {   ++n;
       sx += x;
       sx2 += x * x;
       sy += y;
       sxy += x * y;
   }
   D = n * sx2 - sx * sx;
   if (D == 0)
      cout << "Incorrect input (determinant = 0)\n";
   else
   {   cout <<
          "The regression line y = a + bx approximates the\n";
      cout << "given points, where\n";
      cout << "a = " << (sy * sx2 - sx * sxy)/D << endl;
      cout << "b = " << (n * sxy - sx * sy)/D << endl;
   }
   return 0;
}
```

Exercise 10.11

```
// p10_11.cpp: Count how many integers there are in a
//             given text file and compute their sum.
//             These integers may be separated by any
//             nonnumeric character sequences.
#include <iostream>
#include <fstream>
#include <string>
using namespace std;

class NumFile {
public:
   NumFile()
   {  okFlag = true;
      n = s = 0;
      string fname;
      cout << "Input file name: ";
      cin >> fname;
      fstream in(fname.c_str());
      if (in.fail())
         okFlag = false;
      else
      {   for (;;)
         {   int x;
            in >> x;
            if (in.fail())
            {   in.clear();
               in.get(); // Try to read a single character
               if (in.eof()) break;
            }
```

```
                else
                {   ++n;
                    s += x;
                }
            }
        }
    }
    bool ok() {return okFlag;}
    int nr(){return n;}
    int sum(){return s;}
private:
    bool okFlag;
    int n, s;
};

int main()
{   NumFile nf;   // Constructor does everything.
    if (nf.ok())
    {   cout << "The input file contains " << nf.nr()
                << " integers.\n";
        cout << "Their sum is " << nf.sum() << endl;
    }
    else
        cout << "Cannot open input file.\n";
    return 0;
}
```

Exercise 10.12

```
// p10_12.cpp: Concordance.
#include <iostream>
#include <fstream>
#include <iomanip>
#include <ctype.h>
#include <string>
#include <set>
#include <map>
using namespace std;

typedef set<int> settype;
typedef map<string, settype> maptype;

bool wordread(ifstream &ifstr, string &word, int &linenr)
{   char ch;
    // scan for first letter:
    for (;;)
    {   ifstr.get(ch);
        if (ifstr.fail()) return false;
        if (isalpha(ch)) break;
        if (ch == '\n') ++linenr;
    }
```

```
    word = "";
    // scan for first non-alpha character:
    do
    {   word += tolower(ch);
        ifstr.get(ch);
    }   while (!ifstr.fail() && isalpha(ch));

    if (ifstr.fail())
        return false;
    ifstr.putback(ch); // ch may be '\n'
    return true;
}


int main()
{   maptype M;
    maptype::iterator im;
    settype::iterator is, isbegin, isend;
    string inpfilename, word;
    ifstream ifstr;
    int linenr = 1;
    cout << "Enter name of input file: ";
    cin >> inpfilename;
    ifstr.open(inpfilename.c_str());
    if (!ifstr)
    {   cout << "Cannot open input file.\n";
        exit(1);
    }

    while (wordread(ifstr, word, linenr))
    {   im = M.find(word);
        if (im == M.end())
            im = M.insert(maptype::value_type(word,
                settype())).first;
        (*im).second.insert(linenr);
    }

    for (im = M.begin(); im != M.end(); ++im)
    {   cout << left
             << setw(15)
             << (*im).first.c_str();
        isbegin = (*im).second.begin();
        isend = (*im).second.end();
        for (is=isbegin; is != isend; ++is)
           cout << " "
                << setw(2)
                << *is;
        cout << endl;
    }
    return 0;
}
```

Exercise 10.13

```cpp
// p10_13.cpp: A textfile and a word are given as program
//             arguments. When reading all lines of the
//             textfile, we display each line that contains
//             the given word.

#include <iostream>
#include <fstream>
#include <string>
#include <cstdlib>

using namespace std;

class FileWord {
public:
   FileWord(const char *s)
   {  in.open(s);
      if (in.fail())
      {  cout << "Cannot open input file.\n";
         exit(1);
      }
   }

   void readlines(const char *w) // We will look for w
   {  string str;

      while (getline(in, str), !in.fail())
      {  if (str.find(w) != string::npos)
            cout << str
                 << endl;
      }
   }

private:
   ifstream in;
};

int main(int argc, char *argv[])
{  if (argc < 3)
   {  cout << "Supply file name and word as "
              "program arguments.\n";
      return 1;
   }

   FileWord fs(argv[1]);
   fs.readlines(argv[2]);
   return 0;
}
```

Exercise 10.15

```
// p10_15.cpp: The longest and the second longest
//              lines of a given textfile are displayed.
#include <iostream>
#include <fstream>
#include <string>
#include <cstdlib>
using namespace std;

class InputLines {
public:
   InputLines(const string &fname)
   {  in.open(fname.c_str());
      if (!in)
      {  cout << "Cannot open input file.\n";
         exit(1);
      }
      n = n1 = -1;
   }

   void readFile()
   {  string s;
      int len;
      for (;;)
      {  getline(in, s);
         if (in.fail())
            break;
         len = s.length();
         if (len > n){max1 = max; n1 = n; max  = s; n = len;}
         else
         if (len < n && len > n1){max1 = s; n1 = len;}
      }
   }

   void showResults()
   {  if (n1 == -1)
      {  cout <<
            "There were no two lines of different length.\n";
         exit(1);
      }
      cout << "Longest line:\n" << max << endl;
      cout << "Second longest line:\n" << max1 << endl;
   }
private:
   ifstream in;
   string max, max1;
   int n, n1;
};
```

```
int main()
{   string fname;
    cout << "Input file name: ";
    cin >> fname;
    InputLines inputlines(fname);
    inputlines.readFile();
    inputlines.showResults();
    return 0;
}
```

Exercise 10.17

```
// p10_17.cpp: Sets of words, read from two files, tested
//              for equality.

#include <iostream>
#include <fstream>
#include <string>
#include <set>
using namespace std;

int main()
{   string nameA, nameB;
    cout << "Enter name of first input file: ";
    cin >> nameA;
    ifstream inA(nameA.c_str());
    if (inA.fail())
    {   cout << "Cannot open this file.\n";
        return 1;
    }
    cout << "Enter name of second input file: ";
    cin >> nameB;
    ifstream inB(nameB.c_str());
    if (inA.fail())
    {   cout << "Cannot open this file.\n";
        return 1;
    }
    set<string> A, B;
    string s;
    while (inA >> s)
        A.insert(s);
    while (inB >> s)
        B.insert(s);
    if (A == B)
        cout << "The files contain the same words.\n";
    else
        cout << "The files do not contain the same words.\n";
    return 0;
}
```

Exercise 10.19

```cpp
// p10_19.cpp: Check if parentheses and {curly} braces match.
#include <iostream>
#include <fstream>
#include <cstdlib>
#include <string>
using namespace std;

class SyntaxCheck {
public:
    SyntaxCheck(const string &fname)
    {  in.open(fname.c_str());
       if (!in)
       {  cout << "Cannot open input file.\n";
          exit(1);
       }
    }

    void validSequence()
    {  while (parentheses() || braces()) ;
    }

    void read(int ch0)
    {  if (!trychar(ch0))
       {  cout << "Parentheses and braces do not match.\n";
          exit(1);
       }
    }

private:
    ifstream in;

    bool trychar(int ch0)
    {  int ch;
       for (;;)
       {  ch = in.peek();
          if (ch == EOF || ch == '(' || ch == '{'
          || ch == ')' || ch == '}')
          break;
          in.get();
       }
       // Everything has been skipped until ch is one
       // of the following five: EOF ( { } ). We now read
       // this if this is the desired character ch0:
       if (ch == ch0)
       {  in.get();
          return true;
       }
       return false;
    }
```

```
    bool parentheses()
    {  if (trychar('('))
       {  validSequence();
          read(')');
          return true;
       }
       return false;
    }
    bool braces()
    {  if (trychar('{'))
       {  validSequence();
          read('}');
          return true;
       }
       return false;
    }
};

int main()
{  string fname;
   cout << "Input file name: ";
   cin >> fname;
   SyntaxCheck check(fname);
   check.validSequence();
   cout << "Input OK.\n";
   return 0;
}
```

Exercise 11.2

```
// p11_02.cpp: Demonstrating C-style output.
#include <stdio.h>

int main()
{  printf("  x             f(x)\n\n");
   for (int i=20; i<=40; i+=2)
   {  double x = i/10.0;
      printf("%3.1f %15.10f\n", x, x * x + x + 1/x);
   }
   return 0;
}
```

Bibliography

Ammeraal, L. (1996) *Algorithms and Data Structures in C++*, Chichester, John Wiley.

Ammeraal, L. (1997) *STL for C++ Programmers*, Chichester, John Wiley.

Coplien, J. O. (1992) *Advanced C++ Programming Styles and Idioms*, Reading, MA: Addison-Wesley.

Ellis, A. E. and B. Stroustrup (1990) *The Annotated C++ Reference Manual*, Reading, MA: Addison-Wesley.

Horstmann, C. (1999) *Computing Concepts with C++ Essentials*, Second Edition, New York: John Wiley.

Kernighan, B. W. and D. M. Ritchie (1988) *The C Programming Language*, Second Edition, Englewood Cliffs, NJ: Prentice-Hall.

Lippman, S. B. and J. Lajoie (1998) *C++ Primer*, Third Edition, Reading, MA: Addison-Wesley.

Musser, D. R. and A. Saini (1996) *STL Tutorial and Reference Guide*, Reading, MA: Addison-Wesley.

Stroustrup, B. (1994) *The Design and Evolution of C++*, Reading, MA: Addison-Wesley.

Stroustrup, B. (1997) *The C++ Programming Language*, Third Edition, Reading, MA: Addison-Wesley.

Index